Remaking Wormsloe Plantation

env ronmental
h story
amer can *and the*
south

Remaking
Wormsloe Plantation

The Environmental History of a
Lowcountry Landscape

Drew A. Swanson

The University of Georgia Press

Athens and London

Small passages of chapters 1, 2, and 3 were published in "Wormsloe's Belly: The History of a Southern Plantation through Food," *Southern Cultures* 15, no. 4 (Winter 2009).

© 2012 by the University of Georgia Press
Athens, Georgia 30602
www.ugapress.org

Set in Adobe Garamond by Graphic Composition, Inc.
Printed and bound by Thomson-Shore
The paper in this book meets the guidelines for
permanence and durability of the Committee on
Production Guidelines for Book Longevity of the
Council on Library Resources.

Printed in the United States of America

16 15 14 13 12 C 5 4 3 2 1

Library of Congress Cataloging-in-Publication Data

Swanson, Drew A., 1979–
    Remaking Wormsloe Plantation : the environmental history of a
Lowcountry landscape / Drew A. Swanson.
        p. cm. — (Environmental history and the American South)
    Includes bibliographical references and index.
    ISBN-13: 978-0-8203-4177-4 (cloth : alk. paper)
    ISBN-10: 0-8203-4177-0 (cloth : alk. paper)
    1. Wormsloe Plantation Site (Ga.)—History. 2. Wormsloe
Plantation Site (Ga.)—Environmental conditions.
3. Plantations—Georgia—Savannah Region—History.
4. Plantation life—Georgia—Savannah Region—History.
5. Landscapes—Georgia—Savannah Region—History. 6. Cultural
landscapes—Georgia—Savannah Region—History. 7. Landscape
changes—Georgia—Savannah Region—History. 8. Archaeology
and history—Georgia—Savannah Region. 9. Excavations
(Archaeology)—Georgia—Savannah Region. I. Title.
    F294.W6S93 2012
    975.8'724—dc23   2011029992

British Library Cataloging-in-Publication Data available

For Margaret and Ethan

CONTENTS

Wormsloe as Palimpsest

Wormsloe Plantation is one of the most significant historical, archaeological, and natural sites in Georgia and the entire Lowcountry, and a major reason for its significance is the property's integrity and long-term proprietorship. Noble Jones, one of the founding English settlers of Savannah in 1733, was also among the first to apply to the Trustees of Georgia for an outlying plantation, and in 1736 he received permission to occupy and improve what would soon become Wormsloe. Since then the property has been owned and managed by his descendants—the Jones, De Renne, and Barrow families—for a remarkable ten generations, which goes a long way toward explaining why Wormsloe remains intact while all around it seems transformed. But Wormsloe is not only a wonder of historic preservation; it has also been a critical site to the preservation of Georgia's history. In the late nineteenth and early twentieth centuries, the De Renne and Barrow families were the most avid and accomplished collectors of Georgiana. Indeed, in 1938 the University of Georgia acquired the bulk of the De Renne Library, which included tens of thousands of rare volumes and precious historical documents. Today that collection forms the core of the university's renowned Hargrett Rare Book and Manuscript Library. The continuing preservation of Wormsloe and the spirit of preservation that has flowed from the place are testaments to the family's unerring stewardship.

But what exactly has been "preserved" at Wormsloe, and how ought the property to be interpreted? When you enter Wormsloe's imposing front gates and drive along the monumental live oak avenue, more than a mile long, you immediately feel a sense of retreat from the sprawl of Savannah lapping at Wormsloe's gates. While the live oaks lining the avenue are clearly products of human design, and of fairly recent provenance, if you wander from their protective tunnel you likely will find yourself in mixed maritime forest and within sight of the expansive marshes characteristic of the Georgia coast. Indeed, Wormsloe seems an island of aboriginal naturalness in a sea of subdivisions and strip malls, and this very naturalness lends the property much of its historical allure. The preservation of this natural landscape, then, surely ranks as another of Wormsloe's central points of significance. Wormsloe also preserves important artifacts of the region's precolonial, colonial, and early national history. A short walk from the end of the live oak avenue are the ruins of the original tabby fortification built in the late 1730s or early 1740s by Jones and the detachment of marines that accompanied him to Wormsloe. This was a site of early military significance because it protected a "backdoor" entrance into Savannah at a time of hostility with Spanish colonies not far to the South. Wander elsewhere and you will find shell middens that betray an even deeper history of Native American occupation and resource use, or substantial earthworks that date to the Civil War, or even a lone surviving slave cabin that speaks of the plantation's significance to the history of slavery and the African American experience. It is the breadth and diversity of these artifacts—and others yet undiscovered—and the tranquil natural setting in which they rest that together make Wormsloe so evocative of the past.

While nature and history seem to have achieved harmony at today's Wormsloe, that apparent accord obscures a complicated environmental history—a history that is the subject of *Remaking Wormsloe Plantation*, Drew Swanson's meticulous reconstruction of the property's many landscape changes since 1733. While others, most notably E. Merton Coulter and William Harris Bragg, have written about the history of Wormsloe's residents, the plantation itself and the history of land use inscribed on it have received little attention, despite the wealth of available documentation. Swanson brings the methods and questions of environmental history to Wormsloe, and what he finds is surprising. The Wormsloe of today, Swanson demonstrates, is the legacy of three centuries of landscape transformation, and its apparently natural condition in fact masks the substantial changes in the land that have occurred during most of its history. *Remaking Wormsloe Plantation* is an effort to unearth that dynamism, to find in the woods and fields the legacies of that rich history, and to make a start at understanding what this history of constant change all means to the preservation of Wormsloe in the twenty-first century.

Contemporary Wormsloe might seem a collection of discrete artifacts fossilized in the amber of undisturbed nature, but it is really a palimpsest, a landscape whose history has been written, erased, and then overwritten again and again. To see it as such is a great interpretive opportunity—and a great conservation challenge. Indeed, the opportunity and the challenge are one and the same during this era of postwilderness conservation. For much of the last century, the wilderness ideal in one form or another has dominated conversations about environmental preservation. By its most basic definition, wilderness is a natural landscape substantially unaffected by human activity where natural processes reign. Americans have protected hundreds of millions of acres of de jure and de facto wilderness over the last century and a half in one of the great triumphs of American environmental conservation. But the last several decades have also seen the rise of various critiques of wilderness as an ahistorical preservationist ideal that prioritizes the protection of large-scale, distant, and relatively undisturbed public lands over the smaller, more complicated patches of wildness that survive in our populated landscapes. In particular, the wilderness ethos has made it difficult for us to appreciate that natural landscapes are themselves products of history and that the nature we often assume to be pristine and untouched is in fact itself an historical artifact akin to a shell midden or tabby ruin or even a slave cabin. The interpretive opportunity at a place like Wormsloe, then, is to teach people to read the landscape as an artifact of history and to give them the tools to imagine the site's past human-environmental relations. To pursue this opportunity, we must disabuse ourselves of the idea of a timeless, original nature, a nature at odds with history.

That leads us to the conservation challenge: if Wormsloe's natural landscapes of the present are the product of a dynamic human-environmental past, what does it mean to preserve and protect them? Should we let nature take its course even if doing so means that the property's historical artifacts become obscured by natural regeneration or compromised by decay? Or should we protect the landscape as an historical artifact, as we would the tabby ruin? If we opt for the latter, what moment in the landscape's history are we protecting and interpreting? Might preservation in this sense look more like a series of environmental reconstructions or restorations? And if we pursue an approach to preservation that recognizes and contends with landscape dynamism, what does that mean for historical preservation? All of these questions lead us to a larger one: what does it look like when we treat natural and historical preservation as essentially the same problem? Right now, we have few clear answers, but this is presently one of the most pressing conservation questions, and the state of the art will be worked out at places such as Wormsloe. *Remaking Wormsloe Plantation* is an environmental history written with all of these questions in mind.

This book had its origins in an innovative effort by the Barrow family to further perpetuate Wormsloe as a natural and historical treasure even as various new pressures for development have threatened the property in recent years. The first step in that effort came in 1961, when the Barrow family, facing the property's escalating tax burden, transferred the bulk of Wormsloe to the nonprofit Wormsloe Foundation, which the family had created a decade earlier. But when the county challenged the Wormsloe Foundation's tax-exempt status, the family donated (in exchange for tax forgiveness and a few other concessions) the foundation's portion of Wormsloe to the Nature Conservancy, which then passed it along to the state of Georgia a year later. Since

1973, the Georgia Department of Natural Resources (DNR) has managed the majority of Wormsloe as a state historic site, and since 1979 those acres have been open to the public. The Barrows retained ownership of the historic main house and about eighty acres along the marsh, and they have continued to make Wormsloe their primary residence.

In recent years, Craig and Diana Barrow, the current residents, have begun thinking about how to pass on their small piece of Wormsloe to another generation, a task made challenging by the ever-increasing market value of the property that remains in their ownership and the inheritance tax burden that comes with it. If one of the things to be preserved at Wormsloe is family stewardship, then we are at a moment when it is severely threatened. So Craig and Diana, with the help of their friend Sarah Ross, decided to bring together a group of scholars to discuss how the remaining family property might be saved from development by transforming it into an important resource for interdisciplinary academic scholarship and education. The result—after a long and thorough series of deliberations among historians, geographers, archeologists, ecologists, and landscape architects—was the creation several years ago of the Wormsloe Institute for Environmental History (WIEH). I have been lucky enough to be part of that continuing conversation, as a member of WIEH's scientific advisory council, and I can say that it has been one of the most fulfilling applied interdisciplinary projects with which I have been associated. All of the scholars involved quickly recognized, as did I, that Wormsloe is a remarkable site for conducting ongoing interdisciplinary research in environmental history, broadly defined, and for educating the public about the environmental history of the Lowcountry.

One of the WIEH's first projects was to fund a couple of postdoctoral fellowships—a program known as the Wormsloe Fellows—to begin the task of conducting baseline research on the site, research that would be critical to establishing WIEH's larger research and education agenda. Drew Swanson, then a PhD candidate in history at the University of Georgia, was an inaugural Wormsloe Fellow, and he was charged with writing a report on Wormsloe's land-use history, using the rich archival resources available in the University of Georgia's Special Collections as well as a few ancillary archives. Moreover, we asked him to assess the value of these substantial archival materials to the broad, interdisciplinary environmental history research that WIEH imagined undertaking on the site. Those archival resources not only made it possible for Swanson to produce his report, but they are going to prove vital to other disciplinary efforts to reconstruct and interpret the landscape history of Wormsloe. To give several examples, Swanson's archival research has already helped archeologists to get a better sense of the locations of historic structures that once existed on Wormsloe; his reconstruction of past land use has aided ecologists in their efforts to explain vegetation patterns at a landscape level; and his data have proven crucial to geographers who are working on sophisticated GIS mapping of the site. The land-use history and the larger archival assessment, then, were to be important baselines in a number of ways, and the results that Swanson delivered have been tremendously useful. Indeed, we quickly realized that he had the makings of a book.

Although it began its life as a contract history designed to provide the WIEH with useful historical data, *Remaking Wormsloe Plantation* is now so much more than that. While Swanson had complete editorial freedom throughout the research and writing process, we nonetheless charged him with the difficult task of transforming a history that was tightly focused on the Wormsloe landscape into one that was also broadly engaged with the larger themes of environmental history. In other words, we asked Swanson to demonstrate why the environmental history of Wormsloe ought to matter to a larger audience and how the WIEH's ongoing research agenda might connect with environmental history's most compelling themes and pressing questions. In that task, Swanson has succeeded admirably. While *Remaking Wormsloe Plantation* has all of the virtues of a focused case study, it is also a book that charts Wormsloe's many historical connections with the larger world and creatively uses the available archival materials to push environmental history in new directions.

Drew Swanson's careful attention to land use and landscape at Wormsloe over several centuries is impressive both in its specificity and in the connections he draws to larger historical themes. Swanson demonstrates that Wormsloe was pulsing with agricultural activity for most of its history and that its current dormant state represents an important departure from the land-use regimes of the past several centuries. Giving us the ability to imagine Wormsloe's past landscapes of agricultural production as we stroll through today's preserved plantation is one of the book's greatest achievements. Swanson also depicts Wormsloe as a place of constant experimentation and reinvention, as a site where idealized visions of agricultural prosperity met the realities of environmental, social, and economic constraints. From Noble Jones's earliest isothermal imaginings that Wormsloe might be a new Mediterranean of exotic agricultural productivity, a cultured node in the larger Atlantic world, to the family's early twentieth-century efforts to remake the failing plantation as "Wormsloe Gardens" and profit from a burgeoning tourist clientele in the thrall of an imagined Old South, Wormsloe has always been a place of active interpretation. Indeed, while it might seem useful to bifurcate the "preserved Wormsloe" of recent decades from the "working Wormsloe" of the previous several centuries, Swanson works against this distinction by smartly pointing out that Wormsloe's residents have consistently reworked their landscape with lasting meaning in mind. In order to preserve and perpetuate Wormsloe as a property, they have constantly changed it. This, ironically, is the secret to its lasting integrity. This is "Wormsloe as palimpsest," a place of multiple and overlapping land-use regimes that have constantly remade the landscape, and a place with layers of meaning that have kept the place whole.

By paying such careful attention to these past efforts at stewardship and the ideas behind them, *Remaking Wormsloe Plantation* historicizes our current efforts to preserve Wormsloe and suggests that they are yet another chapter in a long history. It thus marks a new interpretive moment, another layer of meaning. And as the perpetuation of the property enters a new phase, perhaps the best way to answer the question with which I began this foreword—what does it mean to preserve Wormsloe?—is to embrace not a single right answer but the conversation that this book will necessarily structure. To an extent, it is a conversation that will be led by the scholars and managers who will work under the auspices of the WIEH and the Georgia DNR. But it is also a conversation that will be open to the public in new and compelling ways. Read this book, come to Wormsloe, join the conversation.

Paul S. Sutter

ACKNOWLEDGMENTS

Many colleagues, family members, and friends have supported this work over the past few years and deserve brief mention here. Chief among them is Paul Sutter. Paul first brought Wormsloe to my attention, encouraged my efforts to transform a research project into a full-fledged book, and offered tireless guidance throughout the process. He did all this while also supervising my dissertation (a completely separate project) and thus read many more of my drafts than any one person should. Much of what is good about this book comes from his insightful questions. The Wormsloe Institute for Environmental History, headed by Sarah Ross, encouraged this work from the beginning and along the way provided many of the resources that made it possible. I owe Craig and Diana Barrow special thanks: They graciously allowed me to explore the history of their family and home with complete academic freedom. My wife, Margaret, also listened with a great deal of patience as I rambled on about salt marshes, mosquitoes, the built environment of slavery, and historical memory, and her practiced eye and keen observations have made this a more readable and cohesive story.

Conversation with a wide range of scholars with various interests helped me refine arguments and avoid embarrassing gaffes. Those who read or discussed various iterations of the book with me include Tommy Jordan, Marguerite Madden, Al Parker, Kathy Parker, Eric MacDonald, David Spooner, Dan Nadenicek, Melissa Tufts, Ervan Garrison, Lindsay Boring, John Inscoe, Jessica Cook Hale, Drew Parker, Chris Manganiello, Tim Johnson, Tom Okie, Kathi Nehls, Michele Lansdown, Levi Van Sant, Lesley-Anne Reed, and Jesse Pope. Audience comments at the 2010 U.S.-International Association of Landscape Ecology Conference, a 2009 Franklin College of Arts and Sciences Dean's Council Meeting, a 2009 seminar at UGA's Center for Remote Sensing and Mapping Science, and a 2008 meeting of the Wormsloe Institute Scientific Advisory Council also helped me hone my arguments. In addition, I thank two anonymous readers for the University of Georgia Press who provided thoughtful, constructive comments that made this a better work.

Librarians and archivists make historical work possible. I relied heavily on the gracious staff of the Hargrett Rare Book and Manuscript Library at the University of Georgia. Mary Linnemann, Skip Hulett, and Nelson Morgan were especially helpful as I combed through mountains of records; they always seemed to have a smile ready even as I made ridiculous demands on their time. I also met with courteous service at the Georgia State Archives in Morrow, the Georgia Historical Society in Savannah, the Southeastern Branch of the National Archives and Records Administration in Morrow, the Special Collections Department of Mitchell Memorial Library at Mississippi State University, and the Virginia Historical Society in Richmond. The interlibrary loan staff at the University of Georgia also did an excellent job of securing rare books, pamphlets, journals, and newspapers critical to my research.

This book could not have found a better home. The staff of the University of Georgia Press made revision and publication a pleasure rather than a chore. Nicole Mitchell, Derek Krissoff, Beth Snead, John Joerschke, and John McLeod deserve special mention. And Ellen D. Goldlust-Gingrich, my copy editor, helped smooth out the wrinkles with a great deal of patience and aplomb. I do not envy her job.

Funding from a variety of sources made writing this book easier and faster. A research award from the Franklin College of Arts and Sciences at UGA supported research and travel. A cooperative effort between the UGA Graduate School and the Wormsloe Institute for Environmental History provided a two-year research fellowship and time away from the classroom that was critical to the completion of this project.

And time is the most valuable asset we all possess. Thanks again to my family and friends, who tolerated my spending so much of it on this book.

INTRODUCTION

The Last Plantation

ONE OF THE MOST ICONIC IMAGES of the Old South is that of a mile-long avenue lined with live oaks leading to a stately, columned plantation house. This tableau conjures up Disneyesque visions of southern belles in hoop skirts, slaves laboring in cotton fields, the clink of julep cups, and fox-hunting on horseback, with just a hint of magnolia and jessamine in the air. Visitors to Wormsloe State Historic Site on the Georgia coast enter just such a drive as they make their way onto the historic plantation to explore one of the state's richest cultural and natural locations. They visit the site for its long history and for its beautiful natural environment. Located on the Isle of Hope peninsula, Wormsloe sits approximately nine miles southeast of downtown Savannah, Georgia. The old plantation is unique in that it is the only tract of land that has remained under the ownership of one family from shortly after the European colonization of Georgia in 1733 to the present. (Though the state currently manages most of the property, the family still lives in the historic plantation house on part of the old demesne.) For much of the twentieth century, Wormsloe has been preserved and interpreted primarily as a colonial site. Despite this interpretation and its impressive Old South appearance, Wormsloe plantation was and remains a dynamic landscape, with both people and environment constantly defining and redefining one another. This is a story, then, of a place like so many other American places, a landscape of invention and reinvention and interpretation and reinterpretation.

Today's Wormsloe visitors experience a varied landscape. The historic live oak avenue cuts through the heart of the 822-acre park. The drive begins at a massive steel and concrete gate and terminates at the ruins of a colonial fort dating to Georgia's earliest European settlement. Along the avenue lie an early-nineteenth-century plantation house with its historic gardens and farmyard, a modern concrete nature museum, and walking trails. Scattered throughout the landscape are vestiges of its past: a restored wooden slave cabin, the foundations of a dairy building and silo, a family cemetery, a network of drainage ditches that snake through the property, and re-creations of colonial and Native American structures. The solid ground is almost entirely cloaked with dense forest. Live oaks and various species of pine block out the brilliant

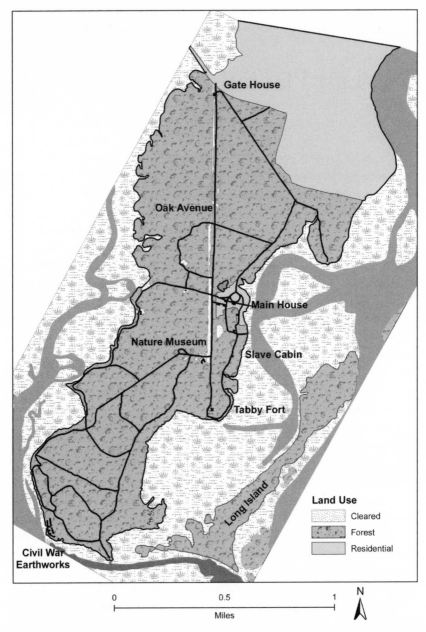

Wormsloe 2010. Map by Dr. Thomas R. Jordan, Center for Remote Sensing and Mapping Science, Department of Geography, University of Georgia, Athens, Georgia.

Lowcountry sun; yaupon holly and saw palmetto fill in the understory; and Spanish moss drapes branches like ghostly streamers. To the north, beyond the entrance gate, the park borders Savannah's suburbs, but on the other three sides the coastal salt marsh envelopes the peninsula. Thousands of acres of salt-marsh cordgrass sway with every breeze, revealing infinite shades of green yet concealing the rich organic muck lying beneath. To the west lies the mainland, to the east Long and Skidaway Islands. This landscape is our setting.

The old plantation is a magnificent example of the Lowcountry environment as well as a cradle of Georgia history. The Lowcountry is a relatively flat, low-lying stretch of coastal ground bordering the Atlantic in South Carolina and Georgia, including both states' sea islands. The region is both geographically and culturally distinct. Wormsloe is one of the few surviving spaces where we can simultaneously glimpse the landscape that witnessed the European settlement of Georgia, the development of the modern coastal South, and the three hundred years of history in between. As fascinating as the property is as an individual southern plantation, it is equally remarkable for its connections to the larger world. Wormsloe has long been tied to the national and transatlantic commerce in goods, people, and ideas, connections revealed in its environment as well as its history. This book captures the ways in which human use of the landscape shaped and was shaped by the environment and, in turn, how memories of history and the land influenced perceptions of a particular plot of earth. This is a tale of how people understood a natural world that simultaneously existed under their feet and in their heads.

Wormsloe is also a productive place to examine the preservation and management of historic and natural landscapes. Why do we preserve particular sites when others fall to developers or the gradual deterioration of time's passage? Or to phrase the question differently, why has Wormsloe survived as a contiguous property when almost every other founding plantation along the Georgia coast has been subdivided and developed? Wormsloe did not become a state property until 1973, yet the roots of its preservation extend into the nineteenth century, when interpretations by its owners characterized the plantation as a site worthy of conservation, though they would not have used that term. Wormsloe is a place to consider what we as a society value in historical sites, green spaces, and the natural world, and the property has the sources to trace the evolution of these evaluations over the centuries. The state historic site is a place to begin to think about how and why we create, conserve, and maintain certain recreational spaces. As one scholar of cultural resource management so passionately exhorts, "This is what a management plan is for. It needs to be descriptive: not to be just a bald list of biological or archaeological features, but to mention everything that is special or wonderful or beautiful, and above all to set out the *meaning* of a place."[1] This book is a preservation case study intended to inform present management and delineate the role of environmental history in the preservation and interpretation of a specific site.

Over a span of almost three centuries, Wormsloe has moved through a wide range of land uses. Indeed, much of the history of the Georgia Lowcountry found expression in the estate's forests, fields, and marshes, and these features still exist on the property today. Colonial Wormsloe was a landscape of discovery and experimentation. Noble Jones, the plantation's first owner, struggled to understand the New World environment he found along the Skidaway River; he sought crops that would survive in the sandy soil and generate profits on world markets; he worried about the Lowcountry disease environment and the compatibility of English bodies, livestock, and crops with the torrid southeastern climate; and he sought a form of labor best adapted to his perceptions of the environment, disease, and plantation economy. Following the American Revolution, Wormsloe became a small node in an emerging worldwide cotton economy that connected Georgia to Lancashire and India. Wormsloe's masters planted sea island cotton, a variety of the fiber especially suited to the Lowcountry environment, and relied exclusively on slave labor to produce their plantation staple. As the antebellum era progressed, Wormsloe became ever more entrenched in the southern cotton economy and racial slavery. Like many southern planters, George W. Jones, Wormsloe's master from 1848 until 1880, grew concerned about the status of plantation agriculture. During the 1850s, he implemented sweeping agricultural reforms designed to make the plantation a more efficient and productive space, reordering land and labor in the process. The Civil War emancipated Wormsloe's slaves and undermined the economic importance of sea island cotton; the crop would disappear from the Isle of Hope by the end of Reconstruction. Negotiations over the form and structure of postwar labor challenged white ownership of the landscape, and though the Joneses (who by this point had changed their name to De Renne) retained control of the physical property, Wormsloe effectively ceased to serve as an agricultural plantation. Following the demise of cotton agriculture on the Isle of Hope, the estate increasingly served as a family retreat, a landscape of pleasure and leisure rather than a place of production. In the same era that the Georgia sea islands became resorts for wealthy New England and midwestern industrialists, the plantation served as an escape for the De Renne family from the world of commerce and investment in which they built their fortune. Wormsloe as a recreational landscape became a public commodity in the late 1920s when the family opened the old plantation's ornamental gardens and historic structures to the public. As a tourist attraction, Wormsloe Gardens marketed a particular past and a particular image of the Lowcountry environment to visitors: The owners and their hired guides emphasized the property's colonial era, and they often portrayed the landscape as a direct reflection of the environment Noble Jones witnessed in the mid-1730s. Like many historically and naturally significant American places, the majority of Wormsloe fell under the management of the state in the second half of the twentieth century: In 1973, Georgia purchased the bulk of the property and created the Wormsloe Historic Site. This government acquisition marked a new chapter in the history of the Wormsloe landscape. State ownership solidified preservation efforts on the plantation, but it also continued many of Wormsloe Gardens' interpretations of the property's natural and cultural history.

Wormsloe as a slice of Georgia coastal environment is equally diverse. The plantation is a place of both hard and fine gradations. The division between Savannah's suburbs and the largely forested property are firm and clear, and the transition from the salt marsh to the maritime forest of the plantation's hammock land is equally abrupt. Other divisions are less noticeable. A foot or so of elevation change creates a shift from a forest dominated by live oaks to a woods characterized by longleaf and various species of shortleaf pine. The soils of the entire property are sandy, but subtle changes in tilth and grain size increase or decrease percolation and drainage, in turn promoting varied plant associations. And throughout the estate, shrubs and trees planted by humans exist side by side with self-propagated vegetation. Wormsloe's cultural and natural history are similarly entwined. The plantation's ecosystems may appear timeless to some visitors, yet they are part of a dynamic environment affected by stochastic processes and human action. A casual survey reveals obvious built portions of the landscape, including the oak avenue and the house and dependencies of the plantation yard, but much of the landscape today appears untouched by human hands. Woods and marsh blanket thousands of years of Native American use and almost three hundred years of Euro- and African American activity. Like the ornamental plantings that still grow side by side with the palmettos, longleaf pines, and live oaks of Wormsloe's forest, past patterns of land use have left their imprint, and this evidence moves us closer to understanding the past of a Lowcountry place and perhaps promises hope for interpreting it in the present and managing its future.

This study is a close ecological history of a particular place over a long period of time. It seeks not to serve as a history of a habitat type, ecosystem, or management idea but rather to be a long-duration examination of the interrelationships of people and place. It is a decidedly cultural exploration of a natural landscape. The cast of characters includes live oaks, oysters, European and African colonists, mosquitoes, viruses, government officials, hogs, chickens, historians, cotton plants, silkworms, and cattle ticks. In some ways, this treatment follows a European model of environmental history in an attempt to bypass some of the inhibitions of American environmental history.[2] At the risk of gross simplification, American environmental history has long been fascinated by the concept of wilderness, thanks in large part to its roots in the history of the West and the environmental movement. Ideas of the wild and domesticated often overshadow long-term interactions between people and anthropogenic landscapes. European history has largely avoided these limitations, in part as a consequence of its long recorded history: Much of the continent has a human history that is almost beyond the comprehension of most Americans, and almost all of that history records a peopled, agricultural landscape.[3] European wilderness disappeared so many centuries in the past as to be all but unrecoverable as an idea. European environmental histories, then, tend to deal with landscapes as anthropogenic spaces, where there is little use in making distinctions between the human and the "natural."[4]

A history of a single event, a singular person, or, in this case, a small landscape requires a brief justification. Why should we care about one southern plantation, one property among millions? In Wormsloe's case, part of the answer lies in its status as a site of historic and natural preservation. To understand what we manage and how it has been managed in the past requires a close and careful study; informed management of the land as a resource benefits from a critical analysis of how the site evolved and why it warranted preservation. The form also permits us to engage with more abstract historical themes and trends on a comprehensible scale. Microhistory is a scalpel with which the historian can peel back the general in search of the specific. As one historian cautions, "We usually look at . . . society from a distance, so that what we see are final results, which often lay beyond the control of the persons involved and indeed outside their very lives. [History] did not happen that way, however. Normative systems, both long established and in process of formation, left gaps, interstices in which both groups and individuals brought into play consequential strategies of their own."[5] Particular people and places existed within larger historical structures, but they also retained a good deal of agency in their daily lives. This caution applies to environmental historians in particular. If individuals influenced the course of history within their sphere, however small, then the local environments in which they lived—full of distinct plants, animals, and weather—were equally influential. The central lesson of ecology echoes this point: While we are all interconnected, we remain individual beings living and acting within specific environments, and microhistory thus does much to illuminate the processes by which landscapes shaped people, and vice versa, in a detail that broad, synthetic studies cannot offer.

Microhistory is not necessarily parochial history. Rather than obscuring broad historical and geographical forces, this focus on one piece of land reveals the reach of regional and global structures. Wormsloe was simultaneously far removed from Liverpool's cotton merchants, Italian and Spanish silk weavers, and the malarial swamps of West Africa yet thoroughly connected to these distant people and landscapes. When fluctuating cotton prices, European silk shortages, and Old World illnesses enter Wormsloe's narrative, they suddenly become more than amorphous market forces or disease exchanges. At Wormsloe as on thousands of other small landscapes throughout the world, these transnational forces encountered individual people and distinct ecologies. This encounter between the plantation's people and landscape and the global tentacles of capitalism and imperialism is the story of the colonial world writ small, but it is also the story writ true, at least for one place. As Wormsloe's history reveals, individuals and specific environments affected development—be it economic, social, or environmental—in profound ways, but multitudinous connections to a larger world always bounded their path.

This book looks at the plantation through a number of interpretive lenses. First, it explores human relationships with the environment through the perspective of agroecology, or the study of agricultural land as an ecosystem. This approach treats farms as places where varied species, including humans, live and interact within the physical environment. Agroecology, according to one definition, is "an attempt by human beings to reorder an ecosystem's relationships to their own benefits."[6] Within this agroecosystem, plants and animals, both domestic and wild, continue to live, reproduce, and die, but they do so as part of a structure created and guided, to a limited extent, by people.[7] Agroecology seeks to offer an alternative to the simplistic dichotomy of environments as either pristine (without humans) or despoiled (sites of human habitation or work). Indeed, agroecology is a potent tool for understanding the ways in which people knew nature through labor.[8] This process by no means destroyed "nature," but it did powerfully influence the ways in which people lived and perceived the land. This work seeks an understanding of the ways in which local ecosystems shaped plantation agriculture, how those agricultural practices in turn affected the environment, and the ways in which ecological undercurrents consistently pervaded all human efforts to rearrange the coastal landscape.

If any American region seems particularly suited to agroecology and a close ecological history that situates humans as an integral part of the agricultural landscape, it is the South. For four centuries (more, if the precontact period is taken into account), much of the South has been an agrarian landscape, a place where farmers, planters, and slaves shaped the environment to a great degree. The Euro-American South began its life as an agricultural region, and the dominance of rural farm life persisted well into the twentieth century. In this regard, Wormsloe was a typical southern space, a place where cotton- and cornfields were as prevalent as woods and marshes and farmwork was the most common way that people interacted with the environment. As a plot of ground that has for almost three hundred years been devoted to agricultural pursuits or the interpretation of historic agriculture, Wormsloe is an inviting case study to deal with regional themes of land use, the preservation of historic and natural landscapes, and the place of agriculture and people within the environment. Any southern environmental history that ignores the centrality of agroecosystems ignores one of the central reasons that places such as Wormsloe have been defined as southern.[9]

This book also explores the institution of slavery and the ways in which it influenced human relationships with nature. Despite the fact that African slavery shaped southern interactions with the environment to a tremendous degree, this system and the plantation agriculture it sustained have received little systematic treatment by environmental historians (with a few notable exceptions).[10] C. S. Lewis's iconic passage asserting the interconnectedness of human domination over both people and the environment—"what we call Man's power over Nature, turns out to be a power exercised by some men over other men with Nature as its instrument"—has not gone unnoticed by historians, but few have gone beyond this observation to examine the ways in which the relationships between environmental and racial domination played out on the ground.[11] On Wormsloe, Lewis's assertion rings true, and we might add that the labors of the plantation also reveal the power of some people over the environment using other people's sweat and blood as fuel.[12] Wormsloe's history not only provides general conclusions regarding an environmental history of slavery but also illuminates the effects of the institution on understandings and land use in a particular environment, a story that originates in the emergence of racial slavery in Georgia and continues until well after emancipation.

Wormsloe's history also reveals a rich tradition of horticultural experimentation, another underappreciated theme in southern environmental history. Beginning in the 1730s, the plantation's owners regularly introduced ornamental and agricultural plants that became integral agents in the landscape and the lives of the people who inhabited it. The plant species that dominated Wormsloe's account books and vistas—among them white mulberry trees, sea island cotton, and camellias—were the products of importation and selective breeding. These plants help illuminate a number of environmental relationships. First, Wormsloe's cultivars were part of a plant traffic across continents and oceans that accompanied colonialism, markets in commodity agriculture, and later the growing popularity of botanical and pleasure gardens. Second, the selection and cultivation of particular plants in particular places reveals a great deal about local environments and perceptions of those landscapes. Which plants (and animals) people introduced were not only products of local climate but also reflections of what sort of landscape the experimenters envisioned. Efforts to establish oranges and pomegranates were simultaneously rooted in the reality of a warm, humid coastal environment and in a Euro-American hope that the Southeast could become a new Mediterranean. Third, Wormsloe's greenery provides another example of the role of science and plant technologies in transforming the environment. Seventy-five years of cotton monoculture and the azalea and camellia understory that currently dominates portions of the old plantation are merely two examples of the transformative power of seed selection, plant breeding, and horticultural nurseries on the land. The story of botanical experimentation on Wormsloe is a tale of modernization, with all of the benefits and ills that it entails.

If agriculture, racial slavery, and the transatlantic traffic in plants and animals shaped Wormsloe's evolution, then disease ecology and perceptions of human health underlay every action on the plantation. Wormsloe's masters and to a certain extent their slaves feared miasmatic diseases, distrusting the humid, subtropical Lowcountry environment. The Joneses worried that the southern sun would strip them of their "Englishness" if not their lives. There is a rich and growing body of literature on the role of diseases and conceptions of health in the colonization and growth of the New World. Colonists often settled on or avoided certain sites because of their understandings of health, diseases paved the way for the European conquest of the New World, and white conceptualizations of illness and immunity contributed to racial slavery.[13] This study applies the lessons of this scholarship to a particular southern place, exploring the role of health, in all its complexity, in topics as diverse as colonial settlement patterns, Georgia's adoption of African slavery, the selection of plantation crops, and patterns of land and labor management. Wormsloe's residents were both attuned to transnational conceptions of disease and environment and intimately concerned with the ground-level details of their small portion of the Lowcountry landscape.

More recently, Wormsloe has become a place of relaxation and recreation, a far cry from a landscape replete with fears of miasmas and disease. The twentieth-century history of the property displays the growing importance of tourism in the South and its role in protecting and interpreting regional history. Wormsloe tourism consistently privileged and linked a particular past and a particular environmental ideal, most often emphasizing the colonial period and a relatively undisturbed woodland. This interpretive framework, forged by visitors' desires as well as the property's owners, masked generations of intensive land use and environmental change, including cotton agriculture, long-term timbering and land clearing, and black and white labor. Although this tourist landscape obscured a great deal of history, it also produced tangible benefits. Wormsloe's popularity encouraged the Barrow family and various outside entities to preserve the continuity of the old plantation, and a focus on the wooded landscape allowed much of the property to escape the intensive development that swept the southeastern coast during the twentieth century. The evolution of Wormsloe tourism connects the plantation past to important management questions of today—that is: How should the property be best preserved and interpreted?

Finally, this story of tourism and cultural resource management on Wormsloe connects to broad themes critical to environmental history. National and state parks and historic sites often emphasize a particular historical event or epoch, and with this interpretive focus comes an attention to a particular, often imagined, sort of environment. As Wormsloe moved from a private tourist attraction to a public park, managers continued to emphasize the property's colonial history and viewed the existing forests and marshes through an eighteenth-century lens. These perceptions permitted mid-twentieth-century landowners and managers boldly to claim, "Wormsloe is much the same today as it was two centuries ago."[14] This interpretive approach to the plantation's past and landscape shapes our present understandings of the property, but it is nothing new. Those who lived and worked on Wormsloe beginning in the 1700s continuously reconceptualized the landscape. Noble Jones's landscape management was guided by his understandings of the English environment; sea island cotton culture remade the land in the nineteenth century in the mold of a southern staple-producing plantation; Reconstruction and the death of coastal cotton brought about a more diversified agriculture and a general nostalgia for an imagined Old South; and a financial crisis in the 1920s and 1930s forced Wormsloe's owners to package the land as a tourist attraction. Wormsloe is not alone in this constant re-creation of both a landscape and its meaning, but it serves as a valuable reminder that memories and perceptions of the environment in a particular place carry just as much baggage as the physical ground itself. Environmental historians would do well to remember that the physical land and our image of it are often difficult to reconcile.

This study has been blessed with an amazing body of primary source materials. Wormsloe is unparalleled as a site for studying long-term environmental changes and land use because of its astonishing records. The members of the Jones/De Renne/Barrow family did much to preserve Georgia history in the nineteenth and twentieth centuries and were equally assiduous in saving family materials. The Hargrett Rare Book and Manuscript Library at the University of Georgia contains hundreds of boxes and thousands of documents relating to Wormsloe's history, sources from the founding of the colony until the acquisition of the bulk of the plantation by the state's Department of Natural Resources in 1973. Hargrett's treasure trove holds a tremendous variety of materials, including journals, account books, photographs, maps, receipts, recipe books, financial papers, letters, newspaper clippings, and all the other ephemera that accumulate over the course of seven generations. Indeed, these collections present a historian with that most pleasant of problems: selecting from an overabundance of sources.[15]

The varied nature of Wormsloe materials made possible the reconstruction of the historic landscape and its associated social and cultural phenomena. Even attentive and preservation-minded landowners failed to constantly record changes in the environment and their attitudes toward nature. While we might wish Noble Jones or George W. De Renne had written letters describing the plantation's fields and forests from one end to the other, followed by reflective passages where they pondered their own understandings of past and present environments and their hopes for the future, such documents are few and far between, if they exist at all. Instead, glimpses of the state of the land and the social and cultural networks that framed it are available through an analysis of less direct sources: receipts for fertilizer and bacon, tax returns, photographs of azalea gardens, wills, blueprints, and family gumbo recipes. These records reveal Wormsloe residents' intimate activities—what they ate at the dining room table in the big house and in small slave cabins and what they saw when they looked across the marsh and fields. Farm journals record the changing of the seasons and notions of agricultural progress, horticultural maps present the ornamental landscape through the pen of the garden planner, medical notes outline fears of disease and a subtropical climate, and lists of slave provisions and farm equipment preserve landowners' attempts to master people and the environment. Piecing together these materials results in a portrait of a plantation and people rooted firmly in the Lowcountry environment yet connected to the broader world.

Wormsloe and its owners have attracted a moderate amount of scholarly attention over the years. The De Renne family collected Georgia historical documents from the mid-nineteenth century on, and their library of rare books and manuscripts drew academics to the plantation starting in the early twentieth century. A few subsequent researchers turned their attention to the library's assemblers. In 1955, venerable southern historian E. Merton Coulter wrote *Wormsloe: Two Centuries of a Georgia Family*, a history of the Jones family from the colony's founding to the early 1800s. More than forty years later, William

Harris Bragg carried this story of Wormsloe's masters from Coulter's conclusion to the mid-twentieth century in a massive tome, *De Renne: Three Generations of a Georgia Family* (1999). (In addition, archeologist William Kelso excavated the tabby fort at Wormsloe in the late 1960s, recording his findings in *Captain Jones's Wormslow: A Historical, Archeological, and Architectural Study of an Eighteenth-Century Plantation Site near Savannah, Georgia* [1979]). In essence, both Coulter's and Bragg's works are family biographies. They are concerned with Wormsloe only as far as the plantation served as the seat for influential Georgians, from Noble Jones to George W. De Renne to Craig and Elfrida Barrow. The Wormsloe landscape takes a backseat to politics and character studies. Coulter and Bragg tell these stories well, but Wormsloe also provides us with other lessons. The land that makes up the plantation is one of the few trustee grants that has survived relatively intact and undeveloped to the present day. Wormsloe has been through many of the transformations that swept the southeastern coast—European settlement, forest clearing, agriculture, tourism, reforestation, and the encroachment of housing developments and paved highways—but the plantation itself survives as an intact property. Have its land, buildings, and people changed in significant ways over the past three hundred years? Of course they have, yet Wormsloe is still intentionally and inadvertently evocative of the eighteenth century and of all the time between then and now. For all its long history, this twisting and convoluted link to colonial Georgia remains one of our most concrete connections to the region's past. On Wormsloe one can still touch the broken remains of the colonial fort, see red cedars leaning over the salt marsh as they did in 1733, and find white mulberry trees descended from those planted by Noble Jones. Wormsloe is a place where we can begin to answer central environmental questions: How did the Lowcountry arrive at its present state, and how might we best manage the natural world that exists today?

Telling this tale is not without its difficulties. Wormsloe's story has few themes that run throughout; it resists neat or blithe summarization. Contemporary Wormsloe is not the sole product of Lowcountry ecology, private landownership, racial slavery, capital-intensive agriculture, investment wealth, historic and natural tourism, or state conservation. The survival of the colonial plantation into the twenty-first century and its present form stems from all of these factors and more, and the surviving landscape is no more an unblemished window into the past than it is a corruption of the pre-Columbian environment. In short, the story of Wormsloe is no more and no less than a tale of a southern landscape, a plot of earth and water and the creatures that rely on it shaped by the historical influences of local, state, national, and global structures. Its past reveals the benefits and the difficulties of historical and natural conservation and the continued value of attempts to understand and preserve portions of the American landscape where human culture is deeply embedded in the natural world.

This book, then, explores the environmental history of a Lowcountry space, but it will provide material that will assist us in managing and preserving similar places. Thoughtful management and preservation entail understanding the natural and cultural histories of particular spaces and the interconnection—indeed, the inextricability—of the two. Wormsloe is a special, wonderful, and beautiful place, worthy of our attention, and this work explores what is meaningful about the site's past and the lessons this history might provide for the future. Wormsloe's story is more than the tale of a single plantation. It is an example of the forces of change and continuity inherent in almost all American landscapes, a palimpsest of land uses and ideas, and a way for us to explore the origins of our present forests, fields, and suburbs, perhaps even our own backyards.

CHAPTER ONE

A Lowcountry Experiment

Creating a Transatlantic Wormsloe

ON NOVEMBER 16, 1732, the ship *Anne* departed England for the New World. The vessel's crew and 115 passengers were bound for the southeastern coast of British North America, for a strip of land between the colony of South Carolina and Spanish Florida where they intended to found a new colony: Georgia. This colonial project was the result of the efforts of a group of twenty-one "ministers, merchants, and parliamentarians"—collectively referred to as the Trustees—intent on creating a new sort of outpost in the Americas.[1] The Trustees envisioned an idyllic and idealistic colony with three principal aims: the Trustees and the English Crown intended Georgia to be a humanitarian colony that would provide opportunities for the expanding English lower class, serve as a buffer between Spanish settlements in Florida and English Carolina, and produce lucrative commodities such as wine and silk. Historian James Cobb has labeled these aims a "seemingly ideal combination of philanthropy, capitalism, and national interest."[2] Among the *Anne*'s passengers was Noble Jones, a physician and architect from Surrey County, just south of London. Jones was among the wealthiest of the colonists aboard the *Anne*, and he traveled with his wife, Sarah; daughter, Mary; and son, Noble Wimberly. After a brief stop in Charleston, South Carolina, the colonists sailed southward, arriving at their destination on a bluff above the south bank of the Savannah River on February 12, 1733.[3] The Joneses and their fellow travelers landed in a Lowcountry environment far different than the English countryside they left behind. They immediately set about changing this stretch of the New World; at the same time, the Georgia coast would alter their thinking about environments across the globe.

The colonists found their preferred site along the Savannah already occupied. A group of several hundred Creek Indians known as the Yamacraw, led by their chief, Tomochichi, lived in a village on the bluff, the last significant section of high ground before the river wends its way through vast tidal marshes and empties into the Atlantic. Through a series of negotiations, James Oglethorpe, the sole Trustee to accompany the settlers, obtained for the

Georgia colony the rights to all of the land within thirty miles of the Atlantic between the southern bank of the Savannah and the Altamaha River. The agreement set aside a village site for the Yamacraw six miles upriver from the colony, and Oglethorpe promised to restrict settler agriculture and timbering to the ceded lands. With the support of the Yamacraw and a relatively secure site, the colonists set about constructing a town that suited the Trustees' ideals.[4]

Part of the allure of the Georgia Colony for England's poor was access to free land. Jones, like his fellow colonists, received one Savannah house lot, a five-acre garden on the outskirts of town, and a forty-five-acre farm beyond the garden belt. In return for this land, he promised to clear and fence at least ten acres, to plant one hundred white mulberry trees to feed silkworms, and not to employ slaves.[5] As these strictures made clear, the Trustees founded the colony with specific ideas about the ways in which settlers ought to interact with the American environment. Oglethorpe and his fellow administrators believed that Englishmen and -women ought to "improve" the southern landscape. Founders charged the settlers with producing agricultural commodities for the mercantile economy of the Atlantic world, and the Trustees also believed that this labor on the land would reform and improve the colonists. Well-off colonists such as Jones could also apply to the Trustees for additional five-hundred-acre plantations more distant from Savannah by demonstrating an ability to cultivate the land, an ability proven by transporting at least ten indentured servants to Georgia. Jones was among the first colonists to request an outlying plantation, presumably after fulfilling these requirements, when he selected a plot of ground along the Skidaway River southeast of town. In 1736, Oglethorpe leased the plantation to Jones. (The Trustees did not grant any property outright.) He named his new estate *Wormsloe* and immediately set about building a home and carving out a farm on the land. Jones recorded no reason for the unusual plantation name. Subsequent speculation tends to attribute the moniker to a similarly named location in southern England or to Jones's hope that silkworms would flourish on the site.[6] Thus began the story of one family's land stewardship: To date, it has lasted almost three centuries.

Jones's activities on his new plantation took place within a particular environment that shaped his planning and cultivation of the landscape. Wormsloe composes the southern end of the Isle of Hope, which, despite its name, is a narrow peninsula roughly ten miles from present-day downtown Savannah. The northwestern end of the Isle of Hope is connected to the mainland by a swampy finger of land, while the other three sides are surrounded by salt marsh flats and channels. The Skidaway River Narrows and Long Island (historically a part of the plantation) lie beyond the marsh to the east of the peninsula, and

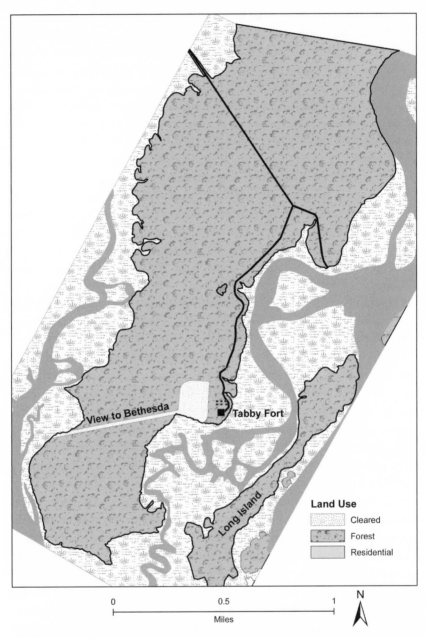

Land Use

Cleared

Forest

Residential

0   0.5   1

Miles

N

Wormsloe 1760. Map by Dr. Thomas R. Jordan, Center for Remote Sensing and Mapping Science, Department of Geography, University of Georgia, Athens, Georgia.

beyond them is Skidaway Island. The Isle of Hope and its environs are part of a maze of waterways, swamps, hammocks, and marshes that lie between Savannah and the Atlantic, a great watery tangle where fresh and salt water merge and mingle. Wormsloe itself was at a strategic location: The Skidaway River formed a water connection between Savannah and the ocean, a potential backdoor for both city residents and Spanish invaders. As a result, when Jones assumed control of the plantation, he also took on a military responsibility. Jones erected the plantation's original structures—a fortified house and garrison huts for marines—to repel soldiers as tensions between Georgia and Spanish Florida climaxed during the War of Jenkins's Ear.[7]

What might the Isle of Hope have looked like upon Jones's arrival, and how had its natural communities been shaped by natural and human history to that point? At the time Jones and his fellow colonists landed, the Isle of Hope was a wooded landscape dominated by two principal forest types: live oak hammock and mixed pine forest. Live oak hammock covered small patches of the poorer-draining soils; on Wormsloe, such areas included portions of the plantation's margins and low-lying sloughs. These live oak hammocks typically formed the forest type closest to the water's edge, where the land was lowest and exposure to salt breezes greatest. Evergreen live oaks and the occasional magnolia dominated the forest canopy, shading an understory of scrub palmetto, saw palmetto, and gallberry. At the ecotone (a place where two ecosystems meet and blend) between live oak hammock and salt marsh, cabbage palms and a few bald cypresses intermingled with the oaks and magnolias. Hammock soils, typically composed of sand and organic muck, tended to drain poorly. The hammocks were shady woods, often with a thick understory and draped in ethereal Spanish moss, an epiphytic plant that grows on trees but does not parasitize its hosts.[8]

Further from the salt marsh, a mixed forest of longleaf and loblolly pines covered the slightly higher, sandier soils with better drainage, with slash pine likely populating swampier patches of ground. These forests were typically more open than live oak hammock, likely as a result of a regular fire regime. Longleaf pines in particular not only tolerate fire but need it to thrive. Along the coastal plain, lightning-generated fires played a vital role in the propagation of longleaf pines. Regular burning, which prevented a buildup of brush, and the precipitation that accompanied most lightning fires led to burns of low to moderate intensity—fires hot enough to kill hardwood and selected coniferous species but too cool to damage longleaf and to a lesser extent other pines. Mature longleaf pines have a thick layer of bark that protects their vascular tissues, and seedlings—or "grass-stage" pines—have densely packed needles that may singe in a fire but protect the tree's bud from all but the most intense conflagrations. Longleaf seed cones rely on these burns to germinate; their scales need contact with bare earth to sprout, a situation created when fire temporarily eliminates ground cover. Centuries of these regular fires produced savanna-like forests of widely spaced mature pines with an understory of wiregrass and herbaceous plants across much of the southeastern coastal plain. The landscape relied heavily on both the generative and destructive powers of fire.[9] From red-cockaded woodpeckers to wiregrass to longleaf pines, life in the vast pine forest revolved around regular burning. Indeed, longleaf forester and land manager Leon Neel writes that "almost everything in the longleaf-grassland ecosystem has some adaptation to fire." Both forest types supported a wide variety of animal life, including deer, turkeys, raccoons, opossums, squirrels, and a host of songbirds and insects.[10]

A substantial portion of the Isle of Hope landscape was not entirely solid land. The surface of the salt marsh that almost encloses the peninsula alternates between water and earth twice each day with the tides. Marsh soil is a rich muck full of organic matter deposited by the endless tide cycle, where Virginia oysters anchor themselves in the intertidal zone and fish feed when the tide flows. Saltmarsh cordgrass dominates the marshland vegetation, rising above the mud and water in all but the most severe tidal surges. The marsh supports an abundance of life: oysters, clams, and other bivalves populate the river banks and flats; estuarial fish—mullet, black drum, sheepshead, saltwater catfish, jackfish, and red drum—feed in the river channel and along the edges of the marsh in high tide; and waterbirds such as marsh hens nest in the cordgrass, while ospreys and herons feed on the abundant marine life.[11] The richness of the marshes reflects the abundance of the meeting of fresh and salt water, soil and sea. According to archeologist Ronald Wallace, the Isle of Hope is an ecotone environment with "a multiplicity of habitats in close congruity."[12] The same ecological relationships that make the marsh and its borders so biologically diverse made the estuarial margin a rich place for Jones to settle.

The Isle of Hope's forests and marshes were shaped by and subject to ongoing natural processes, including fire, tidal deposition, shoreline erosion, and movement of the river and creek channels. Although the landscape was characterized by certain fairly stable animal and plant communities, it was also an environment constantly in flux. Among the most dramatic of these landscape-altering ecological forces were the periodic hurricanes that swept the Georgia coast. These hurricanes were destructive, but the peninsula's environment was also grounded in the ecology of the periodic storms. The landscape that became Wormsloe plantation was shaped over millennia by hundreds of tropical systems. Hurricanes affected the composition and structure of the plantation's forests. For example, storms damage or uproot large numbers of mature trees, opening the forest floor to increased levels of sunlight, which in turn temporarily promote the growth of understory saplings and herbaceous vegetation and thus increase forest diversity.[13] Powerful currents associated with the storms also alter river and creek channels, cut new outlets between sounds and the sea, and overwash salt marshes and low-lying land with storm surges. These waves can deposit layers of sand that can kill plant populations in stretches of marsh and lessen the numbers of some species while promoting the growth of others in other locations. Hurricanes also directly affect animal life, as when storm damage forces marsh and maritime forest-nesting shorebirds to seek undisturbed habitat elsewhere.[14] A hurricane is a dramatic and punctuated period of environmental change, but it is also an extreme but representative example of the environmental processes that created the Isle of Hope, an interaction of ocean, rivers, weather, land, and plant and animal life. The location of the Skidaway channel, the extent of the marsh surrounding Wormsloe, and the boundaries of hammock and pineland on the peninsula were in part the legacy of countless hurricanes. A full appreciation and assessment of the changes to Wormsloe's historical ecology that would occur over the next quarter millennium requires understanding how these competing forces of stability and dynamism created the particular landscape that Jones and his men encountered.

Natural environments thousands of miles removed from the southeastern coast also proved important in shaping Noble Jones's land. Colonial Wormsloe was dramatically influenced by the impress of distant landscapes on the Georgia Lowcountry. Settlers who landed on the coast saw the forests and marshes of their new home and coupled their understandings of this environment with their ideas concerning distant lands. For example, Georgia's latitude convinced the Trustees that the colony might share in the wealth of the West Indies; Chesapeake and South Carolina success with staple agriculture encouraged settlers' visions of tobacco or rice; England's desire to free itself from a dependence on Chinese, Italian, and Spanish silk brought sericulture to the Lowcountry; and the Trustees entertained visions of tropical and subtropical fruit culture that replicated the vineyards and orchards of the Mediterranean. The influence of the English countryside also overlaid all these dreams and desires. Colonists from the British Isles looked at Georgia's forests, fields, roving livestock, and even the health of their own bodies through a distinctly English lens, making New World decisions firmly rooted in the historical practices of the Old World.[15] Alfred Crosby has labeled these colonial empires situated in the temperate regions of the world "Neo-Europes," places where "the plants on which Europeans historically have depended for food and fiber, and the animals on which they have depended for food, fiber, power, leather, bone, and manure, tend to prosper."[16] But in the minds of Georgia's colonists, the Lowcountry was also a Neo-Africa, a Neo-Asia, and a Neo-Caribbean, a landscape in which they hoped to combine the production and wealth of decidedly un-English places and the animals and plants that made that production possible with the more familiar characteristics of home.[17] Only by recognizing the combined influences of distant landscapes and the particularities of the Lowcountry environment can we begin to reconstruct colonial Wormsloe, a place that existed both in the natural world and in the minds of Noble Jones and his fellow colonists.

When Noble Jones obtained a lease for Wormsloe and set about creating a plantation in 1736, he did not begin by altering a "wilderness" frozen in time. In addition to a dynamic natural history, Wormsloe's forests and marshes had a long history of human use. Before Jones's arrival, the Yamacraw had only briefly made the Savannah area their home. Prior to the arrival of Tomochichi and his followers from western Georgia, the Guale people inhabited a stretch of the southeastern coast from northern Florida to the mouth of the Savannah River, including the Isle of Hope. The Guale, who lived in small village complexes, were Muskhogean speakers who likely had political and social ties to the proto-Creek peoples of inland Georgia and Alabama. Spanish accounts from the late 1500s and early 1600s indicate that at the turn of the seventeenth century, more than twelve hundred Guale lived along the coast between St. Augustine and Savannah, a substantial population supported by the natural bounty of the Lowcountry. The Guale situated their villages on the barrier islands and near the deltas of tidal creeks and rivers, where they could access inland resources as well as take advantage of the abundance of the coast's estuarial environment.[18] The landscape surrounding the Isle of Hope provided many of the resources necessary for Guale life, and prior to European contact, the village of Satuache was located a few miles west of the peninsula.[19]

The Guale relied heavily on coastal resources, combining hunting, fishing, and gathering with small-scale maize agriculture. Archeological investigations have described a diet of deer, marine fish, shellfish, small mammals, birds, and maize, a food culture that drew resources from the water, earth, and air. Although oysters were an important source of nutrition, excavations at a St. Simons Island site have revealed that the two most important food items were whitetail deer and Atlantic sturgeon.[20] This diet reflected a long-established relationship with the coastal environment. The excavation of the Irene Mound on the outskirts of Savannah, which dates to several centuries before European contact, has revealed similar diets. Irene peoples consumed deer and seafood; made awls, pins, and fishhooks from deer and fish bones;

and decorated their bodies with carved pieces of conch shells, though there is no evidence that they practiced any systematized agriculture.[21] In addition to their limited agricultural practices, the Guale modified local environments in other ways to increase their production of foodstuffs. Historic accounts and modern vegetative studies suggest that coastal Indians augmented the effects of lightning-generated fires by regularly burning the understory of live oak and pine forests, promoting the growth of useful herbaceous plants and fostering open, grassy conditions that attracted deer and turkey, provided clear lines of sight around villages, and reduced populations of insect pests.[22] Native American firing of the coastal woods was so common that geographer Michael Williams refers to the region's open pine stands as "a man-induced fire subclimax" of a mixed or hardwood forest.[23] Guale burning reflected an understanding and appreciation of the effects of fire on coastal woods and a significant modification of the environment.

Although Guale life centered on village complexes, these peoples made seasonal moves to utilize sites of natural abundance. For most of the spring and summer, they led a relatively sedentary life in fixed villages, where they planted the annual maize crop and hunted and foraged locally. After the maize harvest, men left the villages to hunt deer for the remainder of the fall and winter, when fewer leaves and the occurrence of the rut made the animals more conspicuous, and women gathered hickory nuts and acorns. The Guale also regularly gathered along river and creek mouths in the spring to capitalize on anadromous fish runs, especially the migration of Atlantic sturgeon. Wallace has described this cyclical strategy as a "six-month semi-nomadism." He explains that "the coastal position (as well as the midden heaps left behind) would seem to indicate that much of the aboriginal technology centered around the procurement of shellfish, but such specialization was not in fact the case. More than anything else, the Guale were a hunting, collecting, and fishing society practicing an incipient cultivation of maize and other cultigens."[24] The Guale were not the "ecological Indians" of myth who lived in complete harmony with the land, leaving no mark—they burned the woods, trapped and killed deer and fish, cut down trees, and cultivated fields.[25] Nor were Guale land uses static. Archeologists are convinced that as agriculture spread throughout the coast, Indians relied more on maize and less on marine life. But these activities took place within the limits of a relatively small population living in an expansive and fruitful landscape.

An attempt to define a Guale "environmental ethic" based on the scant sources available would be foolhardy, but we can draw some basic conclusions about the Guale's relationships with the Lowcountry landscape. The seasonal nature of their diet and the natural fluctuations of plant and animal populations meant that the Guale must have carefully studied and learned environmental processes. They had to know when the sturgeon ran, where to find deer and oysters, and which plants were edible and which were toxic. They also had to determine when conditions were right to fire the woods. While limited maize agriculture and regular burning increased the food productivity of selected Lowcountry spaces and food storage limited the hardships of late winter and early spring, the Guale for the most part lived within the limits of local ecosystems. As William Cronon has described this seasonal subsistence cycle for New England, the Guale learned to survive "seasons of want and plenty."[26]

Contact with Europeans brought changes to Guale relationships with the environment. Beginning in 1566, Spanish missionaries established posts along the Georgia coast in an attempt to convert the natives to Christianity and, after the founding of Roanoke Colony in 1585, to establish favorable relationships with potential allies against England's colonial aspirations.[27] For at least a few years prior to 1575, the Spanish operated the Santa Catalina de Gualle mission on or near Skidaway Island, within a few miles of Wormsloe, though they subsequently moved the mission south to St. Catherines Island for reasons that are unclear.[28] These missionaries and their brethren scattered along the Georgia coast found the Guale's seminomadism troubling—sedentary Spaniards found it difficult to trade with and preach to Indians who refused to remain in one location all year round. As a consequence, the missionaries encouraged permanent villages and intensified agriculture. These Spanish entreaties accelerated the Guale's ongoing shifts to agriculture, a turn to "cultivation which was becoming more extensive at the time of European contact."[29] In response, the Guale planted more pumpkins, maize, and beans (crops that had arrived from Central America not too long prior to the Spaniards) and began to raise plants and animals introduced by the Spanish, including cowpeas, "onions, peppers, garlic, limes, peaches, figs, oranges, swine, and chickens."[30] This increased focus on agriculture led to a concurrent diminishment of the importance of oysters and other marine life in Guale diets. Isotopic studies of Guale remains from before and during the mission period indicate that after contact with the Spanish, deer, fish, and oysters remained important food items, but maize consumption increased while marine food consumption declined.[31] Whether this increase in maize consumption at the expense of hunting, fishing, and foraging resulted from an ongoing agricultural revolution, the influence of Spanish missionary activities, or some combination of the two, Guale life was changing. "Hunting and fishing were still carried on," archeologist Lewis Larson explains, "but their importance was sharply diminished."[32]

The disappearance of the Guale from the Georgia coast was not a product of their changing relationship with the Lowcountry environment. Rather, the Guale removal was in part the result of English land use, transatlantic trade, and perceptions of the value of natural resources, the same sorts of economic and social connections that would govern the next three-plus centuries at Wormsloe. In 1670, English colonists settled Charleston, and within a few years they began trading with inland Creek, Yamasee, and Cherokee peoples for deerskins to export to Europe. The South Carolina colonists also desired slaves, eagerly purchasing war captives and slave-raid victims from their trading partners, often in exchange for firearms. Armed with guns, the Yamasee in particular turned to the Guale, whom the Spanish had refused to arm, as a source of slaves. By the 1680s, Creek and Yamasee raids on Guale settlements and Spanish missions were regular occurrences. In response to the continual harassment, the Spanish missionaries abandoned their Georgia outposts and retreated to the vicinity of St. Augustine, Florida, and by 1684 the mission system and its associated Guale complexes "had collapsed."[33] The majority of the surviving Guale population fled to Florida with the Spanish, though a few individuals moved into the Georgia and South Carolina interior, where they were adopted into Yamasee villages. Following the Guale removal, the Georgia coast remained largely unpopulated for two decades. By the early 1700s, the Yamasee began to occupy several abandoned coastal sites, and during the 1720s, the Yamacraw, a group of two hundred Lower Creeks led by Tomochichi, settled near the mouth of the Savannah River.[34]

There is ample if imprecise evidence that Guale-era Native Americans visited and perhaps lived on the portion of the Isle of Hope that would become Wormsloe plantation. Numerous shell middens composed of the detritus of decades if not centuries of hunting and fishing line the peninsula's shores and sloughs. There are at least five recognizable middens along one two-thousand-foot stretch of Wormsloe's eastern shore alone, though none have been subjected to a thorough archeological excavation.[35] Additional evidence of precontact use came during a 1968–69 archeological exploration of the first European settlement on the plantation. While sifting through the artifacts found within the earth of the early-eighteenth-century fort built by Noble Jones, a team of archeologists discovered evidence of prehistoric and contact-era clay pottery. Excavation leader William Kelso wrote that "all deposits [on the Wormsloe site], except those dating after circa 1790, contained sherds of plain, sand-tempered Colono-Indian pottery."[36] Small-scale explorations of other shell middens by a Georgia Department of Natural Resources archeologist during the 1970s yielded similar prehistoric artifacts.[37] The presence of middens and pottery do not prove exactly how the Guale utilized the

Wormsloe landscape, but at the very least it seems safe to conclude that Native Americans visited the peninsula at least periodically to camp, hunt, fish, and collect oysters.

Guale land uses undoubtedly affected the Isle of Hope environment, but the arrival of English settlers in the 1730s marked a new period of land use. Euro-American legal and cultural institutions commodified the land itself in ways that native groups had not, and this new approach to landownership and control would have substantial ecological implications. Beginning with the Trustees' 1736 grant of five hundred acres on the Isle of Hope to Jones, the Wormsloe landscape became private property, managed according to English customs and laws governing natural resources but adapted to the New World environment. The colonial period saw great qualitative if not always quantitative change to Wormsloe's landscape. Among their many activities, the Joneses introduced livestock, cut timber, cleared fields, hunted and fished, introduced indentured servants and later African slave labor, and tried their hands at a variety of crops, including silk and corn. These actions eventually transformed the Isle of Hope peninsula from a landscape characterized by wildness and transient use to a place defined by ownership and agricultural activity, but this transition remained incomplete at the end of the American Revolution.

The location of Wormsloe plantation was determined in part by the same environmental conditions that had shaped Guale land use. Jones sought a good site for his plantation, and on the Isle of Hope he found well-drained ground with promising soil, thick forests, and access to fresh and salt water. While Jones admired the possibilities of the plantation's natural resources, the Trustees appreciated Wormsloe's situation, a term that geographers employ to explain a particular site's relationship to other landscapes. The plantation's position ten miles southeast of Savannah along a water approach to the city, where a fort might provide early warning of a Spanish attack from East Florida, made it a valuable and useful piece of property.[38] On a more intimate scale, the situation of Jones's original fort within the boundaries of the plantation was the product of natural resource distribution. He and his marines built their fortified house on a small bluff in a bend of the tidal Skidaway River, where they had a commanding view of the Isle of Hope salt marsh and the open water beyond. Jones placed the fort in a location with abundant evidence of past human use, situated as it was near several shell middens left by Indian inhabitants who had relied on the abundant oysters of the river bend and the surrounding marshes. Connecting the plantation to the immediate environment even more concretely, Jones and his men built their small fort out of tabby, a material composed exclusively of local resources. To make tabby, the settlers mixed equal measures of sand, which they dug from the river bank and washed in fresh water to remove as much salt as possible, with water, oyster shells recycled from the nearby middens, and lime made by burning additional shells in a rick built of local hardwood logs and pine knots. They poured this conglomerate material into wooden forms to harden and then surface coated it with a lime wash composed of quicklime, water, and sand.[39] The Isle of Hope's natural abundance thus became the fabric of the first plantation structure. This was more than just a fleeting or symbolic connection between Jones's settlement and a specific spot in the Lowcountry landscape. Over subsequent centuries, the Joneses would draw time and again on the natural resources of Wormsloe's marsh, river, and forests in efforts to create and maintain a coastal estate.[40]

In many ways, the tabby fort represented both the parochialism and the cosmopolitan nature of Wormsloe plantation. On the one hand, the physical materials of the fort reflected the necessities of life in a newly settled land, a place where colonists invented a new building form from the natural materials on hand: oysters, sand, water, wood, and their physical labor. On the other hand, the fort's purpose stemmed from the international relationships of the Atlantic world. Jones and his marines cleared the woods and built their fort where they did and when they did because of tensions between the colonial ambitions of Spain and England, made manifest in the War of Jenkins's Ear (1739–48). Decisions made thousands of miles away over the course of centuries resulted in the situation of one small structure in a particular place on the Georgia landscape. These intersections of the Lowcountry environment with the greater Atlantic world would occur repeatedly over Wormsloe's subsequent history.

From the cultural perspective of the new colony's administrators and settlers, one of Georgia's most impressive natural features was its abundant forestland. For the most part, when English settlers arrived, coastal Georgia was a land of mature woods intermixed with salt marshes and the occasional grassy clearing. Surviving colonial documents provide some details about Wormsloe's forests, the property's most valuable asset during its early years. In February 1736, a Salzburger immigrant described the woods lining the Savannah River as "great forests in which the trees reach a great age and represent the earliest times of the creation."[41] Noble Jones took note of the results of regular lightning fires and Indian burning, commenting that the woods were for the most part open and "extremely agreeable," with large widely spaced trees overarching an open understory.[42] More than a century later, in 1867, John Muir wandered among the remaining mature longleaf pine stands near Savannah and gave an account of the impressive remnants of the vast pine savannas, a scene perhaps similar to the one that met Jones. According to Muir, the forests were "low, level, sandy tracts; the pines wide apart; the sunny spaces between full of beautiful abounding grasses, liatris [blazing star], long, wand-like solidago [goldenrod], saw palmettos, etc., covering the ground in garden style."[43] Among the many titles the Trustees bestowed on Jones was that of the colony's first forest ranger, and he noted that almost immediately after landing, Georgians began using the expansive forests in ways that he believed threatened the colony's future wood supply. Jones warned Oglethorpe of a rumor circulating that certain individuals had placed a bounty on live oak timber, probably for sale as ship masts or barrel staves, encouraging colonists to cut trees off private lands or inside the preserve guaranteed to the Yamacraw. Despite his best efforts to prevent this culling of the best live oaks and equally desirable cypress, Jones feared that "great Wast hath been made, and if not prevented would in Short time Disapoint every one of the Great Advantages [the colonists] would otherways Enjoy in having Timber so Near ye Town."[44] Jones might also have been concerned that wanton timbering threatened his natural resources on Wormsloe.

Many early English settlers appreciated the value of Lowcountry timber. Jones and his compatriots viewed massive live oaks and towering longleaf pines as signs of the land's fertility, believing that ground that produced such abundant timber must be able to grow equally luxuriant crops. This esteem for thick Lowcountry forests also resulted from historic timber shortages in England; it was no coincidence that the Trustees created the post of forest ranger despite settling in a landscape blanketed with woods. Settlers arriving in Savannah in the early 1700s came from one of "Europe's least wooded countries," a land of open fields, pastures, moors, and fens only rarely broken by small woodlots and with few remaining large trees.[45] In the early 1700s, the few surviving English forests were parks and hunting preserves for the Crown and the nobility or were intensively managed town commons regulated by the rules of customary use. Small landowners and laborers used timber resources in a regimented fashion: Trees were pollarded (severely limbed) or coppiced (cut to the ground and allowed to grow back from the stool, or stump) rather than cut and cleared, and livestock access was limited to certain times of the year when grazing animals would not damage forest regeneration. English woodlands were thus community rather than private resources, and to a certain degree, Georgia's settlers would treat their woodlands similarly, although the abundance of timber would challenge that communal stewardship.[46]

This English wood shortage was not a recent development. Botanist Oliver Rackham estimates that as early as the Domesday survey of 1086, woodlands covered more than a third of only two of England's counties. More than six hundred years prior to Georgia's settlement, no large forests remained, and "it was nowhere possible in Norman England to penetrate into woodland further than four miles from some habitation." Surrey, Jones's home county, was typically open, with only 20 percent of its land covered in forest.[47] This dearth of timber only increased leading up to 1733. According to historian Leigh Shaw-Taylor, "By 1500 no more than 10% of England was woodland."[48] This downward trend was exacerbated by rapid English economic and population growth during the seventeenth and early eighteenth centuries: London's population almost tripled between 1600 and 1700, agricultural enclosures eliminated woodland, and the demand for timber in the emerging glass, iron, and dye industries placed further pressures on surviving forests. By the late eighteenth century, woodlands covered just 4 percent of Surrey.[49]

As a result of conditions across England, colonial Georgians such as Jones must have struggled with alternate impulses: the temptation to use the forest with abandon in the face of such abundance, and a reluctance to abuse the forest based on their experiences in a homeland of timber shortage. As Jones's worries about the use of timber around Savannah make clear, most colonists quickly adopted a free and easy approach to wood usage, either as a consequence of the incredible abundance or out of a desire to remake the landscape along a European model. Wormsloe ultimately would prove no exception to the general campaign to clear coastal forests. However, Jones's concerns as well as his position as ranger reflected the initial tensions between the English forest experience and Georgia's timber resources.

Despite his worry that Savannah residents were going through the surrounding forest resources too rapidly, clearing and settlement went hand in hand on Wormsloe, and Jones set about timbering portions of the plantation soon after staking a claim to the land. Jones and the small contingent of marines under his command cleared space for the fortified tabby house and surrounding dependencies, chopped out a fourteen-acre tract of agricultural land, and cut an avenue west across the wooded peninsula, providing a clear line of sight from the fort to Bethesda orphanage across the marsh.[50] George Whitefield, a famous Methodist evangelist, founded Bethesda in 1740 as a center for care and instruction of the colony's orphans, and throughout the colonial era, the facility would remain one of Wormsloe's closest neighbors.[51] This work of clearing trees and brush continued on Wormsloe throughout the eighteenth century, though not at the rapid rate of the later antebellum period.[52]

Human activity was not the only agent of forest disturbance during the colonial period. Natural occurrences, such as storms and wildfire, periodically altered the property's woods, as had been the case for millennia. The occasional hurricane toppled or snapped numerous trees at various points in Wormsloe's history: Between the colony's founding and the American Revolution, at least five major tropical cyclones lashed the Savannah area.[53] Summer thunderstorms also could prove to be agents of disturbance. An anonymous 1743 traveler through Wormsloe on the way to Bethesda described the trip as pleasant and extremely scenic but noted the havoc caused in the expansive pine woods by a powerful "Storm of Thunder and Lightening, that happened the day before."[54]

Although colonial activities had begun to change the land, coastal Georgia remained a place of astonishing biological diversity, replete with plants and animals that amazed European travelers and settlers. Englishman Edward Kimber, who visited Wormsloe in 1743, commented extensively on the beautiful wildness of the surrounding coastline, which he found so "romantically pleasing" that it made the "Imagination sick with Wonder." Kimber remarked on the region's rivers and streams and the abundance of coastal marshes and prairies, and he listed in great detail the animals and plants he viewed while traveling. His account furnishes one of the most thorough inventories of mid-eighteenth-century Lowcountry species. Among the wild plants that caught Kimber's eye were live oak, water oak, swamp oak, marsh oak, holly oak, cedar, cypress, hickory, sassafras, prickly pear, walnut, wild grapes, and Spanish moss. He also commented on introduced plants that already grew on Wormsloe and surrounding plantations—pomegranates, mulberry trees, grapes, peaches, and olives. He took careful notes concerning the wildlife visible during his trip, describing deer, squirrels, opossums, raccoons, mockingbirds, mourning doves, snipe, mullet, bass, stingrays, catfish, oysters, alligators, porpoises, bears, and wolves. While most of Kimber's account heaped lavish praise on the Georgia Lowcountry's natural abundance, he did complain that the mosquitoes came close to driving him mad: "I have felt them, and heard their cursed Humming too often for it ever to be obliterated from my Memory." He also warned prospective travelers to watch out for sand flies, cockroaches, and wood ticks, all of which were plentiful.[55]

A few years earlier, Philip Georg Friedrich von Reck, a Salzburger leader, had recorded similar perceptions of the environment near Savannah. Von Reck was quite impressed with the coast's plant and animal life and its potential uses. He praised Georgia's buffalo, catfish ("a most delicious fish without scales"), and eels, among other species. Like Kimber, Von Reck acknowledged that the coastal environment posed some challenges to Europeans. He wrote of the dangers of alligators, rattlesnakes, and wolves and complained that "a kind of small fly discomforts strangers very much by biting them so painfully that they swell up quite a bit at first." Far worse were the swarms of mosquitoes, whose bites were "so painful you cannot possibly sleep through it or refrain from scratching."[56]

Like most early Georgia colonists, Kimber and von Reck felt an unease with the new Lowcountry environment along with their appreciation of its abundance. Although their accounts described beneficial plants and animals, from towering oaks to multitudinous schools of fish, they did not avoid listing more threatening species. Underlying all of these descriptions is a sense that the two men found the coastal environment so fascinating because some of its elements would not have been out of place in the English Lowlands or Austrian forests, while others were romantically (or disturbingly) exotic. These accounts of the coast illustrate the way in which the Lowcountry was both familiar and alien to colonists. Georgia was simultaneously a "Neo-Europe" and truly a New World.

Although the deep forests and wildlife of coastal Georgia, which differed greatly from the pastoral English countryside, filled many early visitors with wonder and some trepidation, the Lowcountry's disease environment posed more daunting challenges for colonists. Georgia harbored New World microbes and bacteria that resulted in such diseases as dysentery, typhoid, and tuberculosis, and settlers complained of frequent illness.[57] The case of William Stephens, a planter and secretary for the Trustees whose Beaulieu plantation along the Vernon River was just southwest of Wormsloe, was typical. In 1737, he wrote that his servants always seemed to be sick: "Ever since my Arrival some or others of them were ailing every Day."[58] Noble Jones himself fell gravely ill while treating sick colonists during his first July in Savannah.[59] The coastal Georgia environment also harbored Old World diseases that had made the transatlantic journey from Europe and Africa, most notably malaria and yellow fever.[60] Malaria, spread by mosquitoes of the *Anopheles* genus, is caused by a microscopic parasite (*Plasmodium*) that attacks the red blood cells of its human host, resulting in fever, weakness, and in some cases death. European colonists had experience with *Plasmodium vivax*, a relatively mild strain of malaria present in England and on portions of the European continent as early as the fifteenth century, and brought the disease with them to the New World. As early as the 1680s, infected sailors or slaves spread a much deadlier African strain of malaria, *Plasmodium falciparum*, to the Lowcountry as well. Both strains of *Plasmodium* thrived along the Georgia coast. A native mosquito, *Anopheles quadramaculatus*, served as a vector for the parasites, and inland swamps coupled with the human-made expanses of standing water in rice impoundments and indigo fermentation tanks to provide fertile breeding grounds for mosquitoes. These swelling mosquito populations paralleled the growth of the colony's human population, providing both the vectors and hosts needed for sustained outbreaks of malaria.[61]

Thanks in part to these two strains of *Plasmodium*, European colonists faced a period of seasoning during their first year in Georgia. In 1738, during Stephens's initial summer on the coast, his son fell ill with what was likely a severe case of malaria:

> My Son's Pains were grown so exceeding sharp and severe by the Contraction of his Nerves in all Parts of his Body, that I had more than enough to do, to give him all the Aid possibly I could, being in such Convulsions, that two Men were scarce sufficient to hold him: But at length through God's Blessing, that Agony began to wear off; and in some little Time after, from the sudden Amendment and Relaxation of Misery which he found, we hoped it was the last Effort of his Distemper; for he grew sensibly more and more easy every Hour. It may not be unworthy to Remark here, to observe what strange Effect Colds frequently have in this Country; this shewing itself first only in an ordinary Tooth-Ach, but by Degrees insinuated into all the tender Nerves, and even deprived him of his Senses, Feeling only excepted.[62]

Stephens's son would recover within a few days, typical of the cyclical nature of malarial fevers, but illness continued to plague the colony as the summer wore on. By mid-August, "the Heats were now grown very sultry, and People began to find ill Effect of them, several falling down frequently in Fevers, &c."[63] Malaria would continue to plague Georgia settlements throughout the colonial era. Olaudah Equiano, perhaps the most famous scribe of eighteenth-century Caribbean slavery, fell ill with "a fever and ague" during a trading trip to Savannah in the 1760s, one among many who suffered from the reoccurring *Plasmodium*.[64]

Periodic epidemics of yellow fever proved even deadlier than malaria. A virus rather than a parasite, yellow fever was also spread by a species of mosquito, *Aedes aegypti*. *A. Aegypti* was a native of Africa but made the journey from the Old World to the New along with other colonizers and quickly established itself in urban portions of the plantation districts of the Caribbean. From there, waves of the fever attacked the southeastern coast in epidemics that could kill as much as 75 percent of local adult populations. *Aedes* mosquitoes could not overwinter in the American Southeast; frost proved fatal to insect and virus. Yellow fever outbreaks thus were the product of the arrival at colonial ports of ships with both infected passengers and the disease's *Aedes* vector. Once the disease made landfall in Charleston or Savannah, it ran rampant until cold weather killed the mosquito population. The Lowcountry's European settlers often failed to realize that these diseases were themselves colonizers, attributing deadly outbreaks of malaria and yellow fever to a general environmental insalubrity.[65]

Oppressive heat and humidity, pervasive malaria, and the annual threat of an outbreak of yellow fever made Georgians wary of the dangers of the surrounding environment. As a practicing physician and the owner of a plantation situated between swampy ground and the coastal marshes, Noble Jones was particularly concerned with the Lowcountry's unhealthy nature.[66] He cupped and bled patients and administered "Draughts," "Drops," and "Powders," but he also believed that a careful diet was vital to maintaining one's health.[67] Writing to ship captain David Murray in 1754, Jones gave a detailed list of medical advice for newcomers to the Savannah area. Jones's prescriptions highlighted the uncertainties of bodily responses to new environments and sought a balance between internal functions and the external world. He warned Murray to shave his head (for the cooling effect), to drink a pint of English beer every morning, and to take three to five laxative pills on a regular basis to keep his system cleansed of harmful impurities. Jones also advised Murray to avoid eating much pork and recommended that the captain abstain "intirely from all kind of Water Fowl, and eat Fish as Sparingly as possibly you can."[68] Colonists such as Jones sought a careful balance of their internal and external environments and worried that extremes of any sort might prove fatal.

Jones's prescriptions reflected a widespread uncertainty concerning the effects of the southern environment on the European body. As historian James D. Rice has noted, "Most English people lived in intimate and complex relationships with nature," but their European understandings of the environment failed to account for the extremes of North America.[69] Indeed, settlers viewed the southern colonies' hot and humid climate with universal trepidation—the English feared a loss of their Englishness, which they believed had been forged by their long residence in a more temperate clime. Tropical and subtropical weather was thought to drain white bodies of energy and health and eventually to lead to death or at least to a degeneration of culture and civilization. Virginia's William Byrd, an inveterate commentator on the colonial southern environment, recorded common perceptions of the dangers of the Georgia climate during the 1730s. He described the new settlement at Savannah as a sickly place where "the land was very unhealthful, and in addition worth nothing, but land rather mostly sand, which the sun heats in such fashion that one must almost faint, indeed, so to speak, burn up."[70] Euro-American beliefs about southern climate also contained a bit of a paradox: The heat and humidity seemed to threaten colonists' lives and culture but were also believed to foster riches by promoting the growth and abundance of "vegetable and mineral" matter. Thus, the luxurious forests and marshes that covered the Isle of Hope both promised potential wealth and harbored deadly diseases. As environmental historian Mart Stewart has noted, such landscapes were "both generative and dangerously destructive." Jones and other prominent settlers must have continually struggled with fears of the consequences of living in coastal Georgia yet simultaneously believed that precisely the things they feared would ultimately make them rich.[71]

In addition to natural conditions that promoted mosquito reproduction and disease replication, Georgia's colonists altered the coastal environment in ways that almost certainly ensured larger *Anopheles* and *Aedes* populations. Clearing forests, establishing farms, building towns, and introducing livestock created additional mosquito habitat. Both *Anopheles* and *Aedes* need stagnant pools of fresh water in which to breed, while *Aedes* also requires water-holding cavities with smooth surfaces, which are most often found in human-made structures. As the Joneses and their fellow colonists timbered, cleared, and plowed their fields, they created thousands of stump holes and furrows that trapped rainwater—perfect *Anopheles* habitat. Rice culture in particular, with its vast sheets of irrigated fields and miles of ditching, created enormous mosquito nurseries. Even the hoofprints of livestock and the tracks of wagons and carts provided pools in which insects could breed.[72] Similar environmental changes supported periodic populations of *Aedes* mosquitoes in Savannah. As colonists erected a town where forest once stood, they created a landscape of gutters, pipes, ditches, and other artificial surfaces that held rainwater. When virus-carrying *Aedes* arrived on ships from the Caribbean, they found these sites ideal for reproducing. With these temporary insect booms came terrifying plagues of yellow fever.[73]

Concerns regarding the Georgia coast's torrid climate and the physiological connections between bodies and the environment also contributed to colonial Georgia's struggles regarding the institution of slavery. The Trustees had banned slavery at the founding of the colony out of a belief that manual labor held redeeming qualities and a worry that a large slave population so close to Spanish Florida was a recipe for insurrection, but from the start, the Trustees' edict faced opposition from a portion of Georgia's population. Pro-slavery colonists, known as "malcontents," believed Africans better adapted to work in hot climates, in large part because they seemed less subject to the fevers that decimated the colony's earliest European settlers.[74] Of course, as Philip Curtin has noted, with the exception of cases of heatstroke or hypothermia, "people die from disease, not from climate," and West African slaves had certain forms of disease resistance absent in the majority of the European population.[75] In particular, West Africans seemed less susceptible to the endemic malaria, particularly the most virulent strain, *P. falciparum*. This relative immunity was, in fact, hereditary. Western Africa was an area of hyperendemic malaria, where almost every individual was exposed to infectious mosquito bites on a regular basis. Tropical Africans had relatively high rates of a sickle-cell blood trait, which often caused anemia and high infant mortality but also provided a degree of protection against *P. falciparum*, "the dominant form of malaria in tropical Africa." Generations of coexistence with malaria had thus selected for individuals carrying the sickle-cell trait.[76] Resistance to yellow fever was also an immunity that had nothing to do with race, but a sufficient number of first-generation slaves brought with them an acquired immunity that led some Europeans to conclude that resistance was a racial characteristic. Unlike the periodic fever epidemics of the southeastern North American coast, yellow fever was an almost constant presence in western Africa. Children who contracted and survived the disease gained lifelong immunity, a protection they carried with them across the Middle Passage, though this immunity could not be passed to succeeding generations. The fever's infrequent appearances in Charleston and Savannah meant that the white population always included some unexposed individuals, leaving the colonial population ripe for an outbreak.[77] Early West African slaves' apparent resistance to disease also resulted in large part from the winnowing processes of the slave trade. Many slaves arriving in Savannah had already been exposed to a broad spectrum of tropical diseases in the slave forts, trading posts, and ships of the Middle Passage, where individuals with lesser immunities perished and only the strongest survived. Some slaves experienced a further disease ordeal when they labored in the Caribbean before being sold to Georgia's rice and indigo planters.[78] Thus, unlike most European colonists, West Africans had already been exposed to diseases from across Africa, Europe, and the New World before setting foot in the Lowcountry, giving those who survived the minor blessing of relative good health.

These white perceptions of slaves' health—perceptions that ignored significant morbidity and mortality—and the dangers of the Lowcountry environment convinced many white settlers that the use of black slaves was only natural. A number of historians have shown that the association of slavery with race was an intellectual construct that gradually took shape in the Americas, but it was also a process deeply influenced by perceptions of the environment and human relationships with the natural world.[79] Arguments about West Africans' ability to withstand the disease environment of the Southeast found parallels in white descriptions of Africans as "savages," as Karl Jacoby has noted. Some southern colonists argued that blacks, like domestic animals, were closer to nature and thus more suited to labor in the heat and humidity of the Lowcountry than were whites. This ideology of race, Jacoby states, grew in part out of historic interactions between people and domestic animals, relationships to which masters commonly referred in period pro-slavery literature.[80] In short, slave owners pointed to both the southern environment and perceived African relationships with nature as justifications for enslaving Africans, arguing that the harsh environment precluded white fieldwork, that Africans were especially suited to withstand common diseases and the climates with which these illnesses were associated, and that blacks' "primitive" natures made them exemplary outdoor laborers. If the disease environment of the Lowcountry challenges Crosby's Neo-Europe argument, these pro-slavery arguments also suggest that colonists often found the Southeast a decidedly un-European place. Tropical diseases, tropical and subtropical insects, and tropical peoples worked to re-create the Lowcountry environment. Environmental arguments for racial slavery essentially posited the incompatibility of Europeans and the Lowcountry landscape: The marshes and swamps of the coast were both attractive (because of the wealth possible through rice and indigo production) and dangerous precisely because they differed so greatly from temperate Europe. Slavery emerged along the Georgia coast partly as a result of this tension.

Although whites' belief that only Africans could labor in the hot Lowcountry sun was grounded in mistaken understandings of disease, environment, and race, the idea nonetheless gained universal currency among Euro-Americans, and the Georgia debates over the legalization of slavery cemented the "environmental argument" for years to come. One historian of colonial slavery, Russell Menard, has pointed to these debates as the instance where widespread environmental arguments supporting the necessity of African slavery in the American South first appeared.[81] The neighbors of John Martin Bolzius, the religious and secular leader of the Salzburger colonists who settled in Ebenezer, informed him that it was "quite impossible and dangerous for white people to plant and manufacture any rice, being a work only for Negroes, not for European people."[82] Thomas Stephens, spokesman for the malcontents, summed up the pro-slavery faction's stance by reaffirming the advice given to Bolzius: Environmental conditions made it "indisputably impossible for White Men alone to carry on Planting to any good Purpose. . . . The poor People of *Georgia*, may as well think of becoming Negroes themselves (from whose Condition at present they seem not to be far removed) as of hoping to be ever able to live without them."[83] On another occasion, Stephens was even blunter: "In Spight of all endeavors to disguise this Point, it is as clear as Light itself, that Negroes are as essentially necessary to the Cultivation of Georgia, as Axes, Hoes, or any other Utensil of Agriculture."[84] And many Georgians indeed wanted to plant, as they cast covetous gazes north toward the wealth amassed by the rice and indigo grandees of the South Carolina Lowcountry. By 1746, a number of Georgia planters had purchased African slaves illegally, and within five years the pro-slavery faction carried the day. Slavery was made legal by a Trustees' edict on January 1, 1751.[85] The legalization of slavery created an economic boom in the colony, and the Georgia Lowcountry population increased rapidly during the 1750s and 1760s. By 1760, more than a third of Georgia's population consisted of black slaves.[86] In Chatham County, where Wormsloe was located, planters also invested heavily in slaves, and by 1790, county residents included 8,201 slaves and just 2,456 whites.[87]

The Joneses were quite active participants in this enormous growth of Low-country slavery. It is not clear exactly when Noble Jones first purchased slaves, but evidence shows that he owned black laborers at least a few months prior to the legalization of slavery (and perhaps much earlier). In an October 1750 petition requesting land along the Little Ogeechee River, roughly six miles south of the Isle of Hope, Jones admitted to owning seven slaves, whom he kept employed at Wormsloe.[88] According to historian Betty Wood, Jones was not a vocal proponent of slavery during the colony's first fifteen years, but he did sympathize with the malcontents and complained about the unreliability of early Georgia laborers.[89] In 1735, Jones wrote to Oglethorpe concerning his "bad Success with Servants." Jones elaborated that his indentured laborers tended to steal, run off, or die from disease and heat. Jones had tried placing one servant in leg irons, but doing so "Retarded me vastly in my bussines."[90] By 1763, Jones had abandoned indentured servants entirely for a growing population of African slaves; a bill from that year recorded Jones's purchase of a large quantity of a type of rough cloth typically used in slave clothing.[91] Jones soon added to his labor force, and when he passed away in 1775, his estate included approximately fifty slaves, with another twenty rented from Governor James Wright. In addition, Noble Wimberly Jones held twenty-eight slaves by 1770, making both father and son substantial planters in the colonial Georgia Lowcountry.[92] Although Noble Jones established Wormsloe as a plantation without African slavery, his rapid adoption of bound labor firmly joined the estate to the developing labor system of the plantation South.

The Joneses' slaves were not confined to Wormsloe but were spread across the Lowcountry. Starting in the mid-1740s, Noble Jones and his son began acquiring property in and around Savannah and in the expanding districts south and west of town. Along with growing slave holdings, these real estate investments and plantation produce would build a family fortune and make the Joneses among Georgia's wealthiest families. Noble received a plantation on Skidaway Island opposite Wormsloe in 1746 from the Trustees; in 1750, he obtained five hundred acres, which he named Lambeth after his old Surrey home, near the mouth of the Little Ogeechee River, a few miles south of the Isle of Hope. Shortly thereafter, he secured title to the 500-acre Wimberly tract adjoining Wormsloe to the north.[93] To these acquisitions, Jones added

1,800 acres in Jefferson County, "1,000 acres in Screven County, 1,150 acres in Bryan County, 500 acres in Liberty County," and some smaller marshland and farm lot holdings scattered around Savannah. By the 1770s, Noble Jones had accumulated a total of 5,500 acres of Georgia land.[94] In 1770, Noble Wimberly Jones also owned a 500-acre plantation and three Savannah town lots, holdings that he parlayed into 3,800 acres by the conclusion of the revolution.[95] These holdings made the younger Jones a substantial landowner and slaveholder and placed his father among the twenty largest Georgia landowners of the colonial era and in the top 6 percent of the colony's slave owners.[96] Wormsloe and the slaves who worked its soil were thus part of an agricultural empire that encompassed thousands of acres scattered across Georgia and a wide variety of land uses, among them rice cultivation and stock raising.

Although worries about the weather, disease, and labor were omnipresent, during the early years of settlement Jones and his neighbors had to attend to more concrete matters, such as how to feed themselves, on a daily basis. One of the earliest and most successful strategies for food production was the introduction of domesticated livestock into the Georgia woods. Colonists imported hogs and cattle, but they also likely rounded up stock that were already roaming the Georgia woods.[97] Spanish explorations and missions during the sixteenth and seventeenth centuries had left behind hogs and cattle, which had gone feral and multiplied rapidly along the coast and in the interior. Conquistador Hernando De Soto's expedition across the Southeast demonstrated the innate fecundity of swine in the New World. De Soto landed in Florida in 1539 with thirteen pigs. At his death, three years later, the Spaniards had a herd of seven hundred animals.[98] This multiplication is all the more impressive in light of the fact that the conquistadors must have eaten pork and lost a number of pigs over that time. Like colonists throughout the rest of the Southeast, Georgians did little to domesticate their introduced stock or the feral animals that roamed the woods, and the animals proliferated when left to their own devices. In his 1743 journey along the coast, Kimber wrote of the presence of "the wild Hog or Boar, who is very dangerous to hunt," and observed that "in some Islands there are also Numbers of wild Horses and Cattle."[99] Indeed, within thirty years of the founding of Savannah, the colony was exporting cattle "to the West Indies, where they are a very profitable article."[100]

This open-range system was a New World adaptation, with colonists such as Jones explicitly rejecting English forms of animal husbandry. Throughout the colonial era, Wormsloe was part of the common range. Georgia law did not require that livestock be fenced in pastures, and almost every stock owner turned his or her animals out to subsist on the commons by foraging for browse in the colony's woods and meadows.[101] English stock-raising systems during the seventeenth and eighteenth centuries were quite varied but typically involved communal ranging of stock on fallow fields, in woods pastures, and on designated meadows, with the animals often under the care of stockmen or protected by fences. Villagers sometimes folded these animals in small pens at night and used the resulting manure to fertilize fields. The most intensive form of English agriculture, convertible husbandry, involved the periodic conversion of arable to pasture and back to arable again, a rotation that preserved soil fertility, reduced plant pathogens, and diversified agricultural practices on a particular piece of land. Although restricted to portions of the English countryside, particularly the southern lowlands, the practice of systematic convertible husbandry was on the rise by 1700. These various stock-management techniques produced quality animals and prolonged the productivity of arable land, but they also required a large population of laborers to herd stock, build fences, and haul dung.[102]

Historians of the southern commons have often described the emergence of American free-range grazing as a product of necessity—early Georgians, like other southern colonists, turned to free-ranging livestock out of a shortage of labor and an abundance of woodland. Labor shortages no doubt encouraged Georgians to let domestic animals fend for themselves, but the abundance of suitable rangeland coupled with ongoing English agricultural trends may also have encouraged colonists to exploit the liberty of property ownership in the New World. English small farmers and rural laborers—the majority of Georgia's early settlers—had long relied on small livestock holdings, often limited to one or two animals, for milk, fiber, butter, cheese, and manure. The increasing enclosures and encroachments of the seventeenth and early eighteenth centuries had steadily reduced livestock ownership among the poorest classes by circumscribing customary grazing rights on woodlands, wastes, and open fields.[103] It seems fair to ask how people used to shrinking stock ownership rights might have thought of a land where the grazing resources of forests, meadows, and marshes seemed infinite and free for the taking. This perception of abundance coupled with the memories of shortage no doubt encouraged colonists to raise as many animals as possible. Faced with the English stock-raising experience and the realities of the Lowcountry environment, colonists, in the words of historian S. Max Edelson, created a "cattle culture" that "bore . . . marks of transatlantic adaptation."[104]

The initial 1733 land grants to Noble Jones and his son in Savannah acknowledged the widespread presence of roaming stock, requiring that Jones fence in his white mulberry trees to "preserve [them] from the bite of Cattle."[105] Although the Lowcountry had little in the way of open ground, the longleaf-wiregrass ecosystem provided abundant forage for grazing herbivores, and

Jones described the existing woodlands as a great resource for domestic animals. Longleaf pine forests subjected to regular burning were relatively brush-free and supported vast stands of edible grasses and herbaceous plants, and even sections of oak hammock were relatively open. These open, grassy forests fed deer and roaming stock alike. Jones's comments on the dangers of heavy timbering also stemmed from his concern that such actions damaged the forest's stock-carrying capacity. He lamented that leaving treetops and branches throughout the woods and opening up the canopy caused formerly open and grassy woodlands to become tangled and shrubby, damaging valuable "Pasture which would otherways be Usefull for the feed of Cattle and in a Great Measure prevent their Rambling."[106] So many animals roamed the woods that they were often sold at estate sales without ever being rounded up. A 1763 advertisement in the *Georgia Gazette* revealed that owners often had no idea how many animals they owned. The notice promised to sell "for ready money, at the Watch-house in Savannah, A large flock of cattle, a flock of hogs and horses, as they run in the woods."[107]

Cattle and hogs also subsisted on the grasses and rushes of the marshes that bordered Wormsloe. Coastal settlers ranged their livestock in marshland as well as forest; cattle foraged anywhere the marshlands were firm enough to support their weight, and hogs ate bivalves, crabs, and dead fish as well as vegetable matter. When traditional forage was scarce or unavailable—in winter and early spring—the marshes became even more important for herds.[108] An antebellum Lowcountry resident noted that in the early spring, the salt-marsh cordgrass was "tender, and eaten with avidity by mules, horses, cows, and sheep." Once the grass toughened in the summer, it could still be "cured and converted into excellent fodder."[109] Animals throughout the Lowcountry flourished in this rich estuarial environment, moving freely between the forest and the water's edge. Surrounded as it was by thousands of acres of marshland and bordered by natural fences of deep water, Wormsloe was ideally suited for raising large herds of cattle and hogs. Early colonists were also preconditioned to think of marshland as potential range. Noble Jones and his fellow Englishmen came from an agricultural system that had long taken advantage of seasonal and permanent wetlands to sustain livestock. English salt marshes were sites of intensive agriculture; landowners often ditched and drained coastal lowlands and built seawalls to prevent tidal inundations. Farmers then plowed or made pasture from these "reclaimed" lands. Southeastern English salt marshes, including the estuaries of the Thames River and the Swale of Kent, were particularly developed. In these areas east of Surrey, cattle and sheep grazing served as one of the primary agricultural activities during the early modern period.[110] Georgia colonists also were likely familiar with other European marshland practices, such as the Dutch and Danish habit of turning cattle and sheep into undrained salt marshes to forage. Farmers in these European lowlands drove their herds into the marshes to graze and cut fodder from the tidal flats.[111]

The use of meadows along inland rivers and streams to support livestock was at least as popular among English farmers as was salt marsh agriculture. This form of wetland agriculture, replicated in portions of New England during the colonial period, relied on river and creek bottom grasslands for winter hay and for grazing livestock. Grassy stretches along floodplains became integral components of New England agriculture rather than wasted expanses. Though the South lacked extensive wetland meadows, southerners also turned to river and creek bottoms and freshwater swamps to supply cattle. Free-ranging southern herds relied on the abundant growth of river cane throughout the region, grazing thousands of acres of the giant grass that flourished along regional watercourses.[112] Coastal Georgia's salt marshes, which were flooded by the tides all year round and produced lower-quality forage than did freshwater meadows, were less suitable than New England wetlands for making hay and lacked the river cane popular with southern stockmen, but they remained green throughout the year, and colonial Lowcountry farmers relied on the marshes to fulfill some of their herds' needs.[113] Although researchers have determined that cattle foraging in southeastern salt marshes are more selective than animals in upland meadows, they can graze effectively on a number of common species, including cordgrass, knotroot bristlegrass, panic grass, needlehead panic grass, and paspalum.[114]

Any number of domestic animals of dubious ownership roamed colonial Wormsloe, but Noble Jones also owned cattle and horses that he turned out on the land and looked after cattle owned by the Trustees. In 1741, Georgia's secretary, William Stephens, noted that Jones managed livestock on the property.[115] These cattle included a lot of one hundred steers the Trustees had imported from South Carolina in 1737 or 1738 and released on the Isle of Hope with the intention of using the herd to supply Savannah with beef.[116] Stephens recorded that Isle of Hope landowners built a sturdy fence across the northern end of the peninsula to keep wolves away not only from their personal cattle but also from the Trustees' animals, making "the Island an entire Possession."[117] This was not a unique stock-raising venture: Coastal islands and peninsulas were popular and favorable locations for contained herds.[118] Stephens also reported, for example, that a colonist named Burnside had "enclosed" nearby "Rotten-Possum" Island as cattle pasture in 1737.[119] As Kimber and Stephens noted, wolves roamed the Lowcountry landscape, and colonists feared the animals and took measures to drive them from settled portions of the coast.

English wolves had disappeared by the end of the Middle Ages, and the last recorded wolf in Scotland was killed in 1621, but the English retained numerous myths and legends concerning the predators. In the New World, colonial governments from New England to Georgia viewed wolf eradication as a vital step in civilizing the countryside. Feral and free-ranging livestock may have led to an increase in wolf populations during the early colonial period, and most town and county governments offered bounties for wolf heads or skins.[120] In New Ebenezer, a few miles north of Savannah, the Salzburger colonists complained that "the wolves are so daring that they fear neither fire nor dogs and often wreak great damage among the cattle and even besiege our dwellings."[121] The Wormsloe fence was at once a barrier to a very real threat and a physical expression of intellectual ideals. Jones's fence simultaneously kept predators out (at least in theory) and defined the land inside as domesticated, in contrast to the untamed acreage beyond the pale.

Predators of a wilier nature than wolves also threatened the herd. In February 1738, the Trustees complained that a man named Bradley had killed "one of the largest Steers of the Trustees that was in the Colony." Bradley complained that he was forced into this action because "Mr. *Jones* did not supply him; and that he could not see [his family] starve."[122] The imported cattle also gave Jones and his fellow Isle of Hope residents difficulties, placing pressure on the fence from the inside. Stephens reported that "a new Fence was made, which was thought sufficient to keep every Thing within it. . . . [T]hose Cattle were driven, as into a Place of Safety; but being exceedingly Wild, and not contented with all that Range (which was very Large) they soon broke out." Jones and his fellow herders located only some of the escapees, and some of Savannah's beef herd thus joined the feral cattle roaming the coastal forest.[123]

As Stephens's 1741 comments indicated, Jones and his neighbors rebuilt the Isle of Hope fence and, at least for a period, attempted to separate their common range from that of the rest of the region. While their fence was certainly intended to keep the South Carolina cattle in, it may also have been maintained because of heavy usage of the woods north of Wormsloe by Savannah's growing cattle herds: A map compiled shortly after the revolution labeled the area between the Isle of Hope and the town as a "cattle park."[124] Jones also sought some control over his stock by purchasing horse- and cowbells that helped him and his slaves locate the animals in the woods.[125] There are no records of hogs on Wormsloe during the colonial era, though it seems certain that the animals must have moved through the property at some point, even if only prior to the construction of the peninsular fence. The most likely explanation for this dearth of references to swine is that the animals were so ubiquitous that Jones felt little need to comment on them; like the auctioneers who sold stock in the Savannah squares, Jones might have viewed hogs as simply animals that ran in the woods.

Livestock on Wormsloe and across the Southeast changed regional ecosystems, often in dramatic fashion. Deb Bennett and Robert Hoffman, experts on introduced livestock in the New World, conclude that because of their relatively large body sizes and herding habits, the "mere physical presence" of cattle and hogs "had an immediate, visible effect upon areas where they were introduced"; herds of these animals "fundamentally changed the ecology of the hemisphere."[126] Cattle and hogs browsed hardwood undergrowth, killing young saplings and thinning understory species; pigs cropped grass-stage longleaf seedlings and rooted out young trees; and cattle compacted the soil where they gathered by streams or under shade trees. Selective grazing altered ecosystems as succulent forage declined and was replaced by less palatable species, a transition most evident along regional waterways, where livestock gradually destroyed the native river canes and reeds. These grazers were particularly attracted to longleaf-wiregrass savannas, such as the stands that covered portions of Wormsloe, as the pine ecosystem produced more forage per acre than any other southeastern woodland environment. Animals recently released into the wild also served as dispersal devices for invasive plant species, since such animals carried Old World seeds in their digestive tracts. Foraging hogs and cattle deposited these seeds, along with a healthy dose of fertilizer, in millions of locations across the Southeast. Although stock numbers as a whole were small in comparison to the vast coastal plain, the animals could be quite destructive at certain gathering sites. Congregations of domestic animals cut paths down creek banks, gobbled canebrakes, and killed favored scratching trees. If herds moved through a given stretch of woodland at least once a year for a decade or more, they could eliminate an entire generation of trees by grazing over each season's fragile saplings, eventually creating forests of mature trees and unpalatable understory plants. The presence of large numbers of free-ranging livestock also affected wild animal populations. Cattle and hogs competed with native foragers, such as whitetail deer and turkey, for the choicest browse and mast, and the growing livestock numbers increased the food supply available to mountain lions and wolves, perhaps temporarily increasing large predator populations. Livestock on Wormsloe engaged in all of these processes, and as they grazed, rooted, defecated, wallowed, and reproduced across the Isle of Hope, they gradually altered hardwood hammocks, longleaf pine stands, creek channels, and salt marsh.[127]

Cattle and hogs were not the only biota colonists intentionally carried from the Old World to the New. Georgia's colonization occurred at a moment of increased global traffic in plant species, and, from the first years of settlement on

Wormsloe, Noble Jones used the property to experiment with introduced botanical species.[128] Reflecting a natural curiosity about and some confusion over the exact climate of coastal Georgia, Jones and other colonists tried to establish various subtropical fruits, including oranges and pomegranates, alongside more climate-appropriate species such as grapes and plums. Many of Georgia's early settlers believed that the Lowcountry had the potential to produce the same species of tropical fruits grown in Southeast Asia and the Middle East, a belief rooted in Georgia's latitude (farther south than the Strait of Gibraltar) and in deceptively favorable early reports of the region's climate circulated by the Trustees.[129] The Joneses were not alone in their horticultural experimentations. The Trustees set aside a portion of Savannah for an experimental garden designed to determine which plants would thrive in the Lowcountry. William Stephens planted 150 mulberry saplings, oranges, and grapes in addition to his corn. Settler Abraham DeLyon, "a Portuguese Jew," planted grapes imported from Portugal on his farm plot, an operation he planned to expand to five thousand vines within a few years of his arrival.[130] These efforts reflected a widespread drive to find cash crops suitable to the colony, but Wormsloe seemed a property of particular diversity, attracting the notice of Savannah residents as well as distinguished outsiders.[131] Jones acquired one thousand grape cuttings from Stephens in 1745 and regularly experimented with a variety of plants, including figs and oranges.[132] Regular winter freezes ultimately doomed citrus fruits and other tropical staples in even the warmest regions of the colony, but for several decades Wormsloe produced a tremendous variety, if not quantity, of fruit.

One of the property's most famous visitors, noted naturalist John Bartram, recorded a detailed description of the horticultural experimentation taking place on Wormsloe. On a 1765 journey through the Southeast, Bartram wrote in his journal,

> We then rode to A gentlemans house which was delightfully scituated on A large tide salt creek where ye oisters is as thick as thay can ly within A stone cast of his house. He hath & is makeing great improvements in fruites which it is properly adapted for. His orange trees, pomegranates, figs, peaches, & nectarins grows and bears prodigiously. I saw one Apricot tree but it looked poorly, & one grape vine, ye fruit of which rotted Just before ripe, like as ours. Ye orange trees here is not hurt with ye frost while young, as in most parts of this countrey & allso at ye Colledge [Bethesda] for a year or two, & his pomegranates is very large, 4 or 5 inches diameter, & very delitious. I eat freely there & he gave us several to eat upon ye road. It was delightfull to see ye lovely scarlet blossoms & ripe fruit at once on ye same tree.[133]

Jones actively looked after these exotic plants, which were more than just casual plantings. According to Bartram, Jones took care with his trees and vines, manuring plants such as oranges in an attempt to produce more fruit.[134] The relatively small scale of these experiments indicates that Jones was intent on discovering species best suited to Wormsloe's environs rather than attempting to grow these crops for sale in the Savannah markets.

The horticultural endeavors of Noble Jones and his son even attracted the attention of one of the greatest of American experimenters, Benjamin Franklin. In a 1772 letter to Noble Wimberly Jones, Franklin enclosed a sample of upland rice from "Cochin China" (Vietnam) and seeds of the Chinese tallow tree. Reflecting the Joneses' desire to produce practical crops for the colony, Franklin described the rice, which could be raised without the elaborate hydrological works of tidal rice, as a potential Georgia staple. Franklin also touted the tallow tree, with its seedpods that produced a wax useful in candle making, as a plant that might become commercially successful.[135] Jones optimistically replied to Franklin that "there is little doubt of [the rice] doing well." Despite his positive reaction, there are no records of upland rice in Georgia again until Thomas Jefferson reintroduced it roughly twenty years later, and there is no concrete evidence that rice of any type was ever cultivated at Wormsloe. Jones was less enthused about the tallow tree, worrying that it might "fail for want of a proper knowledge of the kind of Land necessary, and the time of sowing and method of Treatment."[136] Again, there is no direct evidence to indicate where the Joneses planted tallow trees on Wormsloe (if at all) or how successful the early introductions were. Jones's worries about the hardiness of the tallow tree were unfounded: The plant has since become a widespread pest species throughout the Southeast, where it has invaded wetlands and crowded out less vigorous native species.[137] A few mature specimens still dot the Wormsloe landscape, linking the present plantation environment to Franklin's gift.

Although timber production, free-ranging livestock, and horticultural experimentation added economic value to Wormsloe, its definition as a plantation rested on staple-crop production. Like many early Georgia planters, Noble Jones sought a staple crop that would produce healthy profits from the sandy coastal soil. On Lambeth Plantation, where the fertile soil "would answer the Expence of Cultivation," he eventually turned to the dominant Lowcountry cash crop, rice. Although he left no record of his reasoning, he believed Wormsloe's soil and situation unsuited to rice culture and sought alternative crops.[138] Unlike Lambeth and many neighboring properties, Wormsloe seems to have moved through a variety of cultivation patterns before the Joneses settled on a major staple crop, sea island cotton, following the revolution. Indeed, the colonial search for a plantation staple was a study in futility.

Wormsloe's first commercial crop was silk. Georgia's Trustees believed that silk would be a natural fit for the colony for several reasons: a native mulberry tree grew in Georgia's coastal forests, and silkworms eat mulberry leaves; the prohibition on slavery favored the less intense labor of sericulture over the demands of staples such as rice and sugar; and English officials actively sought a colonial source of silk that would lessen dependence on foreign supplies. Although Asian silk was one of the fabled bounties of the Far East that drew European ships into their great voyages of exploration, by the eighteenth century, England had become dependent on foreign sources closer to home. Almost all silk used in English weaving came from the Italian Piedmont or Spain, a situation the Crown hoped to alleviate with the help of its overseas colonies. Lying slightly farther south than southern Spain and Italy, Georgia seemed a natural place to attempt English sericulture. The emphasis on Georgia silk production only increased in 1750, when the Italian and Spanish states "prohibited the exportation of raw silk" to stimulate domestic textile industries, almost entirely cutting off English silk weavers from their sources of supply.[139] Like colonial conceptions of disease, fruits, livestock, and forests, silk culture in Georgia relied on English ideas about European places and relationships as well as the specific conditions of the Georgia environment.

At first settlement, the Trustees believed that silkworms might feed on the abundant native red mulberry trees of the coast, an assumption that proved false—the worms refused to eat those leaves. When it became apparent that red mulberries would not sustain silkworms, colonial officials imported white mulberry seedlings and established rules and bounties promoting silk production. As a condition of all of the original land grants, Trustees would provide Georgia colonists with one hundred white mulberry trees to be planted on the grantees' forty-four-acre farm plots, and an equal number of trees were to be planted on any additional rural plantation grants, such as Wormsloe. Silk producers interplanted their mulberry trees with corn, carefully harvesting leaves to serve as food for their silkworms, "a constant process during the feeding period."[140] The original plantings at Wormsloe near the fortified house must have been relatively successful, as within a few years Jones was ready to produce silk. A 1750 account of local silk operations recorded that "Mr. Patrick Graham and Mr. Noble Jones who have both a pretty parcel of Trees, intend likewise to wind the cocoons they raise at their plantations."[141]

Exchanges from the following year indicate that silk cultivation was still very much a tenuous undertaking and suggest that Wormsloe's production, under the direction of Noble Jones's daughter, Mary, was of central importance to the colony's silk aspirations. In January 1751, colonial official James Habersham noted that the silkworm supply for the Savannah region was based on Wormsloe's production.[142] By March, he worried that the colony's silk-worm "seed" would be in short supply for the upcoming year, as Mary Jones had "suffered her worms to issue from the Cocoons without sorting them" (selecting an equal number of male and female cocoons to ensure maximum reproduction).[143] Just as Wormsloe struggled to produce profits from silk, Georgia as a whole found little success with the venture. Silk workers were typically poorly trained and more interested in securing their own tracts of land for farming than in learning sericulture; the coastal climate was alternately too hot or too cold for the best growth of silkworms; and white mulberries proved susceptible to damage from spring frosts. A late freeze in 1739 struck the young trees, creating a shortage of leaves that reduced Georgia's silkworm population by three-quarters.[144] Attempts at silk production were kept alive largely by a royal bounty. By 1750, the colonial government was so concerned about the state of Georgia sericulture that it offered a healthy incentive package designed to encourage production. The legislation promised homes built exclusively for silk makers, furnished weaving machines, and offered a bounty of two pounds to each woman willing to learn the craft of silk making.[145] Between 1755 and 1761, the colony exported an average of 450 pounds of silk a year, but in no year did the export equal the amount of imported silk finished goods.[146]

Mary Jones's supervision of Wormsloe's sericulture was not an unusual arrangement: Women made up the bulk of the colony's silk workers. The Trustees considered silkworm management to be female work, and it was often undertaken by the colony's poorest laborers or by hired servants. Even after the legalization of slavery in 1751, sericulture remained women's work. The Trustees required that masters train one female slave in the techniques of silk winding for every four male slaves owned.[147] Despite these prescriptions, few planters saw the value in teaching their slaves silkworm care, and poor women still undertook the majority of the work.[148] While Mary was clearly in charge of Wormsloe's silk work, the Joneses may also have had servants who worked with silk. Noble Jones's 1735 letter to Oglethorpe indicated that Jones employed indentured servants and was dissatisfied with the results, though the document does not describe exactly what sort of tasks demanded their labor.[149] In the end, silk culture on Wormsloe and in the Lowcountry was doomed not by labor troubles but rather by the combination of the unpredictable growth patterns of white mulberry trees in the Georgia climate, the elimination of the royal bounty on silk, and the increasing profitability of agricultural alternatives, such as rice, indigo, and eventually cotton. Although fleeting sericultural efforts reappeared across the South through the Civil War, the American Revolution effectively spelled the end of organized attempts to produce silk along the Georgia coast. Lowcountry sericulture may have died with the eighteenth century in part because the white mulberry was poorly adapted to reliable spring leaf production, but the tree naturalized and spread from sites such as Wormsloe across the Southeast, where today it is a relatively common tree of second-growth thickets. Indeed, white mulberries still grow across the Isle of Hope, where they have become a part of the forest complex and their abundant sticky fruits provide a valuable food source for birds and raccoons.[150]

The surviving fragmentary records often hint at additional agricultural activity on the property while avoiding any substantial details. Jones and his marines cleared at least fourteen acres of field within the first years of settlement, Jones invested in slaves even before the Trustees declared slavery legal, and the few surviving receipts from the period prove that he purchased agricultural implements, such as hoes and sickles, in substantial quantities, indicating an active interest in producing crops.[151] But the records fail to indicate what Jones was raising. Sickles indicate the production of at least some small grains, and it seems safe to presume that Jones produced corn, the most common southern food crop. Most accounts of farming on Wormsloe are impressionistic rather than specific, such as Jones's 1746 petition for a tract of land on Skidaway Island. The Trustees supported the petition, believing that he would stock and cultivate the new land in accordance with his actions at Wormsloe.[152] This decision indicates that Jones must have farmed his first property to the Trustees' satisfaction but furnishes no clue as to what he planted other than the requisite one hundred white mulberries. A 1750 petition for land along the Little Ogeechee River gives a few more details. Jones stated that his seven slaves working at Wormsloe were engaged in food production but that "he had not rais'd more than Food to feed them the ensuing Year."[153] Although this document suggests agriculture of only limited scale, it ignores Wormsloe activities for which we have other evidence, such as fruit culture, sericulture, and livestock production. These petitions demonstrate that Jones grew at least some subsistence crops for his family and slaves, though that sort of produce rarely made its way into records. But a great mystery surrounds the question of two famous Lowcountry staples. Did Wormsloe ever produce rice or indigo?[154]

Rice was the most important colonial staple in the Lowcountry, providing the greatest opportunity for planters to amass fortunes. According to geographer Judith Carney, rice was "the first cereal to be globally traded." South Carolina began exporting rice during the 1690s, and by the mid-1700s, the cereal grew in popularity in Europe, especially among Catholics, who consumed it during Lent. Prior to 1763, English trade laws required that Georgia planters export their rice directly to England for transshipment to other English colonies and the European continent. After the Crown eased this restriction, rice became a key export in trade between the American Lowcountry and Caribbean sugar, indigo, and cotton plantations, where it served as a central component of slave diets.[155] With its elaborate demands on both labor and landscape, rice shaped the developing plantation world of the Lowcountry to a great degree, ordering everything from the slave task system to the hydrologic flows of tidal rivers. The Jones family raised rice on Lambeth Plantation during the colonial era and after the revolution created a new rice estate, Newton, south of Savannah. Records also reveal that the Joneses experimented with small amounts of the cereal on another property, Poplar Grove. But the evidence suggests that they never grew the crop on Wormsloe. Records from the plantation detail the presence of numerous ditches, an earthen dam, and a rice mill, and Jones commissioned local craftsmen to make trunks and gates, which controlled the flow of water. All of these structures were common on Lowcountry rice plantations, but with the exception of the rice mill (which processed grain from adjoining properties), these works seem to have been solely for drainage and/or flood control on Wormsloe.[156] The records fail to mention rice culture, and the property itself lacks evidence of the carefully constructed impoundments and leveling necessary for the grain. If Wormsloe's fields ever grew rice, it was probably associated with Noble W. Jones's experimentation with the upland variety provided by Franklin.

There are more enticing hints that Wormsloe may have produced indigo at some point during or just after the colonial period, but as with rice, no definitive proof exists. Indigo is a large, leafy plant that produces a vivid blue/purple dye that was popular with European textile manufacturers, and the crop often served as a secondary staple on plantations focused on rice production. Like silk and rice production, indigo cultivation in Georgia was connected to foreign markets and imperial desires as well as to the Lowcountry landscape. The Navigation Act of 1660 prohibited colonial producers from selling indigo to any foreign merchants but created a steady English market for the dye, and Jamaican planters' shift from indigo to more lucrative sugar production in the 1670s resulted in an indigo shortage that South Carolina planters slowly began to fill. Two varieties of indigo, *Indigofera carolinians* and *Indigofera lespotsepala*, were indigenous to the South Carolina and Georgia coasts, and although these species did not produce high-quality dye, they suggested that the Caribbean commercial species would grow in the region. A depression in rice prices and a 1748 royal bounty of six pence a pound revived indigo culture in South Carolina, and the crop spread across the Georgia line by 1750. Ongoing English hostilities with France and Spain had cut English textile producers off from much of their foreign dye supply and stimulated colonial indigo production. An extremely demanding crop, indigo relied on the same sorts of exacting slave labor structures as rice, an expensive processing facility, and "a high degree of technical knowledge" and was thus almost exclusively a crop of the larger planters.[157] Producing the dye involved slaves in land clearing, plowing, weeding, cutting, fermenting (an incredibly malodorous process), long periods of stirring the solution, and straining, bagging, and pressing the dye, activities that took place from well before first frost to early winter. Although Georgia and Carolina indigo produced a passable dye, the area's production was never as pure or as efficient as that of tropical plantations, such as those in Guatemala, where rich soil, abundant moisture, and a longer growing season meant that Central American planters could harvest up to eight cuttings a year, compared to just two along the Georgia coast. As was the case with sericulture, the American Revolution largely spelled the end of Lowcountry indigo cultivation. The end of the Crown bounty, the loss of English trade, increased competition from the French West Indies and Guatemala, and the greater profitability of cotton following the invention of the cotton gin relegated indigo to the status of a historic commodity.[158]

Noble Jones certainly raised indigo on at least one of his regional properties. In 1760, he took out an insurance policy on a cask of indigo shipped to London, but his slaves could have raised the crop on Skidaway or another Lowcountry plantation. Indigo was most likely on Lambeth, where Jones also produced rice.[159] A 1796 letter to George Jones (Noble Wimberly Jones's son) from his wife, Sarah, strongly implied that they were raising indigo at that point, but George and Sarah were living on nearby Newton plantation at the time.[160] Although the Joneses raised some indigo, had the labor force to produce the dye in substantial quantities, and mentioned the crop during years they actively cultivated Wormsloe, indigo production on the property can only be described as a possibility based on the surviving sources.

The onset of the American Revolution put a pause to planting and experimenting on Wormsloe and throughout the surrounding Lowcountry. Wartime struggles for control of Savannah affected agricultural produce and livestock in the plantation's vicinity. British officials promised emancipation to slaves who took up arms against the rebels, a move that struck fear into the scions of the colony's plantation economy.[161] British forces also consumed the produce of Lowcountry agriculture. When a royal expedition led by Archibald Campbell captured Savannah in December 1778, commissary agents scoured the countryside for provisions and requisitioned rice, corn, and livestock, especially from suspected rebels. A British officer stationed in the city reported to his superiors, "All the Rebel cattle within reach of our posts, have been ordered for slaughter, and to be salted up for the use of the navy and army." Officials offered to purchase "bullocks, hogs, sheep, poultry, &c." from farmers and planters who had managed to escape the requisition drives.[162] Countryside plantations also suffered at the hands of rebel guerrillas, who operated in the swamps, marshes, and back creeks south of the town. These irregulars confiscated supplies, destroyed the homes and farm buildings of suspected loyalists, and collected food wherever they could find it. Shortly after the British captured the city, this intermittent violence halted most agricultural operations in the vicinity of Savannah, with the exception of the production of naval stores, which the British strongly encouraged.[163]

The turmoil of the revolutionary period had a direct impact on the Jones family and Wormsloe. Noble W. Jones, an ardent revolutionary, fled Savannah ahead of the British occupation, losing most of his books and personal papers in the process, and he left Wormsloe in the hands of his sister, Mary.[164] British agents likely searched the property for supplies, and American and French forces marched just west of the estate in an unsuccessful 1779 campaign to retake Savannah.[165] Even though Mary Jones had inherited the property from her father at his death in 1775, Noble Wimberly's patriot activities made his family a target of British retribution. In 1780, royal officials attached Noble W. Jones's Savannah-area property, though it is unclear if they made moves to confiscate Wormsloe as well.[166] Loyalist neighbors or simply individuals seeking to take advantage of wartime circumstances also exploited Wormsloe's resources during the war. In 1780, James Bulloch, who had married Mary Jones, issued a notice in the *Georgia Gazette* forbidding Skidaway Island residents from continuing to cross Wormsloe as a shortcut to their homes, trespasses resulting from wartime disruptions of the ferry just north of the plantation.[167] Wormsloe's forests also tempted some unscrupulous neighbors. In a postwar lawsuit, Noble W. Jones charged John Fox and Martin Toller with cutting "white Oak staves and other lumber" from Noble Jones's estate, presumably including Wormsloe, during the British occupation. Jones asserted that Fox and Toller had illegally carted off timber worth an astonishing five hundred pounds sterling.[168] While the Joneses' case may have been extreme, illicit cutting of live oak timber during the turmoil of the revolution was a widespread problem along the Georgia coast.[169]

The British occupation forces withdrew from Savannah in 1782, and residents of the surrounding countryside returned to their estates to resume agricultural activity. Accounts of the lasting effects of the revolution on the region vary. Kenneth Coleman argues that the war had little effect on Savannah and its environs: He claims that the British evacuated Savannah without doing a great deal of damage to the town's physical infrastructure, that relatively few Georgia slaves escaped bondage during the war, and that agricultural capital remained largely intact. Despite the great potential for economic and social disruption, little lasting change took place.[170] Conversely, Walter Fraser Jr. describes the revolution as a transformative event in the Lowcountry. He argues that a substantial portion of the region's slave labor left with their Tory masters or took advantage of wartime turmoil to escape, that the conflict stripped the region of livestock, and that plantation infrastructure such as buildings and rice impoundments suffered from general neglect and direct damage.[171]

On Wormsloe, the revolution was significant but did not create lasting changes in the landscape. Agricultural activities ceased for a few years, military forces likely seized the plantation's domestic animals, neighbors crossed the property and cut live oaks, and perhaps a few of the plantation's slaves fled the estate along with the evacuating British forces, but when the revolution ended, the Joneses resumed their prewar activities. Indeed, as the war wound to a close, Noble W. Jones penned a poem that emphasized his aspirations for the postwar economic situation and connected American mastery of the land, commerce, and slaves to the new nation's imminent freedom from English political domination:

> Hail! brave Columbians, sons of heaven,
> To whose all conquering hands tis given,
> To bend proud tyrants down;
> To burst vile Slavry's Iron bands,
> Guard sacred freedom, save your lands;
> There fix the God in his Throne.
>
> Nomore shall Albion rule the waves;
> For you, the wide Atlantic heaves,
> And own your proud controul;
> For you she visits every shore,
> Wafts Indias treasure, Africs ore,
> And wealth, from pole to pole.[172]

Unlike damaged or neglected rice plantations, with their elaborate maintenance requirements, Wormsloe's diverse agriculture was easily resurrected, and the family's slaveholdings seemed largely unscathed. Rather, Wormsloe's revolution was a dramatic but discrete event, a punctuated period of change and disruption that, once ended, left few permanent marks yet presented numerous economic possibilities.[173] The next war to engulf the plantation would be a far more momentous occurrence.

The revolution emphasized Wormsloe's continued connections to Savannah. The estate's proximity to the town, a port of growing importance, tied the plantation to the urban center's markets, but these connections also bound the property to the rest of the Atlantic world. Like other plantations surrounding the port, Wormsloe became a target of British forces intent on securing the region. The plantation's location along a channel that connected the town to the ocean also placed Wormsloe in the way of military activity, as invading armies sought avenues of surprise attack; thus, the marshland geography that provided the site with economic advantages also posed concurrent risks. Hogs, cattle, sheep, and rice flowed out of the region to feed armies on both sides, smallpox outbreaks spread by British occupiers marked disease cultures moving in, and the violence of war slowed agricultural activities but accelerated other uses of the environment, including the production of naval stores and earthmoving for trenches and fortifications.[174] Like horticultural experimentation, staple crops, transatlantic diseases, and colonial conceptions of forests and livestock, the war reinforced Wormsloe's ties to distant landscapes.

The surviving documents help piece together a picture of colonial Wormsloe undergoing a series of changes. The Joneses and their servants and slaves cut the property's woods and cleared a few fields and built a fort and marine and slave huts; livestock moved freely through the standing forest; servants and slaves labored to produce crops; and a number of exotic species grew next to the native live oaks and pines. Noble Jones had also expanded the boundaries of the property. While these changes were dramatic, Wormsloe in the 1780s in many ways closely resembled the Wormsloe of the 1730s: Most of the property remained covered in mature timber, relatively few structures dotted the landscape, and the expansive salt marsh still surrounded the plantation. The 1785 tax returns of Noble Jones's estate summarized the situation. The tax assessor described the Jones family's landholdings in newly formed Chatham County, which included Wormsloe, simply as 437 acres of "pineland" and 1,200 acres of "marsh."[175] At the end of the colonial period, Wormsloe was still a landscape dominated by forest and salt marsh rather than agricultural fields.

The fragmentary colonial sources allow us to construct a sketch of Wormsloe as a farm/plantation during the prerevolutionary era, though the image is foggy at best. Noble Jones and his children raised cattle and swine, which ranged in the coastal woods and marshes, changing coastal ecosystems as they grazed, rooted, and reproduced across the landscape. Jones also grew a number of tropical and subtropical fruits and shared his horticultural methods with neighbors and guests. With these experiments, Jones sought crops best suited to the extremes of the coastal environment. From the early decades of settlement, Wormsloe was the site of sericulture. The plantation produced some silk and served as a source of young silkworms used by Georgia's other sericulturalists. The Joneses also raised some field crops on Wormsloe, though this produce (with the possible exception of indigo) was likely intended for subsistence rather than for local markets. The Joneses also experimented with various forms of agricultural labor—marines, family members, indentured servants, and finally massive purchases of African slaves. By midcentury, Wormsloe's labor system came to resemble that of the rest of the plantation South, though that evolution was by no means predetermined.

As this sketch indicates, colonial Wormsloe was a site of conscious experimentation. Noble Jones spent his first years on the property discovering coastal Georgia's natural resources, from broad forests to feral livestock to abundant fish and game. The Joneses also began exploring potential staple crops in a search for produce well suited to the landscape, a search that was not resolved during the colonial era despite the economic success of tidal rice culture and indigo in the surrounding Lowcountry. These experiments and transitions epitomized the ideological and physical struggles of colonization. Jones and his neighbors had to learn not only how to live in the New World but also how to conceptualize a new environment and their place in a natural world that proved to be a distinct place despite preconceived notions about "Neo-Europes."

Although unique in its details, Wormsloe's process of experimentation was a typical New World colonial experience. Settlers in the Chesapeake and the English West Indies had explored their local environments and conducted economic experiments during the first half of the seventeenth century before settling on tobacco and sugar, respectively, and similar activities took place in the Carolina Lowcountry in the second half of that century before the region's planters turned to large-scale rice production. That coastal Georgia still struggled to find revenue-producing agricultural products in the mid-eighteenth century despite these earlier examples illustrates the power of local environments over colonists' minds and efforts. Thus, despite the strong similarities between the founding of older English colonies and the settlement of the mouth of the Savannah, the specific characteristics of Wormsloe's environment resulted in the postrevolutionary adoption of a plantation staple that was largely limited to portions of the Georgia and South Carolina Lowcountry.

Perhaps most important, Jones's fashioning of a plantation in the colonial Lowcountry combined his knowledge of local environmental conditions with his conceptions of the greater world. Jones's understandings of Wormsloe's crops, fields, forests, marshes, diseases, slaves, and situation all reflected an expanding English empire, limited and tempered by the environmental constraints and resources of the Isle of Hope. He experimented with silk because white mulberries grew in Georgia and because of the needs of English textile producers and politics in Italy and Spain; he worried about profligate timbering around Savannah because such actions harmed the local range and because of the collective English experience of timber shortage; and he feared the seasonal fevers of the Lowcountry because of a local mosquito and because of the transatlantic trade that carried slaves and African diseases from the Old World to the New. Wormsloe would remain a cosmopolitan place over the next two and a half centuries, but the global influence on the Lowcountry plantation would never be greater than it was during the colonial era.

CHAPTER TWO

Becoming a Plantation

*Wormsloe from the Revolution
to the Civil War*

A CROW FLYING across the Skidaway Road and down the Isle of Hope peninsula in the spring of 1783 would have passed over a coastal live oak and mixed pine forest, with an occasional palmetto or marshy slough breaking up the canopy. Moving south, the bird might have wheeled once over Noble Jones's tabby fort and an adjacent cornfield or two, edged by small wooden slave huts and perhaps dotted by a few foraging cattle or hogs, but from the air, most of Wormsloe plantation would have looked little different from the surrounding marshes and woods. A similar crow soaring over the landscape in 1861 would have encountered a far different prospect. Expansive fields of corn and hay edged the Skidaway Road at the property's northern border, surrounded by wooden rail fences and dissected by arrow-straight drainage ditches. A large new wooden plantation house stood prominently in a clearing at the center of the property, near a bend in the Skidaway River. An expansive farmyard, flower and vegetable gardens, and more than a dozen wooden barns, sheds, stables, and other structures, including a new cotton gin and a rice mill, surrounded the house. A wooden dock jutted into the river with a view east across the marsh to Long Island, which was largely open and cultivated as well. Although little more than crumbling walls remained of the old fort south of the plantation house, the old colonial fields grew sea island cotton cultivated by more than fifty slaves, who might have looked up and wished that they too could escape the plantation as easily as our crow.

By the onset of the Civil War, Wormsloe was a far different place than it had been eighty years earlier, and the changes to both people and landscape were more than superficial. After the revolution's end, the Jones family turned to sea island cotton as the plantation's staple crop. Cultivation of the fiber emerged out of the agricultural experimentation that had dominated the colonial plantation and largely replaced diversified horticultural activities with a profitable but demanding global staple. The fiber quickly dominated the rhythms of plantation life, structuring daily activities around the seasons of planting, hoeing, and harvesting, and the needs of the crop and its culture shaped both usage and perceptions of the Lowcountry environment. With the adoption of sea island cotton, slavery became even more central to Wormsloe's operation. By the mid-1800s, the plantation was a landscape shaped by race as well as crops. Slaves tended sea island cotton under a division of labor known as the task system, a form of management that divided both land and labor into agricultural units and on most days provided slaves with some personal time (and along with it the master's expectation that black workers would provide a portion of their own subsistence). The task system, coupled with an antebellum remodeling of the plantation's built landscape, divided Wormsloe into distinct white and black landscapes. By the 1850s, the growth of the plantation led to an agricultural improvement campaign by planter George W. Jones, Noble Jones's great-grandson. George sought to make Wormsloe more efficient and profitable through the application of scientific agricultural principles. These efforts produced more cotton, but they also reordered the landscape in ways that placed a great emphasis on Jones's mastery over both slaves and the environment. Factors largely beyond Jones's control ultimately would render his improvement campaign unsuccessful, but changes in the Wormsloe landscape would prove more lasting.

Following the turmoil of the revolution, Wormsloe once again became a landscape of modest agricultural production. Noble Jones's daughter, Mary, and her husband, James Bulloch, inherited the plantation in 1775 and controlled Wormsloe for two decades. The Bullochs farmed the plantation on a relatively small scale until 1796, when Mary's death transferred the property to her brother, Noble Wimberly Jones. Farm activities during this period most likely mirrored colonial agriculture. The Bullochs continued to range livestock on Wormsloe and probably cultivated at least a few row crops in addition to raising a portion of their own food. Plantation agriculture during this period seems to have been almost identical to prewar labor on the property, absent sericulture and the horticultural experimentation of Noble Jones. An estate inventory and a sale notice in the *Georgia Gazette* reveal that at the time of Mary's death, she owned twelve slaves and a small herd of cattle.[1] Noble W. Jones likely used the estate in a similar manner, working a few slaves and hunting or relaxing on the property when he had the chance to get away from his Savannah home and relying on real estate deals and the produce of his other plantations for his primary income. Jones did not keep control of Wormsloe for long; in 1804, he passed the property along to his son, George, who would oversee the plantation for more than three decades.[2]

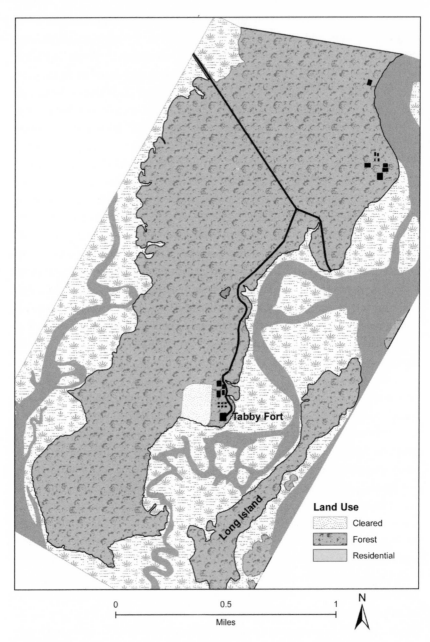

Land Use

Cleared

Forest

Residential

Long Island

Tabby Fort

0   0.5   1

Miles

N

Wormsloe 1810. Map by Dr. Thomas R. Jordan, Center for Remote Sensing and Mapping Science, Department of Geography, University of Georgia, Athens, Georgia.

Even after more than half a century of human settlement, parts of Worms-loe and the surrounding coast were timbered and seemingly wild places. Despite its proximity to Savannah, postrevolution Wormsloe remained a distinctly rural estate, a place where Noble W. Jones could escape to enjoy "the exercise of hunting Deer by hounds."[3] A more in-depth look at the area's fauna comes from famous entomologist and ornithologist John Abbot. Recording his observations across the Georgia Lowcountry near the end of the eighteenth century, he compiled a particularly revealing notebook describing local birds and their habitats. Abbot's notes were an exploration of the avifaunal diversity of the Lowcountry, from his comments on crested flycatchers to his observations of prothonotary warblers and least bitterns. Several species soar from the pages. Abbot recorded flocks of passenger pigeons and majestic sandhill cranes in the region's pinewood flats. He noted the presence of chattering congregations of the Carolina "Parroquet" in lowland swamps and abandoned apple orchards and reported that the fabled ivory-billed woodpecker "has a bill like bone or Ivory, They cry is said to be a sign of or foretell rain." In all, Abbot recorded and described the appearance and habits of 153 regional species in his notebook.[4]

The Lowcountry world that Abbot described at least superficially resembled the broad forests present at the founding of Savannah, but Abbot included a cautionary note at the end of his journal. Worried about increasing agricultural activity and the expansion of Savannah and other regional towns, Abbot feared that the days of abundant wildlife and broad expanses of undisturbed coastal woods were numbered. In a brief passage following his bird observations, he warned of the end of certain aquatic habitats at the hands of rice and cotton planters: "The Pine woods of this country abounding with Ponds of various sizes, in the summer these dry's away when a multitude of small Cat fish & other kinds & Tadpoles may be observed in the shallow holes of them, affords a plentiful repast to the Aquatick Birds which then visit us & breed here, but it is probable these will be much rarer as the country becomes more settled, Indeed I think they already decrease (as [Lowcountry residents] already drain & plant many of these ponds) annually."[5] Abbot's words would prove prescient over the next century. His observations of Georgia's coastal avian life took place during the region's last few decades of superabundant bird populations.[6] When the next extant inventory of bird species found in and around Wormsloe appeared nearly a hundred years later, the passenger pigeon, sandhill crane, Carolina parakeet, and ivory-billed woodpecker were nowhere to be found. Human and domestic animal population growth, farm clearing, town building, and timbering across the southeastern coast had changed millions of acres of natural habitat, extirpating or greatly reducing a number of regional bird species. Though less common, the Lowcountry's growing agricultural and urban landscapes also led to population increases in certain species. Deer and rabbits benefited from an increase in edge habitat along field and pasture borders, and bobolink and crow populations boomed as rice and corn production increased. These sweeping environmental changes resulted largely from an exponential human population increase. In 1800, Georgia had only 162,686 residents, but a century later that number had increased to 2,216,331. Because of its early settlement, Chatham County's population did not increase at the same astronomical rate as the state as a whole, but the county still expanded from 12,946 residents in 1800 to 71,239 people by the end of the nineteenth century.[7]

Much of this growth had taken place in Chatham by the onset of the Civil War. Between the first federal census of 1790 and the 1860 count, the county's population expanded from 10,769 to 31,043. This booming population was composed of a wide variety of people in an increasingly diverse countryside. Just prior to the Civil War, Chatham had 14,807 slaves, more than in any other Georgia county, and the total population was also almost 10,000 greater than that of Richmond, the next most populous county. The white population had grown much faster than the number of slaves since 1790, when the enslaved outnumbered whites almost four to one. This white population growth resulted in large part from Savannah's expansion. The port city spread south from the river into the county's agricultural land, bringing work for store merchants, shipbuilders, drayers, and countless other craftsmen and laborers—both free and slave—as well as northern tourists seeking an escape from harsh winter climes. In 1860, the county also boasted thirty-eight manufacturing establishments that employed 674 men and women. Although relative slave numbers declined following the revolution, the absolute numbers of bound workers grew, and agriculture remained a vital segment of the county economy. By 1860, Chatham was dominated by large plantations and small market garden plots, with relatively few middling farms. Of the county's 215 recorded farms, 60 percent were either larger than five hundred acres or smaller than fifty acres; statewide, more than 60 percent of all farms fell between those two figures. Influential planters remained some of the wealthiest individuals in local society; in 1860, county residents included forty-nine planters who owned fifty or more slaves. At the other end of the spectrum, the free black population stood at 725 by the close of the decade, by far Georgia's largest concentration of free people of color. These free blacks labored for wages in the city and toiled in small market gardens in the rural portions of the county. These census figures sketch out a complex, relatively developed mosaic of a landscape. Savannah had grown to be a true port city of manufacturing establishments, docks, and markets, ringed by small farms producing livestock and produce for urban residents and large plantations producing staples for national and international markets. All of these uses cleared and developed the pines and ponds that Abbot had so admired.[8]

Wormsloe was nestled into this landscape, a substantial plantation on the outskirts of the city, and by the nineteenth century was producing a staple for global markets. The growth of both urban and rural Chatham County revolved around the spread of cotton across Georgia and the Deep South, a trend in which Wormsloe took part. Although surviving evidence suggests that the Joneses never found a staple crop for Wormsloe during the colonial period, after the revolution they began to cultivate long-staple cotton on a significant scale. (By the late eighteenth century, the crop had become known in the Southeast as sea island cotton, thanks to its reliance on the coastal climate.) Definitely by 1806 and probably as early as the last decade of the eighteenth century, George Jones was planting the crop on Wormsloe.[9] With Mary Bulloch's death in 1796, George Jones, who operated a plantation near Augusta, returned to the Savannah area to manage Wormsloe for his father as part of a burgeoning agricultural estate; in addition to the old homesite on the Isle of Hope, George purchased a plantation near the Little Ogeechee River, which he named Newton, and bought land just south of Savannah, christening the parcel Poplar Grove. Each of the three plantations had a distinct form of cultivation adapted to its location and soil. George grew rice at Newton, where he used the waters of the Little Ogeechee to inundate impoundments, and he first grew short-staple (upland) cotton on Poplar Grove's landlocked fields, later adding such truck crops as watermelons and peanuts to sell in Savannah's expanding markets. Both properties would prove profitable. On Wormsloe, Jones, like many of his neighbors, turned to a new staple crop particularly suited to the Isle of Hope's maritime environment: sea island cotton.[10] This crop and its culture would rule the plantation for the next seven decades, fading only with the dramatic labor changes wrought by Reconstruction.

Sea island cotton as a commercial crop in the Georgia Lowcountry was a relatively recent development in 1800. Although the colonists occasionally planted sea island cotton throughout Georgia's early years—it was even included in the Trustees' garden—prior to the revolution it was strictly a home-use product. The occasional experimenter, such as George Whitefield, who employed some of the wards of Bethesda orphanage under his care in picking cotton as early as 1740, attempted small-scale sale of the fiber, but there was little profit in its cultivation.[11] Originating in Anguilla, sea island cotton as it first arrived in the Lowcountry was a short-day, perennial species. This cotton was adapted to tropical warmth and relatively even day length, and it flowered in the fall in the Southeast. As a result, it often produced little floss before being killed by frost.[12] This fragile "tree-cotton," with its uncertain production, was ill suited to plantation agriculture. While traveling along the Georgia coast during a 1774 journey to East Florida, naturalist William Bartram provided one of the best sketches of early sea island cotton and its role in Lowcountry life. Noting a relative lack of cotton and indigo plantations on Georgia's barrier islands, he elaborated,

> The cotton is planted only by the poorer class of people, just enough for their family consumption: they plant two species of it, the annual and West-Indian; the former is low, and planted every year; the balls of this are very large, and the phlox long, strong, and perfectly white; the West-Indian is a tall perennial plant, the stalk somewhat shrubby, several of which rise up from the root for several years successively, the stems of the former year being killed by the winter frosts. The balls of this latter species are not quite so large as those of the herbaceous cotton; but the phlox, or wool, is long, extremely fine, silky, and white. A plantation of this kind will last several years, with moderate labour and care, whereas the annual sort is planted every year.[13]

Following the revolution, cotton culture spread across the Lowcountry and the Upstate, in part due to Georgians' wartime realization of their overdependence on foreign textiles.[14] In 1786, a plant breeder on Skidaway Island changed sea island cotton in a way that soon made it a valuable southern staple crop. Just across the river from Wormsloe, planter James Spaulding experimented with a day-neutral version of sea island cotton, probably selected from a random mutation in the short-day species. Unlike tropical varieties of cotton that need long days of relatively even length to trigger their production of fiber, day-neutral cotton plants grow and bloom independent of the changing duration of light that occurs in temperate locales over the course of the year. Drawing on earlier trials conducted by his neighbor, John Earle, Spaulding perfected a sea island variety that did well in Georgia's climate, maturing independent of the photoperiod fluctuations of the southeastern seasons. Unlike the perennial Anguilla variety, which frost threatened every year, Spaulding's plants flowered much earlier and produced a reliable crop each season. This new strain lost its parents' perennial habit and had to be replanted every year, but its reliable production of high-quality fiber revolutionized cotton growing along the southeastern coast.[15]

Earle's and Spaulding's experiments with Caribbean cotton were part of a general late-eighteenth-century interest in transplanting crops across the globe and breeding improved varieties. Cotton experimentation existed at the intersection of colonial plant diffusion and new, scientific methods of plant breeding. Although the Columbian Exchange of plant material had been ongoing for almost three hundred years by the conclusion of the American Revolution, European colonialism and commodity plantation agriculture continued to fuel the transfer of plants (and animals) across oceans and continents. At roughly the same time that Spaulding perfected sea island cotton, French colonists transplanted clove and nutmeg trees from Southeast Asia to Mauritius and to the French African possessions, Russian agriculturalists spread potatoes across the steppes, corn penetrated the farms of northern China, Caribbean planters introduced a new Asian sugarcane variety, Joseph Banks engineered the movement of breadfruit trees from Tahiti to Jamaica, and Russian fur traders planted rhubarb in Alaska.[16] Closer to Wormsloe, old and new apple varieties moved across the East Coast and the American South as farmers and planters moved to fresh lands, and European horse chestnuts became popular edible ornamentals in southern plantation gardens.[17] Plant breeders also modified plants in more direct ways than through simple relocation. The last years of the eighteenth century were, as one botanist defines them, "the dawn of plant breeding."[18] Experimenters selected for the hardiest and most productive individuals in each plant generation, as agriculturalists had done for centuries, but they also began to explore the intentional cross-breeding of plant varieties to produce hybrid crops. (Hybridization produces offspring that are larger and hardier than either parental type, but the resulting hybrids cannot pass these superior traits on to the succeeding generation.)[19] Across the new United States, breeders began work on hybridizing plant varieties: Northeastern nurseryman William Prince developed new plums, Joseph Cooper grew and marketed more productive vegetables in New Jersey, and Pennsylvania's Peter Legaux worked with native grape stocks.[20] When Spaulding introduced a foreign cotton variety to Skidaway soil and selected for the hardiest, best adapted plants (Spaulding probably did not engage in hybridization), he took part in horticultural processes occurring across the nation and the globe.

Whatever his technique, Spaulding did his work well. The new variety of cotton was a success on the coast, and it spread rapidly over sandy lands suited for its growth. Acre for acre, a well-managed sea island cotton plantation was twice as profitable as a rice plantation in 1800, and cotton cultivation did not require the construction and maintenance of the elaborate earthworks and irrigation ditches that rice culture demanded. By 1828, demand was such that exceptional sea island cotton could bring an extraordinary two dollars per pound, and average fiber sold for twice as much as short-staple cotton.[21]

Like the silk, rice, and indigo that preceded it, sea island cotton was an agricultural commodity very much entangled within the economics of empire and transatlantic trade. The variety planted in Wormsloe's fields was an offshoot of a West Indian cultivar that had entered European markets as early as the mid-seventeenth century. This Georgia cotton, like its Caribbean predecessor, produced exceptionally long fiber—at 1.5 to 2 inches in length, the floss was considerably longer than short-staple cotton, the fibers of which averaged less than an inch in length—that made spinning the individual strands into thread much easier. This ease of spinning combined with its silky texture to make sea island cotton a favorite of English and French weavers, who transformed the staple into expensive laces and muslins for resale in Europe or export to growing colonial outposts: Even Queen Victoria blew her nose into lace handkerchiefs woven from sea island cotton. Indeed, almost all of the high-quality cotton raised on coastal plantations such as Wormsloe during the early national period was bound for European markets, and prices and gossip on the Liverpool market meant more to these Lowcountry planters than the demand in New York or Boston.[22] By the 1850s, the interests of cotton planters in the American South were firmly joined with the spinners and weavers of Lancashire, France, and Germany, and cotton weaving had become the most important manufacturing industry in the world. Although Georgia's planters relied on foreign manufacturers, the reverse was true as well, as booming European manufacturing centers grew dependent on American long- and short-staple cotton. Whereas southern growers shipped a paltry ten bales of cotton to England in 1784, by 1820 exports destined for Lancashire alone topped 300,000 bales.[23] According to historian Sven Beckert, even specialized cotton cultivation, such as that on Wormsloe, was "ensnared in a global system and could not be made sense of without it."[24]

While cotton marketing and manufacture was an international business, cultivation of the plant relied on understandings of particular local landscapes. Sea island cotton was a relatively demanding plant; it required a specific microclimate similar to the one found on Wormsloe to thrive. Plantations adapted to sea island culture needed warm summers and at least 260 frost-free days over the course of the growing season for the fiber to fully mature. Sea island fields also had to be located close enough to coastal waters to receive regular humid salt breezes, which were vital in producing the silky texture that made the variety so valuable. Although the plants would grow farther inland, quality declined in proportion to a field's distance from salt water. Indeed, early "planters believed that the best fields had an ocean exposure."[25] In addition, sea island cotton needed regular rainfall—around four inches each month—during its first three growing months, followed by drier conditions during the late fall and early winter harvest season, when inclement weather might damage the floss. These climatic demands closely matched the typical weather patterns of the southeastern coast (with the notable exception of the occasional fall hurricane, which proved to be a significant annual threat). The crop also did best on level sandy land that drained well, terrain often indicated by stretches of coastal woods that grew tall stands of longleaf or loblolly pines. Sea island cotton relied heavily on the natural abundance of nearby saltwater marshes. Planters used crushed oyster shells from the marshes and associated prehistoric middens for field roads and to reduce soil acidity, and they employed their slaves in seasonal hauling of rich marsh muck and "the drifted reck, that is thrown up by the tides" to poor spots in their fields. The environmental conditions of Wormsloe that made it a poor site for rice—a lack of naturally swampy ground and a location too close to the coast to ensure the availability of fresh water with which to flood impoundments—proved to be advantages for cotton cultivation. With its location along the tidal Skidaway River, wide marshes, regular salt breezes, substantial labor force, adequate drainage, and broad pine woods, Wormsloe was well adapted to this new form of cotton culture.[26]

The cultivation of Wormsloe's sea island cotton fields was the work of the Jones family's slaves under the supervision of a white overseer. Although slaves were probably less influential in the shaping of sea island cotton culture than in tidal rice development, they were nevertheless the individuals with the most intimate knowledge of cotton from planting to bagging. In short, they were key to the success of the Joneses' experiments with the new staple.[27] Many slaves imported into colonial Georgia came from cosmopolitan backgrounds. A portion of the early Lowcountry slave population had experienced coastal African trade centers and slave markets that gathered together Europeans and Africans. After surviving the Middle Passage, they had then labored in the Caribbean, where sea island cotton flourished in a plantation economy. And finally, they had survived transit and sale to plantation owners along the Georgia coast. In addition to a level of acquired disease immunity, at each step along the way these Africans gained language skills, foodways, and agricultural knowledge. These "Atlantic creoles," to borrow a term from Ira Berlin, may have served a critical role in teaching Lowcountry planters the finer points of sea island cotton cultivation.[28] There is direct evidence of this technology transfer on Sapelo Island to the south of Wormsloe. In the late 1700s, planter Thomas Spalding purchased a Muslim slave named Bilali and his family, all of whom had worked on a cotton plantation in the Bahamas. An educated man who could read and write Arabic and who celebrated Islamic holy days throughout his captivity, Bilali and his kin also knew cotton culture. By 1800, drawing on his slaves' expertise, Spalding had created one of the Southeast's first large sea island cotton plantations.[29]

Historians Peter Wood and Daniel Littlefield and geographer Judith Carney, among other scholars, have described a similar transfer of agricultural techniques across the Atlantic basin in the form of rice culture. Beginning in the early 1700s, rice plantations in the American South planted African as well as Asian rice varieties; planters built elaborate ditches, embankments, and gates that echoed African forms to control and direct field hydrology; and slaves performed agricultural tasks in ways that mimicked West African fieldwork. As Wood has noted, "When New World slaves planted rice in the spring by pressing a hole with the heel and covering the seeds with the foot, the motion used was demonstrably similar to that employed in West Africa. In summer, when Carolina blacks moved through the rice fields in a row, hoeing in unison to work songs, the pattern of cultivation was not one imposed by European owners but rather one retained from West African forebears. And in October when the threshed grain was 'fanned' in the wind, the wide, flat winnowing baskets were made by black hands after an African design."[30] Although no similar analysis exists of the role of enslaved Africans and creoles in the origins of sea island cotton culture, the story of American rice and the experience of many Caribbean slaves with cotton culture prior to their arrival in Georgia suggests that creole and African slaves may have been important agents in the adoption and success of the new staple.

The histories of Wormsloe's slave workforce are all but impossible to reconstruct, but there are hints that the plantation's laborers came from diverse backgrounds that may have contributed to cotton's success on the plantation. The Savannah area was the epicenter of Muslim slaves in the New World, many of them from Sierra Leone, where cotton was a popular crop, and the region retained strong ties with slave markets and economies in the Caribbean, virtually ensuring a varied slave population with exposure to a variety of agricultural systems.[31] Inventories in Noble Jones's 1767 will and George W. Jones's antebellum papers provide lists of names at two points in the plantation's history. In both instances, the documents record names of African and perhaps Spanish origin (for example, Tenah, Jeedy, Loomba, and Tony) as well as a few with Arabic roots (Mingo and Sam[bo]) or derived from Sierra Leone (Binah).[32] Names are, of course, in no way definitive indicators of a person's background, religion, or agricultural experience. Many Lowcountry slaves had both English and African names, and slaves from Arabic or Spanish backgrounds or who had spent time on plantations in the British and French Indies could bear almost any name imaginable.[33] But names do hint at the stores of knowledge that the plantation's slaves brought with them to the Isle of Hope.

As with the cultivation of most other southern staple crops, tending sea island cotton was hard work. Although slaves on cotton plantations avoided the noxious fumes of indigo production and the ever-present swarms of mosquitoes that hovered over rice impoundments, the crop demanded difficult, steady labor throughout much of the year. Slaves on sea island cotton plantations, including Wormsloe, often prepared the sandy soil of cotton fields with hoes rather than plows—backbreaking work—and after planting the cotton regularly hoed the rows to keep the fields clear of weeds and promote drainage. Oak hammock lands were particularly difficult to cultivate. Thomas Spalding wrote that "it takes many years before the Palmetto, and the collateral roots of the Live Oak, make hammock land free to the plow."[34] One northern visitor to the Savannah area commented on the intense cultivation that planters demanded: "The slaves watch over [the cotton plants] with such paternal care, that every stalk seems obliged to grow to the same stature, and not a noxious weed ventures to show its head."[35] Eminent agricultural historian Lewis Gray has argued that the demands of producing exceptional sea island cotton resulted in a crop culture fundamentally different from that found in short-staple regions of the South: "Sea-island cotton became a highly intensive industry, with essential emphasis on quality, as contrasted with the extensive methods and striving for quantity characteristic of the production of short-staple."[36] This attention to detail was most evident during the late September–early December picking time, the most demanding part of the season, as slaves young and old, male and female, worked to harvest the fiber before the exposure of the opening bolls (the flowering structure that contains the fibers) to the weather could damage it. While short-staple producers usually picked over their crops three times, sea island planters had their hands pick each field as many as a dozen times, gathering in the fragile floss before it could be "injured by dust, rain, and wind."[37] The work continued in ginning and packing. During ginning, a labor primarily performed by male slaves, planters expected each hand to produce thirty pounds of clean cotton per day.[38] Sea island cotton was then packed in large bags rather than in bales, as upland cotton was. Workers suspended a heavy sack from the upper story of a packing house or gin, "and while one colored person stands in it to tread the cotton down, others throw it into the sack."[39] In winter, after the cotton was safely picked and packed, slaves still faced endless plantation tasks—building and repairing fences, clearing new ground, preparing fields for the following season's crops, and taking care of livestock.

Although Wormsloe was always a place of varied agricultural production, from the first years of the nineteenth century, sea island cotton identified the property as a plantation. Cotton was the plantation's primary source of revenue, but it was also more than just an economic product. For most of six decades, cotton governed Wormsloe's annual work cycles. George Jones and his son, George W. Jones, supervised planting and geared their agricultural plans around the fiber, slaves labored to the rhythms of the crop, and plantation residents black and white thought of the surrounding environment in terms of planting, weeding, fertilizing, and harvesting cotton. This cotton-centered worldview extended beyond the perimeters of Wormsloe's fields. The Joneses bought seed from South Carolina planters with the Isle of Hope's sandy soil in mind; as the enterprise grew, slaves cut lumber from the plantation's pines and oaks to build a cotton gin, packing house, storage sheds, and quarters; and workers hauled mud from the marshes bordering the estate to renew the fertility of cotton lands. The cotton plant's tentacles thus connected all aspects of the plantation, from its ecosystems to the minds of its inhabitants, in a web centered on producing bags of fine white floss each fall.

It is unclear exactly how many slaves lived on Wormsloe at any given time, but it was probably a significant number throughout the nineteenth century. By 1812, George Jones owned 102 slaves spread out over plantations in five counties, with the bulk working at Poplar Grove and Wormsloe in Chatham County.[40] Jones was also a judge, too busy with his judicial duties to attend to daily plantation operations, and like many Lowcountry planters, he seemed reluctant to live near the coastal marshes year-round for fear of malaria and other endemic diseases.[41] Jones resided in the Lowcountry from the fall through spring and traveled to cooler climes during the summer; a typical trip in 1803 took him to New England and then to Virginia's Sweet Springs resort before he returned to Georgia in late September.[42] As a consequence of Jones's annual migrations and his aversion to the coastal climate during the peak months of the growing season, he contracted with neighbors, relatives, or independent white overseers, such as James Sims, John Rawls, and Noble Glen, to manage Wormsloe during the first decade of the nineteenth century.[43] An 1810 agreement with Rawls to oversee Wormsloe was probably typical. Rawls promised to manage all facets of the plantation's agriculture, including the production of six hundred pounds of cleaned cotton per hand. In return, Jones agreed to pay Rawls two hundred dollars and provide him with "Corn & such other Bread kind as may be raised on the said plantation" as well as "a wench named Flora to cook" for him.[44] Jones likely permitted Rawls to live in the old tabby house, where he could be near the cotton fields and keep a close watch on the slaves in their huts.[45] While Wormsloe's overseers did not grow rich from overseeing Jones's slaves, their contracts compared favorably with similar positions in the Lowcountry. According to historian Timothy Lockley, the majority of the region's overseers were relatively poor, laboring for as little as fifty dollars a year plus board.[46]

Managing a sea island cotton plantation was a daunting task made all the more complex by the use of slave labor. Of primary importance to planters was maintaining discipline among their slaves; landowners attempted to master their slaves just as they sought to shape the landscape. The Joneses, like other Lowcountry slaveholders, sought a balance between the harsh dictates of a disciplinarian and the softer compulsion of paternalism, a balance that seemed impossible to find. In 1796, Sarah Jones, writing to her husband, George, revealed both the difficulties of managing human property and the differences planters believed existed between themselves and their bound laborers. Sarah, who was managing the Joneses' Savannah area plantations while George was away, warned that they should be magnanimous with their slave, Lancaster, who wanted his children to accompany him on a reassignment from one family plantation to another. If "you chuse to indulge him with one" child, she wrote, "he can not be so unreasonable as to want the whole of them."[47] Sarah believed that Lancaster would appreciate such a gesture of paternalism but seemed hesitant to believe that he could feel the same parental bond as a white person. The tone of her letter suggested that a "childlike" slave could hardly feel as a white father would.

Sarah's letter equated the struggle to manage slave labor with the efforts of overseeing an agricultural landscape and revealed some of the daily tasks involved in creating and maintaining a coastal plantation. She directed slaves in ditching, digging potatoes, sowing small grains, and cutting and selling timber for barrel staves (probably intended for export to the sugar plantations of the West Indies). She also oversaw management of the family's livestock, specifically mentioning cattle and turkeys.[48] Among many tasks, plantation workers rounded up hogs in the winter for killing, cleared and drained cropland, spun and wove wool into cloth, fanned rice to remove the husks, and hauled cotton to the gin on the Joneses' nearby Skidaway plantation.[49] Sarah's administration of Newton and Wormsloe plantations demonstrated the important role women played in the creation and maintenance of the Jones family's properties. Like Mary Jones's supervision of colonial Wormsloe's sericulture, Sarah's work exhibited a pragmatic approach to improving the family's fortunes and a willingness to step into traditionally masculine roles. Still, managing both people and the environment was a task with which she preferred help. Her letter chastised George for delaying his trip to the coast since his "presence is very much wanted here."[50]

Sarah and George's direction of slave labor took place within the task system of management, a style of work governance that regulated both people and landscapes. Philip D. Morgan, a historian of Lowcountry slavery, has concluded that the task system was firmly entrenched on the region's sea island cotton plantations by the end of the eighteenth century. Under the task system, masters or overseers assigned each slave a specific daily task. Rather than working as a gang under direct supervision, each slave had a certain amount of cotton to plant, weed, or pick, depending on the season, and these tasks were usually divided up based on a specific plot of land. For example, a slave might be assigned a half acre of cotton to weed as one task (the work an overseer expected could be done in one day), and managers adjusted the amount of land covered by each task according to a slave's age and sex. Though the size of a given task occasionally varied, agricultural labor on Lowcountry cotton plantations was often unisex; Betty Wood has determined that in sea island cotton culture, both men and women often performed the same field tasks. Morgan argues that most sea island cotton planters adopted this task system in the 1790s as a natural outgrowth of their experience with that form of management during earlier indigo cultivation. When the task was done, the slave was free for the remainder of the day, but failure to complete an assigned task could result in punishment. Planters appreciated the system because it required less direct supervision than did gang labor, and slaves enjoyed having time most afternoons to work their small gardens, hunt and fish, or visit neighboring plantations. Although this arrangement provided slaves with valuable periods of respite from direct supervision, on many plantations masters expected slaves to spend this time provisioning themselves and adjusted rations accordingly. Despite this possibility of additional labor, Morgan concludes that the task system was a less chafing form of slavery than the gang system common in the Chesapeake.[51]

This task system was vital in shaping black and white understandings of the Lowcountry landscape. As Mart Stewart has pointed out, masters' expectations that slaves would provide a portion of their own provisions contributed to the latter's knowledge of the coastal environment. Slaves who cultivated their own produce in food plots—dubbed "Botanical Gardens of the Dispossessed" by two scholars—kept alive traditional African food crops in a new land, from okra and cowpeas to eggplant and sesame.[52] Like field labor, work in these food gardens fostered an intimate familiarity with a plantation's agricultural spaces, where slaves worked day after day; moreover, thanks in part to the task system, African Americans also developed an intimate knowledge of stretches of marsh and woodland. In essence, sections of riverbank and forest where slaves fished, collected oysters, and trapped rabbits to round out their diet became black spaces, utilized by slaves and avoided by whites. While masters often considered these spaces marginal or waste lands, these portions of the plantation landscape were vital to the overall functioning of a task-based agricultural system, and the use and management of these spaces were exclusively black activities. Plantation lands thus formed a continuum of racial control, from the cotton and rice fields watched closely by masters to the cultivated gardens full of African and New World crops lining the margins of the plantation proper to the woodlots and forests where slaves worked under no gaze but their own. This environmental knowledge gave slaves a degree of power over their daily lives: black fishermen, hunters, and foragers used their knowledge of the surrounding landscape to supplement their diets, to surreptitiously visit other plantations, or even to shirk onerous work.[53] Although direct evidence of slaves' free-time activities during the early nineteenth century cannot be found in Wormsloe's records, the marshside location of the plantation's slave huts and subsequently its cabins provided the estate's workforce with easy access to the bounty of the estuarial environment and the wooded southern end of the property.

The task system reflected the demands of coastal agriculture and became a way for planters and slaves to conceptualize space. Stewart has also made an intriguing observation about the way in which the task system became rooted in particular Lowcountry landscapes. After years of assigning a certain plot of land as a task, planters began to dig their drainage ditches and form field borders based on the dimensions of the task. Thus, the term *task* took on two meanings. It was shorthand for both a specific amount of labor and for a particular quantity of land, forging an inextricable tie between Lowcountry labor and the built landscape. Although there is little in the way of surviving evidence to establish the conditions of slave labor on Wormsloe in the early 1800s, the Joneses' experience growing indigo on at least some of their colonial-era plantations and the prevalence of the system among their Lowcountry neighbors probably meant that Wormsloe's slaves labored under the task system.[54]

If managing the time and labor of slaves was a demanding exercise, feeding and clothing a large number of human chattel was also a significant challenge. As during the colonial era, Wormsloe's residents produced a portion of their food and clothing on site and relied on local and regional markets for the balance. Slaves grew some of their own foodstuffs, including corn and pork, and gardening provided fresh vegetables, but accounts also reveal that the Joneses regularly purchased staples from outside sources. In just one 1813 purchase—perhaps several months of rations for Wormsloe's slaves—George Jones bought 130 bushels of "rough rice," the bacon from five hogs, a barrel of flour, and 200 bushels of corn.[55] Jones also made efforts to clothe his slaves with plantation-made garments, in some cases buying cloth and needles for home assembly of purchased osnaburgs and other cloth. Jones also encouraged the overseer of one of his plantations to have the slaves make new clothing "as soon as they can spin & weave the cloth."[56] Plantation self-sufficiency was an ideal for Jones and other masters, who sought to make their properties as independent as possible. Despite such efforts at domestic production, however, the markets of Savannah remained important sources for keeping both masters and slaves clothed and fed.

Even relatively large-scale production of sea island cotton did not immediately make dramatic changes in the Wormsloe landscape. In a brief 1815 inventory of the plantation, George Jones revealed how little had changed since the colonial period. There were a few new wooden structures—a cotton house, corn building, pea shed, and fodder barn—but the old fort remained the dwelling house, and the slaves resided in huts that probably hailed back to the original rude structures erected for Noble Jones's marines. Although the inventory does not tabulate improved land, some new ground had undoubtedly been cleared for cotton- and cornfields to occupy and feed the growing slave population. Structures for storing fodder and peas also point to increased livestock numbers, more intensive management of the existing herds, or both.[57] The northern portion of Wormsloe, separated as Wimberly Plantation at Noble W. Jones's death, was similarly lightly developed. In 1815, it held one plantation house, an overseer's house, a barn, a corn shed, and a few wooden slave huts.[58] The transition to a staple crop was quick, but its effects on the landscape were more gradual. Over the following decades, the Joneses would slowly clear more forest, drain low grounds, and build new farm structures, gradually transforming the colonial property into an antebellum cotton estate.

Most of the 1820s are a blank period in the Wormsloe sources—the family alternately rented the plantation and hired overseers to manage its cotton crops, and few estate records survive from the decade—but we can make a few guesses concerning land use. In 1819, George Jones rented the plantation to a widow, Ann Reid, for the meager sum of twenty dollars. The language of the agreement suggests that there were roughly twenty acres of open land for Reid to tend, though the document is not entirely clear as to whether Reid rented all or only a part of the property.[59] Jones may have retained the use of some portion of Wormsloe during this period. If so, it seems likely that he had his slaves tend market gardens or cut firewood to haul to Savannah, the activities he pursued at Poplar Grove during the same period.[60] Archeologist William Kelso's research suggests the possibility that Reid continued to rent Wormsloe until Jones and his family made the plantation their permanent home in 1828.[61] All indications are that Reid lived in the old tabby fortified house and farmed the same fields that the Joneses and their slaves had cultivated during the previous decades. Cotton production likely continued on the plantation during

Reid's tenure, though in the early 1820s the crop brought low profits. The sea island cotton market boomed following renewed access to European markets at the conclusion of the War of 1812, but the bubble collapsed in the Panic of 1819, and prices remained depressed for several years.[62]

An 1825 accident altered the family's management of Wormsloe in an important way, bringing the Joneses into more frequent contact with the plantation and its daily operation. That year, George Jones's house at Newton burned down, and he decided to build a new plantation house on Wormsloe rather than to rebuild at Newton, perhaps because of the Isle of Hope's proximity to Savannah.[63] Jones may also have believed that moving the family home from Newton, with its stagnant waterscape necessary for rice culture, to the sea island cotton fields of Wormsloe would benefit his dependents' health.[64] He commissioned Savannah's Alexander Shaw to build a frame house several hundred yards north of the old tabby fort, where it would share the older structure's commanding view of the river. In 1829, the family moved into a wooden structure that represented a marked improvement over the old house. Forty feet wide by twenty feet deep, the two-story house sat on a tabby foundation built from materials taken from the old fort. The Joneses also erected a servants' house and a new stable nearby at the same time, moving the center of plantation operations to the new farmyard.[65] This structure remains the core of the plantation house that still exists on the same site, though the house has been expanded and remodeled numerous times. Jones's move to Wormsloe intensified agricultural operations on the estate—records of sea island cotton and foodstuff production increase following the move—and initiated a period of more than three decades where the cultivation of sea island cotton governed the activities of the plantation's seasons.

Throughout the 1830s and the 1840s, Wormsloe remained an active sea island cotton plantation, but in many years, the property did not produce tremendous revenues. George Jones remained tied up in nonagricultural pursuits until his death in 1838, busy managing his Savannah real estate and working as a judge. Following his passing, his minor son, George Wimberly Jones, lived either at Poplar Grove or in Savannah, and George Jones's grandson, George Noble Jones (who was sixteen years older than his uncle, George Wimberly Jones), administered the estate. George Noble relied on an overseer to look after Wormsloe, Poplar Grove, and Newton until George Wimberly came of age in 1848.[66] The records of George Jones's estate illuminate the variety of plantation types and farming strategies present within a relatively small portion of the Lowcountry landscape. Between 1839 and 1849, Newton produced rice, rice flour, and the occasional crop of corn for sale. The rice, packed in large wooden casks, was an international trade good, while the rice flour, produced from inferior or broken grains, and the corn were commodities for local markets, where they fed slaves and livestock. At Poplar Grove, the overseer and slaves grew short-staple cotton, corn, and livestock and produced a variety of market garden crops for sale in Savannah, including pumpkins, seed potatoes, and cowpeas. Throughout this period, Wormsloe's workers primarily produced sea island cotton.[67]

Although sea island cotton could bring high returns, Wormsloe's production seems to have been irregular. Cotton production fluctuated from seven to twenty-one bags per year based on weather conditions (and perhaps inattentive management of the estate), with the crop grossing anywhere from a low of $524.59 in 1841 to a high of $1248.46 in 1849. In comparison, nearby Poplar Grove sold crops worth three times as much in a typical year, and Newton's rice crop sold for the substantial sum of $3,380.13 in 1848. Although Wormsloe's modest cotton crops did not produce a large profit, the Joneses incurred relatively little in the way of expenses on the plantation. They purchased rough osnaburg and other cloth for slave clothing, replaced worn-out slave shoes, bought bagging and twine for packing the cotton crop for market, and purchased such basic farm staples as nails, seed, and hand tools. Although the Joneses certainly purchased some provisions, such as salt and molasses, from local merchants, all indications are that most of the plantation's slave supplies were grown on site during this period. With this limited overhead, even moderate amounts of cotton resulted in a small profit. In an 1853 memo, George W. Jones estimated the plantation's average gross from 1838 to 1848 at $768.63 and average expenses at just over $250. The Jones family's investment in a variety of plantation strategies provided a degree of economic security, as a poor year for sea island cotton was not necessarily a bad season for rice or short-staple cotton. In 1839, Wormsloe's sea island crop turned out poorly, but Poplar Grove's fields of upland cotton sold for almost $2,500; in 1847, when Poplar Grove produced little more than $1,000 worth of cotton, Newton sold 163.5 casks of rice for $3,311.29.[68] Although a major regional disaster, such as a hurricane or war, could affect all three plantations, the Joneses' diversified staple crops provided modest protection against more typical market and environmental fluctuations. What remains unclear is whether this diversification was an intentional decision to minimize risk or whether managing the three plantations was a simple matter of selecting the crop best suited to each microenvironment.

Aside from rice culture, plantation farming in the Georgia Lowcountry remained an enterprise based on the application of large amounts of bound labor rather than on agricultural innovation and improvement. An inventory of the slaves and agricultural supplies George Wimberly inherited in

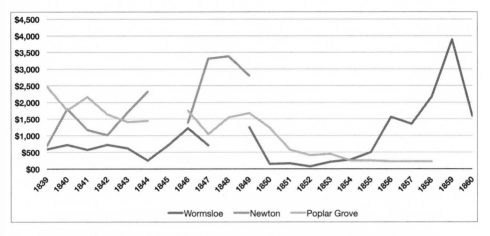

Figure 1. Value of Jones Family's plantations produce, 1839–1860. In 1848, George Wimberly Jones acquired Wormsloe and Poplar Grove from his father's estate, and Newton was either sold out of the family or passed to a relative. Gaps in the chart reflect missing accounts.

the 1849 estate liquidation reveals much about the basic nature of agriculture on Wormsloe. Jones received thirty-four slaves to divide between Wormsloe and Poplar Grove. He also inherited five mules, seventy head of cattle, and seventy-five sheep. Most of the farm tools listed were relatively simple hand instruments, from thirty hoes to a collection of axes and spades. The plantation equipment included six plows, a wagon, and two millstones for grinding corn and wheat. Jones also inherited a thousand dollars worth of corn, peas, potatoes, and fodder to feed his slaves and stock.[69] His inheritance reveals the relatively simple nature of regional agriculture, even on large plantations. The tools and methods of the late 1840s were remarkably similar to their colonial counterparts. Over the following decade, Jones would take steps to intensify and modernize agricultural operations on his Lowcountry plantations, and his efforts would remake the southern end of the Isle of Hope. Although sea island cotton remained the center of agricultural endeavors on Wormsloe, these efforts ushered in a new era of capital-intensive farming.

The growth of Wormsloe as a staple-producing plantation did little to lessen its inhabitants' dependence on the surrounding woods and waters for sustenance. Although the Joneses or their overseers purchased some of the plantation's foodstuffs, the forests and marshes still provided much of plantation residents' diets. Ducks, terrapins, and palmetto joined beef, sweet potatoes, and rice in plantation dishes, and two surviving recipe books from the first half of the nineteenth century reinforce the centrality of the surrounding marshes and rivers in Wormsloe's food culture. The seafood prominent in these manuals included soft-shell turtles, shrimp, crabs, blackfish, rockfish, shad, oysters, sea bass, haddock, turbot, and herring. Whether prepared simply or through elaborate methods, dishes from stewed oysters to shrimp pie frequently graced the Joneses' table.[70] The exact origin and purpose of these recipe books are unclear. Plantation cooks were almost always slaves, and a printed record of recipes seem to make little sense when slaves were legally prohibited from reading and writing. The Joneses may have used these books to preserve favorite recipes, Wormsloe's cooks may indeed have been literate, or Mary Jones (George Wimberly's wife) may have enjoyed working in the kitchen on occasion. One page lists "Terrapins, Flora's recipe," almost certainly a dish drawn from the slave "wench" who cooked for overseer John Rawls in the early years of the century.[71]

Period recipes reveal the extent to which Wormsloe residents' diets were the product of a fusion of Native American, African, and European cultural influences. Dishes that utilized local shellfish or maize hearkened back to the native groups that once inhabited the property. The arrowroot puddings, griddle cakes, custards, gumbos, sweet potato starches, and benne (sesame) dishes that frequently graced Wormsloe's tables were adaptations of traditional African foods. The combination of these ingredients with such vegetables as English peas or carrots, often stewed or baked with cream or spirits such as madeira and sherry, was a decidedly European twist on fusion foods. Indeed, the surviving Wormsloe recipes from the nineteenth century suggest a household that combined a reliance on local resources with influences and ingredients from three continents.[72]

Particularly important to the developing food culture of Wormsloe and similar Lowcountry plantations were the black cooks who prepared meals for the planters and their families. Just as slaves, such as Bilali, had brought their knowledge of crop systems and agriculture across the Atlantic littoral to the American Southeast, creole cooks brought African ingredients and methods of preparation to the plantation. Although, as culinary scholar Jessica B. Harris has noted, "it is impossible not to be amazed at the similarity of methods of preparation, ingredients, and tastes" in West African and southern cuisines, the connection between Africa and the American South was "not static; it [was] mutable—a lifeline—an umbilicus."[73] "The *warp* of cookery" in Georgia may have been English, but African-born slaves and their descendants strongly influenced the shape of southern cooking, from the names of dishes to regional residents' affinity for spicy food.[74]

One recipe from the Wormsloe records demonstrates the typical creole nature of food on the plantation:

Terrapin—White Stew

Cut off heads, and throw terrapins into cold water for about an hour to draw out blood. Then scald in boiling water to take off skin and nails. Boil slowly until thoroughly done so that legs may be pulled off. While boiling season with allspice, black pepper, thyme, salt & onion. Drain, open, and take out gall and intestines, keeping liver. Cut up fine, rejecting coarse white meat. Put in a stew pan with some of the liquor in which they have been boiled. Put in a tablespoonful of butter to each terrapin and season with salt & red pepper. Boil eggs—three to each terrapin fourteen minutes. Smash yolks thoroughly and stir in. Put in by degree a wineglass of cream to each terrapin, to which when stewed down and well incorporated, add a wine glass of Sherry to each terrapin. The eggs should be removed when the terrapin is opened, and only put into the stew one minute before dishing.[75]

This dish contained ingredients that were obviously of European derivation— cream, sherry, butter—but it also reflected the black hands that prepared it. The cook used capsicum (red) pepper, popular in African dishes, as well as the black pepper common in European cooking and relied on a tough native meat that needed slow cooking to tenderize the flesh. In addition, the dish's structure as a stew was conducive to serving over rice, a common West African practice that was transferred to the cuisine of the Lowcountry.[76]

This recipe and similar records concerning eating at Wormsloe highlight the immense value of foodways studies for environmental historians. Nicolaas Mink has noted that "food, at least at the beginning of its journey to the stomach, represents the quintessential embodiment of that enormously complex idea we call nature."[77] Marcie Cohen Ferris has observed that "food is entangled in forces that have shaped southern history and culture for more than four centuries. . . . When we study food in the South, we unveil a web of social relations defined by race, class, ethnicity, gender, and shifting economic forces."[78] She might also have added that food sheds light on the shaping power of local environments. The study of foodways connects production and consumption—acts all too often regarded as discrete—in meaningful ways. Planters, their families, and slaves often ate food that they raised, caught, or collected; thus, what they consumed and how they prepared it reflected an intimate understanding of the natural and agricultural world.[79] This viewpoint is often all but impossible to reconstruct without exploring foodways sources. For environmental historians of the American South, foodways are also a fruitful medium for exploring connections and dissonances between black and white southerners. Although southern tables were among the most segregated of regional spaces, food itself often crossed racial lines and thus connected blacks and whites to similar crops, animals, and wild spaces. Examining regional foods and their preparation is a starting point for thinking about southern landscapes and the people that inhabited them in a holistic way. When Noble Jones advised travelers on the health effects of Lowcountry food and when Flora and other African cooks blended Old and New World ingredients into Wormsloe's cuisine, food served as both nourishment and as a medium for their explanations and interpretations of the Isle of Hope environment. For Jones and Flora, food served as nature and culture writ small.

Paying attention to food reveals a plethora of additional historical sources. For example, limning antebellum slave relationships with the environment is a challenging task: Few slaves wrote about nature, few whites were interested in recording such relationships, and the overwhelming paternalism and/or brutality of the institution of slavery obscured a great deal about daily interactions between blacks and the environment. A careful examination of foodways can begin to bridge this gap in the sources. Mention of slave consumption of certain wild animals not only reveals what creatures they considered palatable but also provides evidence of what portions of the landscape slaves used for recreation and subsistence. Garden lists that include benne planted at the end of rows demonstrate the presence and use of an "African" crop in the New World but also suggest that African cultural traditions survived—at least in part—along with food crops. (Africans considered benne planted at the end of a row to be good luck.)[80] Likewise, antebellum plantation recipes that combine African and European ingredients and methods reveal the hands of the black cooks who stirred pots and tended fires. These documents demonstrate that black women incorporated their own tastes with the produce of the South, in the process shaping white ideas about "southern" food and cooking. Recipe books, provision lists, garden journals, store receipts, and meal plans open a door to the most elemental of human ties to the natural world: the act of eating. That foodways often represented a direct expression of black and white environmental understandings should come as no surprise, but historians would do well to explore the plantation's belly in more detail.[81]

The summer of 1854 marked a dramatic change in Wormsloe's operation. George W. Jones moved his base of agricultural operations from Poplar Grove to Wormsloe and began a determined campaign to make the property a more innovative and profitable sea island cotton plantation. Although it is unclear exactly what provoked Jones's move, it is quite apparent that he committed a great deal of time and energy to making Wormsloe a model estate. Years later, Jones acknowledged that he had been "ignorant and averse to agriculture" prior to 1854, and his frequent travels coupled with less-than-diligent overseers had resulted in the deterioration of the old home place. Looking over his books following the Civil War, he recalled his determination to make a change. "An examination of these accounts, with inquiry into the experience of others, determined me to abandon Poplar Grove on account of its proximity to town, to move my people to Wormsloe and to erect there suitable plantation buildings for cotton-planting. The accounts from 1856 to the end of the book will show the advantage of the change."[82] Whether because of Wormsloe's natural advantages, such as light soil and access to the rich marshes, or because of a desire to more fully control his slaves by limiting their proximity to the temptations of Savannah, Jones turned to the Isle of Hope plantation as the center of his agricultural endeavors. Over the next five years, Jones would devote most of his time and energy to remaking Wormsloe as an exemplary cotton plantation.

Jones brought with him to Wormsloe an avid interest in modern, "scientific" farming. Despite his later claims that he knew little about agriculture before the mid-1850s, he had already begun experimenting with new and innovative farm practices at Poplar Grove. A farm notebook from the 1840s reveals some of his interests. Jones took notes on traditional corn and cotton culture, wrote about the value of careful soil preparation, and pondered the profitability of alternative crops such as rutabagas (which he believed would make "good food for horses") while keeping track of plantings. The notebook also reflected Jones's reliance on outside expertise to improve his agricultural endeavors. Carefully tucked between the pages of handwritten notes were pasted clippings from agrarian journals and newspapers on such topics as pest control, crop rotation, and the importance of fertilizers and other soil amendments. One article suggests that the writings of Virginia agronomist and agricultural reformer Edmund Ruffin influenced Jones's farming efforts. The author advised readers to "get Mr. Ruffin's book on Calcareous Manures, or his survey of South Carolina, and read his directions with care."[83] Jones's interest in agriculture was one of his many avocations. He loved to travel and was a shrewd businessman, a writer, and a bibliophile deeply interested in Georgia's early history (and especially in collecting colonial documents). His approach to planting mirrored his pursuit of his other pleasures; he brought an active and penetrating mind, deep pockets, and endless enthusiasm to Wormsloe's grounds.[84] By the 1840s, Jones was on his way to developing a good "book knowledge" of farming, and his cultivation of Wormsloe during the following decade suggests that he took seriously at least some of Ruffin's prescriptions.[85]

The agricultural reform movement that inspired Jones had slowly spread throughout the South over the four decades preceding the Civil War. Grounded in the work of such English agriculturalists as Charles Townshend and Jethro

Tull as well as the experiments of prominent founding fathers including George Washington and Thomas Jefferson, southern planters such as Virginia's John Taylor touted systematic and scientific farming as key to the region's future. Following Taylor, Ruffin epitomized the southern agricultural reform movement. From Shellbanks, his Tidewater Virginia plantation, Ruffin published books and an agricultural journal, the *Farmers' Register*, that advocated new farming methods and laws that benefited rural landowners. Ruffin and his cohorts were most concerned with outmigration from the southern seaboard and Piedmont to the West, and they believed that soil exhaustion, erosion, and a lack of rural economic opportunity were the primary roadblocks to regional prosperity. Reformers pressed a broad agenda. They advocated contour plowing, terracing, and ditching to slow erosion; they promoted crop rotation, the use of such nitrogen-fixing crops as clover, and applying fertilizers to increase soil fertility; they urged farmers to use marl (fossilized sea shells) to lessen soil acidity; they pushed for a fence law to end the open range and reduce the costs associated with protecting cropland from free-ranging livestock; and they touted alternative crops that might lessen the South's dependence on cotton and tobacco. Southern agricultural reform was far from universally successful, but the discourse of improvement permeated southern agricultural thinking from Virginia to Georgia. As Jones intensified and expanded agricultural operations on Wormsloe, he drew heavily on the advice of agricultural reformers, but he modified their agenda to meet his personal goals and the particularities of the Isle of Hope landscape.[86]

Like Ruffin, Jones first turned to increasing the plantation's soil fertility. Decades of cotton and corn cultivation had diminished the nutrient levels of Wormsloe's fields, as plants drew nitrogen, phosphorus, potassium, and traces of other minerals from the sandy soils. Under Jones's direction, the plantation's slaves continued to amend fields and gardens in traditional ways; they hauled mud rich in organic matter from the salt marsh to cotton fields, tilled ginned cotton seed back into the land, carted manure from livestock barns and pens to cropland, and spread crushed oyster and other marine shells on cleared land to lessen soil acidity.[87] Jones also turned to distant sources to renew the plantation's fertility. By the late 1850s, he joined a substantial number of southern planters and farmers who imported South American guano for use as fertilizer. Guano is the dried droppings of seabirds, found most frequently on the arid islands of the southeastern Pacific. The dried, chalky material was tremendously abundant on such archipelagoes as the Chincha Islands off the Peruvian coast, where the guano mounds were two hundred feet high in spots.[88] Beginning in the early nineteenth century, European and American agriculturalists discovered that guano was an extremely rich source of nitrogen and phosphorus and began experimenting with using it to fertilize agricultural crops. A steady trade brought guano to East Coast ports by the mid-1840s, when the United States claimed sovereignty over a number of the guano islands and American companies organized to exploit the natural (but limited) resource. Use of guano became quite popular with farmers and planters in the older Tidewater agricultural districts from Maryland to South Carolina. Peruvian exports peaked in the mid-1850s, when American farmers spread 140,000 tons of droppings on their fields each year and when Jones first began using the fertilizer on Wormsloe.[89] Within a year of his first purchase, he made a significant financial investment in guano, spending almost seven hundred dollars on 10.5 tons of the Peruvian product.[90]

With his move to Wormsloe, Jones demonstrated a keen interest in improving the plantation's livestock and crops by purchasing outside stock and selective breeding. Reflecting the advice of such agricultural improvers as Ruffin and South Carolina's James Henry Hammond, Jones sought out varieties of animals and plants that might increase the property's production, "occupying [himself] in agricultural experiments."[91] During his first few years at Wormsloe, he introduced Newport chickens and cattle, merino sheep, guineas, a Devon bull, and an Alderney cow. In addition to these purebred imports, Jones augmented the plantation stock by buying more local cattle, mules, chickens, and turkeys. Reflecting his cosmopolitan interests and knowledge, he also freely experimented with new breeds and crosses of various crops from around the nation and the globe. He tried peanuts, Rhode Island yellow flint corn, Maryland white corn, two types of sea island cotton seed from Charleston, Wyandot corn, and Chinese sugarcane.[92]

Some of Jones's experiments were more successful than others. The turkeys multiplied well enough that Jones sold a number on local markets each year; the merino sheep produced enough wool that he sent some to market in 1856 and 1857; and the sugarcane was "as good, in the opinion of several persons, as any molasses; though of a lighter colour." Jones took a great deal of pride in particularly successful experiments. For example, he exuberantly described the results of a corn trial: "The Wyandot corn planted in March last succeeded perfectly. But *one* seed (grain) was planted in a hole, and from this *single* grain, 4, 5, 6, and even 7 *stalks* (*not* suckers), grew—each stalk bearing one, two, or three ears, and tillering, like wheat, from the roots. The overseer—Henderson—informs me that he counted *thirty-one* ears—the product of one bunch of stalks, which all grew from one single grain!"[93] Not all of Jones's experiments went so well. He eventually sold the merino sheep, probably because they were ill suited to the southern heat, and the Devon bull he purchased died within two months of arrival, prompting Jones to warn against buying "stock from a 'gentleman,' relying upon his uprightness."[94] Although Jones criticized the honesty of the seller, there is a good chance that the bull died of Texas fever, an endemic southern disease caused by a parasite (*Pyrosoma bigeminum*) and spread by the cattle tick (*Boophilus annulatus*). Until its eradication in the twentieth century, Texas fever infected southern herds and killed as many as two-thirds of introduced northern cattle, which had little resistance to the parasite.[95] More significant than the loss or underperformance of livestock, Wormsloe's cotton production fluctuated widely, ranging from 2,295 pounds in 1856 to 10,155 pounds in 1859 and then back to 5,843 pounds in 1860.[96]

Some of these crop variations can be attributed to the weather fluctuations that affect all farming—good conditions obviously produced more cotton than years that were too wet or too dry, that suffered from severe insect infestations, or that featured ill-timed destructive storms. Sea island cotton was a particularly fragile crop. Even in otherwise favorable years, spring drought, a hurricane, or an early frost threatened to turn healthy profits into devastating losses. The boll weevil had not yet arrived in the South, but other insects still posed a serious risk to maturing cotton, as in 1804, when a plague of cotton caterpillars stripped sea island fields bare and an unknown rust affected some crops. Even if a hurricane or insect infestation failed to destroy the crop outright, these calamities threatened to turn clean, white cotton into "stained" cotton, which sold for a fraction of the price of pure white fiber: In 1860, for example, Jones sold his clean cotton for forty cents per pound, while three bags of stained fiber brought a meager sixteen cents per pound.[97] If Jones's surviving accounts for the period are complete, part of the fluctuation may also have resulted from the uneven application of manures and amendments. His largest guano purchases took place in 1858, when he spread 26,728 pounds on Wormsloe's fields, so it is perhaps no coincidence that Wormsloe produced its largest cotton crop the following year (although 1859 was generally a good year for all sorts of agricultural production across the South). Crops such as cotton received the most benefit from guano during the year following its application.[98] Despite the claim by historians Richard Porcher and Sarah Fick that commercial fertilizers were "wholly unknown before the war" on sea island cotton plantations, Jones relied heavily on purchased amendments during the late 1850s.[99] He brought in superphosphate of lime in 1855, and from 1856 to 1859 he spent almost a thousand dollars on his efforts to spread guano, quite a substantial sum for the time.[100] Jones may subsequently have decided that the extra cotton produced by fertilizing the land was simply not worth the added cost and labor of large-scale guano application. Jones also devoted a great deal of energy to his alternative crops, selling small amounts of other produce, including wool and peanuts, and though these activities turned little profit, they

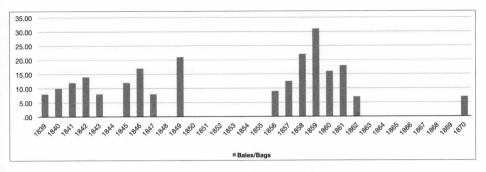

Figure 2. Sea island cotton production on Wormsloe, based on surviving records. Compiled from George W. J. De Renne's Account Book and Jones Estate Records Ledger, 1839–1849.

periodically drew his attention away from sea island cotton. Wide variations in cotton production may also have been endemic to the exercise of growing such a demanding staple—Wormsloe's production had fluctuated rather severely during the 1830s and 1840s as well. It seems unlikely that production fluctuations represented drastic swings in cotton acreage on the plantation, as Jones recorded the same fields each year in the planting cycle.

Although his experiments with various plant and animal breeds reflected the same agronomic curiosity as his predecessors possessed, Jones's agricultural endeavors also reflected his wide travels. He had spent substantial time roaming Europe in his early life, including regular visits with relatives in Montpellier, France. His honeymoon trip spanned part of 1852 and 1853 and featured sojourns in Germany, England, France, Austria, Czechoslovakia, and Italy, where he and his wife traveled with "a Swiss courier and a French maidservant." Until the mid-1850s, his family summered in the wealthy enclave of Newport, Rhode Island, taking an active part in the upper-class social scene. Jones also had business interests in Philadelphia (where he owned railroad and bank stocks), and his wife, Mary, had family in northern Florida.[101] The Newport stock, merino sheep, and his various corn varieties were more common in the northeastern United States than in the South, and his decisions to experiment with these varieties perhaps reflected observations during Rhode Island summers or business trips to Pennsylvania. The Wyandot corn, for example, came from a broker in Staten Island, New York. Many of his other improved breeds were European introductions: Alderney and Devon cattle were popular English breeds.[102] Even purchases made closer to home reflected his careful tracking of markets and trends. In the spring of 1857, Jones purchased select sea island cotton seed from Beckett and Company of South Carolina because he heard cotton from that seed had brought ninety-five cents per pound in Charleston the previous year.[103] Like Noble Jones at colonial Wormsloe, George W. Jones used the plantation as a laboratory for experiments with crops and animals drawn from a variety of habitats, intent on creating the best of all possible farms: an agricultural space particularly suited to the Low-country environment.

Jones did not limit his modernizing efforts to living things. He also purchased new farm implements and equipment designed to make Wormsloe's agricultural production more efficient. Every year prior to the Civil War, he acquired new hoes, pitchforks, mule collars and traces, wheelbarrows, sweep and shovel plows, axes, plow points, carts, and shovels—in short, the basic tools of southern plantation labor. In addition to these implements, Jones spent money on newer and more elaborate mechanical equipment. In 1856, Jones invested in a horse-powered cotton gin for Wormsloe, and a year later, he procured a machine designed to speed up the process of packing cotton into bags. According to Jones's notes, the packer was the first of its kind shipped to Georgia. Apparently unsatisfied with his first gin, he bought an entirely new Fones McCarthy roller gin in 1858. By 1860, Jones was determined to mechanize the gin and other farm operations as much as possible, commissioning an eight-horsepower steam engine from Louisville, Georgia, to run the gin, a small sawmill, and a corn sheller (and perhaps for use in a rice mill he had built in 1859).[104] Although these purchases were far from cheap, Jones saw them as long-term investments in Wormsloe's agricultural future.

Jones's purchase of livestock breeds, new seed varieties, tools, equipment, and external soil amendments were part of a capital-intensive approach to agricultural improvement. Like other large planters across the South, Jones seemed to be a firm believer in the maxim that one must spend money to make money, and he willingly invested not only in the necessities of agricultural operations but also in the plantation's growth and expansion. These efforts by capitalist planters at agricultural conservation sought to replace "any part of their agroecosystem [that] was not maximizing production" with purchased alternatives. These wealthy agriculturalists replaced poor soil with fertilizers and underperforming plants and animals with new varieties and breeds. Such attempts to refashion the landscape disrupted established ecological relationships, but planters undertook them in an attempt to conserve soil, fertility, and the plantation unit itself.[105] In many ways, the conflict between outside resources and internal sustainability on Wormsloe and similar southern plantations reflected tensions between the insular, internal economies of staple plantations and the world commodity markets that made such plantations possible. Jones desired independence and self-sufficiency on his plot of Lowcountry ground, but the cotton that made Wormsloe's cultivation possible also drew the plantation into distant markets and made the purchase of external resources all but irresistible. Thus, the same international trade that carried cotton from Savannah to Liverpool led to the economic rationalization of moving dried bird droppings from Peru to Georgia. Wormsloe's cotton production failed to return Jones's investments in the late 1850s, and the Civil War cut short his experiments. Applications of shell, lime, guano, and marsh mud, along with larger livestock herds, more efficient farm equipment, and new varieties of food crops, certainly increased Wormsloe's productivity. Whether these expenditures would have resulted in a profitable and sustainable cotton plantation remains an unanswered question. What is certain is that Jones's approach to agricultural improvement was a route open to only a few southern landowners. Outside investment and family wealth allowed Jones to take a long-term approach to restructuring the plantation; few of his fellow planters, much less the region's small farmers, could afford to forgo profits or even lose money for several years in the hopes of building a more efficient landscape. Jones's effort at cotton planting, as William Harris Bragg has argued, "was essentially an avocation, never a livelihood."[106]

Wormsloe's accounts made clear the high cost of agricultural improvement. Between 1854, when Jones began his intensive investment in the estate, and 1861, Wormsloe farm operations turned a profit in only one year; for most of this period, the plantation lost more than a thousand dollars annually. In 1859, an unusually large cotton crop resulted in a net profit of $1,112.45, but this income paled beside the $10,442.63 that Jones made from railroad stocks, bank investments, and renting his Savannah property. Poor returns at Wormsloe were a direct reflection of Jones's heavy investment in the property rather than poor productivity, as the plantation's gross agricultural revenue climbed from a mere $276.80 in 1854 to a robust $3,888.84 in 1859. Heavy capital investment in purebred livestock, soil amendments, equipment, and building construction created the deficits.[107] Jones seemed to envision these expenditures as investments in future agricultural returns and thus sought to exchange a few years of lost profit for future wealth. In practice, these deficits ensured that Jones remained committed to large-scale sea island cotton agriculture and the slavery that sustained it. As Jones spent more and more money on the plantation, Wormsloe's agriculture became locked into cotton production. So much had been invested in the staple that it made little sense to seek an alternative.[108] On Wormsloe, money spent clearing cotton fields, building a gin and packing house, feeding and housing slaves, and spreading guano increased the likelihood that cotton would dominate the future landscape. Only a cataclysmic war and the resulting emancipation of the slaves would break the capital-cotton cycle.

A willingness to pour money into Wormsloe did not preclude Jones's interest in certain aspects of plantation self-sufficiency. As his program of modernization progressed, Jones increasingly focused on Wormsloe's ability to feed his family and slaves. Although fortuitous real estate, railroad, and bank investments meant that the Joneses were wealthy enough to purchase all their food if they so desired, the family saw the plantation's fruitfulness as evidence of good stewardship. In an 1856 farm journal entry, Jones celebrated the success of his diversification programs, noting with pleasure the food produced or gathered on the plantation during the month of November: "We have of eatables—the produce of this place—this month, the following: oysters, crabs, shrimp, fish (whiting), wild ducks, turkeys, chickens, eggs, milk, butter, English walnuts, hickory nuts, persimmons, pomegranates, hominy, sweet potatoes, Irish potatoes, [illegible], turnips, carrots, beets, cow peas, green peas, Lima beans, eggplant, tomatoes, okra, spinach, besides benne and arrowroot, and syrup from the chinese sugar cane—to say nothing of cabbage & pumpkins. We had also as fine a watermelon as I ever tasted on the 11th of this month." This and similar passages reflected Jones's belief that a "good" plantation provided for its residents, and as part of the reciprocal relationship between landowner and nature, a good master took care of the land.[109] The tone of these entries demonstrates that Jones took a good deal of pride in his ability to make the Isle of Hope landscape a place of abundant and diverse production. With his wealth, he could easily have purchased food for his family and slaves from Savannah's markets; for that matter, he could have forsaken planting and gardening altogether and used his family estate as a place of occasional retreat from his business ventures. Jones's interest in making the plantation landscape productive and efficient reflected a deep sense of paternalism: As a "good" master of both land and people, he sought to "improve" both. Food lists were ways of tallying his relative success in bettering the soil and, in his mind, those who worked it.

As during earlier periods, the diet of Wormsloe's residents reflected a meshing of African, North American, and European foods. The seafood, persimmons, hickory nuts, and ducks were wild products of the Georgia coast; pumpkins, potatoes, tomatoes, turkeys, and corn for the hominy were Native American staples; benne, arrowroot, okra, and eggplant were of African origin; and walnuts, dairy products, and many of the garden crops reflected the Joneses' English ancestry. Adding to the culinary mix were neotropical fruits and Chinese sugarcane. What Jones celebrated as local independence was actually the product of international food fusion, connections between the Georgia coast and landscapes far removed that were mediated through local environmental conditions.

While the plantation's white residents were eating local food influenced by global exchanges, Wormsloe's slaves existed on a somewhat less diversified diet, though one equally grounded in history and the surrounding landscape. Jones's farm journal entries and purchases indicate that his slaves seem to have subsisted largely on salt-cured pork and some sort of starch accompaniment, usually rice, sweet potatoes, or cornmeal. Jones regularly supplemented these basic rations with molasses, brown sugar, peanuts, and cowpeas. The sweet potatoes, peanuts, corn, and cowpeas usually came from Wormsloe's fields and were cultivated by the slaves themselves, while Jones purchased the other staples from Savannah merchants. In a gesture of paternalism, he also recorded giving out boxes of salted herring as "presents for the negroes" each holiday season.[110]

This basic diet was certainly augmented by fresh vegetables from slave gardens and fish and game caught in the surrounding woodlands and marshes. Squirrels, rabbits, raccoons, and opossums roamed the live oak and pine forests, and the local rivers and creeks were still thick with oysters, crabs, waterfowl, and various fish.[111] Although no surviving records document the exact ways in which Wormsloe's slaves engaged in gardening and self-sufficiency, an 1854 statement by a Savannah-area slave likely captures the domestic economy of Jones's laborers. When questioned by northern reporter James Redpath, who was traveling the South incognito, the anonymous slave described the efforts of regional blacks to augment the standard plantation diet: "We has a little piece of ground dat we digs and plants. We raises vegetables, and we has a few chickens," the sale of which allowed slaves to purchase vegetables and eggs, and "a piece of bacon wid de money when we kin."[112] Emily Burke, a northern teacher who spent time on a sea island cotton plantation in the Georgia Lowcountry around 1840, similarly observed that slaves "often raise considerable crops of corn, tobacco, and potatoes, besides various kinds of garden vegetables. Their object in doing this is to have something with which to purchase tea, coffee, sugar, flour, and all such articles of diet as are not provided by their masters."[113] Frederick Law Olmsted, the most famous northern observer of the antebellum South, also remarked on the slave houses near the city, with their "gardens and pig-yards, enclosed by palings, between them."[114] According to Betty Wood, gardens had a "dual importance . . . in the domestic economy of the quarters: the contribution they made to the diet, and thereby to the health, of plantation bondpeople and the possibility they presented of producing surpluses that could be bartered or sold."[115]

Wild seafood was also an important resource within easy reach of Wormsloe's slaves. With their cabins fronting the salt marsh and the Skidaway River, the plantation's black men and women could harvest oysters; catch fish, crabs, and shrimp; and hunt for marsh hen eggs. Archeologists researching other Lowcountry sites have emphasized the importance of marine life in slave diets. Evidence from one South Carolina site indicates that antebellum slaves consumed at least thirty-two aquatic species, and another excavation on St. Simons Island, Georgia, revealed that 70 percent of the meat slaves consumed was fish.[116] A writer in the *Southern Cultivator*, an Augusta agricultural journal, commented that Lowcountry slaves "consume [fresh oysters] in enormous quantities."[117] There is little reason to believe that Wormsloe's slaves, with their close proximity to river and marsh, were any less reliant on aquatic resources. The differences in local black and white diets suggest different views of the importance of Wormsloe's fertility. For masters such as Jones, productivity provided an independence that was at its heart a luxury. Jones sought certain forms of self-sufficiency, but he had the money and freedom to look beyond Wormsloe's boundaries for goods that he needed or desired. For his slaves, the property's fruitfulness was often a matter of necessity. The task system and attendant masters' expectations made the productive spaces of plantation borders, forests, and slave gardens integral to the slaves' quality of life.

While Jones was intent on making qualitative improvements to the plantation's fields and pastures, he also engaged in a quantitative increase of Wormsloe's acreage during the late 1850s. He purchased a portion of Wimberly plantation, land to the north of Wormsloe that had been joined to the property prior to Noble Jones's death in 1775. George Wimberly Jones also bought Long Island from Frederick Waring in May 1856 for seven hundred dollars.[118] Noble Jones had sold the island at some point during the colonial era, and George Wimberly had desired its return for several years. In 1853, he had noted in his farm journal that under Waring's cultivation, the island's fertile soil produced thirty bags of cotton from only sixty acres. Although no documents record what Jones did with Long Island's fields immediately after purchasing the property, he built a shanty for a crew of local woodcutters under John McConnell and began clearing the Wimberly tract for cropland in 1858.[119] Both purchases moved Wormsloe's bounds closer to their late colonial limits.

At first glance, George Wimberly Jones's efforts on Wormsloe during the 1850s seem a bit irrational. The family's primary sources of income clearly lay elsewhere, and much of the effort and money invested in the old plantation disappeared as if down a drain. Jones had the financial resources to do as he liked, but the plantation was more than just a hobby or diversion. Jones's passion for improving Wormsloe seemed to come from a deep emotional attachment to the land. The estate was a physical tie to his family's start in the New World, the oldest of his properties scattered across the state and nation. Wormsloe was Noble Jones's seat, and more than a century after Noble received the Trustees' grant, his great-grandson had come to view the plantation as hallowed ground. As George would write following the war, his love of owning land came "from reflecting on the history of our family," and no piece of ground symbolized the Jones family history better than Wormsloe.[120] His efforts to manage land and labor, to build the ideal plantation, were always tied to his understanding and love of family history, and his devotion to Wormsloe would only grow as he poured himself, monetarily and emotionally, into bettering the landscape.

Jones's avid interest in modern farming methods seemed independent of his views on slavery. Like Ruffin and Hammond, Jones seemed to see no conflict between capital-intensive farming and chattel slavery, though unlike those reformers, he seemed to have little interest in vehement apologies for the institution. As William Bragg has determined, Jones's voluminous library focused on Georgia history but held only two titles relating to slavery: Theodore Canot's *Captain Canot; or, Twenty Years of an African Slaver*, which painted a rather rosy picture of the Middle Passage; and Samuel George Morton's *Crania Aegyptiaca*, "an ethnological defense of slavery."[121] While neither text was remotely abolitionist, together they hardly formed a canon for the hard-core slavery apologist. If his library lacked substantial references to slavery, Jones's agricultural journal is equally silent concerning his slaves. They appear only as the recipients of gestures he felt demonstrated his paternalism. Jones built new slave houses during the last years of the 1850s, double frame cabins with central fireplaces, raised plank floors, and entrances on each end to accommodate two families. This housing design, with variations in brick, stone, and tabby, was typical on large Georgia and South Carolina coastal cotton plantations of the period and must have been an improvement over the colonial-era huts. Jones's new cabins also reflected widespread appeals of southern reformers for better slave dwellings.[122] In large part, the regional campaign for improved slave housing that emerged during the 1840s and 1850s drew on old and mistaken conceptions of the Lowcountry disease environment. Planters such as Jones believed that modern, well-ventilated frame cabins with wooden floors and brick chimneys would ensure healthy slave populations by reducing their residents' exposure to the "bad air" thought to provoke illnesses.[123] Once a year he made surprise inspections of the slave quarters, awarding prizes such as furniture, clothing, and small mirrors to the women who kept the neatest houses. Aside from these brief references, however, Wormsloe's slaves remain in the background of the journal; they provided the blood and sweat that made the plantation work but were seemingly of only small interest in George W. Jones's larger scheme of things. The depth of Wormsloe's reliance on these hidden figures can be glimpsed only in a list compiled in 1861. Recording the slaves he owned and the individuals his wife had inherited from her father's El Destino plantation in Florida, Jones carefully inscribed the names of London and Celia, Nathan and Old Effie, and sixty other people who tilled Wormsloe's land and cared for its crops, the human elements of Jones's landscape experiments. As the Civil War began, Jones might have created a modern farm, but it still relied on a backbone of cotton and slaves.[124]

Jones's lack of discussion regarding his slaves suggests an ambivalence concerning the place of slavery in his remade plantation, a stance reflected in the built environment of antebellum Wormsloe. He located the new double slave cabins, with their tidy whitewashed walls and symmetrical arrangement in two rows along a central road, several hundred yards south of the main plantation house. Like Jones's house, the new quarters had a pleasant situation, located as they were under the shade of live oaks along the riverbank, with a prospect of the marsh, the Skidaway channel, and Long Island. These new cabins, with their plank floors, solid roofs, and large windows, fit Jones's improver ideals: Healthy slaves were productive slaves. Unlike Noble Jones, who had built his colonial slave huts close to his fortified house, George W. Jones created a nucleated slave village that was a distinctly separate entity from the house grounds and the farmyard. The clustering of all of Wormsloe's slave quarters in one location reinforced the notion that the plantation's slaves were a single unit, under the command of Jones, rather than individuals or families and ensured that although out of sight, his laborers were never more than a few minutes' walk away. In fact, a white presence was ubiquitous in the quarters, as the overseer's house stood next to the slave village. The new plantation landscaping further separated master and slaves, as ornamental plantings and new outbuildings screened the quarters from the house, just as shade trees created a symbolic barrier between the house and the crop fields located to the north, west, and south. This structuring of the plantation landscape was typical of large Lowcountry plantations prior to the Civil War, a carefully designed and circumscribed terrain that John Vlach has labeled the world "back of the big house," where planters attempted to assert their mastery of both people and land.[125] Viewed in this light, Jones's decisions regarding his slave quarters and slave management were just as calculated to ensure an efficient and modern plantation as were his introductions of new strains of livestock and crops or his efforts to mechanize elements of agricultural production. These decisions reflected a willingness, common in the South, to conceptualize slaves as simply one cog in the plantation machine.

These antebellum building and landscape projects reoriented the productive and residential landscape with an eye toward race and labor. The productive portion of the colonial plantation had been a compact space. The Joneses' house (the fort) was located next to the cluster of small slave huts and surrounded by agricultural clearings, with the commons of the forest and marsh beyond; both blacks and whites lived at Wormsloe's center. On the late 1850s plantation, the big house existed at the core of the agricultural and social landscape. Surrounding the house, ornamental and vegetable gardens flanked by hedges, camellias, and jessamine divided the master's living space from the working landscape. Beyond these plantings were clusters of plantation buildings: stables, sheds, the rice mill, barns, and a cotton gin. Past these structures, further still from the main house, were the fields, where the slaves lived in rows of cabins lining the quarters field and lying just north of the old fort field. The overseer's house served as a buffer between the village and the farmyard to the north. As on plantations where slave cabins lined entrance drives or flanked orchards and gardens, the slaves and their housing were integral in the productive portion of the landscape. George W. Jones still lived at the center of the plantation world, but his house was now insulated from his slaves and agricultural operations. Although this realignment of plantation space at first seems inimical to Jones's improvement campaign, it was in fact part and parcel of his modernization efforts. Even though Jones could no longer easily overlook slaves' living and working spaces, the plantation house's location at the center of the property reinforced Jones's command of his estate. Family and guests arriving at Wormsloe rode down the long oak avenue, surrounded on both sides by neat cotton, corn, and sweet potato fields, then moved through a series of carefully landscaped gardens and yards before halting at the big house. Progression through the agricultural and ornamental landscape carried an obvious message: Wormsloe was an orderly place, and its master lived in the most beautiful and orderly space on the plantation. Despite this landscape redesign, however, the big house and the quarters remained "inseparably and dreadfully linked."[126]

Jones's relegation of the slave quarters to a plot of land out of sight of the big house did not mean that he monopolized the definition of the plantation's geography. Just as slaves shaped their diets to a great degree, they also held a certain power to define living and working spaces as their own. As Vlach has noted, "When viewed from the outside, slave quarters can be seen as instruments of control, as material devices used by planters to demean and brutalize their slaves," but slaves "subtly modified their cabins and the spaces around them to serve needs of their own."[127] This slave determination to manage elements of time and space combined with the task system to transform certain portions of the plantation into black spaces.[128] In theory, the master may have controlled all aspects of the estate, but in practice the slave quarters and much of the rest of the plantation were occupied and cultivated almost exclusively by slaves. Although these laborers were far from free to manage the land as they desired, this tacit division of the landscape into black and white spheres gave slaves on large holdings, such as Wormsloe, a modicum of latitude. Hunting, fishing, gardening, and even resting were no doubt easier undertakings away from the master's gaze. While masters were to some degree complicit in this partitioning of the landscape—Jones and others must have understood the value in providing their slaves with time and space to attend to personal needs—it would be a mistake to minimize slave agency in using the plantation margins. Jones may have viewed his slaves and slave housing as essential elements of a modern plantation, but the division of Wormsloe's built environment and black desires to use and control small pieces of the natural world created plots of ground bounded by the master's desires but shaped by black culture.

The conscious and subconscious reasoning behind this division of the landscape into racial spheres is perhaps best explained by Eugene Genovese, who attributes the tensions that shaped plantation spaces and relationships to an overwhelming planter paternalism that "afforded a fragile bridge across the intolerable contradictions inherent in a society based on racism, slavery, and class exploitation that had to depend on the willing reproduction and productivity of its victims."[129] When Jones built neat, spacious slave cabins, planned a nucleated slave village, and distributed annual prizes to the women who kept the neatest households, he sought both a peaceful labor force and peace of mind: An ordered and productive landscape symbolized a contented and stable slave population. Use of the term *paternalism* does not imply that Jones's efforts were beneficent or that they overwhelmed his slaves' ability to control aspects of their lives. Just as Jones acted in a way calculated to obtain his aims, Wormsloe's slaves used the paternalistic system and the resulting paternalistic landscape to gain small concessions. Slaves used the same slave village plan and location that Jones designed for maximum beauty and efficiency to exert increased control over their provisioning and personal time, and slave gardens that saved planters money provided slave cultivators with a sense of independence and even furnished them limited opportunities to enter a basic market economy when they sold vegetables or poultry in Savannah. As Genovese argues, progressive planters may have constructed modern slave cabins and houses across the South during the antebellum era, but slaves worked to their own ends within these paternalistic acts, building a black world within white walls.[130]

Among antebellum planters intent on agricultural reform, Jones was hardly alone in his willingness to meld slavery and modern farming methods. Ruffin and other proponents of more intensive southern agriculture failed to see slavery and reform as incompatible—indeed, these reformers often defined modernization as slavery's savior.[131] Despite many planters' willingness to associate bound labor and reform, slavery at times hindered agricultural modernization. Most planters, Jones included, invested a large portion of their wealth in slaves, so actions that stressed labor rather than soil conservation made a certain economic sense, especially when cheap land was available elsewhere, as it was in the antebellum South. However, as historian William Mathew has pointed out, reform could also serve as "a protective and conservative exercise" for planters intent on proving that the plantation system could be a durable form of agriculture. For landowners such as Jones, who held especially strong feelings for family estates, any program that promised to save the plantation without radically altering southern society held tremendous appeal. Although reform-minded planters associated improvement, slavery, and permanence, it is difficult to disagree with Mathew's declaration that "slavery not only hindered much reform but was itself intrinsically unreformable."[132]

On Wormsloe, as across the South, slavery posed challenges for reform-minded planters and farmers. The slave system valued labor over land, and even on plantations such as Wormsloe where historic family ties and independent wealth made westward migration unlikely and unnecessary, the calculus of slave ownership and staple agriculture pressured planters to make conservation decisions in certain ways. With slave labor so valuable, external amendments such as guano made a sort of sense: Guano cost more than salt marsh mud only if the black labor used to dig, move, and spread the muck was not factored into its cost. Slaves freed from laboring in the marshes could devote their time and energy to clearing new land, plowing cotton fields, or working with livestock and other crops. Just as important, Jones and his fellow planters believed that ownership of slaves placed certain limitations on the selection of crops. At the crux of this problem was a belief that few crops were profitable enough to support large-scale slave ownership; as a consequence, rice and cotton dominated the Lowcountry agricultural landscape. According to this logic, plantation-scale cotton production required slaves, and slave ownership necessitated cotton (or rice) cultivation. Breaking this Faustian cycle required that planters either sell their slaves or find alternate cash crops. The first option went against the paternalism that many planters—including, it seems, George W. Jones—held dear, while the second proved a fruitless task in the antebellum South. Slavery was not antimodern, but its existence placed real limits on the types of reform and improvement southern planters believed practical.

Jones's simple refusal to acknowledge or discuss, at least in writing, the tensions of combining progressive farming with slave labor was but one of agricultural reformers' strategies regarding slavery. Although few reformers went as far as Virginian slavery apologist George Fitzhugh, who touted the institution as a "positive good," most accepted slavery as an integral part of southern agriculture and sought ways to work around or with slaveholding.[133] In *An Essay on Calcareous Manures*, Ruffin wrote of his fear that southern slave populations were growing too rapidly, yet he included instructions on how to dig and apply marl with slave labor and remained a steadfast supporter of the southern right to own slaves.[134] Even southern reformers who believed that slavery was the key obstacle to regional agricultural modernization struggled to divorce themselves from a reliance on the institution. For example, in an 1847 address to an agricultural club, Virginia's James Bruce, a prominent Upper South reformer, called for southern planters to sell their slaves and invest in farm mechanization and regional industry, yet he failed to follow his own advice. At the onset of the Civil War, Bruce remained the master of several hundred slaves.[135] Ruffin's and Bruce's vocal struggles to reconcile slavery and agricultural reform were mirrored in Jones's reconstruction of the Wormsloe landscape. Jones sought to preserve the old order of slavery and mastery while creating a new plantation, efforts that constantly chafed against one another.

In the last decade before the Civil War, Wormsloe seemed to be mirroring Chatham's countywide movement toward an even more intensive plantation society. Although Jones's focus on innovative farming methods and self-sufficiency on Wormsloe may have been unusual, his neighbors were also raising more sea island cotton, working more slaves, and cultivating more land than ever before. By the 1850s, the region and the nation had fully recovered from the Panic of 1837 and the ensuing five-year depression, and commodity markets in general were strong. Tobacco farmers in Virginia and North Carolina, upland cotton producers in the fresh lands of the Mississippi Delta and Texas, and sugar producers in the river parishes of Louisiana experienced a period of relative prosperity.[136] Sea island cotton reflected this trend, selling for more than thirty cents per pound throughout the decade.[137] Cotton production (the majority of it the sea island variety) almost doubled in Chatham County from 580 bales in 1850 to 933 bales ten years later, and there was a substantial, though less dramatic, increase in rice production as well. There was also an attendant rise in crops typically associated with slave provisions, such as sweet potatoes, cowpeas, and corn. Unlike on Wormsloe, this growth of plantation culture threatened to replace subsistence cultivation with ever larger staple-producing plantations. Mules increased at the expense of milk cows, and farmers raised more beef cows and hogs but produced less butter and owned fewer sheep.[138] As on Jones's estate, Chatham County's landowners increasingly focused on cotton and plantation production in the 1850s. Although Jones's actions brought Wormsloe more and more into the sphere of global cotton markets, he simultaneously sought to increase his connections with the local landscape, struggling at times with these disparate goals.

These efforts at intensification on Wormsloe and surrounding plantations were in large part the product of the growth and prosperity of Savannah. Between 1840 and the outbreak of the Civil War, the city experienced a period of robust economic expansion. The new Central of Georgia Railroad and its feeder branches connected the port city to inland Georgia, and as Piedmont cotton culture increased, these rail lines hauled thousands of bales of short-staple cotton into Savannah for export. Between 1844 and 1849, the number of cotton bales hauled annually by the Central of Georgia increased more than fivefold, from 77,437 to 391,000. The Savannah, Albany, and Gulf Railroad joined the Central of Georgia in bringing cotton to the city in 1857, and the Savannah and Ogeechee Canal, built in the early 1830s and improved in 1840, also moved timber, cotton, and rice north to Savannah's wharves. This influx of raw materials promoted the development of industry, and during the antebellum period, city businessmen invested in lumberyards, sawmills, four shipyards, cotton presses, rice mills, a locomotive shop, and a number of mercantile businesses. Between 1830 and 1860, the city's population tripled, reaching 22,292.[139] All of these people and industries required agricultural products, and Chatham County planters and farmers expanded their production to meet these needs. Riding around Savannah's outskirts during his visit, Olmsted met with "long teams of mules, driven by negroes . . . with loads of rices or cotton," and roads were choked with small carts burdened with cotton or "an assorted cargo of maize, sweet potatoes, poultry, game, hides, and peltry, with always, some bundles of corn-leaves, to be fed to the horse."[140] These wares made their way to Savannah's docks and market stalls, feeding both the city's international cotton trade and workers' stomachs.

The Wormsloe landscape underwent a dramatic transformation between the end of the American Revolution and the outbreak of the Civil War. Large corn and cotton fields covered the northern portion of the property where a broad oak and pine forest had once stood. A new plantation house and numerous dependencies dotted the cleared land, and a population of more than seventy people lived and worked on Wormsloe, more than had inhabited the property since Noble Jones's settlement. Although 1860 Wormsloe could not match the opulence of the Lowcountry rice estates, such as those ringing Charleston or the Hermitage a few miles away along the Savannah River in Chatham

County, the Joneses' holdings had become a modern and impressive sea island cotton plantation.[141] When he rode across his estate, George W. Jones surveyed neat white-painted slave houses, a new rice mill with a towering brick chimney, a complex of barns and stables, a modern gin, pastures full of cattle and sheep, and dozens of slaves. The composition of local plant and animal life had changed as well. New ornamentals such as camellias and figs replaced the older century plants and oranges, deer and turkeys seemed to have largely disappeared from the surrounding woods, perhaps as a result of overhunting, and although an alligator occasionally made an appearance in the plantation's sloughs and terrapins remained a fixture in plantation cookbooks, pigs and chickens had become a more common sight than wild animals.[142] Under Jones's active stewardship, Wormsloe had become more farm than forest, more manicured landscape than marsh, but the coming war would shape the property in even more profound and uncontrollable ways.

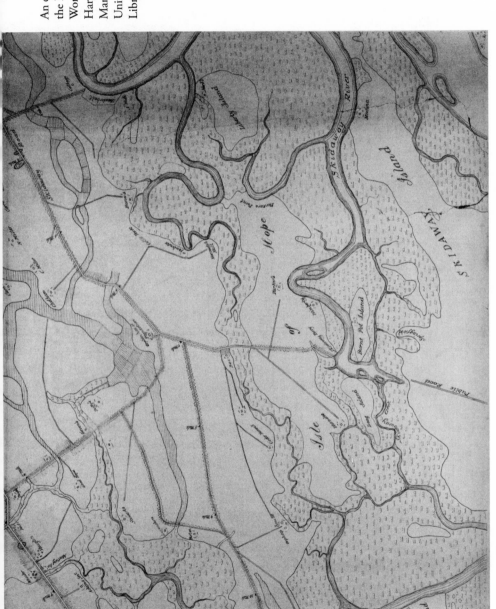

An early map showing the Isle of Hope and Wormsloe. Courtesy of Hargrett Rare Book and Manuscript Library/ University of Georgia Libraries.

330 ft.

No. 2 is the residence of a confidential servant drawn
Inch to ten feet as also its Distance from the Dwelling
20 ft by 15 ft one story
No. 3 is a carriage house & stable 23 ft by 21 ft one story
an inch to ten ft as also its Distances from the Servant
the Dwelling house 134 ft. No. 5 is a Spring distant
Passing directly in front of the Dwelling is a large
the house 330 ft

This Dwelling house as here described No. 1 is drawn by Sea
forty feet front & 20 feet deep two stories high of wood standing
together with a room in the rear of 17 ft by 15 ft one story
basement of 7 ft high there will be 3 fire places in the
of wood & 2 do in the second story of wood No. 4 is
above is 7 ft by 5 ft one story

After George Jones's house on a neighboring plantation burned, he built a new home on Wormsloe in 1828–1829. Courtesy of Hargrett Rare Book and Manuscript Library/University of Georgia Libraries.

No 2
Servants house
20 ft   92 ft ½

No 3
Stable
23 ft

1/8 of an inch to the foot is
... a basement of tables 7 ft high
... of wood resting on A table
... ment 3 D° in the first Story
... room Drawn by Scale as

this Room is one Story
on a basement
17 by 15 ft

No 1

No 4
Store room
5 ft   7 ft

... scale of 1/8 of an ...
... say 95 ft 9 inches
... own by Scale of 1/4 ...
... 92 7/8 ft & from
... the Dwelling 165 ft
... or river distant from

No 5
Spring

African Americans picking cotton near Savannah, Foltz Studio, Savannah, Georgia. Courtesy of Hargrett Rare Book and Manuscript Library/University of Georgia Libraries.

Sea island cotton grew on the quarter's field, seen here with the plantation's slave cabins in the background. Courtesy of Hargrett Rare Book and Manuscript Library/University of Georgia Libraries.

The plantation house with its Victorian trappings as it appeared in 1895, Goebel-Salterbach Studio. Courtesy of Hargrett Rare Book and Manuscript Library/University of Georgia Libraries.

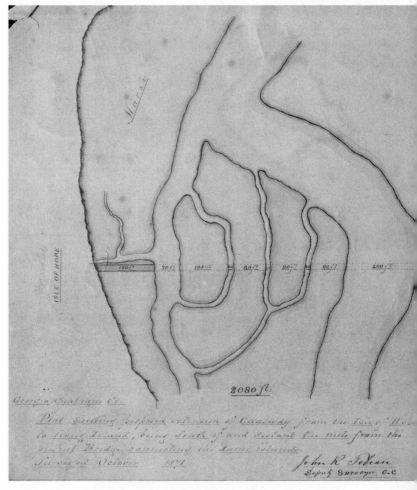

A plat of the proposed causeway between the Isle of Hope and
Skidaway Island, 1871. Courtesy of Hargrett Rare Book and
Manuscript Library/University of Georgia Libraries.

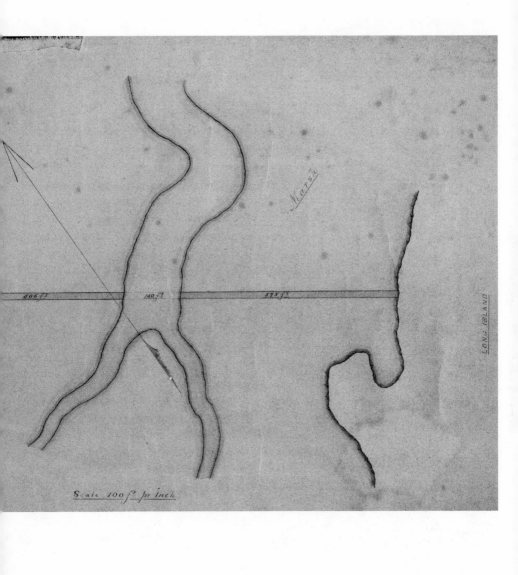

Marsh

LONG ISLAND

605 f²   160 f²   575 f²

Scale 100 f² pr inch.

The original live oak avenue leading from Skidaway Road to the Joneses' house, Goebel-Salterback Studio, 1895. Courtesy of Hargrett Rare Book and Manuscript Library/University of Georgia Libraries.

Wormsloe was home to a variety of livestock, including pleasure and work horses, 1899. Courtesy of Hargrett Rare Book and Manuscript Library/University of Georgia Libraries.

M. Edw. Wilson.
Photo.   13.

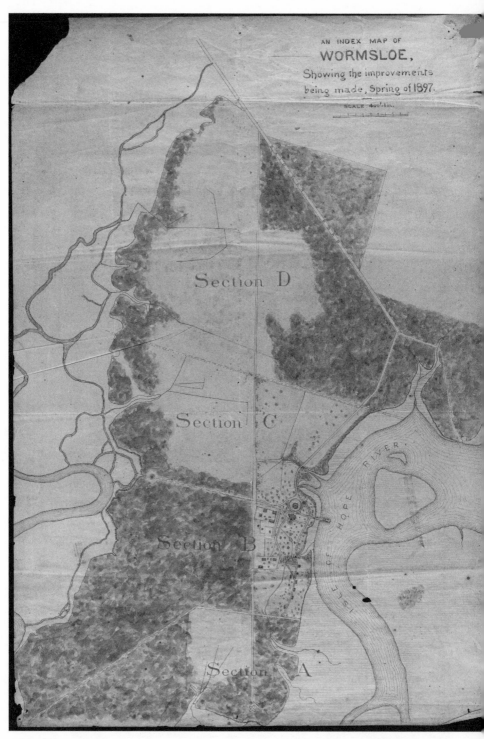

During the late 1890s, Wymberley J. De Renne undertook a large-scale effort to beautify the plantation grounds, part of which was recorded in a series of landscaping maps, 1897. Courtesy of Hargrett Rare Book and Manuscript Library/ University of Georgia Libraries.

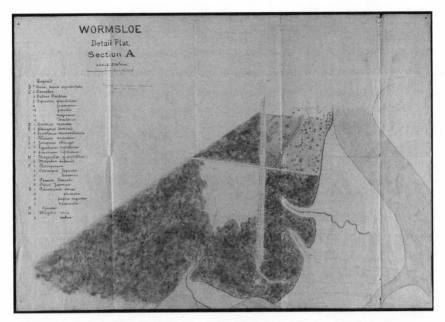

Detail of the 1897 landscaping map. Courtesy of Hargrett Rare Book and Manuscript Library/University of Georgia Libraries.

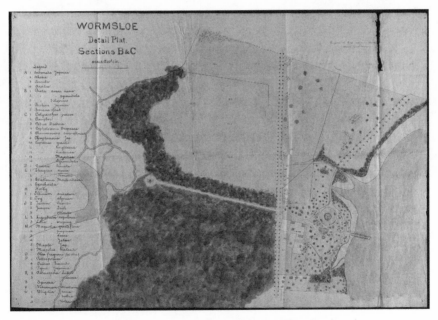

Detail of the 1897 landscaping map. Courtesy of Hargrett Rare Book and Manuscript Library/University of Georgia Libraries.

By the turn of the century a modern concrete pier projected over the marsh to the Skidaway River. Courtesy of Hargrett Rare Book and Manuscript Library/ University of Georgia Libraries.

Wormsloe's agricultural operations included a modern dairy by the early twentieth century. Courtesy of Hargrett Rare Book and Manuscript Library/University of Georgia Libraries.

The plantation mansion in all its
Victorian glory, 1899. Courtesy
of Hargrett Rare Book and
Manuscript Library/University of
Georgia Libraries.

"WORMSLOE" 1899.

M.C.W. WILSON
PHOTO. 17.

At the turn of the century, Wormsloe's landscaped grounds included reflecting pools, fountains, a gazebo, foot bridges, and garden gnomes, 1899. Courtesy of Hargrett Rare Book and Manuscript Library/ University of Georgia Libraries.

"WORMSLOE" 1877.

The slave village by the marsh served after the war as housing for African American renters, sharecroppers, and wage laborers, often former slaves and their families, 1899. Courtesy of Hargrett Rare Book and Manuscript Library/ University of Georgia Libraries.

Wormsloe's grand dining room was the scene of white leisure and black labor, 1899. Courtesy of Hargrett Rare Book and Manuscript Library/University of Georgia Libraries.

Local African American craftsmen built the impressive fireproof library.
Courtesy of Hargrett Rare Book and Manuscript Library/University of
Georgia Libraries.

Wymberley J. De Renne amassed an impressive collection of taxidermy mounts of Lowcountry species, a few of which are displayed here, alongside a statue of a boy. Courtesy of Hargrett Rare Book and Manuscript Library/University of Georgia Libraries.

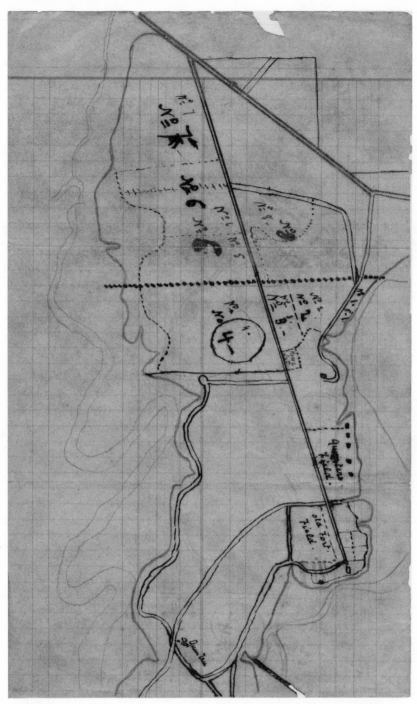

A sketch of the plantation's fields, diagramming a crop of hay, peas, and potatoes, ca. 1910s. Courtesy of Hargrett Rare Book and Manuscript Library/University of Georgia Libraries.

Successional pine forest on Wormsloe—note longleaf pine sapling in the foreground—early twentieth century. Courtesy of Hargrett Rare Book and Manuscript Library/University of Georgia Libraries.

Formal Garden.
Wormsloe. Georgia.
By Augusta De Renne.

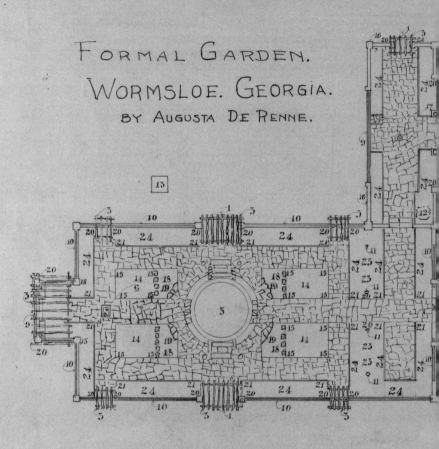

Legend

1 GATE	9 GRILL WORK	17 URN
2 DOOR	10 IRON FENCE	18 AZALEAS
3 ARBOR	11 COLUMN	19 ROSES
4 BENCH	12 TREE	20 CLIMBING ROSE
5 FOUNTAIN.	13 DOVE COTE	21 FLOWERING ALMO
6 BIRD BATH	14 TURF	22 ROCK GARDEN
7 GNOMES	15 CYPRESS	23 OLEANDER
8 STATUETTE	16 BRICK WALL	24 HERBACEOUS B

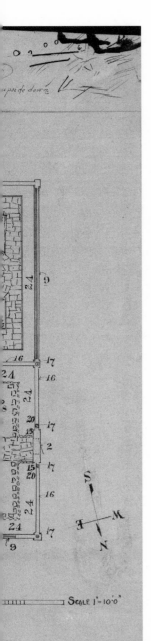

A horticultural diagram of the walled formal garden at Wormsloe, Augusta De Renne, 1928. Courtesy of Hargrett Rare Book and Manuscript Library/University of Georgia Libraries.

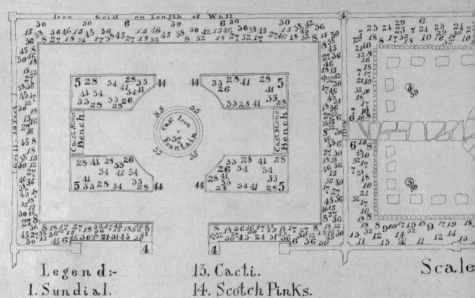

Scale

Legend:-

1. Sundial.
2. Fountain.
3. Statuettes.
4. Urns, Yucca.
5. Arbor Vitae.
6. Climbing Rose.
7. Azalea, Dwarf.
8. Row of Violets.
9. Heartsease.
10. Pansies.
11. Rock plants.
12. Columbine.
44. White Spider Lily.

13. Cacti.
14. Scotch Pinks.
15. Larkspur.
16. Iris.
17. Jonquils.
18. Verbena.
19. Forgetmenots.
20. Tuberoses.
21. Blue Sage.
22. Hollyhocks.
23. African Daisies.
24. Shasta Daisies.
25. Bougainvillea.
45. Montbrisa.

26. Dwarf Cedar.
27. Marigolds.
28. Strawberries.
29. Guernsey Lili
30 Rubeckia,
    Grandiflora.
31. Chrysanthem
32. Callendulas.
33. Gnomes & Ju
34. Hemero calli
    Double Orang
46. Nasturtium

The 1928 additions to the formal garden, Augusta De Renne, 1928. Courtesy of Hargrett Rare Book and Manuscript Library/University of Georgia Libraries.

View of a corner of the formal gardens, Foltz Studio, Savannah, Georgia. Courtesy of Hargrett Rare Book and Manuscript Library/University of Georgia Libraries.

A detail of Wormsloe's formal walled garden, Bayard Wooten, 1934. Courtesy of Hargrett Rare Book and Manuscript Library/University of Georgia Libraries.

The ruins of the Colonial tabby fort as they appeared to Wormsloe Garden visitors, Bayard Wooten, 1934. Courtesy of Hargrett Rare Book and Manuscript Library/University of Georgia Libraries.

Liza, who claimed to have been born on Wormsloe, furnished park guests with refreshments from a restored slave cabin, ca. 1930, Foltz Studio, Savannah, Georgia. Courtesy of Hargrett Rare Book and Manuscript Library/University of Georgia Libraries.

This aerial photograph of Wormsloe
(ca. late 1930s?) captured the forces of
succession at work on the plantation's
fields and pastures, U.S. Army Air
Corps. Courtesy of Hargrett Rare Book
and Manuscript Library/University of
Georgia Libraries.

A map of Wormsloe and
vicinity as they appeared in
1958, Thomas & Hutton,
Engineers, 1958. Courtesy
of Hargrett Rare Book and
Manuscript Library/University
of Georgia Libraries.

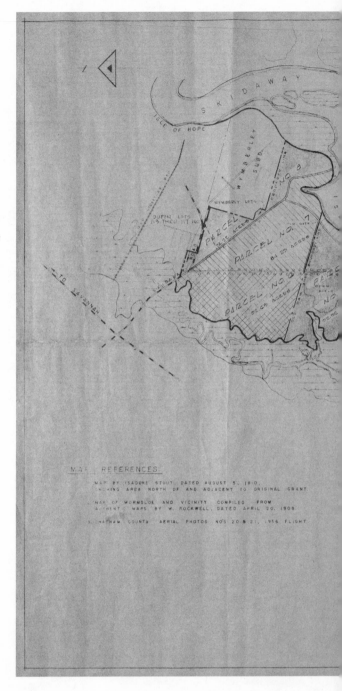

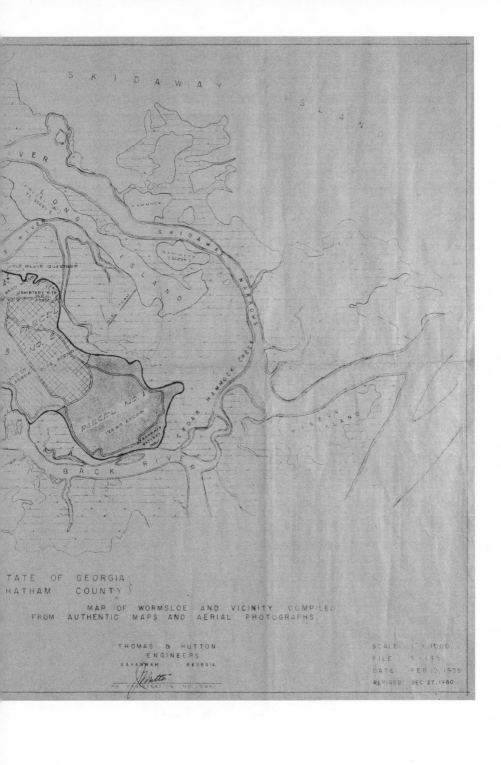

S K I D A W A Y

I S L A N D

R I V E R

L O N G

HAMMOCK

S K I D A W A Y

R I V E R

I S L A N D

HAMMOCK

OLD SLAVE QUARTERS

CEMETERY SITE
OLD
FORT

SKIDAWAY NARROWS

PARCEL
NO. 2

PARCEL NO. 1
174.80 ACRES

CEDAR HAMMOCK CREEK

PIGEON ISLAND

B A C K   R I V E R

TATE OF GEORGIA
HATHAM   COUNTY

MAP OF WORMSLOE AND VICINITY COMPILED
FROM AUTHENTIC MAPS AND AERIAL PHOTOGRAPHS.

THOMAS & HUTTON
ENGINEERS
SAVANNAH   GEORGIA

SCALE 1" = 1000'
FILE S-145
DATE FEB 12, 1958
REVISED DEC 27, 1960

Wormsloe's live oak avenue, planted in the 1890s, still welcomes tourists to Wormsloe State Historic Site. Photograph by the author, 2008.

The modern house and grounds retain elements of the plantation past.
Photograph by the author, 2008.

The coastal saltmarsh still surrounds the estate with tidal abundance. Long Island is across the marsh. Photograph by the author, 2008.

The restored slave cabin, today housing for researchers, stands as a reminder of Wormsloe's long human history. Photograph by the author, 2008.

Wormsloe Remade

Plantation Culture from the Civil War to the Twentieth Century

IN OCTOBER 1861, Confederate artillery at Port Royal opened fire on Union gunboats along the southeastern South Carolina coast. The roar of the cannons shook Wormsloe's plantation house "from cellar to garret, though the firing was at forty miles distance."[1] With that thunderous barrage, the Civil War came to Wormsloe. The conflict disrupted cotton planting and the Joneses' normal routines over the next four years, temporarily leaving the plantation in the hands of Confederate troops guarding Savannah. But the Union victory in the war spelled the end of slavery and ultimately sea island cotton on Wormsloe and threatened the Joneses' ownership of the plantation. The Civil War and its aftermath would also be a watershed in Wormsloe's environmental history.

Although the war temporarily altered agricultural routines on Wormsloe, emancipation proved to be the most important force in transforming relationships between the plantation's people and the land. During Reconstruction, George W. Jones experimented with renting the property to northern investors, made sharecropping arrangements, and leased small subsistence plots to freedpeople, all in attempts to reconcile his antebellum agricultural ideal of an efficient, staple-producing plantation with the realities of emancipation. In the end, all of these efforts failed. If the war's consequences meant that the Joneses had to face a new plantation order, the outcome was at least as portentous for the Lowcountry's former slaves. Freedpeople throughout the Lowcountry sought their own pieces of land and struggled to define the exact meaning of emancipation. In many instances, these former slaves believed that they had a right to a portion of plantations built with their labor, and the federal government agreed—temporarily. At war's end, four freedmen laid claim to a section of Wormsloe, though their claims were short-lived. As wage laborers, sharecroppers, and tenants, African Americans also continued to use the landscape in traditional ways, gardening, fishing, oystering, and hunting

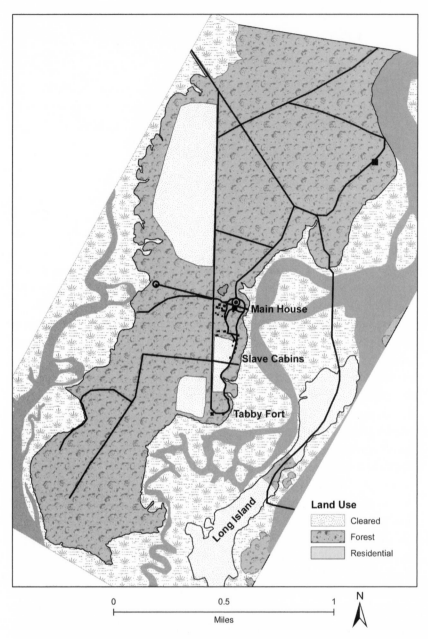

Wormsloe 1860. Map by Dr. Thomas R. Jordan, Center for Remote Sensing and Mapping Science, Department of Geography, University of Georgia, Athens, Georgia.

in the forests and marshes. By 1900, the Jones family still firmly held onto Wormsloe's grounds, but former slaves and other local African Americans consistently acted to utilize the plantation's resources in ways that simultaneously hearkened back to the antebellum era and reflected the new postbellum economic order.

Wormsloe's commercial connections to the larger world also changed during the four decades following the war. Sea island cotton disappeared, replaced by fodder crops, pasture grasses, Irish and sweet potatoes, and an increasing quantity of corn. This shift from a staple crop to a more diversified agriculture reoriented Wormsloe's market relationships, replacing transatlantic ties with more regional markets. The Joneses remained a cosmopolitan family, tied to the American Northeast and Europe through family, taste, and travel, but the transatlantic economic connections rooted in the land and its produce that had contributed so much to their global perspective had vanished forever.

The postwar decades also marked a physical and mental refashioning of the plantation landscape. Wormsloe remained an agricultural property, but the grounds became increasingly centered on pleasurable and relaxing activities, from horseback riding to gardening. George W. Jones, followed by his son, Wymberley, undertook these changes with an idealized image of the antebellum plantation in mind. Father and son planted gardens, remodeled the main house, and attempted to preserve the ruins of the colonial tabby fort with an eye toward conserving and interpreting the past, a process that slowly shaped family and visitor impressions of the estate. At the turn of the twentieth century, Wormsloe appeared an impressively preserved piece of the Old South, but it was a plantation as the family wanted it to be rather than as it had actually been. This process of reinterpreting the landscape was nothing new. Noble Jones had remade the coastal forest with early modern England in mind, and sea island cotton transformed a landscape of mixed agriculture and horticultural experimentation into a staple-crop-producing plantation, but the land use changes that took place on late-nineteenth-century Wormsloe were a much more self-conscious refashioning of the landscape. These efforts at re-creating the colonial and Old South continued antebellum trends and persisted into the late twentieth century. They continue to affect current perceptions of the landscape, complicating what the preservation of Wormsloe plantation entails.

George W. Jones continued to raise sea island cotton as the war approached, and he persevered in his improvement and modernization campaign, purchasing additional slaves, soil amendments, and agricultural equipment during the last boom years of the antebellum period.[2] Although Jones was unable to transform the plantation into a lucrative cotton estate on the scale of some sea island planters, he had managed to increase production of the fiber above the level of the 1830s and 1840s. Despite the outbreak of the war, Wormsloe's 1861 cotton crop totaled eighteen bags (roughly nine thousand pounds), a similar size to the moderate crops of the late 1850s, though the Union naval blockade meant that Jones was able to sell only a portion of the crop.[3] While agricultural operations continued in some fashion throughout the war, 1861 was the last year for both the Joneses and cotton on the plantation until after the Confederate surrender at Appomattox.

Following the southern assault on Fort Sumter, the Jones family departed Wormsloe in July 1861 for the safety of the Blue Ridge Mountains, leaving an overseer in charge of managing the plantation and its slave population. As self-imposed refugees, the family split time that summer between Greenville, South Carolina, and Flat Rock, North Carolina, antebellum playgrounds for lowland planters where families such as the Joneses had long escaped the coastal summer heat. The mountains of the Appalachian South served as a haven for a number of wealthy southerners, many of whom brought along their human property to prevent the slaves from falling into Union hands. In October, the Joneses left the mountains and attempted a return to Wormsloe, perhaps to oversee the autumn cotton harvest. Greeted by the Port Royal cannons, the family was again forced to trek inland; on this second, longer sojourn, the Joneses spent time as refugees in Augusta, Georgia, and Greenville, South Carolina.[4] Soon after this second flight from Wormsloe, Union troops occupied Tybee Island and established a blockade of the mouth of the Savannah River, close to the Isle of Hope.[5] From the end of 1861 until the Union campaign that captured Savannah in December 1864, Wormsloe existed as an armed camp, land under Confederate control yet between the main enemy lines and never far from harm's way.

Although hostilities near Wormsloe and the Union naval blockade spelled a temporary end to cotton production on the property, the war did not bring agricultural activities to a complete halt.[6] Cattle, horses, mules, and poultry still ranged the plantation's woods and pastures, slaves still labored in the fields and in their gardens, and George W. Jones still attempted to direct daily routines from afar. He retained an overseer early in the war and continued to produce provision crops that found ready buyers in Savannah's Confederate quartermasters. Corn, peas, fodder, and hay replaced sea island cotton in the fields, and Jones recorded profitable sales of Wormsloe's crops in 1862 and 1863, thanks to the dramatic inflation of foodstuffs. In fact, he later marveled at the way in which "agricultural productions rose in price greatly" during the war. His 1863 crops alone grossed more than twenty thousand dollars (albeit in inflated Confederate currency).[7] Wartime inflation and the risks of working so close to the front made plantation management more costly as well. In January 1864, Jones hired Edward Nelson to oversee Wormsloe for six hundred dollars (three times the antebellum rate), the services of a cook, and "the usual plantation fare."[8] Jones had good luck selling his crops, but he also risked periodic seizure of the plantation's produce, as when Confederate quartermasters requisitioned sixty-four bales of hay from Wormsloe in February 1862.[9]

The Civil War also temporarily increased Wormsloe's human population. The Joneses had fled the property, but their slaves and the overseer who remained were joined by a large contingent of Confederate troops. More than fifty soldiers were stationed at earthworks on the southern tip of Wormsloe guarding the Moon River, and rebel engineers constructed another armed garrison at Bell's Point, on the northeastern corner of the plantation, overlooking the Skidaway River. These military activities brought their own changes to the Wormsloe landscape. At both locations, soldiers moved massive quantities of dirt to protect their artillery emplacements. At Fort Wimberly, along the southern point of Wormsloe, these fortifications rose more than twenty feet high and stretched for more than a hundred yards along the marsh. The earthworks themselves displaced soil, replaced forested land with clearings, created borrow pits that would have filled with stagnant water, and changed drainage patterns. Soldiers also built an earthen causeway across the marsh, connecting the Isle of Hope with Long Island and Skidaway Island, to serve as a potential escape route for coastal defense forces. This earthmoving certainly affected the hydrology of the river channel and the population of the dominant marsh plant, saltmarsh cordgrass.[10] To this day, the old earthworks remain a distinct microhabitat within Wormsloe's maritime forest—the embankments of the fort at the southern tip of the plantation support a thriving stand of hickories that rely on the old fort's elevation above the water table for dry, well-drained soil. The daily routines of the soldiers who manned these works almost certainly had a temporary effect on the local environment as well, through their fishing, hunting, or gathering oysters during idle hours and cutting timber for cooking and heating.

Forced separation from Wormsloe was a difficult experience for the Joneses to endure. Early in the war, George and Mary sent their young son, Wymberley, through the Union blockade to France, whence he expressed his homesickness. Writing his "autobiography" for an 1865 school assignment, Wymberley described his home as "a beautiful country place named Wormsloe," a "very large plantation with a beautiful river." He rhapsodized, "Oh! Oh! You dont know how pleasant in sumer it is to sit out on the balcony and look at the garden which runs around the house and take the fresh brize."[11] Wymberley's parents likely felt the same sentimental longing for the Isle of Hope landscape as they passed the war in the Upcountry. It is easy to imagine George Jones lamenting the abandonment of an estate in which he had invested so much energy and money and expressing his longing for a landscape and way of life challenged so directly by the struggles of the war.

While the Joneses missed their Lowcountry estate, their exile to the Piedmont and the mountains was hardly without its comforts. They visited with family in Augusta, and while in Greenville they stayed at the luxurious Mansion House Hotel, where they had vacationed before the war. The Mansion House was an expensive retreat that catered to wealthy planters and their families; four months of food and lodging in the fall of 1862 cost the Joneses more than fourteen hundred dollars. The family also traveled with a portion of their Wormsloe comforts. Throughout their stay in Greenville they were attended by two slaves and a white nurse and her child, they ate quite well in the hotel's dining room, and they rented horses for explorations of the countryside. Although the war restricted access to their primary residence, the Joneses moved through familiar spaces. Indeed, these sojourns to the mountains echoed the family's antebellum pattern of traveling during the Lowcountry's torrid summers, though their wartime exile was a forced one. George W. Jones fell into a familiar pattern of absentee ownership, directing the plantation from afar, but for the duration of the conflict, he was not free physically to return to the plantation.[12]

Jones's feelings about the security of his home plantation are easier to divine than his thoughts on the war in general. He was never an ardent secessionist; indeed, he seems to have shunned politics and public office whenever possible, and little in the way of family correspondence survives from the war years. Jones also avoided service in the Confederate Army as a result of what his doctors diagnosed as a chronic kidney ailment.[13] Despite this general apathy toward the South's political and military cause, Jones's actions suggest that he wholeheartedly sided with southern economic and social interests during the conflict. He was fully invested in cotton cultivation and the institution of slavery; the topic of manumission makes no appearance in his antebellum or wartime documents, and, if anything, Wormsloe was becoming more dependent on cotton as the war approached. After the armistice, Jones embraced investment opportunities in banks, railroads, and insurance companies in both the North and the South, but his growing interest in southern history also suggests that he found Old South social and economic customs to be romantic. During the war, then, Jones was a bystander with an abiding interest in the Confederacy's success.

While family members in France and in the South Carolina mountains pined for Wormsloe, the events of the war closed in on the coastal estate. In mid-December 1864, the U.S. Army moved on Savannah, and the garrisons of Wormsloe's batteries pulled back, surrendering the Isle of Hope to Union forces without a prolonged fight. Savannah fell soon thereafter, and with the capture of the city, the long stalemate in the Georgia Lowcountry was effectively over. Union cavalry ransacked Wormsloe on November 28 as part of preliminary operations against the city. As during the revolution, the invading soldiers struck at the plantation's agricultural base. A neighbor wrote that the cavalrymen "burned all [Jones's] cotton, [and] took off his Horses & mules." Confederate pickets engaged the Union cavalry, and a brief skirmish took place near the mansion house. The retreating Union forces carried off some of the family silver and furnishings and defaced the plantation house's mantels but did little else in the way of lasting damage to the plantation's buildings and grounds.[14]

The greatest challenge to the Joneses' control over Wormsloe came from a pen rather than the point of a bayonet. General William T. Sherman's Special Field Order 15, issued when Union forces occupied the Georgia Lowcountry in January 1865, ceded all of the barrier islands from Charleston, South Carolina, to the St. Johns River in northern Florida as well as all abandoned coastal rice plantations within thirty miles of the ocean to former Lowcountry slaves and African American veterans of the Union Army. Under the terms of the order, freedpeople could lay claim to tracts of up to forty acres within this reserve. A new federal agency, the Freedmen's Bureau, then furnished the new landowners with written title to their farms.[15] The bulk of Wormsloe fell outside the technical boundaries of the confiscation order—Wormsloe was a cotton rather than rice plantation, and the Isle of Hope was connected to the mainland by a narrow neck of land and thus despite its name was not a true sea island—but the Long Island portion of the plantation was a different matter. In the summer of 1865, Federal authorities seized Long Island and divided it among four freedmen, Simus Howell, Bristol Drayton, Prince Jackson, and Charles Steele, each of whom received a tract of between twenty and forty acres.[16] At least three of the four freedmen may have been former Wormsloe slaves. A slave inventory prepared by Jones near the outbreak of war listed "Charles," "Sim," and two men named Prince among the plantation's hands.[17]

Howell's Freedmen's Bureau deed indicates that he was an active agent in securing title to his forty-acre tract of Long Island. The bureau granted Howell the legal right "to hold and occupy" the small farm, but this formal permission merely codified the freedman's unilateral actions. A note written by a bureau official on the back of the title declared that the Freedmen's Court of Chatham County granted the land to Howell because he had already built a "shanty or house on the Lot" and "was in possession of the land" at the conclusion of the war.[18] Neither Howell nor his fellow Long Island landowners wrote down their thoughts regarding their claim to a piece of the Lowcountry, but their actions suggest that they agreed with Aaron Bradley, a Savannah freedman who spoke publicly about the former slaves' right to land in the fall of 1865: "Who does the property of this country belong to if not to negroes!—they have earned it all!" He believed that men such as Howell "had an unquestioned right to squat upon" the plantations of former slave owners.[19]

Observers commented on the degree to which Wormsloe's environs were temporarily ceded to freedmen and northerners as well as on the absence of antebellum landowners. Steaming up the mouth of the Savannah in 1865, Yankee traveler Whitelaw Reid described the local plantations as "mainly given over to the negroes," and he and his companions "did not see one white man" for miles on end.[20] This dominance of former slaves was supported by Union Army regulations. For the plantations located on sea islands, Special Field Order 15 stipulated that "on the islands, no white person, unless military . . . will be permitted to reside."[21] Although Wormsloe proper escaped outright confiscation, it was "occupied" under the direction "of the Authorities" by "a very good man, who will take care of it, whilst cultivating the land." In all likelihood, the "very good man" was a northern official or Union sympathizer given control of the estate by federal authorities until Congress decided the legal status of Lowcountry landownership.[22]

Jones's freedom to manage Wormsloe's land, even if the federal government relinquished all claims to the plantation as part of the Sherman tract, remained in question in the summer of 1865. President Andrew Johnson issued a general amnesty to most southerners at the conclusion of the war; exceptions included individuals who had served as "high-ranking Confederate military [or] civil officials" and those whose estimated personal wealth exceeded twenty thousand dollars.[23] Jones and his neighboring planters worried about the fate of their plantations, writing to each other concerning the disposition of coastal lands.[24] Jones had never served as a leader in the rebellion in any capacity, but his estate clearly exceeded the wealth clause; by 1860, his annual net income surpassed eleven thousand dollars. Not even wartime losses and emancipation could diminish the value of his real estate, bank investments, and railroad shares below the federal bar.[25] Thus Wormsloe, with the exception of Long Island, was technically Jones's property, but under the provisions of Johnson's amnesty proclamation, the plantation remained under federal control. By June, Jones obtained permission from the local authorities to rent Wormsloe if he could find a tenant. His next step was to apply for a presidential pardon, an all but pro forma exercise, and government officials granted

Jones's application on August 29. With the restoration of his citizenship came a guarantee that Wormsloe would remain in the Jones family for the foreseeable future. Although Georgia Freedmen's Bureau officials were often slow to return occupied land to wealthy Lowcountry planters, including those with presidential pardons in hand, Jones seemed to have little difficulty reclaiming Wormsloe.[26] The restoration of Long Island likely occurred in 1867. Although Long Island does not appear by name in Savannah-area restoration orders, on January 19 of that year, Freedmen's Bureau Special Order 6 restored all confiscated lands on Skidaway Island to former owners. If the federal government had not already restored the property to Jones, Long Island may have fallen under this order's umbrella. In any case, Jones had regained control of all of his former plantation along the Skidaway River by 1867.[27]

The surviving records reveal little about what became of the four freedmen who had fleetingly owned their own piece of Lowcountry soil. Only Charles Steele appeared in the 1870 Chatham County census agricultural schedule, which listed him as the owner or renter of twenty acres of improved land. By that date, Steele had acquired a mule, a milk cow, and five pigs (worth an estimated two hundred dollars), and his small farm had produced fifty-five bushels of corn and forty bushels of sweet potatoes during the year. These crops and livestock—and the land, if Steele owned it—represented a modest but promising start toward economic independence.[28] Jackson, Drayton, and Howell do not seem to have had the same fortune, at least in Chatham County, as none appeared in the postwar censuses, and they may have left the county in search of economic opportunities elsewhere.

Despite the struggles of Long Island's freedmen to establish an economic foothold, freedpeople in the Georgia Lowcountry were more successful at obtaining land following the war than were African Americans in most regions of the South. Historian J. William Harris has calculated that 57 percent of black farmers along the Georgia coast owned their own land by 1879. Harris and other scholars attribute this high frequency of landownership to several factors: a strong desire among most former slaves to own their own property; the abundance of cheap piney woodland within a few miles of the coast; planters' general economic struggles, which led to their willingness to sell small plots of ground to former slaves in exchange for cash; and the availability of regular wage work in towns and on the surviving rice plantations that supplied freedpeople with seasonal income to fund purchases and supplement their subsistence-farming efforts.[29] Freedpeople in and around Savannah had a more difficult time obtaining land, which was more expensive near the city, but a number of African Americans parlayed their antebellum experience as skilled laborers into postwar work as masons, blacksmiths, butchers, coopers, and carpenters.[30] Aided by the availability of skilled work, Chatham County's black residents gradually accumulated real estate. Between 1875 and 1905, the amount of black-owned land in the county grew from 1,491 acres to 7,207 acres.[31]

Freedpeople rarely obtained prime tracts of land. Their small farms were often located on marginal lands, from swampy ground to relatively infertile piney flats, but no matter what its quality, land offered a measure of independence and security unavailable to wage workers and renters. The former slaves who owned land could put their agricultural and environmental knowledge to work on their own plot of ground. Owning land instilled pride in the owner. An article in the *Southern Workman*, a journal published in Hampton, Virginia, by and for freedpeople, declared that the landowner's "soil may be poor, and the cabin rude and small, but its owner feels it to be like a firm footing in a boundless swamp."[32] Black landowners used their property for a variety of agricultural purposes and relied on the Lowcountry environment for sustenance in ways similar to antebellum practices. Whether or not they owned land, freedpeople's knowledge of the region's forests and wetlands provided them with the ability to make a living following emancipation. African Americans hunted deer, raccoons, and alligators; caught fish; gathered oysters from rivers and marshes; and used such plants as palmetto and mayapple for medicinal purposes.[33] In addition to fishing, foraging, and hunting, former slaves raised large gardens on their own land or plots of rented ground, and, mirroring earlier slave economic activity, they found a ready market for surplus vegetables and meat in Savannah. A postwar estimate placed the number of black street vendors and oyster hawkers in the city at five hundred, and groceries catering to African American customers bought raccoon and venison from the surrounding countryside.[34]

Although the U.S. government restored Wormsloe's physical landscape to Jones, the work of reestablishing the social and agricultural order of the antebellum plantation would be a difficult if not impossible task. As if to symbolize the profound changes that had taken place with the war, George W. Jones legally changed his name to George Wymberley Jones De Renne in 1866, adopting a modified version of his maternal grandmother's surname. Jones declared that the change came out of a desire to distinguish himself from his older nephew and onetime executor of his father's estate, George Noble Jones, who also lived in Savannah and vacationed in Newport. George Wymberley Jones had previously experimented with his name; he was born George Frederick Tilghman Jones but starting in 1847 referred to himself as George Wymberley Jones, insisted that friends and family call him Wymberley, and signed his correspondence as G. Wymberley Jones.[35] Jones's impulse to remake himself following the war may also have reflected his lifelong interest in history and improvement of all types. He had long been an avid collector of Georgia and family history, and both Wymberley and De Renne were versions of old family names. His willingness to re-create his family's past bore remarkable parallels to his efforts to establish Wormsloe, so long a landscape at the center of Jones family history, as a viable plantation. Wormsloe, like the De Renne name, was a link to the past remade to suit Jones's desires.

Once De Renne resecured title to Wormsloe and Long Island, he faced a decision. How should he manage the plantation under the new free labor system? De Renne decided to lease the plantation out for the first few postbellum years while getting his financial affairs in order, a relatively common practice among Lowcountry planters during the early days of Reconstruction.[36] Shortly after Appomattox, he made a rental agreement with Robert T. Smillie and Company, a group of northern opportunists who intended to prove that sea island cotton could be profitably cultivated with free labor. In exchange for a payment of twelve hundred dollars, De Renne gave Smillie the right of "planting and raising cotton, corn and other produce" on Wormsloe, in essence temporarily relinquishing complete control of the property. This arrangement continued for the next three crop seasons.[37] Although De Renne must have been pleased to receive some income from the plantation's fields, Wormsloe's rental rates were quite low considering the size and location of the property. Rental rates and terms fluctuated a great deal across the postwar South. Districts with promising crops, such as bright leaf tobacco, witnessed high rental prices, while other sections were depressed. In 1867, a six-hundred-acre plantation on ground suitable for tobacco in the North Carolina Piedmont leased for one thousand dollars, with the renters promising to build two barns and a new fence "at their own proper expense" as a condition of the lease.[38] Closer to the Isle of Hope, the rental situation was not as promising, as planters worried about the uncertainties of free labor and government plans to redistribute land. Louis Manigault leased his substantial Savannah River rice plantation for between thirty-two hundred and thirty-five hundred dollars per year during Reconstruction, even though the property had netted nearly ten thousand dollars annually before the war.[39] With more than a thousand acres of land, a proven record of producing fine cotton, an elaborate house, a large complex of farm buildings, and close proximity to Savannah, Wormsloe's rent of twelve hundred dollars seems extremely modest. It is not entirely clear why De Renne leased the plantation for such a low amount. The most likely explanation is that Smillie's management of Wormsloe relieved De Renne of some of the burdens of resuming planting following the war, a benefit he found greater than maximizing the property's returns. With a renter tending to the land, he could take time to get his business affairs in order, matters that included securing antebellum debts and regaining ownership of Long Island.

The agreement between De Renne and Smillie mirrored similar arrangements taking place across the conquered South. From the cotton lands of the Mississippi Delta to the rice impoundments of the sea islands to the tobacco plantations of the Upper South, northern opportunists rented or purchased plantations with the intention of profiting from regional disorganization. Lawrence Powell, a historian of these northern/southern planters, estimates that "anywhere from twenty thousand to fifty thousand northerners tried their hands at planting" between the start of the Civil War and 1870. These migratory businessmen believed that money could still be made in southern staple-crop agriculture, particularly cotton, and that as experienced free labor entrepreneurs, they could make the old crops work under the new conditions of emancipation. Northern planters leased lands considered spoils of war from the federal government, but they also made thousands of arrangements similar to that at Wormsloe, as southern landowners beset by a shortage of cash and with little access to lines of credit turned to the only available source of income, northern capital.[40] No records of the Smillie Company's efforts to raise cotton on Wormsloe survive, but the project, like so many similar northern experiments in the plantation South, must have been unsuccessful. De Renne and Smillie failed to renew the rental agreement in 1869, probably as a consequence of the northerner's refusal to plant another year as De Renne still sought a tenant for Wormsloe. A man named Neely eventually paid six hundred dollars for the season's rent.[41] Although a later writer claimed that the Smillie Company's attempts to make a profit at Wormsloe failed because management "soon tired of the existing labor conditions," there is little evidence to pinpoint exactly why the northern investors gave up on cultivating the plantation.[42]

De Renne's northern renters were not alone in their struggles to reestablish sea island cotton along the Georgia coast. As a plantation staple, the crop largely disappeared from Georgia and South Carolina within two decades of the South's surrender. Few freedpeople wanted to work in gangs hauling marsh muck to the cotton fields for relatively poor wages, and declining cotton prices and a general shortage of specie kept landowners from paying higher rates. Competition for labor from the region's surviving rice planters, the relative availability of land, and more appealing wage work in Savannah also hurt large cotton planters. Sea island cotton largely became a crop of small farmers who raised an acre or two of the fiber, tended by family labor and cleaned on small hand rollers, to supplement their subsistence crops and livestock. A number of these small farmers were freedpeople who had acquired land; though unwilling to labor on large plantations under the eye of a boss or overseer, these farmers recognized the value of a readily salable commodity.[43]

The Civil War had wrought equally important changes to global cotton markets that challenged the profitability of Lowcountry cotton. Temporarily bereft of American cotton while the war raged, British manufacturers had turned to other nations to satisfy their textile mills' demands. At the behest of Lancashire's mills, cotton production grew dramatically between 1861 and 1865 in India, in the Nile Delta, and along the Brazilian coast, with smaller cotton centers emerging in Argentina and China. Following the war, cotton production remained well above antebellum levels in Egypt and Brazil and continued to grow in India. In Egypt in particular, a portion of the new cotton acreage grew long-staple cotton that could compete in quality with the best fiber from the sea islands.[44] American cotton growers also developed several varieties of long-staple upland cotton after the war. Although these new cottons did not command the same prices as the best sea island cotton, they were more productive and would grow on fertile upland soils, such as the new land opened by planters in the extraordinarily rich Mississippi-Yazoo Delta.[45] This increased competition depressed long-staple cotton prices as Reconstruction progressed. Sea island cotton sold for eighty-six cents per pound in 1867–68, but the price steadily declined to twenty-nine cents per pound in 1877–78 and would not exceed forty cents per pound again until a brief resurgence of the crop during World War I. As South Carolina planter William Lawton recognized in 1870, sea island cotton production was increasingly unremunerative: "The competition by other countries now producing sea island cotton at cheaper rates, similar to that of Carolina, Georgia and Florida, and the fact that spinners are discontinuing the use of American sea island varieties, are serious admonitions and undoubted evidences to those in the trade" that coastal cotton plantations "have ceased to afford a money profit."[46] Together, new labor realities throughout the Lowcountry, increasing national and international competition, and declining cotton prices spelled the end of large-scale sea island cotton cultivation, and the arrival of the boll weevil in the early twentieth century finished off the remaining coastal long-staple cotton.[47]

Despite the writing on the wall, De Renne attempted for several more years to produce cotton on Wormsloe. These efforts and the inevitable struggles over labor and race resulting from a resumption of cotton planting under a new political order reflected De Renne's attempts to gain control over the land as well as people. Making the old fields productive and profitable and even the act of maintaining the plantation and its boundaries created friction between landowner and former slaves. Disenchanted with the results of leasing the plantation or perhaps unable to find a renter, De Renne turned to sharecropping arrangements to return the plantation to productivity. Although this shift arose in part because of the failure of other management systems, freedpeople's desire for greater autonomy was also an important force in spurring the rise of sharecropping. Concurrent to Neely's lease of Wormsloe proper, De Renne entered a share arrangement with one of his former slaves, Brutus Butler, to cultivate Long Island in 1869. Butler promised to raise at least twenty acres of sea island cotton on the island—a substantial crop that implied that he commanded the labor of several hands—and to deliver half to De Renne in Savannah, "ginned and packed in good merchantable order." Seizing this opportunity to work his own piece of productive ground, Butler signed the contract in a jerky but firm and legible hand.[48] De Renne renewed Butler's contract under the same terms for 1870 and, apparently satisfied with Butler's work, sought a similar agreement for Wormsloe when the Neely contract expired. De Renne eventually signed a share agreement with freedman James W. Jones, perhaps another former Wormsloe slave. In a contract similar to that of Butler, Jones promised to cultivate at least twenty-five acres of cotton and to give De Renne half at the end of the year.[49]

Sharecropping arrangements resulted in a greater autonomy for freedpeople but did not mean that De Renne divested himself of all elements of plantation management. The renters of the late 1860s and the general neglect of the Civil War years apparently left the plantation in poor condition, as De Renne invested heavily in repairing the farm's infrastructure in an attempt to restore the estate to its late 1850s condition. In 1870, he repaired Wormsloe's buildings and fences, resurveyed the plantation's boundaries, and spent almost two hundred dollars—roughly two years of wages for an agricultural laborer—on guano to fertilize the depleted fields. Although these actions might have been part of De Renne's agreement with James Jones, they were more likely attributable to a continuation of his antebellum desire to improve the property. These efforts at improvement brought the plantation into shape, but they were also costly. After Jones delivered De Renne's share of the 1870 cotton crop—seven bales—De Renne's accounts revealed that he lost $1,740 on Wormsloe during the year.[50]

George De Renne's efforts to lease Wormsloe to central white management and his experiments with sharecropping seem to have finally convinced him that his continued attempts to make a profit from sea island cotton cultivation were more of a headache than they were worth. Seeking a less complicated way to profit from the land, from 1871 until some point during the 1880s, De Renne rented a portion of Wormsloe to a group of black tenants, each of whom promised to pay him three dollars per month.[51] De Renne recorded few details about this black tenancy at Wormsloe, but more detailed contracts for similar rentals at Poplar Grove during the mid-1870s provide clues to rental terms. At Poplar Grove in 1876, De Renne allotted each freedman five acres of land for two dollars a month, plus one dollar up front as "earnest money," and gave the tenants free hand "to make all improvements." He also agreed to provide boards and nails for new fencing if the tenants would furnish the posts (cut from the plantation woods) and labor. Perhaps reflecting a reversal of his antebellum paternalism, De Renne's terms for freedmen at Poplar Grove were less generous than a rental agreement forged for a white tenant who cultivated an adjacent portion of the plantation. De Renne charged a German farmer, Charles Frederick, three dollars per acre for a year's rental of a ten-acre tract on the eastern side of Poplar Grove. At the recorded rate, a similar tract would have cost a freedman forty-nine dollars per year. The same year, De Renne gave similarly favorable rates to white farmer Joseph Claghorn, who rented fifty acres of prime cropland along Wormsloe's northern line for only two and a half dollars per acre.[52]

The 1880 agricultural census offers a bare outline of Wormsloe's tenants and their land use for a single year. According to the census taker, there were eight tenants living on the plantation during the 1879 season: Jesse Beach, Matilda Lewton, London Singleton, Peter Campbell, Isaac Walker, Archy Griffin, Isaiah Jones, and Tom Thomas. The number of tenants corresponded exactly to the number of standing slave cabins, and the freedpeople almost certainly lived in the antebellum structures. This was a significant departure from the tenancy settlement pattern on many postwar plantations, in which concentrated antebellum housing quarters were broken up in favor of cabins spaced evenly across the landscape, placing each tenant in close proximity to his or her tract of rental land.[53] This continued housing concentration likely reflected De Renne's intention to again manage Wormsloe as an entire property. On Wormsloe, each tenant cultivated five acres of improved land. Beach owned a horse, and Lewton had a milk cow and a beef cow, but the rest of the tenants possessed no livestock. Three tenants grew small patches of corn, led by Beach's four acres, all grew enough sweet potatoes to sell a few bushels, and Campbell must have had access to a marshy piece of ground, as he had raised 510 pounds of rice.[54] This modest agricultural production suggests that Wormsloe's tenants lived a hardscrabble existence. The sale of a few bushels of sweet potatoes or corn could hardly have covered the monthly rents, and the tenants must have regularly performed wage work for the De Renne family or for neighboring landowners to make ends meet.

It is unclear what portion of Wormsloe the tenants cultivated during the 1870s and early 1880s, but the former slaves' plots were probably located close to their rental cabins. The old quarters field just west of the cabins remained open after the war, along with the old fort field farther to the south, and together the two plots may have served as the primary tenant fields. A set of contemporary photographs also supports the supposition that black tenants lived in the old slave cabins during and following Reconstruction. One image shows freedmen working near the cabins, with neatly swept dooryards, a lack of undergrowth, and supplies of firewood stacked tidily against the sides of the cabins indicating permanent occupation of the structures.[55] Several photographs also demonstrate that small lots near the cabins were fenced in with wooden palings. Richard Westmacott, a historian of African American gardening practices, has described these paling fences as a common form of protection for slaves' and former slaves' gardens, though they were used with equal frequency for one of two purposes: to fence livestock out or to keep chickens and pigs contained within the yard.[56] It is unclear for which purpose Wormsloe's tenants erected their fences, though the relative lack of livestock in the 1880 census suggests that the fences were designed to protect kitchen gardens rather than to keep animals. What is clear is that as tenants, just as they had as slaves, African Americans worked Wormsloe's soil and relied on its resources for the basics of life. The De Rennes remained attached to the plantation, but the tenants knew the ground through labor. This knowledge meant that, along with the De Rennes, the period's black tenants shaped the face of the plantation. George De Renne determined the overall land use plan for Wormsloe, structuring tenant contracts, permitting and forbidding certain activities, and retaining legal ownership of the soil, but field by field and day by day, freedpeople guided life on the land much as they had as slaves.

De Renne's struggles to determine the most profitable form of plantation management under the terms of emancipation were not unique. Planters across the Lowcountry and throughout the South sought firm control of labor and a reestablishment of the antebellum social order. As on Wormsloe, this process of labor negotiation took multiple forms, often progressing quickly from some form of wage work—as under Wormsloe's northern renters—to sharecropping arrangements. Sharecropping dominated most regions of the South by the late 1860s for a number of reasons, most prominently black desires for autonomy, a lack of available hard currency or credit to back cash wages, and a realization among white landowners that sharecropping, through the iron chains of crop liens and ensuing debt peonage, offered a means of controlling black and white laborers.[57]

Planters and freedpeople living on portions of the Lowcountry where rice and sea island cotton had dominated the antebellum landscape often entered into a more flexible sort of tenancy that reflected the legacy of the task system.

Under this "labor rent" form of tenantry, freedpeople promised to work for a landowner for a fixed number of days each week in exchange for the use of a house and a few acres of land. As they had under the task system, workers tended their own gardens, fields, and livestock and hunted and fished after fulfilling their obligations to the landowner. During the early years of Reconstruction, freedpeople across the Lowcountry often refused to work for landowners under any other system.[58] Eric Foner notes that the legacy of the task system also took another regional form, in which former planters leased entire plantations to large groups of freedpeople in exchange for a portion of the crop, with the freedpeople allowed to determine how they managed their labor over the course of the year.[59] Although on an exceptionally large scale, William Gibbon's contract with 120 freedpeople at his Shaftsbury plantation was representative of this form of arrangement in Chatham County. In 1866, Gibbon gave the group of freedpeople the right to farm four hundred acres of rice land and promised the former slaves housing, woodcutting rights, medical care, and the use of farm equipment in exchange for one-quarter of the total rice crop.[60]

These labor rent arrangements were in no small part an expression of African Americans' knowledge of the coastal environment. Landowners knew that their former slaves understood the requirements of cultivating rice and sea island cotton far better than any other potential laborers, even if an alternative labor pool could have been found. Gibbon and other planters made contracts on such flexible terms because they were often the only way to secure a capable and experienced workforce. If landowners refused to meet at least some of their former slaves' demands, African Americans could survive off the land using their knowledge of forests, marshes, and waterways—experience acquired during their free time under the task system. Freedpeople used this leverage to retain a degree of independence and applied their intimacy with the landscape to raise subsistence and market crops during their personal time. Thus, the same environmental knowledge that served slaves under the task system continued to shape black and white relationships and land use for decades following emancipation. The region remained a landscape divided into spatial and temporal bounds, always underwritten by racial relationships, with ground and its use demarcated into landowners' and tenants' spaces and masters' and laborers' time.[61]

After a few years of sharecropping, Wormsloe's cessation of cotton production and De Renne's willingness to rent small plots of land to freedmen meant that the plantation avoided the worst ills of southern sharecropping and provided the tenants with a modicum of independence similar to that of labor rents, but for most of Reconstruction, De Renne's struggle with eman-

cipation and the remaking of the plantation world was a common southern story of changing labor forms. The plantation's tenants never acquired a
long-term stake in the land, largely as a result of the family's wealth, which
removed the necessity of making the property pay but also avoided the harsh
relationships between landowner and laborer that developed across much of
the South. Wormsloe's labor transitions seem to have taken place without significant violence. At the end of the war, Savannah was overwhelmed by more
than forty thousand former slave refugees, and the region was plagued with
cases of whites killing emancipated slaves and freedmen striking back against
their oppressors, but there is no evidence of this sort of physical tension on the
plantation.[62] All in all, Wormsloe apparently escaped the worst of Reconstruction violence and the oppression of prolonged wage labor and sharecropping,
but the landscape remained owned and controlled by a white landowner, with
no space for black dreams of landownership.

De Renne was willing to allow portions of Wormsloe to fall under the temporary control of white and black renters and in many cases even encouraged
these arrangements, but he strongly resisted any permanent loss of control
over the property. Just as the Civil War had threatened De Renne's ownership
of the property, the changes wrought by the conflict continued to plague his
plantation management throughout Reconstruction. Transportation routes to
Skidaway Island were a particular problem. The antebellum road from Savannah to Skidaway Island had passed along Wormsloe's northern line, through
the Wimberly tract, and had bridged the Jones River near the northern end of
Long Island. During the upheaval of the war, the Jones River bridge fell into
disrepair, and Skidaway residents began using a plantation road that cut south
across Wormsloe to the old colonial fort ruins, where they then crossed the
marsh on the earthen causeway built by Confederate forces. Chatham County
repaired the Jones River bridge following the war, but some traffic apparently
continued to use the route through the heart of Wormsloe, which provided
more direct access to the southern end of Skidaway.[63] In 1870, a group of Skidaway residents, mostly freedmen, petitioned to have the southern route designated the permanent county road, a move De Renne fiercely opposed. He
argued that it was unfair to destroy Wormsloe's privacy for the benefit of a few
individuals who already had an existing road to their property. The region's
struggles with postemancipation labor and race relations were reflected in De
Renne's further comments on the petition. He complained to a relative that
the "road is chiefly travelled by the Skidaway negroes, the most disreputable in
the country" and worried that he might have to build four miles of new fence
to keep his property safe from these travelers and their animals.[64] Although
De Renne's arguments about the cost of the fencing associated with the poten-

tial road were legitimate—the southern route would have necessitated miles of wooden fences to protect crops and livestock from road traffic, and the new route would greatly reduce the continuity of the plantation and thus its usefulness for agriculture—his argument also reflected a struggle to come to grips with the postemancipation South's new racial dynamics. In this debate, De Renne's inability to control black labor seemed tangled with his desire to control the plantation landscape.

The rental of portions of Wormsloe to freedmen for small subsistence plots marked the end of De Renne's attempts to manage the property as a plantation. Like other Lowcountry planters, De Renne had experimented with various labor and rental strategies during Reconstruction in an effort to revitalize cotton production, but, as was the case with most of his fellow sea island cotton planters, De Renne ultimately failed to restore some semblance of plantation order.[65] Agriculture would remain an important part of Wormsloe's story throughout the remainder of the nineteenth century and through the first few decades of the 1900s, but the property would never again be a staple-producing plantation. In the end, emancipation broke De Renne's antebellum vision of expansive cotton fields supported by a well-ordered pastoral landscape.

By the second half of the 1870s, George De Renne's personal finances were in good enough order to allow his increased interest in Wormsloe's management. Thanks to his judicious investments in railroads, bonds, and Savannah rental properties, from 1876 to 1879 De Renne's annual net income topped fifty thousand dollars, roughly ten times his income during the last few antebellum years. In fact, from 1867 onward, his income was higher than at any point prior to the Civil War.[66] These figures were at odds with comments De Renne made in one of his postwar account books, where he claimed that "as a result of the war, the value of bankstocks and negroes was annihilated. . . . Fortunately for my children, I early adopted opinions in favor of real estate, from reflecting on the history of our family; and always steadily adhered to the policy of increasing and improving it. . . . That we were not reduced to poverty by the results of the war was owing mainly to this." He went on to assert that farm ownership was a vital component of his real estate holdings.[67]

These statements clearly ignored postwar financial reality. Wormsloe produced very little income; indeed, plantation operations often lost money during both the antebellum and postwar periods. And the wartime occupation of Savannah and Reconstruction debates regarding the redistribution of land had threatened De Renne's real estate just as much as wartime upheavals endangered his less tangible investments. Although by 1880 Wormsloe, Long Island, and all improvements on the two properties—"736 acres of land with dwelling house, Overseers residence, stables, Barnes, Plantation houses etc."—were valued at $21,000, a substantial sum, their value was only a small fraction of the $1,277,634.01 assessment of De Renne's estate. This phenomenal fortune consisted of stocks and interest in Pennsylvania and Georgia companies as well as Chatham County urban real estate. The estate included stock in twelve railroads, among them the Augusta and Savannah Railroad and the Sunbury and Erie Railroad; interest in three canal companies, including the Schuylkill Navigation Company and the Chesapeake and Delaware Canal Company; and shares in ten banks and several insurance companies scattered across the eastern United States, from Louisville to Philadelphia. In addition to Wormsloe and Poplar Grove, De Renne owned a house in Philadelphia and properties in the Savannah area: twelve tenement buildings, three wharf lots, four store buildings, a brick warehouse, eight wooden and six brick buildings of unlisted purpose, and three brick rental houses. The Savannah wharf lots alone were valued at $200,000.[68] Thus, bank stocks and business property rental fees restored the family's fortune so soon after the war. Despite its inaccuracy, De Renne's statement revealed his attachment to landownership and especially his fondness for Wormsloe. The property's value lay as much in its connections to his family's history and legacy as in the land's ability to produce a profit. De Renne treasured the plantation's ties to Noble Jones, colonial Georgia, and the antebellum era, and he saw Wormsloe as a symbol of his family's durability and permanence. The plantation's survival of the war symbolized his own lasting success.

This affection for the old plantation led to both deliberate and unconscious efforts on the part of the family to re-create the antebellum landscape—or, more accurately, to shape a landscape that conformed to their notions of the Old South plantation. In practice, these efforts created a burnished and beautified estate that celebrated but did not always accurately represent Wormsloe's past. De Renne held an avid interest in family and state history—following the war he was an active member of the Georgia Historical Society and briefly served as the organization's president—and he sought an estate that lived up to his memories of a glorious past.[69] Tenants continued to cultivate a portion of the land in the late 1870s, but De Renne used the plantation house and grounds as a country retreat, much as Noble W. Jones had seventy years earlier, and De Renne took an active hand in making alterations to the property. De Renne owned a fine house in Savannah proper, and by the end of Reconstruction, Wormsloe's house and grounds were showing the ill effects of almost two decades of absentee ownership. A series of photographs from around the 1870s reveals peeling paint and overgrown shrubbery. Continuing his relationship with the family, freedman Brutus Butler contracted to serve as manager of Wormsloe's daily agricultural activities, but De Renne involved himself in various plantation projects.[70] He commissioned a new stable, carriage house, and servants' hall for the house yard and worked to repair other structures. He also built new fence lines and a gate to limit access to the Wimberly fields from Skidaway Road, and he paid laborers to buttress the walls of the old fort and patch holes in the tabby, "not to repair, but to preserve the old ruin." In 1878, seeking a permanent and impressive emblem of his renewed estate, he planted carved granite gateposts at the mouth of the live oak avenue leading from Skidaway Road to his "country house."[71]

De Renne also revitalized Wormsloe's horticultural tradition dating back to Noble Jones's botanical experiments. In 1879, De Renne "marked out [an] enlargement of [the] garden at Wormsloe" and began purchasing plants to ornament the plantation grounds. Over the following year, he planted aloe, camellias, and roses around the house and hired laborers to clear out undergrowth and open up the yard. These plantings were larger-scale continuations of his antebellum efforts to beautify the grounds. He also went to great lengths to bring Wormsloe's natural beauty to his Savannah house. He transplanted several full-grown palmetto trees from Wormsloe to his city residence and created an expansive urban garden of camellias and roses. De Renne also retained his antebellum interest in scientific agriculture. He took careful notes on the importance of mulching and paid one hundred dollars for his gardener, J. J. Cadogau, to attend the horticultural exhibitions at the Philadelphia Centennial Exposition of 1876.[72]

Unlike Noble Jones's interest in colonial horticulture, De Renne seemed more interested in the aesthetics of his cultivars and botanical landscapes than in their practicality or commercial possibilities. Jones sought new crops to stimulate the plantation economy, while De Renne desired plants that pleased the eye and astonished guests. He cut down trees that blocked certain views at Wormsloe and his Savannah home and employed hired hands in elaborate landscaping projects, such as moving a full-grown tulip tree six feet "using a derrick and guys" to create a more pleasing panorama. He also enjoyed demonstrating his wealth by sharing botanical gifts with friends, as when he sent an acquaintance an astonishing "100 olive trees from France as a present" in 1879.[73] In his postwar landscaping, De Renne sought beautiful vistas and peaceful retreats, but he also attempted to reconstruct the plantation's antebellum grandeur, real or imagined. Lavish plantings and construction projects transformed the dilapidated estate of the early 1870s, wracked by the exigencies of war, neglect, and the harsh Lowcountry climate, into a new showplace that evoked the prewar South.

These efforts were in keeping with a desire to repair damage while modernizing the estate, but they also seem a conscious attempt on the part of George De Renne to celebrate and glorify his family's history. Wormsloe had long served as a site central to the definition of the Jones family, and De Renne's efforts to modify and preserve the place drew on this reservoir of familial affection. Family friend Charles C. Jones Jr. commented on the beautification campaign at Wormsloe in his 1883 eulogy to De Renne:

> In this youthful country so careless of and indifferent to the memories of former days . . . where no law of primogeniture encourages in the son the conservation of the abode and the heirlooms of his father, where new fields, cheap lands, and novel enterprises at remote points are luring the loves of succeeding generations from the gardens which delighted, the hoary oaks which sheltered, and the fertile fields which nourished their ancestors . . . it was a beautiful sight—this preservation of the old homestead, this filial devotion to tree and ruin and tradition, this maintenance around the ancient hearth-stone of cultured memories and inherited civilization. Love of home and kindred and State lay at the root of it all.[74]

Jones's comments firmly connected De Renne's landscaping activities to his antebellum improvement efforts and to his passion for state and family history.

George's son, Wymberley, continued this planting and gardening campaign on the old estate. In the early 1890s, along the disputed route once used by Skidaway residents, Wymberley created the plantation's most dramatic landscaping feature, a new infinity live oak avenue lining the historic road connecting the tabby fort ruins to the Skidaway Road. Under his direction, workers widened the path, laid crushed oyster shells on the roadbed, and planted oak saplings on either side of the avenue, where they would eventually overarch the drive, their monumental moss-draped trunks and limbs shading out the Lowcountry sun. This avenue has become the iconic symbol of the modern Wormsloe State Historic Site, the road that leads thousands of visitors annually into the old plantation. Family biographer William Bragg suggests that the avenue reflected the De Rennes' European travels, as a French custom called for the planting of a wood to honor and enrich the first-born son (in this case, Wymberley's son, Wymberley Wormsloe De Renne).[75] This may very well have been the case, but the avenue also fit in nicely with the family's efforts to shape the plantation landscape in the image of an idealized Old South. The drive bore a remarkable resemblance to nearby stretches of Savannah's famed old Bonaventure cemetery, where the De Rennes owned a family vault.[76] Live oaks lined Bonaventure's walks and paths, impressing visitors with the graveyard's shady majesty and tranquility. Visiting in 1867, John Muir declared the oak-mantled cemetery a uniquely southern landscape as well as "one of the most impressive assemblages of animal and plant creatures I ever met."[77] The new drive also mimicked an antebellum live oak avenue that led from the Skidaway Road to the frame mansion house, though the new route surpassed the old in conception and scale; it was wider, longer, and arrow-straight for its entire 1.5-mile length. The location of the new avenue also emphasized the interpretive focus of much of the plantation's horticultural landscaping. Rather than terminating at the house or the contemporary farmyard, the avenue led directly to the site of colonial Wormsloe, drawing visitors toward the land's celebrated past. The impressive corridor worked to shift the estate's cultural geography, transforming the family's home from the center of the plantation into a more secluded enclave tucked beside the new landscape showpiece.

Less formulaic landscapes persisted on Wormsloe during this period as well. The Isle of Hope's marshes and their abundant aquatic life continued to provide for plantation residents during the postwar years, much as they had for centuries. The oyster banks that clustered along the tidal channels were a particularly important source of food. As early as 1765, John Bartram had commented on the abundance of the local bivalves, describing banks where "oisters is as thick as they can ly within A stone cast of [Noble Jones's] house."[78] The same massive shell middens that proved Native American reliance on local bivalves had served as the basis of tabby construction during the colonial era. During the 1870s, George De Renne and his family continued to consume tremendous quantities of Wormsloe oysters both at the plantation and at their Savannah house. In an 1878 diary entry, De Renne noted that the household ate an average of a gallon and a half of oysters every week.[79]

De Renne also used the abundant oyster banks to turn a small profit while continuing to support individuals previously connected with the plantation. At least as early as 1870, De Renne leased oyster harvesting rights for a modest sum to former Wormsloe overseer Edward Nelson, who sold the shellfish at local markets. From 1870 until 1874, Nelson took oysters from the surrounding marshes for a fee of only one dollar a year, and after that date, he continued the arrangement for five dollars a year over the next twenty years. De Renne and Nelson also ensured the continued abundance of oysters in Wormsloe's waters. Overfishing can rapidly deplete oyster beds, especially if it involves dredging methods that remove dead oyster shells. Old shells are necessary for the successful establishment and growth of young oysters (also known as spat), which need solid, protected sites on which to anchor.[80] Nelson promised to "plant" or "seed" oysters in the marshes after harvest to replace his catch and to return shells to the water to create suitable oyster habitat. During a three-year period in the 1890s alone, he planted at least four thousand bushels. Nelson also refrained from taking oysters within one hundred yards of Wormsloe's dock to avoid infringing on the De Rennes' personal supplies. Much like antebellum efforts to better the landscape, De Renne and Nelson worked to improve the banks' productivity. These aquaculture efforts seem to have worked well, pleasing both the family and Nelson and keeping oyster numbers relatively stable, and the agreements persisted until well into the twentieth century with little change except in amount of the annual rent.[81]

The De Rennes' claims on the marsh and river oysters and their manipulation of both had legal standing. According to Georgia's oyster laws, under certain circumstances, shellfish were the private property of the owner of the adjacent river and creek banks. Between 1855 and 1895, private landowners retained legal rights to natural oyster banks along waterways if they owned the property on both banks of the creek or river and if the waterway was not a traditional navigational channel. The body of water between the Wormsloe mainland and Long Island met these requirements. Much of the estate's western waters fell under another legislative clause. Landowners also had private property rights to artificial or "planted" oyster beds, such as the banks where Nelson seeded oysters, that lay within one thousand feet of their shore and were clearly marked. Under the state legal codes of 1867, 1873, and 1882, watermen had the right to collect oysters from all other oyster beds as long as they used only tongs (hand harvesting tools that resembled two rakes fastened together near their heads), which limited the catch and minimized damage to the shell beds.[82] The 1895 oyster code was much more elaborate, reflecting the growing coastal oyster industry. The new laws established a closed season (May–August), prohibited nighttime tonging, and allowed mechanical dredging and raking on beds more than one thousand feet from shore. The regulations also established a leasing program, in which applicants could purchase the right to plant oysters on barren portions of the public waters in exchange for annual payments of one dollar per acre and a promise to seed the leased ground. The new oyster code left in place the old laws governing private oyster banks and planted beds, so the laws applying to Wormsloe's oyster grounds, with the exception of the new closed season, remained largely the same.[83]

Although Georgia's oystering statutes codified De Renne's control over Wormsloe's marshes and the oysters that grew within them, some locals held different ideas about wetland ownership and property rights. Over their five-decade-long business relationship, the Nelsons and the De Rennes constantly struggled to prevent unlicensed oystering and fishing in the plantation's marshes. For poor local residents—white and black—the enclosure of what had been a watery commons for much of the antebellum era transformed accepted practices into criminal acts. Even oystermen intent on following the law might have become confused as the oyster code grew more complex or as property ownership changed. For example, the beds between Long Island and Wormsloe proper were technically public during the years that freedmen owned the island but became private with the island's restoration to George De Renne. Watermen who were unaware of the ownership of property facing the oyster beds might have believed that they were within their rights since the law declared that "the natural oyster-beds of the State shall forever remain the property of [Georgia], open to all her citizens for the procuring of oysters for consumption, sale, seed, or propagating purposes."[84]

Illegal oystering grew more prevalent around the turn of the twentieth century, and Wymberley J. De Renne was determined to reduce trespassing and poaching. In 1901, he sent an employee, Jesse Beach, to Savannah to swear out a warrant against Frank Tyler and Quirus Frazier, whom Beach had witnessed harvesting oysters near the ruins of the old fort. The oystermen fled the scene but left behind their catch, equipment, and boat. In his personal notes, De Renne complained that a neighbor, likely Edward N. Hargrave, had loaned the boat to the trespassers and that Hargrave had been caught in the Wormsloe marshes the previous year, though he was acquitted of poaching when brought to trial.[85] Though Frazier's race is unknown, both Tyler and Hargrave were black, suggesting that opposition to marsh enclosure was common among local African Americans. Both men were young and landless: Tyler was an eighteen-year-old waiter, and Hargrave was a twenty-year-old day laborer.[86]

De Renne's campaign against trespassers continued throughout the first decade of the twentieth century. Between 1903 and 1905, he filed complaints before the Chatham County court on at least twelve occasions, and the defendants were found guilty in six of the incidents. Several of the defendants were repeat offenders, and conviction meant they had to pay twenty-five dollars and court costs. The low fines and the repeated actions of local oystermen suggest that the trade was lucrative enough that the fines were not dissuasive. In fact, in 1911, when Nelson was paying one hundred dollars per year for oystering rights, a poacher could afford to be found guilty in court and fined twice and still harvest oysters illegally for less than Nelson paid.[87] Although De Renne doggedly prosecuted neighbors he believed stole Wormsloe's natural resources, he could be more lenient to trespassers with connections to the family or the plantation. In 1907, he caught "Julius Williams, son of Mauruel Williams," fishing in the marshes. Probably because of his familiarity with the elder Williams, De Renne allowed Julius to continue fishing on Wormsloe if he promised to furnish the family "fish at Market prices."[88]

The rise in oystering in the waters surrounding Wormsloe was likely connected to the growing regional oyster-packing industry. During the last two decades of the nineteenth century, seafood demand in the United States increased along with the nation's population, and watermen along the mid-Atlantic coast faced the twin specters of shellfish overharvesting and declines in oyster populations as a consequence of water pollution. In response to these national trends, oystering along the southeastern coast increased in importance, as Georgia and Florida fisheries gradually supplemented such traditional oyster centers as New Jersey and the Chesapeake Bay.[89] During this era, Savannah became a regional seafood-processing hub. The community of Thunderbolt, only a few miles from Wormsloe, had two oyster-packing plants that processed 2.5 million pounds of oysters each season. In addition, two smaller plants had operated on nearby Wilmington Island since the 1890s. The Thunderbolt works relied largely on African American packers and watermen, as local blacks such as Tyler and Hargrave knew the oyster beds from generations of use. A correspondent for the *Southern Workman* who visited Thunderbolt in 1908 remarked on the degree to which local African Americans relied on oystering to make a living. Many black watermen operated under a system similar to sharecropping, in which they leased their boats and equipment from the packing plant in exchange for a third of their catch, and their wives often worked in the packing plants. This complete economic reliance on oystering must have pushed a number of watermen to bend or break the oyster laws, as an activity that was once geared around subsistence and Savannah street sales became increasingly industrial and market-oriented.[90] At Wormsloe's margins, this growing seafood industry, which exploited entrenched African American understandings of the maritime environment, grated against traditions of private oyster resources.

Oyster poaching in the Isle of Hope marshes not only challenged De Renne's control of the edges of Wormsloe but also threatened his notions of conservation and management of marsh oyster stocks. From De Renne's point of view, local oystermen took a natural resource without paying; perhaps more important, they upset the balance of harvest and restocking he had worked out with Nelson. This viewpoint regarded Wormsloe's oysters as both the fruit of private property and the produce of aquaculture.[91] This struggle over oysters highlights three fundamentally distinct views of the marsh. De Renne believed the marsh to be a part of Wormsloe, a stretch of ground defined by property boundaries delineated by surveyors and recorded in the Chatham County courthouse and further privatized through his and Nelson's seeding efforts. According to this perspective, Wormsloe's oysters and cattle were all but interchangeable as parts of the agricultural landscape. This conception of ownership created both an obligation and a legal right to manage the marsh in the same way as the family managed the plantation's fields and forest. For local oystermen, the marsh was a liminal space; neither land nor river, the marsh was "a community property system owned and managed by its users," where all had usufruct rights to its abundance.[92] Further complicating struggles over Isle of Hope oysters, the growing regional packing industry consumed thousands of tons of shellfish each season, treating oysters as raw material and pushing watermen to increase their harvests. In the end, these three ways of conceptualizing the marsh proved incompatible.

The oyster banks remained a part of everyday life on Wormsloe, and other elements of the plantation's food culture remained tied to tradition while remodeling earlier eating habits in new ways. The family continued to provide lavish meals for estate guests, much as had been the case during the antebellum era, but, like the family's landscaping efforts, postwar spreads reached an entirely new scale. Befitting De Renne's conception of Wormsloe as a country retreat, he threw fantastic parties for city friends. The menu for an 1880 luncheon on the plantation's grounds included "Oysters on the shell, Boned turkey truffled, sandwiches, crab salad, ice cream and orange sherbet, cakes, strawberries, Oranges, apples, Prunes, Dried ginger, coffee, Burnt almond, sugared almonds, chocolate caramels: everything cold but coffee. Wines were sherry, and champagne."[93] Although these large dinners resembled De Renne's antebellum descriptions of abundance on the plantation table, he no longer focused on food with local origins. Rather than symbolizing the Wormsloe landscape as the source of wealth, the estate had become a showpiece that demonstrated its owner's wealth and hospitality. These meals, then, were the culinary equivalent of the family's horticultural designs, as the De Rennes used bounteous tables to reinterpret an imagined gracious Old South.

The De Rennes regulated oyster harvests in the marshes and foot traffic through Wormsloe to the best of their ability but struggled with other challenges to the primacy of their private property rights. During the postwar period, coastal Georgia remained an open-range landscape. Stock owners turned their hogs and cattle into the woods to forage for at least a portion of the year, and farmers were still responsible for protecting their crops by building fences. Although the Isle of Hope had undergone countless social and environmental changes since the colonial era, the legal relationships between livestock and land remained essentially the same as in the eighteenth century. All indications are that portions of Wormsloe's northern property line were fenced throughout the late 1800s, but a breach in the fence from a fallen tree, a rotted board, or an open gate left the plantation's fields open to marauding animals and the De Rennes with no legal recourse. Upkeep of these external fences was both tedious and expensive. In one year's repairs alone, Wormsloe workers planted

454 cedar fence posts.[94] Across the South during the late 1800s, landowners challenged these old fence laws for a variety of reasons.

When a campaign to end the open range in Chatham County developed in 1894, Wymberley De Renne took active notice. As articles arguing for and against changing the law appeared in local newspapers, he carefully cut out the columns and pasted them in his personal scrapbook. With his recent struggles over controlling access to Wormsloe and its natural resources, it is no surprise that he selected more articles in favor of closing the open range than pieces supporting the status quo. One of the final fencing articles in the scrapbook proclaimed a victory for landowners over stockmen: On July 5, 1895, Chatham County voters voted to do away with the old law and to require stock owners to fence in their animals, with the new law going into effect six months later.[95]

Scholars have debated the intent of postwar laws closing the open range across the South. The first school of thought, epitomized by the work of Steven Hahn, characterizes southern fence laws as a tool of white landowners and merchants to control the labor of free blacks and poor whites. Closing the range, along with the game laws passed around the same time, cut down on the poor's ability to hunt, fish, and range livestock—that is, to live outside a wage labor and credit economy. Without the all-important cushion of an extensive commons, freedpeople were forced to labor on plantations for wages or shares and small white cotton farmers had to sign crop liens with town merchants to survive.[96] A second viewpoint, led by the work of Shawn Kantor and J. Morgan Kousser, argues that range closure was the natural outcome of southern population and economic growth. Just as residents of the Northeast and the Midwest had passed fence laws when regional populations reached certain levels, southerners closed their range when urban and row-crop interests surpassed the economic influence of small farmers and herders. According to Kantor and Kousser, race and class were much less important factors than demographic and economic calculus in legislative movements to end the open range.[97]

The public debates in Chatham County seem to support Kantor's and Kousser's claims for the roots if not the results of range closure. The Savannah-area articles collected by De Renne argued that a stock law was necessary in the urbanizing county. Advocates of changing the existing law declared the cattle and swine that defecated in the city's streets and drank from its open gutters a health nuisance and worried that the cost of fencing all cropland retarded the county's emerging truck farming enterprises.[98] Calling for a "practical and progressive" law, residents favoring range closure also linked urban and suburban infrastructural problems with free-ranging stock.[99] They argued that roaming cattle and hogs damaged roads, ditches, and culverts throughout the county, thereby inhibiting drainage and sewerage works, and county officials supported these claims by stating that new infrastructural bonds were unlikely until the electorate resolved the fence issue.[100] Although a few writers declared that the new law would benefit poor farmers by relieving them of the burden of fencing their fields, range closure undoubtedly harmed the landless poor who relied on livestock. The end result then, mirrors Hahn's description of the consequences of the stock law, but if the public dialogue is taken at face value—and there seems little reason to suggest that it should not be—the reasoning behind the law reflected the economic interests of the majority of the county's population.

Photographs of Wormsloe before and after passage of the new law revealed the environmental changes wrought by farmers penning their livestock. During the 1870s and 1880s, wire fences surrounded the plantation house and outbuildings to exclude passing animals, and the forest was relatively open, with little understory as high as a cow could reach. Few seedlings grew between the larger trees, and longleaf pines in their fragile grass stage were noticeably absent. Pictures from the early twentieth century reveal a much different landscape. With the plantation herds and neighboring livestock safely in pastures and pens, the fences surrounding Wormsloe's buildings were gone, and portions of the woods were much thicker. In one detailed photograph of the piney woodlands, young longleaf seedlings crowd the foreground of the frame.[101] Not all of Wormsloe faced this transition. Portions of the estate remained in dairy pasture, and workers kept the landscaped grounds surrounding the house open and orderly, but other areas of the plantation underwent ecological succession in the absence of the pressure of continual grazing. Young pines and live oaks recolonized sandy and hammock land, and understory shrubs repopulated the forest. If anything, the post-stock-law woods were thicker than the forest had been two centuries earlier and were more akin to current successional forests as contemporary southern agricultural and forestry practices all but excluded regular burning. The shift from woods pasture to enclosure marked an end to more than a century and a half of livestock rule in the plantation's forests. For Isle of Hope residents, a new fence law might have seemed a minor political development, but for Wormsloe's woods, the end of the open range brought dramatic ecological changes.

By the mid-1890s, Wormsloe was also the site of commercial dairy operations. The plantation facility was part of a small but growing group of suburban dairies that supplied Savannah's markets and homes. Proximity to the city was vital to the success of these operations, since the age of refrigeration had not yet arrived and most dairy products were perishable. In addition to Wormsloe, local dairymen founded at least five herds around the turn of the century, but none seem to have predated De Renne's dairy.[102] The growth of rural dairies on the outskirts of the city reflected changes in the dairy industry throughout the United States around the turn of the century. As the nation's urban population grew, city residents worried about the quality of their dairy supplies. Progressive health inspectors and agricultural scientists criticized cramped urban dairies for unsanitary practices, and as a consequence, many consumers came to associate rural dairies with pure milk. Southern cities lagged behind their northern counterparts in milk cleanliness campaigns—New York City required dairy inspections by 1902, while Georgia failed to initiate a milk sanitation campaign until 1943—yet common consumer perceptions of dairy products existed across the nation. As historian Kendra Smith-Howard writes, many urban consumers saw "milk as bottled sunshine and fresh air" from the country.[103] Wormsloe existed in a perfect location to exploit this perception, far enough from the urban center to qualify as rural yet close enough to furnish perishable products to city dwellers. Tapping into the growing popularity of rural dairies, De Renne built a substantial low brick dairy house, purchased chickens and milk cows, and marketed the dairy's products in such Savannah groceries as M. S. Gardner's on Whitaker Street.[104] De Renne also used his connections in Asheville, North Carolina, where the family often vacationed, to market eggs and butter, which traveled relatively well, in the mountains.

The De Rennes' stock were likely mixed-bloodline crosses between coastal landraces (cattle that have evolved in one location over several generations) and the improved breeds from the Northeast and England that George W. Jones had introduced in the 1850s. (The black-and-white Holsteins that typify modern dairies were a twentieth-century introduction to the South.) The Devon cattle that Jones brought to Wormsloe were a notable early dual-purpose breed: Farmers raised Devons for both their beef and milk-producing characteristics.[105] Another import to the plantation, English Alderney cattle (the descendants of which are now known as Jerseys) were even more adapted to milk production. They were brought to the United States in the mid-nineteenth century as a "strictly dairy" breed that gave "exceptionally rich milk" suitable for butter and cheese production.[106] Wymberley De Renne continued stock introductions around the turn of the century. In 1899 and again in 1905, he ordered young bulls for the dairy. Though De Renne did not record the breed of either animal, his dairy manager described the second bull as "full blooded."[107] These stock improvement efforts bore a marked similarity to De Renne's father's attempt to improve Wormsloe's herds and flocks before the Civil War.

In addition to the introduction of such pure dairy and multipurpose breeds as Alderneys and Devons, the Wormsloe herd almost certainly benefited from the most common method of increasing cattle productivity, selective breeding. Dairy farmers kept note of the individual cows who produced the greatest quantity of milk or whose milk contained the most butterfat and then bred those animals each year while culling poor producers from the farm. This gradual selection was perhaps the most general and important factor in the increasing efficiency of America's dairy herds around the turn of the century.[108] Wymberley De Renne engaged in selective cattle breeding practices throughout the early years of the plantation dairy. He collected journal and newspaper clippings on the topic of successful cow breeding and kept records of individual cows, when they were bred, and to which bull. Even while traveling, he wrote to his dairy hands regarding herd management and breeding schedules.[109]

Dairy cattle, whether specialized or multipurpose breeds, need more feed per animal than beef cattle to produce substantial quantities of milk, and these nutritional demands shaped Wormsloe's cultivation practices.[110] Dairy cattle required fenced pasture—farmhands had to round the animals up for milking every day and could not chase them through the woods and marshes—and high-protein feed. As Chatham County's open range ended, De Renne could remove the fences surrounding his crops, but he also had to build new barriers to contain his cattle. By the early 1900s, Wormsloe's old cotton fields grew a range of fodder crops, including hay, several types of peas, beans, rye, oats, and corn. The dairy also purchased supplementary feed, perhaps more corn, to round out the herd's diet. De Renne also recorded manuring the plantation's cropland, returning some of the waste produced by the dairy cattle to the land.[111]

The dairy employed a relatively new agricultural technology, the silo, for long-term storage of cattle feed. The low-oxygen environment inside a silo promoted the slow fermentation of plant matter, and the resulting acidic conditions slowed spoilage. Farmers could make silage from a number of crops, including corn, grass, beans, and peas, and feed kept in silos retained a much greater nutrient value than did dried hay. Silos first appeared in significant numbers in the dairy belt of the Upper Midwest in the late 1800s, but the structures were much slower to gain popularity in the South, where there were fewer dairies and milder winters required less feed storage.[112] At some point in the early history of the Wormsloe dairy, De Renne built a substantial concrete silo, the remains of which still stand near the foundation of the dairy barn. The majority of the plantation's fodder crops were well suited to ensilage:

Cowpeas, hay, corn, rye, oats, and velvet beans would have kept well in the silo during the brief Lowcountry winters. The silo was another way that De Renne rationalized and managed the produce of Wormsloe's fields. The silo made peas and hay from the summer available throughout the winter and did so in a more efficient and predictable manner than older methods of curing hay and storing fodder. De Renne developed elaborate field-rotation plans in the first years of the twentieth century to fill the silo. He divided the plantation's fields into at least eleven blocks, numbered each division, and mapped out which plots grew peas, hay, sweet potatoes, and other feed crops each season.

While some northern dairy cooperatives sold milk direct to customers' doors, early Georgia dairy operations, like other southern dairies, sold very little fluid milk directly to consumers. Instead, these facilities sold their raw milk to creameries or produced butter, cheese, and cream, which could survive unrefrigerated shipping.[113] The Wormsloe dairy was no different, as it seems to have specialized in these relatively stable commodities. In one month in 1894, De Renne recorded the sale of two thousand dozen eggs, two thousand pounds of butter, and one thousand pounds of cheese.[114] These numbers indicate that the dairy had already become a substantial operation. Following the turn of the century, Wormsloe's dairy business would expand, though the activity never became a major revenue producer. Instead, dairy operations and truck farming provided the family with a tie to the plantation's agricultural past, even if the connections to the staple-crop system that had dominated the site a half century earlier were tenuous at best.

Dairy operations on Wormsloe represented the broad late-nineteenth-century changes taking place in the Lowcountry surrounding Savannah. As during the antebellum period, Chatham County's agriculture was undergoing a transition. Sea island cotton and rice culture declined sharply in favor of truck gardens as Savannah grew and expanded into the rural countryside, and the city's transportation connections with the East Coast via rail and steamer improved. Where slaves once labored chopping cotton or pulling weeds in flooded rice impoundments, freedmen worked market garden crops of early potatoes, beets, cabbage, corn, and hay. In 1860, Chatham County had produced almost a thousand bales of sea island cotton and more than 25 million pounds of rice. By 1900, production of these antebellum staples had fallen to a meager 1,556,674 pounds of rice and only ten bales of cotton. Offsetting the diminishing acreage in rice and cotton was a tremendous growth in root crops and green vegetables, which could be planted and harvested more than once each year in the mild coastal climate. An 1896 promotional pamphlet stressed the newfound importance of truck farming, claiming that Savannah had become the "largest vegetable, fruit and melon shipping port in the South."[115] By the dawn of the twentieth century, Chatham County led Georgia in the production of Irish potatoes and in the value of its market garden produce, and local farmers also raised large quantities of cabbages, string beans, cantaloupes, green peas, strawberries, and tomatoes.[116]

In part, the growth of truck farming in the Savannah vicinity reflected local landowners' attempts to make a living when faced with the disintegration of the plantation system. Truck farms supplied the city's markets and kitchens, railroads hauled coastal produce inland, and packet steamers carried vegetables to mid-Atlantic and northeastern ports. Chatham truck farming, like similar agricultural activity in other well-defined portions of the South, benefited from the region's climate and its past agricultural legacies. In its African American population, the county had a large pool of skilled agricultural labor with experience growing various vegetable crops for market. Although one government report described truck labor as "nearly all negro and in many cases . . . unskilled," black agricultural expertise was a vital component of truck farming, as the emerging agricultural system demanded in-depth environmental knowledge to control pests, select plant varieties, and read Lowcountry weather. The situation of Wormsloe and similar farms also contributed to the success of truck farming. Thanks to the Georgia coast's unusually long growing season—nearly ten months in Savannah—Chatham truck farmers could deliver cabbages, strawberries, beans, and potatoes to northern markets before similar crops were ready in other locales. Vegetable and fruit prices fluctuated dramatically by season, and coastal Georgia's climatic advantage over more northerly ports made truck farming profitable.[117]

Wormsloe's small-scale production of potatoes and beans as well as its dairy operations contributed to this expanding truck trade. This form of agriculture resulted from the efforts of both white plantation owners such as the De Rennes and freedpeople. The old master class struggled to adapt its holdings to the new labor realities of the late nineteenth century; as slaves, Lowcountry African Americans had worked within the task system to produce market crops, and following emancipation, freedpeople used this experience to make a living, often outside the sharecropping/wage work economy. Such agriculture was made possible by the continued expansion of Savannah as a city and a port. Wormsloe was a landscape rapidly being surrounded by the city, and though the plantation would escape the development that swallowed much of the agricultural land ringing Savannah, changes in the usage of the land reflected the proximity of the suburbs. Wormsloe as a dairy was an extension of the urban landscape only a few miles north on Skidaway Road, and the plantation's truck farming activities reflected growth in Savannah and in urban markets up and down the Atlantic coast.

Both dairying and truck farming were dramatic reorientations of Wormsloe's plantation economy. Where sea island cotton, an export staple, once grew, fields of fodder and food crops covered the landscape. The De Rennes raised these crops largely for local and regional rather than international consumption; potatoes moved through Savannah markets or traveled up the Atlantic coast to neighboring ports, while beans, peas, and hay remained on the plantation to nourish the dairy herd, which in turn produced butter, cheese, and cream for Savannah's grocers. These agricultural changes on Wormsloe moved counter to the general southern trend. Following Reconstruction, the rural South, already centered on cotton, tobacco, rice, and sugar, became increasingly dependent on staple-crop production, and sharecropping arrangements and crop liens led small cotton and tobacco farmers deeper and deeper into debt peonage, furthering their ties to cash crop cultivation.[118] In fact, the production of cotton and tobacco almost doubled between 1860 and 1900.[119] Chatham's agricultural shift was, however, in keeping with the general trend of the Georgia Lowcountry, where large-scale plantation agriculture was in general decline, to be replaced by timber and tourism in the new century.

With its move away from sea island cotton and toward subsistence crops and small-scale production of vegetable crops following Reconstruction, Wormsloe mirrored these larger county trends. Wormsloe's farm diversification would continue in the early twentieth century, as the suburbs of Savannah gradually enveloped the estate. Dairy operations grew, and the De Rennes continued to plant sweet potatoes, Irish potatoes, peas, and hay on a substantial scale. Four decades after George Jones strove to create a plantation centered on cotton cultivation, Wormsloe had become a landscape of agricultural diversity with no cotton in sight. This transition had been long and difficult. Both the De Renne family and the region's former slaves struggled to define the form of the postwar plantation. As with the sea island cotton plantation, this farm landscape ultimately proved unsuccessful; agriculture as a way of life would be completely gone on the old plantation by the late 1930s. Although the plantation's agricultural track mirrored local and Lowcountry trends, its surviving landscapes and history were also unique in ways that would enable the next chapter in the estate's history. Wormsloe became more and more a place of pleasure and retreat, culminating in the estate's inclusion in the burgeoning coastal tourist economy. Wormsloe as a tourist attraction would gradually erase not only agricultural production on the old plantation but also its memory.

CHAPTER FOUR

"Worth Crossing Oceans to See"

The Transition from an Agricultural to an Ornamental Landscape

AROUND MIDDAY ON SEPTEMBER 29, 1896, a hurricane made land-fall near Tybee Island, packing sustained winds of close to 110 miles per hour. The storm surged up the Savannah River, destroying homes, uprooting trees, swamping rice impoundments, and leveling cotton fields as it went. The hurricane had earlier made a circuitous passage across the Florida peninsula from the Gulf of Mexico to the Atlantic, leaving severe damage in Jacksonville, Brunswick, and Darien as it skirted the bight of northeastern Florida and coastal Georgia. As the storm plowed over Savannah, it drove boats ashore on the Isle of Hope, destroyed churches and warehouses, and toppled "more than half the trees" in Forsyth Park. Ferocious winds forced salt water over low-lying stretches of the coast, temporarily blurring the boundaries between sea and land. When the hurricane had passed, it left in its wake at least seventeen dead in the city's vicinity and more than a million dollars in property damage. On Wormsloe, the powerful storm ripped through the plantation's forests, snapping the tops off longleaf pines and downing trees.[1] The 1896 hurricane was but one of a regular parade of tropical storms that periodically swept over the Georgia Lowcountry. Every few years, ocean currents, winds, and tropical lows combined to bring the storms ashore somewhere along the southern Atlantic coast, but several monstrous storms stand out. A "Great Hurricane" killed five sailors off the mouth of the Savannah River in 1752. A massive 1804 cyclone sent a tidal surge over the Georgia and South Carolina barrier islands, washing away crops of rice and cotton and killing more than five hundred Lowcountry residents. Another storm blasted Wormsloe in 1854 as George W. Jones was moving his base of agricultural operations to the plantation, leaving "a terrible path behind it of crops destroyed, & property of every kind injured."[2] These powerful storms destroyed property and disrupted human, animal, and plant life, but they also continued to replenish and renew coastal ecosystems, as storms had for thousands of years. Wind-toppled trees created

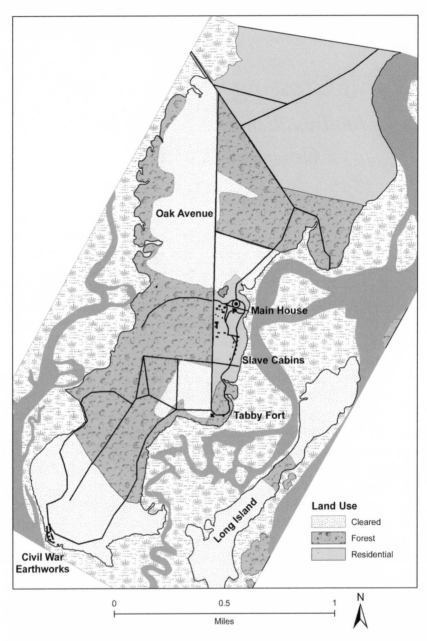

Wormsloe 1910. Map by Dr. Thomas R. Jordan, Center for Remote Sensing and Mapping Science, Department of Geography, University of Georgia, Athens, Georgia.

openings for new understory growth, certain bird and insect species relied on the resulting downed logs and dead snags, and storm surges deposited loads of nutrients across the salt marsh.

Equally important as the tropical storms that periodically pounded the Low-country coast, human social and economic activity continued on Wormsloe. The decades following the 1896 hurricane highlighted the plantation's historic role as a secondary property—a place of escape. By the end of the nineteenth century, after a brief period when the family had tried to make Wormsloe a productive centerpiece, the old plantation had become a family resort, a place where the De Rennes could rest and relax in the salty air away from the urban bustle of Savannah or residences in the cities of the Northeast and Europe. The De Rennes had built a substantial dairy on the property and expanded their market garden production, and they eventually invited tourists onto their historic plantation. Paths of crushed oyster shells and thousands of azaleas, camellias, and roses transformed the former cotton plantation into a flowering fantasyland. Over the next four decades, gradually diminishing wealth limited the De Rennes' use of Wormsloe as a vacation spot—Wymberley W. De Renne (Noble Jones's great-great-great-grandson) and his family lived on the plantation year-round—and caused the family to open what was once a private playground to the admission-paying public by the late 1920s. Visitors from across Georgia and beyond traveled to Wormsloe to glimpse the preserved majesty of an old plantation South, often unaware that the decay of an old southern fortune had made possible their exploration and enjoyment of Wormsloe. And for all this transformation, hurricanes still swept the marshes and fields and woods, moving in patterns that predated human changes to the land.

In addition to the constancy of hurricanes, human residents' continual efforts to reinterpret the landscape remained a feature of early-twentieth-century Wormsloe, as it had in the preceding century. Wymberley J. De Renne continued to remodel the plantation's house and grounds after 1900, continuing work begun by his father before the Civil War. Wymberley's landscaping and construction emphasized the property's long cultural history, even as it worked to change the plantation's appearance. After Wymberley's death, his son, Wymberley Wormsloe, and daughter-in-law, Augusta, actively continued (re)creating an Old South plantation as they saw fit. Among their efforts, Wymberley and Augusta expanded the formal gardens behind the main house, continued planting horticultural specimens throughout the estate, and actively sought to preserve, refashion, and celebrate elements of the property's colonial and antebellum past. Efforts to interpret Wormsloe as one of Georgia's most pristine colonial sites reached a crescendo in the late 1920s and 1930s, when financial setbacks forced the couple to open the estate to the public as a tourist attraction, Wormsloe Gardens. Tourists were invited to stroll through a fragment of the Old South even as ongoing planting and landscaping efforts actively transformed the woods and grounds through which the visitors walked. Despite Wormsloe's popularity, the tourist trade failed to rescue Wymberley's and Augusta's fortunes, and in 1938, Elfrida De Renne Barrow, Wymberley Wormsloe De Renne's sister, took control of the estate to prevent its sale outside the family. Like all of Wormsloe's previous masters, Elfrida and her husband, Craig, brought their own ideas about what the Isle of Hope landscape meant and set about their own reinterpretation.

Underneath Wormsloe's multiple layers of interpretation, the physical environment of the southeastern coast continued to influence life on the Isle of Hope. In 1940, as Elfrida and Craig settled in at Wormsloe, another hurricane swept across coastal Georgia. The storm snapped off hardwoods, toppled pines, and blew away ornamental shrubbery and garden walls. The fierce winds even toppled a few of the substantial live oaks that lined the plantation avenue. Damage in Savannah alone was estimated to be in the neighborhood of four million dollars, despite the fact that the worst quadrant of the storm tracked north of the city.[3] Unlike earlier hurricanes, this tempest had no effect on the plantation's agricultural activities for the simple reason that none remained. The Barrow branch of the family had closed the dairy, and its demise also spelled the end of the plantation's field crops. As the world spiraled into war, Wormsloe had become a landscape of formal gardens, manicured walks, and vistas that emphasized the property's colonial past. The fields of the nineteenth and early twentieth centuries were slowly reforesting, and the damage wrought by hurricane winds affected lines of sight and aesthetics rather than fences and crops. The Barrows had completed Wymberley J. De Renne's efforts to establish Wormsloe as a place of rural retreat that celebrated family and state history. Although the 1940 storm lashed a Wormsloe far different than the estate of the mid-1890s, the storm served as a reminder that for all the cultural and environmental changes that had taken place on Wormsloe, ecological processes continued to shape the Isle of Hope landscape, often in dramatic fashion.[4]

George W. De Renne's 1880 will left Wormsloe in a trust, administered by the Pennsylvania Company for Insurance on Lives and Granting Annuities, that denied his children—the fifth generation of the family to live at Wormsloe—outright ownership of the property. Apparently suspicious of his children's business acumen and worried that they might squander their inheritance or sell Wormsloe outside the family, De Renne made arrangements that granted his wife and children yearly annuities drawn from the interest of the estate but left legal control of the land in the hands of the Pennsylvania Company. With the deaths of his mother and siblings from age and illness, Wymberley Jones De Renne took over control of Wormsloe, though to live on the plantation he was required to pay an annual rent in excess of one thousand dollars. Although Wymberley lacked the power to sell or rent Wormsloe, once he made the property his home, he set about adapting the landscape to suit his needs and desires.[5]

Despite the frustrating legal stipulations of the trust, Wymberley became as enamored of the historic family seat as his ancestors had been. He and his family returned to Wormsloe in 1891 from sojourns in Texas and France, settling into the plantation house as their primary residence, though they still traveled extensively in the Northeast and abroad. Soon after returning to the Isle of Hope, Wymberley began a massive campaign to remodel the main house and the property's grounds. Over the next several years, he enlarged the house and added decks, verandas, and even a fanciful tower on the facade facing the river, transforming the conservative federal-style home into an elaborate mansion in line with contemporary Victorian tastes. These additions were also in keeping with the family's tradition of continually modifying the house; over the years, George Jones's relatively simple 1828 frame home had been transformed into a sprawling three-story structure replete with porches, decks, and multiple entrances. De Renne's building campaign also extended beyond the main house. He had workers construct a house for a farm supervisor, a modern steel water tower, and a new concrete dock with a pavilion overlooking the river. He also built a magnificent fireproof Grecian library, completed in 1908, that housed his extensive treasury of Georgia history, a collection begun by his father before the Civil War. Among these structures was a substantial log cabin playhouse in the forest for Wymberley's children, Elfrida, Audrey, and Wymberley Wormsloe. These improvements came at a cost to the property's older buildings. Wymberley built his new estate on the rubble of his father's 1850s plantation, much as George W. Jones had altered the antebellum landscape to suit his whims. Construction crews working on the new pier tore down the old sea island cotton gin and used scrap iron from the demolition in their new structure, and after 1899, the family began razing some of the wooden antebellum slave cabins and using the materials for other construction projects. Although this building campaign erased some physical features of the antebellum landscape, many of the plantation's social structures remained intact in modified form. For example, African American labor built the estate's new structures, and as the old slave/tenant cabins came down, they were replaced by a newly remodeled servants' wing attached to the main house.[6]

While the addition of new structures and the removal of old ones changed Wormsloe's appearance, the De Rennes' landscaping efforts during the same period altered the land in less dramatic but perhaps more significant ways. The most notable new landscaping feature was the second oak avenue leading along the old path connecting the colonial fort to Skidaway Road. This is the live oak avenue that park visitors experience today. The older entrance to the plantation house lay along the eastern edge of the property, flanking the Skidaway salt marsh, but the new drive cut arrow-straight through the heart of the old plantation, and its double rows of live oaks created a formal feature in the center of the property.[7] Both drives remained in use, but the new avenue provided an impressive vista for distinguished guests. De Renne also accelerated the pace of ornamental planting, a hobby of all his Wormsloe ancestors. He continued to favor the traditional camellias, roses, magnolias, and jessamine to which his father had been so partial, but he also purchased a wide variety of new cultivars. An 1897 map of the improvements and plantings on the estate reveals that he had planted fifty-eight species of shrubs and trees, including new ornamentals such as deodar cedars, Japanese maples, and weeping lilacs, as well as herbaceous plants that overflowed beds, lined walks, and carpeted open glades. These banks and stands of cultivars flanked the new avenue, dotted the open park along the entry drive to the house, and surrounded the old plantation structures and slave cabins.[8] De Renne hired a professional full-time gardener to oversee this landscaping and built a substantial coal-heated glass greenhouse in which he could start ornamentals and keep tropical plants alive through the winter.[9] Although few of these species were natives, De Renne specified that they be planted in a naturalistic manner, scattered throughout the woods or clumped in asymmetrical bunches. Wormsloe had old-fashioned formal gardens, most notably one located near the rear of the main house that featured roses, hedges, eucalyptus, and jessamine, but the majority of De Renne's energy and money went into integrating domesticated plants into the surrounding woods and agricultural lands.[10]

This built environment that mimicked natural patterns was inspired, at least in part, by the work of landscape architect Frederick Law Olmsted at George Vanderbilt's immense Biltmore Estate near Asheville, North Carolina. During one of his family's Appalachian vacations in the early 1890s, De Renne visited the Biltmore while it was still under construction, and he came away deeply impressed by both the chateau (the largest private residence in the United States) and its ornamental grounds. At the Biltmore, Olmsted brought together on a massive scale elements of estate and landscape design that interested De Renne. By the time Vanderbilt opened the chateau in 1895, he had assembled a 125,000-acre estate. Like Wormsloe, the mountain property included forests, formal gardens, lawns, landscaped drives, and agricultural spaces. Olmsted, the designer of New York City's Central Park and Boston's Fens and Riverway, among other projects, landscaped much of the Biltmore property so that "designed and deliberately constructed" grounds appeared to be "works of nature or felicitous, serendipitous products of culture."[11] Of particular interest was the long, winding entrance drive. The route made its way through heavily logged hills and vales, but Olmsted's landscaping created a wooded road that convinced many visitors that they were passing through untouched forest. Olmsted, along with professional forester Gifford Pinchot and his successor, Carl Schenck, who operated the nation's first forestry school on the grounds, also worked to combine aesthetic beauty with economic use.[12] By carefully shaping the grounds surrounding his house, De Renne mimicked these various Biltmore campaigns as he sought to blur the lines between his home and the woods and marshes beyond. Like Olmsted, De Renne "had the designer's faith that he could make something better, not worse." His workers dredged reflecting pools, installed fountains, and built gazebos, benches, and bridges designed to lure walkers into the gardens and used shrubs and trees to screen farm structures and direct foot traffic. The end result was a pleasingly parklike landscape that hid much of the tremendous effort and expense behind its creation.[13]

These landscaping efforts distinguished Wymberley's horticultural endeavors from the family's numerous earlier planting and gardening efforts. Whereas the formal gardens and neatly ordered agricultural spaces of George W. Jones created a landscape that conveyed the authority and power of the plantation's master, Wymberley's gardens and groves sought to create the image of an old, established estate. The former efforts highlighted the vigorous productivity of an innovative plantation, with its new buildings, busy workforce, and rich fields, while the latter landscaping celebrated the historic elements of the property by screening new structures with vegetation, funneling visitors to the old tabby fort, and replacing vegetable gardens and functional designs with plantings of camellias and azaleas that appeared natural. Although these plantings appeared to be vestiges of the antebellum or even colonial past, they required more planning, money, and professional advice than any of Wormsloe's previous horticultural efforts. Commercial nurseries supplied many of the plants, a full-time gardener supervised the grounds, and black workers dug, planted, and watered on a daily basis. A set of elaborate landscaping plats from 1897 demonstrates the plantation-wide extent of this planting campaign and De Renne's rigorous attention to detail. Whereas George W. Jones's plantings were part of an essentially modern worldview in which horticulture and agriculture worked together in pursuit of an "improved" landscape, Wymberley's efforts were much more romantic. He sought not a better future estate but rather the creation and conservation of an idealized image of the land as he imagined it had been.

Wymberley also sought to make Wormsloe a place of vigorous outdoor recreation. He loved to hunt both on the estate and across the Northeast, keeping memberships at hunting clubs near Asheville, North Carolina, and in southeastern Canada, where he vacationed on a regular basis. In 1906, De Renne became a charter member of the Chatham Hunt Club, which endeavored "to promote and cultivate social recreation and intercourse among its members and to encourage and stimulate interest in fox-hunting, riding and other country sports."[14] Like his ancestors, he enjoyed hunting Wormsloe's woods and marshes, though the deer Noble Wimberly Jones had once chased with hounds were gone, a victim of overhunting (though they would return to the area in the twentieth century).[15] Reflecting his love of equestrian sports, De Renne built a new stable near the main house where he kept horses and ponies for the family and guests, and he was involved in hunt club horse shows.[16] In the early 1910s, he also drafted plans for a quarter-mile racing oval to be built in the pine woods near the property's northern line. Equestrian groups such as the Georgia Hussars, a Savannah-based martial cavalry unit that dated back to the age of Oglethorpe, were attracted to Wormsloe's facilities and regularly met at the plantation, where they toured Wymberley's remodeled home and grounds and staged shooting competitions.[17]

Much as Wymberley sought to shape Wormsloe's physical landscape into an idyllic wonderland that treasured an invented past, he also impressed on his children the value and mystique of the country estate. Audrey, Elfrida, and Wymberley Wormsloe attended school in Pennsylvania and spent much of the year away from their Georgia home, but it was never far from their minds. Wymberley and his children frequently mentioned Wormsloe in nearly every letter they exchanged, often treating the property as a magical place where they could escape the frenetic pace of the outside world. Elfrida discussed the cattle, commented on her father's drive to make "alterations," and had him send her snips of jessamine to remind her of the lush Lowcountry.[18] Audrey and Wymberley Wormsloe similarly adored the old plantation, writing longingly of the land's domestic and wild animals and counting the days until they could return to Wormsloe to ride horses, play in their log cabin, or wander in the woods and along the marshes.[19] Audrey wrote to her father of "hunting eggs" in the Wormsloe farmyard, while Elfrida informed him that she planned to take a boat out on a creek near her school in the hopes that "it will remind just a little of Wormsloe."[20] Like their father and his predecessors, the De Renne children seemed always to have the Wormsloe landscape in their thoughts when they journeyed outside the Lowcountry. Part of this strong attraction to Wormsloe as an idyllic space may have stemmed from the property's role as a vacation estate. Memories of pleasurable stays in Wormsloe's rambling house along the Skidaway marshes proved durable and enticing incentives to preserve the plantation as a landscape of relaxation.

By the early 1900s, however, the rapid growth of Savannah and its surrounding communities threatened to envelope the old plantation with suburbs. In 1903, workers began construction of the Dupon subdivision just north of Skidaway Road. Much of this new development was on a former portion of the Wimberly tract.[21] Pressed tightly against Wormsloe's boundary, Dupon included 127 house lots, a park, a school, two churches, and a depot of the City Suburban Railway Line that connected new homeowners to their jobs and shopping downtown. The clearing, draining, and paving that accompanied suburban construction transformed the live oak and pine forest, replacing the woods with asphalt streets, grass lawns, and tract homes.[22] Dupon was part of the larger growth of the Isle of Hope community, which by the early twentieth century had developed into a substantial village complete with a yacht club and new houses in Caribbean, "Old English," and "French Provincial" styles.[23] Within a few years, only a thin screen of trees separated Wormsloe's northern fields from the busy energy of town life. The De Rennes had long been connected to Savannah and its commercial growth, but they must have felt some anxiety as development spread east from the city. Along these lines, as part of the landscaping accompanying the new oak avenue, the family built a massive entrance gate and wall fronting Wormsloe's northern line. This concrete and iron barrier served as both architectural adornment and as a partition between the tranquility of the plantation and the hustle and bustle of the world beyond.

One of Wymberley's hobbies revealed these environmental changes taking place throughout the Savannah River delta. At some point around the turn of the century, De Renne had begun collecting taxidermy mounts of local birds, and he eventually built a massive collection of at least 165 species. In many cases, he had mounts of male, female, and juvenile examples of each species. Ornithologist Walter John Hoxie, who lived in Savannah from 1901 until 1927, acquired at least one of these specimens for De Renne.[24] Although the formal practice of taxidermy dated to at least the 1700s, the late nineteenth and early twentieth centuries were a period of growing interest in the preservation of wildlife mounts, especially those of birds. Collectors tended to be members of the upper class; wealthy Victorian aficionados such as Wymberley exhibited their interest and education in natural history (or in some cases their hunting prowess) by displaying taxidermy mounts. These objects often served as household decorations that beautified indoor environments as they revealed their owners' erudition or accomplishments. In addition, stuffed birds became fashion objects for adorning hats as well as homes during this era, though members of the fashionable set were less interested in displaying their interest in nature than in capturing a bit of its beauty. Taxidermy collections not acquired through hunting were often assembled and sold by professional dealers who marketed their ability to find and preserve wildlife specimens to discerning collectors, and De Renne's relationship with Hoxie seems typical of this trend.[25]

Comparing De Renne's collection to John Abbot's observations of regional avifauna from a century earlier reveals some changes in Lowcountry biodiversity. Songbirds persisted in great numbers in the early 1900s: De Renne's collection included ten warblers, eight sparrows, and four varieties of wren. Despite heavy hunting, wading birds, shorebirds, and waterfowl remained numerous, if perhaps less plentiful than before, and the collection included sixty varieties of these waterbirds. Even predatory hawks, eagles, and owls, farmers' perpetual nemeses, were represented, their numbers sustained by the populations of squirrels, rabbits, and rats that accompany any agricultural landscape. De Renne owned mounts of ten such species, including apex raptors such as the great horned owl and bald eagle. Nevertheless, several of the Lowcountry's distinctive species that had proven vulnerable to increasing habitat destruction and hunting pressure were missing from the early-twentieth-century collection. Passenger pigeons and Carolina parakeets had gone extinct, done in by farmers' resentment of their damage to crops and flocking habits that made them vulnerable to market hunters. The ivory-billed woodpecker and sandhill crane had also disappeared from Wormsloe's vicinity, unable to survive in the midst of heavy timbering, wetland drainage, and land clearing for agriculture and towns. In the place of these extinct or extirpated species, bobolinks and grackles feasted on rice and corn, and yellow-bellied sapsuckers and downy woodpeckers survived in tree cavities too small for ivory-billed woodpeckers.[26]

De Renne's collection of stuffed animals also included mammals and reptiles. He owned mounts of groundhogs, eastern cottontails, opossums, raccoons, gray squirrels, and several species of rats, all common creatures in the South's agrarian landscapes. The collection also included rarer local inhabitants such as bobcats, eastern diamondback rattlesnakes, fox squirrels, and long-tailed bats. Noticeably absent were whitetail deer, a once-common species that had grown scarce along the coast as indiscriminate hunting lessened its numbers.[27] Despite the missing species, the diversity of the wildlife that still lived in and around Wormsloe was impressive. The farm was increasingly under development pressure, with the woods beyond its margins shrinking yearly, but it would be easy to overstate the pace of ecological change on the plantation itself. Even during the early years of the twentieth century, Wormsloe retained some quality wildlife habitat. Waterfowl and other birds that relied on aquatic habitat still had thousands of acres of marshland, bays, estuarial channels, and river to use in and around the plantation; the borders of fields and pastures provided food and shelter for edge dwellers, such as rabbits, and the predatory birds that fed on them; and despite almost two centuries of agriculture, much of the property remained wooded.[28]

By the early 1900s, Wormsloe may have no longer been a plantation, but it was still a landscape heavily populated with domestic animals. Letters, account books, and feed receipts flesh out the farm's animal populations. Among the stock were beef cattle and the herd of dairy cattle, chickens, donkeys, at least twenty-five sheep, mules, pleasure and work horses, a few goats, bronze and white turkeys, ponies, pigeons, dogs, and cats. While many of these animals were working or food stock, others, such as the ponies, pigeons, dogs, and cats, provided family members with enjoyment as they relaxed at their country estate.[29] As during the eighteenth and nineteenth centuries, these domestic animals would have placed demands on the plantation environment, grazing and foraging in the fields and woods. Even when contained in pastures, cattle, horses, and pigs would have competed with turkeys and the few surviving deer for browse, and cats and dogs would have pursued small mammals and birds.

The largest and most economically important group of animals on the farm remained the dairy herd. To house the expanded dairy herd and milking equipment, De Renne built a low brick and concrete dairy house and a silo between the plantation house and the rice mill. He also stocked the facility with modern, work-saving machinery, such as a "Baby" no. 1 cream separator.[30] Although never a large operation, the Wormsloe dairy kept a number of Savannah groceries in cream, butter, and cheese curds during the early nineteenth century. Records of sales are spotty, but in August 1906, the dairy sold 93.5 quarts of cream, 14.5 pounds of butter, 180 cheese curds, and perhaps some milk. The De Rennes also kept laying hens in association with the dairy and sold hundreds of eggs each month along with their milk-based products.[31] While these dairy products flowed out of the estate, certain by-products were returned to the land. The herd's waste was put to use, as cattle manure fertilized the various forage crops.

The herd of dairy cattle and a large and diverse population of other domesticated animals required an equally substantial quantity of feed. During the early twentieth century, much of Wormsloe's cropland was devoted to producing food for its flocks and herds. The broad fields that lined the oak avenue on the northern portion of the property were planted in rotations of field peas, pea vines (probably field peas planted extra thick to produce more vines and fewer seeds), potatoes, and hay. Farm laborers hauled the potatoes to Savannah markets for resale, but the vast majority of the peas and hay likely fed the farm's animals.[32] The De Rennes also planted turnips, cowpeas, rye, oats, sweet potatoes, corn, cassava, and velvet beans. Even with a substantial portion of the farm's land in feed crop cultivation, Wymberley De Renne had to buy some of his livestock supplies from local merchants. His account books regularly recorded purchases of cracked corn for chickens and ground feed for his horses, mules, and cattle.[33] These purchases reflected the plantation's continued reliance on outside markets for day-to-day operations. Despite various self-sufficiency campaigns over the centuries, including Noble Jones's horticultural experiments, George W. Jones's agricultural improvement campaign, and Wymberley J. De Renne's attempts to plant livestock food and return manure to the land, Wormsloe always relied on purchases to fulfill its needs.

As during all previous eras on Wormsloe following the legalization of slavery in 1751, African American workers provided the labor that ran dairy and livestock operations. Jesse Beach, who began living as a tenant on the property shortly after Reconstruction, was particularly instrumental in the farm's daily operations while the De Rennes were vacationing in the Northeast or Europe during the summer.[34] Beach oversaw ten full-time and seven part-time workers who lived in a newly constructed servants' quarters or in neighboring communities; managed dairy production and sales; looked after the farm's other stock; policed Wormsloe's boundaries against poachers and trespassers; and did any other maintenance required. In his monthly reports to De Renne, Beach recorded plantings and crop rotation, made notes on breeding supervision, commented on the health and productivity of stock, and advised his employer of initiatives regarding plowing and cutting wood. Beach was a jack-of-all-trades; De Renne expected him to handle any and all farm tasks, among them converting returned cream into salable butter and inspecting the dairy cattle for the cattle ticks that carried Texas fever, a disease that diminished milk production. As the De Rennes toured Rhode Island and Upstate New York, enjoying cooler summer climes, Beach ensured that agricultural work on Wormsloe proceeded smoothly.[35]

Beach's correspondence reveals an astute farming sense mated to an intimate understanding of the coastal landscape. He understood the importance of crop rotations on the sandy ground, shifting fields between crops that were net nitrogen extractors, such as Irish potatoes and turnips, and plants such as velvet beans that fixed nitrogen in the soil. This agricultural skill extended to Beach's care of Wormsloe's livestock. In addition to maintaining the health of the herds, he also supervised selective breeding with an eye to producing superior dairy cattle, writing to De Renne with both requests for instructions and his keen observations.[36] De Renne seemed to trust Beach's aesthetic eye as well as his farming acumen, giving Beach at least some leeway to direct horticultural gardening and planting on the estate when De Renne was not in residence. Beach supervised the gardener and other workers as they planted palmettos, thinned out wood lots, and set roses and chrysanthemums.[37] Although his letters are silent concerning his perceptions of the plantation landscape, Beach's correspondence raises certain questions about how he perceived his labor and, by extension, how all of Wormsloe's African American workers felt about their work on the land. Was he proud of Wormsloe as an estate? Was he pleased with his management skills yet ambivalent about a landscape that he would never own? These questions remain unanswerable, but they reinforce the continued importance of African Americans in the shaping of the Isle of Hope landscape long after slavery's demise.

The pervasiveness of African American labor was not limited to dairy work during the early 1900s. Full-time and temporary black laborers performed the tasks that built and maintained Wormsloe's landscape and structures. They sweated in the Lowcountry sun, digging and cleaning the thousands of yards of drainage ditching that kept the farm fields arable; they planted thousands of shrubs, trees, and flowers; and they worked as carpenters and masons. A set of photographs from early in the century captured these workers at some of their daily tasks—serving food, pushing wheelbarrows, working in the fields, and driving mule-drawn wagons. Skilled African American craftsmen also erected the impressive Wormsloe library, which housed a collection of Georgia documents that did relatively little to acknowledge the importance of slaves and freedpeople in the state's history.[38] Though much had changed—and improved—on Wormsloe since the days of slavery, the old relationship between white supervision and black labor remained in place (with the notable exception of Jesse Beach). Although black workers in the early 1900s received wages, no longer cultivated cotton, and were free to look for other work at any point, their economic survival still rested largely in the hands of white landowners. Their presence and their physical labor continued to define the plantation as a white retreat.

Although Wormsloe plantation had long attracted visitors with its beautiful grounds, the De Rennes' collection of Georgiana housed in the plantation library, and the family's support of historical research and publication, in the late 1920s the property became even more widely known. Wymberley died in 1916, and his son, Wymberley Wormsloe, assumed stewardship of the land for which he was named, becoming the sixth generation of Noble Jones's family to manage the site. By the summer of 1927, the younger Wymberley and his wife, Augusta, opened the old plantation to the paying public as Wormsloe Gardens. Spurred on by economic difficulties—Wymberley had made some unsuccessful real estate investments—and a desire to display the family's horticultural activities, the couple advertised the new tourist attraction in the regional and national press.[39] Wymberley and Augusta's public garden was an extension of the turn-of-the-century landscaping of Wormsloe, but it also modified older horticultural traditions. The attraction maintained Wymberley J. De Renne's rambling landscapes in which the artifice of construction remained hidden from the observer, but Wormsloe Gardens also emphasized the showy and elaborate. Augusta designed a series of formal gardens that relied on symmetry and regular plantings, with exotic cultivars contained within geometric walls and borders. These displays showed nature controlled and harnessed, a sharp contrast to the older gardens' emphasis on mimicking natural vistas.

Touring Wormsloe during the interwar years was in keeping with an expansion in public access to and the particular presentation of southern plantation homes. For the price of a ticket—one dollar in 1927—a visitor to the gardens gained access to much of the historic plantation. Guests entered the plantation at the elaborate stone gate fronting the live oak avenue planted in the 1890s, where a small house had been built and filled with a collection of Wormsloe memorabilia and postcards. The gatehouse also featured the elder Wymberley's collection of nearly four hundred taxidermy mounts, on display for visitors interested in the fauna of Chatham County, and sold potted camellias and ivy cuttings from the gardens.[40] After leaving the gatehouse, guests proceeded down the avenue, lined with the crop fields still in use for dairy operations, and turned off at the entrance to the plantation house. On foot, visitors could explore the sculpted hedges, pools, fountains, and marsh views of the house yard; wander through the walled formal gardens that Augusta had built just south of the house; and peer through a protective metal grate at the massive collection of rare Georgia books and manuscripts collected in the neoclassical library. They might even catch a noted historian, such as Ulrich Bonnell Phillips, exploring the collection. Guests interested in walking farther afield could make their way along winding paths of crushed oyster shells lined with azaleas, roses, flowering annuals, and "camellia trees . . . unequalled anywhere in the South" to the ruins of the old colonial fort or visit the site where Noble Jones had been buried before his body was moved to the family plot in Bonaventure Cemetery during the nineteenth century. Benches marked periodic resting points and pleasing views, statues of female nudes and "quaint though formal" garden gnomes dotted the grounds, and the soft cooing of Augusta's pigeons and the startlingly ethereal cries of peafowl pierced the air. Hiking back to the house, guests passed the old slave cemetery with its wooden grave markers and the sole surviving antebellum slave cabin before returning to the parking lot near the house.[41] Many guests, among them magazine writer Herschel Brickell, left the property spellbound. After his 1933 visit, Brickell praised Wormsloe's "great oaks covered with Algerian ivy, and japonicas [camellias] of large size and brilliant color, and all the other flowers that make the gardens of this part of the South worth crossing oceans to see."[42]

Wormsloe Gardens was a popular attraction from its opening season. Visitors came from Savannah and other coastal towns as well as from across the state, throughout the nation, and even from overseas. By the mid-1930s, the majority of the garden's guests came from the Northeast and the Midwest. Reflecting the effectiveness of the attraction's advertising campaigns, a visitors' register from the 1934 and 1935 seasons reveals that the garden drew as many tourists from Massachusetts as it did from Savannah.[43] The number of paying guests from all regions increased dramatically during the middle of the decade as a consequence of increased publicity. In 1935, the gardens drew 5,287 tourists, a figure that had almost doubled to 10,273 attendees by 1937.[44]

The thousands of guests who visited the garden arrived in a variety of ways. Bus tours from Savannah brought groups of tourists attracted by the history of the city and its surroundings. The De Rennes also arranged for special promotions through the railroad lines that fed Savannah. For example, in 1928, both the Seaboard Air Line Railway and the Central of Georgia Railway advertised the garden and offered package trips that included round-trip rail fare and tickets to Wormsloe. Residents of Atlanta and other cities could catch the train and make a convenient weekend of touring Wormsloe and neighboring Savannah sites.[45] The railroad advertising and specials were successful enough that they were repeated. The following year, Georgia's *Albany Herald* announced that the "railroads of Georgia and Alabama are putting on special rates during the azalea season" for Wormsloe tourists.[46]

More important, however, the increase in private automobile ownership made large crowds possible throughout the year. During the 1920s and 1930s, automobile tourism grew rapidly, as office and factory workers from urban areas took their families on long-distance vacations, formerly an activity reserved exclusively for the wealthy. The growing practices of vacationing and automobile ownership went hand in hand, and these waves of new middle-class vacationers were especially attracted to America's great outdoors.[47] As Wormsloe Gardens opened its gates to the public, national, state, and private parks across the Southeast were becoming increasingly popular destinations for both day trips and longer excursions.[48] Wormsloe advertisements frequently touted the plantation's accessibility by automobile. Pieces pitching the gardens as a destination for auto tourists appeared in *AAA Travel*, *Delaware Motorist*, and *Ohio Motorist*, among other forums targeting car owners.[49] Advertisements emphasized that the attraction lay on good roads, and Wymberley Wormsloe De Renne pitched the site as a natural excursion for automobile tourists taking the popular coastal route to or from Florida.[50] A 1930 article in the *Motor Bus Traveler* alluded to the property's long history yet declared that modern amenities made the past more palatable for the twentieth-century tourist: "Smooth concrete roads have replaced the ancient trails, and the automobile accomplished in a few minutes the toilsome journey of the pioneer."[51] The convenience of modern transportation thus made the serenity of the Wormsloe landscape both more appealing and more accessible to the growing body of American tourists.

Symbolic of this development, among the first visitors to Wormsloe Gardens was the father of America's automobile industry, Henry Ford, who motored to the estate from his nearby retreat, Richmond Hill.[52] Ford was a new Lowcountry landowner, having purchased twelve thousand acres along the lower Ogeechee River in 1925. Along with his friend, Thomas Edison, Ford was interested in the coastal Georgia environment and its potential for chemurgy—the process of producing industrial materials from agricultural crops. On the Richmond Hill plantation, his farm manager raised goldenrod, from which Ford and Edison hoped they could produce rubber.[53] Ford was also attracted to the coast's "nostalgic, rural values" and its suitability as a retreat from Detroit's harsh winters. Fascinated by the legacy of local plantation agriculture, Ford eventually accumulated almost seventy thousand acres in Chatham and Bryan Counties, where he raised sweet potatoes and safflower in addition to goldenrod, and he built a substantial mansion house in part from bricks taken from the Hermitage's old plantation house, which he bought and razed.[54] Ford was just one of Wormsloe Gardens' early tourists, but he was a potent symbol of the intersection of the legacy of nineteenth-century Lowcountry agriculture and the dynamic change brought by the early twentieth century.

New graded and paved highways were instrumental in bringing ever-increasing numbers of automobiles to the Georgia coast during the late 1920s. Perhaps the most important of these new arteries was the Dixie Highway, a series of well-marked roads built between 1915 and 1927 that connected Chicago to Miami via Chattanooga, Atlanta, and Jacksonville. According to historian Tammy Ingram, the Dixie Highway was the nation's first "interstate highway system." An eastern branch of this road network passed through Savannah before turning south to follow the Georgia coast. This spur came about largely at the behest of Savannah's industry and civic leaders, who were firmly convinced that the road would fuel the region's growing historical and recreational tourism industry.[55] By 1927, more than one out of every three Americans took an annual pleasure trip in an automobile, and these twenty-nine million vacationers spent five hundred million dollars on their roadside recreation. This massive moving cash flow encouraged entrepreneurs to flock to the nation's roadways, where they opened restaurants, filling stations, motels, and tourist attractions of all sorts. Motorists traveling along the Dixie Highway and other routes sought entertainment, diversion, and, as roadways geographers John Jakle and Keith Sculle explain, "authentic" experiences in "natural areas and historic sites."[56] With its location near historic Savannah, the beaches and outdoor playgrounds of the coast, and the new Dixie Highway, Wormsloe was perfectly positioned to tap into Americans' new obsession with motoring.

Ford's visit, the Dixie Highway's linkage of the coastal South to the Upper Midwest, and Wormsloe's popularity with guests from the Northeast and Midwest reflected the Georgia Lowcountry's increasing reputation as a playground for wealthy northerners. By the 1930s, the state's barrier islands from Savannah to the Florida state line contained a number of ostentatious estates owned by wealthy businessmen from the urban North, attracted by the region's balmy weather and relative seclusion. Like the northern refugees Olmsted observed in antebellum Savannah, well-off Yankees fled south during the interwar years to escape the winter snows. South of Savannah, Philadelphia's Wanamaker family purchased Ossabaw Island as a private hunting resort in the 1890s. Slightly further south, northern investors purchased St. Catherines Island and began developing its fields and forests as a tourist destination in the late 1920s, though the deepening depression halted work around 1930. Further down the coast, Howard Coffin, a Detroit automobile entrepreneur, developed portions of Sapelo before selling the property in the 1930s to Richard J. Reynolds Jr., heir to the RJR tobacco fortune. Reynolds carved out a grand estate on Sapelo, complete with a bowling alley, indoor swimming pool, and a circus tent in which he could entertain guests. Coffin and fellow Detroit businessman Eugene Lewis also owned St. Simons Island, where in the 1920s they built a golf course and cottage community on old cotton fields, attracting such famous guests as Calvin Coolidge, Herbert Hoover, and a young Dwight Eisenhower.[57] In 1886, Georgian John Eugene Du Bignon and northerner Newton Finney purchased Jekyll Island in its entirety and founded "what would become the most elite and inaccessible social club in the United States," the Jekyll Island Club. By the 1930s, Jekyll Island was a retreat associated "with such names as Vanderbilt, Rockefeller, Astor, and Gould."[58] The farthest south of any Georgia barrier island, Cumberland was also home to rich northerners. In 1881, the Carnegie family bought a portion of the island, and it would remain their hunting preserve—stocked with imported elk, antelope, mule deer, and pheasants—and escape from Pittsburgh well into the twentieth century.[59] The situation in the South Carolina Lowcountry was similar. By the early 1930s, nearly eighty estates owned by wealthy northerners dotted the land between Savannah and Georgetown.[60]

Wormsloe Gardens was certainly not the same sort of exclusive destination as the Jekyll Island Club or Cumberland Island, but the old plantation offered middle-class northerners as well as local residents a glimpse into the natural and cultural past. The estate's quiet forests, fields, and gardens provided a welcome retreat from the urban and suburban South that existed just outside the gates, and the tabby ruins, slave cabin, and plantation house served as antiquarian counterpoints to the automobiles and trains that carried tourists to the gardens. Modern transportation technology thus made Wormsloe more appealing even as it made the historic plantation accessible to the masses.

The De Rennes' opening of Wormsloe to the public was also in keeping with a growing interest in Savannah and its surrounding plantations. Wormsloe's formula of elaborate botanical and ornamental gardens centered on a historic southern plantation had direct regional competition, as along the South Carolina coast both Magnolia Gardens and Middleton Estate opened their grounds to the paying public.[61] Closer to home, historic plantation tours in the Savannah area became popular. By the interwar years, the chamber of commerce and local boosters publicized the city and the surrounding Lowcountry as a destination for tourists interested in southern history. Guides such as one prepared by the depression-era Federal Writers' Project listed the city's attractions and provided guests with well-marked foot and motor tours. Outlying plantations, Wormsloe among them, tapped into this tourism market, offering their natural beauty and historic structures for public consumption. By 1937, tourists had access to at least fifteen plantations surrounding Savannah, a group that included Beaulieu, Hermitage, Whitehall, and Mulberry Grove as well as the De Renne family home. These promotional efforts made Wormsloe part of a larger network of sites that tapped into Georgia's history and coastal environment. The 1933 designation of Fort Pulaski, a Civil War–era fortification located along the Savannah River east of the city, as a national monument provided an additional boon to local tourism.[62]

Wormsloe and similar coastal plantations turned tourist attractions were more than middle-class imitations of the new recreational demesnes of northern millionaires. Wymberley Wormsloe De Renne and Augusta De Renne's public gardens were at once an effort to reverse declining economic fortunes and a natural extension of the family's long history of designing and displaying the environment. The development of neighboring sea islands at the hands of industrial barons was in places revolutionary—building palatial chateaus in the coastal forest and replacing marsh and hammock with instant golf courses—whereas the creation of Wormsloe Gardens was evolutionary. Landscaping and celebrating the site's history drew on well-established Isle of Hope traditions. Tourism on Wormsloe thus became an essential part of a spirit of preservation that had been important to George W. Jones's efforts to improve plantation agriculture and record his family's history and to Wymberley J. De Renne's book collecting and ornamental gardening. The role of tourism as a preservation tool would only increase as the twentieth century progressed.

Like George W. Jones with his antebellum attempts to intensify Wormsloe's agricultural operations, the De Rennes often turned to outside professionals for advice and expertise when expanding the property's ornamental plantings and landscaping. As early as 1917, Wymberley Wormsloe De Renne's father had asked professional landscaper T. Bignault to increase and diversify the flowering plants on the grounds. Bignault responded with an elaborate plan to plant deciduous and evergreen shrubs, flowering trees and vines, and borders of herbaceous perennials.[63] These connections with professionals continued through the 1930s, with the De Rennes particularly interested in using their connections to collect rare plants, often varieties associated with the colonial South or Wormsloe's history. In 1929, R. A. Young, a horticulturalist with the U.S. Department of Agriculture (USDA) Bureau of Plant Industry, sent Wymberley Wormsloe three different species of *Elaeagnus*, an Asian shrub that Young thought might interest De Renne as a collector.[64] Augusta also tried to track down a specimen of *Gordonia alatamaha* (now known as *Franklinia alatamaha*), a rare flowering tree that William Bartram observed during his travels along the Georgia coast. In 1930, Augusta turned to University of Georgia horticulturalist T. H. McHatton for help in her quest.[65] The following year, she contacted a representative of the Henry Mitchell Seed Company as well as a botanist and horticulturalist at the Bureau of Plant Industry in an unsuccessful search for three rare varieties of *Leucojum* (snowflake amaryllids).[66]

The family also sought professional land- and farm-management advice. Augusta requested information about designating Wormsloe a bird sanctuary, and Wymberley Wormsloe worked with his brother-in-law, Craig Barrow, to have a Georgia state forester ship a hundred slash pine seedlings for an experimental planting on the property.[67] The attempt to introduce slash pines may have been connected to the Union Bag and Paper Company's construction of a pulp paper mill, the first of its kind in the South, in Chatham County in 1935. Union Bag and its competitors soon began harvesting and planting pines throughout the county and broad swaths of the South.[68] The De Rennes and the Barrows also requested advice on raising a variety of animals, from the horses and cattle that had long roamed the landscape to more exotic fantail pigeons and peacocks that Augusta kept in her formal garden. The family even contemplated bringing sheep back to Wormsloe during the 1930s, writing off for USDA farmers' bulletins on sheep husbandry.[69] The De Rennes and Barrows were not alone in their growing reliance on professional foresters, horticulturalists, and agricultural scientists, as the early twentieth century witnessed the growth of agricultural extension services, USDA programs, and forest management services even in the relatively benighted South.[70]

Through her contacts and interactions with horticulturalists, botanists, and nurserymen as well as by autodidactic experimentation, Augusta De Renne became a well-known expert in ornamental garden design and the plants associated with historic southern gardens. In 1930, she wrote an article for the *Junior League Magazine* in which she described her horticultural efforts at Wormsloe and outlined her tastes in landscape design.[71] Augusta also went on to become the first vice president of the Garden Club of Georgia as well as a member of the Garden Club of America (founded in 1913), and she corresponded regularly with officials of garden clubs across the nation.[72] As part of her horticultural work, Augusta kept detailed records of her plantings and orders, sketched plans of the plantation's formal gardens, and noted which nurseries carried interesting or unusual stock. Among her far-flung plant suppliers were companies in New York, Ohio, Michigan, and California as well as the Fruitlands Nursery, closer to home in Augusta, Georgia, and later transformed into the Augusta National Golf Course.[73]

Augusta De Renne's garden club activities provide an interesting window into the gendered nature of early natural resource management and conservation. Even if women were on the whole "muffled and cosseted" in the early years of the conservation movement, as one historian claims, they could freely express their landscaping and management philosophies in their garden spaces and clubs.[74] Often considered a part of the domestic sphere of the home, gardens were outdoor spaces in which women could exercise power and control over nature without threatening the authority of men concerned with managing the nation's forests and agricultural lands. Club women such as Augusta worked to beautify domestic, urban, and suburban settings, often in the best tradition of the conservation movement, seeking to put landscapes to their highest, most aesthetically pleasing uses. The creation of Wormsloe's grounds and similar gardens encouraged women to engage in landscape design and management, and they did so from New England to the Deep South to California.[75] These activities were not reserved solely for garden clubs, however, as female members of such organizations as the Daughters of the American Revolution and the Audubon Society also engaged in garden and landscape design along with preservation of historic homes or bird populations. A few women, among them Beatrix Farrand, who worked on famous estates across the nation in the early twentieth century, even entered the ranks of professional landscape architects. These activities united women in the common exercise of creating and preserving beauty of all sorts, linking gardens, forests, and homes as places of creation and conservation.[76]

The women of southern garden clubs also often proved influential interpreters of historic landscapes and their connection to an imagined social order. Steven Hoelscher has shown that Natchez, Mississippi, garden clubs did much to shape the city's interpretation of its past in the early twentieth century. Club women beautified Natchez's historic homes and crafted showy southern garden spaces, but they also worked to portray the city as an idealized remnant of a romantic Old South. Club women published guides to the city's gardens and history and hosted Confederate balls with images of black cotton hands as the backdrop for the celebrations.[77] Augusta De Renne's efforts on Wormsloe shared much with these labors of the Natchez clubs, as she worked simultaneously to beautify the plantation's grounds and its past.

Although modern landscapers and horticulturalists provided much of the knowledge and skill vital to creating Wormsloe's expansive gardens, the De Rennes were just as intent on maintaining connections between the contemporary grounds and the plantation's past, both real and imagined. Much like the Natchez ladies, who treasured the city's idealized history, the De Rennes envisioned their new gardens as a continuation of the family's horticultural efforts beginning with Noble Jones's oranges, pomegranates, and century plants. As part of this renewed emphasis on historic Wormsloe, the gardens hosted a number of historic events and re-creations.

One way that Augusta and Wymberley tried to connect twentieth-century Wormsloe to its antebellum and colonial past was by weaving old materials into their new landscapes. Augusta's 1920s design for the formal walled garden just south of the main house prominently featured antique bricks, some of which came from the foundation piers of the slave cabins.[78] Masons built other portions of the wall from English-fired bricks that Augusta salvaged from the ruins of colonial Lowcountry homes facing demolition and from ballast stones that had crossed the Atlantic in the holds of English ships.[79] Along these lines, a marble pillar rescued from the ruins of the Spalding House on Sapelo Island occupied a prominent spot in one block of the garden, ironwork from historic Savannah homes framed other sections of the garden, and historic cobbles from the city's wharf district flanked a fountain.[80] The couple also stressed the presence of old mulberry trees near the remains of the colonial tabby fort, claiming that these trees were survivors of Noble Jones's eighteenth-century sericultural efforts. In her personal garden notebook, Augusta even made the unlikely assertion that one large mulberry near the main house dated to 1736.[81] Recalling memories of a genteel colonial and antebellum South, Augusta used the gardens and grounds to host members of the Savannah Junior League. Socialites would visit the garden for tea, conversation, and old-fashioned delicacies, recalling an Old South image that might or might not have reflected Wormsloe's actual history.[82]

The family's promotional efforts seem to have paid off, and many guests apparently believed that they enjoyed a landscape that had remained largely unchanged since the days of Oglethorpe. Among the first visitors to remark on this effect, Elizabeth Wade White of *Junior League Magazine* wrote in 1930 of the historical associations that draped the attraction's formal gardens: "There is in this air and in the quiet sound of fountain-water falling, the essence distilled of memory, the ghostly rustling of silk which is the eighteenth century."[83] Travel writer Erland Bates reiterated this perception in 1933, praising "the world famed Wormsloe Gardens, preserved in all of their beauty from Colonial times."[84] A guide to Savannah's tourist attractions prepared by the Federal Writers' Project presented similar sentiments: "Here the spectator recalls those pioneer Georgians whose voices once rang through this quiet. He sees Noble Jones crashing through the underbrush and Mary Jones cocking her rifle through a fort embrasure; he sees Oglethorpe riding up the path to inspect the marines. Time at Wormsloe becomes a long avenue, down which moves the early history of Georgia."[85] These and similar testimonies emphasized Wormsloe's colonial history as part of its charm and found evidence of the plantation's storied past in the Isle of Hope's natural environment. Much as new avenues and gardens channeled historic structures, the woods and marshes that had changed a great deal since the 1730s came to represent the landscapes of centuries past.

Perhaps most important in conjuring Old South fantasies was the presence of black labor. Although Wormsloe had been staffed by African American workers—often former slaves or their descendants—continuously since emancipation, Wymberley Wormsloe De Renne believed that garden tourists wanted to see even more explicit connections to antebellum labor arrangements. In the winter of 1928, he began renovating the remaining slave cabin, and by the following spring the restored cabin, complete with antique furnishings and a new paling fence that replicated the old slave enclosures that surrounded small kitchen gardens, was ready for tourists. Touting Wormsloe's attractions, the *Savannah Morning News* noted the grand opening of the cabin, informing readers that "refreshments will be served by a nice old-fashioned mammy, bandanaed and imported for the event." Curious passers-by could sample coffee and hoecakes prepared by the reenactor.[86] The "mammy" was apparently a hit. By March, she was a regular employee of the gardens, and press releases stated that "Aunt Liza" had been born into slavery on Wormsloe two years before the start of the Civil War. Liza regaled visitors with tales of the Old South, reenacted various slave tasks, and claimed that she had been born in the same cabin in which she now worked.[87] The De Rennes planted azaleas and camellias around Liza's cabin and featured the humble structure on postcards available at the garden gift shop.[88]

Most Wormsloe visitors, especially native southerners, would have instantly recognized Liza as a stock character of literature and advertising. Mammy figures were popular tropes in the Jim Crow South, where they were often associated with food and domestic labor—it was no coincidence that Liza's role in the gardens was to serve snacks to guests. White Americans in the 1920s and 1930s were bombarded with advertising images of mammies selling soap, Aunt Jemima pancake mix, and numerous other products.[89] These stereotypical advertising figures promised black service for white needs, whether through an actual mammy or through modern conveniences that took her place.[90] According to historian Grace Elizabeth Hale, many whites found the mammy persona comforting because it served as an "image of racial and gendered yet asexual subservience."[91] For those who remembered the Old South, mammy was a safe stock figure who "never doubted that the Good Lord intended blacks for slavery, and while she could adopt the manner of a stern disciplinarian with the white children in her care, she was more deeply devoted to her master's family than her own."[92] For the De Rennes and other southerners intent on remembering the food and service of the antebellum South, Liza offered a reassuring figure that emphasized the continuity of Wormsloe traditions and, by implication, the permanence of the landscape itself.

Liza was a figure of at least equal importance for northern visitors. Guests from the Northeast and the Midwest sought a classically "southern" experience, one difficult to imagine without the presence of black laborers, mammy chief among them. According to Reiko Hillyer, northern tourists were particularly attracted to African Americans "in highly controlled and contained environments," where "the apparently contented and contained status of black people . . . suggested that the Old South had made a successful transition to the New."[93] Benevolent mammy, smiling as she comforted whites of all ages with a mix of sass, deference, and generosity, reassured northerners that the South was not so bad; white families looked after and even loved loyal African Americans, who in turn were content with their station in life. Happy slaves had been replaced by happy freedpeople.[94] This impression was especially enticing to Yankees as the North and the South buried memories of the divisive

Civil War. During the last years of the nineteenth century, many northern whites had grown increasingly willing to accept Jim Crow, with its characterization of southern blacks as beastly, ignorant, and most of all different, and the image of the happy mammy seemed to assure visitors from above the Mason-Dixon Line that conditions in the South were just fine.[95] For northern tourists determined to catch a glimpse of the Old South in the New, then, Liza's presence, along with her hoecakes and coffee, nourished both body and imagination.

Liza's cabin appealed to visitors' mental geography, but it also carved out a small piece of the plantation's physical landscape in an attempt to interpret the ground through the lens of a particular era. Like efforts to cast the garden and grounds as specifically colonial spaces, the cabin played on the growing mystique of a gracious and timeless Old South. The paling fence surrounding the cabin separated the structure's grounds from the larger garden, demarcating temporal as well as physical spheres. Liza's abode was a conscious effort on the part of De Renne to re-create the antebellum landscape, even if on a tiny scale and even if it ignored the larger context of the past landscape. There were no broad cotton fields beyond mammy's fence by the 1930s; no slave workforce digging marsh muck and hauling oyster shells; no humming, vibrating gin stripping seed from floss. Most important, there was no slave order to legitimate mammy's captivity within the bournes of the cabin, though the strictures of the Jim Crow South must have seemed almost as binding. What remained was a small plot of ground meant to look homey and inviting, an interpretation of a former slave abode and by extension the antebellum social order as a comforting domestic space.

While Liza provided white guests with a traditional image of the relationships between African Americans and the southern plantation landscape, some black workers also interacted with guests in a more modern capacity. Black experts on Wormsloe's grounds and plantings were available as guides for visitors. Probably workers such as Jesse Beach or other groundskeepers and farmhands, these workers knew the gardens and surrounding landscape intimately through years of laboring on the land. Garden guides served guests but did so by demonstrating their intellectual capabilities and understanding of the landscape rather than through brute labor. Virginia Cullen, a writer for a Savannah magazine, recorded a mixture of condescension and admiration for the staff when she noted that "Through [Wormsloe's] verdant aisles walk many wonderstruck visitors, some accompanied by capable darkey cicerones who furnish enlightening moments about various flowers, plants and shrubs that beautify the estate."[96] Northern journalist J. C. Cook questioned black expertise more directly when he mocked the "old colored guide" who told him,

"Yes suh, we have three kinds of ivy—English, German an'—er poison ivy."[97] Though it may seem surprising that white visitors (especially those who lived in the South) accepted black workers as experts and advisers, historian Scott Giltner has provided a possible explanation. In his examination of southern field sports, Giltner has shown that whites generally found black hunting and fishing expertise to be threatening expressions of independence but that the same abilities became acceptable and even commendable when they were employed in the service of whites.[98] Unlike mammy, black guides served whites in a nontraditional capacity, but in Wormsloe's gardens as well as in southern forests and streams, the act of service may have outweighed the implicit threat of black intellectual ability.

One visitor who was enchanted by Wormsloe's gardens and the plantation's real and imagined past was well-known North Carolina photographer Bayard Wooten. Wooten reached the height of her popularity in the 1930s, and she visited Wormsloe in 1934 to take landscape photographs as part of her collection of images of coastal plantations. The De Rennes threw an oyster roast to celebrate the photographer's arrival and gave Wooten free range of the property.[99] She took numerous pictures of Wormsloe's colonial fort but focused primarily on the landscaping, formal gardens, and masses of showy azaleas, camellias, and wisteria that edged the property's trails and drives. Following her visit, Wooten transferred these images to glass lantern slides, which could be projected onto a large screen, and used the pictures in a series of lectures she presented across the country. In her presentations, Wooten associated Wormsloe with North and South Carolina properties such as Middleton, Magnolia, Cypress, Belle Island, and Orton, portraying Wormsloe as part of the stereotypical Old South, an elegant but sleepy land forgotten by the frenetic pace of modern life but still in possession of the culture and gentility that enshrouded the plantation South. Such representations constituted precisely the image that Augusta and Wymberley Wormsloe De Renne sought to cultivate.[100]

The development of Wormsloe Gardens as a tourist attraction did not completely end agricultural operations on the property. The Wormsloe dairy continued to produce milk, cream, butter, and cheese for the local market, expanding in the late 1920s and throughout the 1930s after the De Rennes turned over operations to Foremost Dairy Products, based in Jacksonville, Florida. A large company that operated twenty-two dairies in urban areas across Florida, Alabama, North and South Carolina, and Georgia, Foremost leased Wormsloe's barns and herd in exchange for a monthly rental fee.[101] Foremost used most of Wormsloe's remaining crop and pasture land—a little over 241 acres, according to a 1920 survey—to raise feed crops and range cattle and, in keeping with the property's role as a tourist attraction, touted the operation as an example of modern agriculture.[102] Foremost managers invited Savannah residents to tour the facility and entertained groups from farther afield, such as the Potato Growers Association of Maine, whose members toured the Wormsloe gardens and the dairy operations and found themselves "pleasantly surprised at the modern, clean unique methods used in this up-to-date dairy plant and to see so many fine animals."[103]

Although the Foremost Dairy may have attracted a few tourists to Wormsloe, the rental income generated was more important to the property's economic health. Indeed, the dairy rental probably proved more profitable than did garden tourism. Prior to 1933, Foremost paid $250 per month for the rights to Wormsloe's fields, but as the depression deepened, the rental fee declined to $150 and finally to just $100 per month by 1935, a loss of income that growing ticket sales at the gardens could not make up.[104] Dairy operations ceased by the end of the decade. Photographs show that as Foremost's business declined, the company gave less effort to carefully managing Wormsloe's croplands and pastures. Trees and shrubs began to invade what was once pastureland across the avenue west of the main house, and the quarters field had shrunk from its most expansive boundaries several decades earlier.[105] This vegetative succession would continue throughout the twentieth century, as thickets and then forests gradually enclosed the plantation's arable land, transforming the open, agricultural landscape of the late nineteenth century back into woods. The general decline of dairy operations marked the last phase of large-scale agricultural operations on Wormsloe, an end to two hundred years of continuous cultivation.

By the 1930s, the Great Depression coupled with poor real estate investments placed Wymberley Wormsloe and Augusta De Renne's ownership of the historic plantation in jeopardy. Among his financial miscalculations, Wymberley had funneled roughly half a million dollars into the construction of an eight-story apartment building on Savannah's Liberty Street erected in 1920. The De Renne Apartments opened just as the city's real estate market collapsed, and the structure proved a liability rather than an income producer.[106] Following the venture's failure, Wymberley mortgaged the title to Wormsloe to secure various outstanding loans despite the insistence of his sisters, Elfrida and Audrey, that the historic plantation never leave the family. Confronted with this threat to Wormsloe's preservation as a family estate, Elfrida and her husband, Craig Barrow, who lived in Savannah, stepped in and took control of Wormsloe's mortgage. Wymberley and Augusta's continued financial difficulties led to tensions between the siblings, a situation that family historian William H. Bragg describes as characterized by "misunderstanding and misinterpretations." By 1938, the De Rennes could no longer meet their obligations to the Barrows, who took control of Wormsloe in March.[107]

The period from 1900 to 1940 witnessed a transformation of Wormsloe. The physical landscape underwent a metamorphosis of sorts. Dairying and truck farming lessened in economic importance, and in the place of these agricultural activities rose a tourist attraction that harvested dollars from visitors intent on witnessing Lowcountry history. Domestic animal numbers declined, and woods crept over agricultural lands. Wymberley Wormsloe and Augusta De Renne built new walls, paths, and gardens and planted horticultural specimens on portions of the estate, continuing and expanding on gardening traditions of the nineteenth century. These physical transformations often took place in familiar ways, however, as African American labor built the gardens, cared for the remaining agricultural tasks, and guided tourists through the grounds.

While these physical changes were important in Wormsloe's refashioning, the early decades of the twentieth century also marked a conceptual evolution of the historic plantation. For the De Renne family, the value of Wormsloe shifted from the productive power of the soil and its suitability for raising marketable commodities to its significance in family, regional, and state history. This interpretive focus on the significance of the plantation as a cultural/historical monument continued nineteenth-century understandings of the landscape but took this emphasis on the value of the estate as a legacy to a new level. Wormsloe's expanding gardens and manicured grounds defined pleasure and recreation as the site's key values, and an undergirding sense of the property's historic value served as a powerful justification for the family's love of the plantation. This shift in thinking reflected not just the De Rennes' attachment to a particular piece of ground but also broader trends. As the importance of agriculture lessened across the Lowcountry, property owners sought new justifications and economic solutions for keeping historic plantations intact. The increasing importance of tourism in Savannah and the sea islands emphasized both natural beauty and history, and economic growth along these lines encouraged struggling property owners to open their estates to a curious public. This emphasis on history and nature in a tourist setting would continue to define Wormsloe throughout the remainder of the twentieth century. Agriculture passed slowly from the old plantation after almost two centuries during which black and white hands had worked the land. With the opening of Wormsloe Gardens and the closure of dairy operations, the 1930s marked the end of an epoch on Wormsloe.

These interpretive efforts did as much to define the plantation's cultural and natural landscapes as had the agricultural labors and vernacular architecture of the preceding centuries. As much as the property's history and beauty warranted preservation, these early-twentieth-century activities defined Wormsloe as a space worthy of tourism. John Sears has argued as much in his examination of early American tourist attractions, writing that "natural phenomena, impressive as they may be, are not productions of culture in the sense that cathedrals are. They become the products of a culture only when transformed by human activities such as painting them, describing them, and building hotels near them."[108] This process held true on Wormsloe: The beauties of the maritime forest and the salt marsh appealed to visitors, but the De Renne family's efforts to portray the plantation as a place where both nature and history mattered shaped the estate's path. From at least the mid-nineteenth century, the past was always on the minds of Wormsloe's owners, but by the end of the Great Depression, Wormsloe had become a landscape all but defined by its history.

CHAPTER FIVE

From Plantation to Park

Wormsloe since 1938

IN THE MID-1970S, Noble Jones's plantation became a state historic site, owned and preserved by the people of Georgia. The state acquired the historic property as a consequence of a belief in the value of its rich history, especially in connection with the colonial era. Officials also appreciated the natural resources and green space that the estate offered in the midst of the rapidly developing coast. The creation of a state historic site was the culmination of family preservation efforts, marking Georgia's declaration that Wormsloe's history and environment were significant enough to warrant government management. Despite this fundamental shift, the shake-ups of the late twentieth century did little to change Wormsloe managers' beliefs concerning the landscape and its past.

Wormsloe's preservation worked to solidify historical interpretations of the site and concurrent interpretations of the Isle of Hope landscape established over the previous decades. Craig and Elfrida Barrow echoed Wymberley Wormsloe and Augusta De Renne's modeling of the plantation landscape on real and imagined pasts; when entertaining guests or the occasional tour group, the Barrows also emphasized the plantation's colonial history as the site's most important epoch. The creation of Wormsloe State Historic Site only solidified these interpretations. Park officials prized Wormsloe for its early history and they drew up interpretive documents and designed programs focused on Noble Jones's era. Park guests were presented with signs and artifacts from the colonial period, and the staff portrayed the plantation's woods and marshes as largely untouched remnants of the world that greeted the eighteenth-century settlers. Together, the family and the state created a Wormsloe myth that was rooted in real but select elements of the plantation's past. The state acquisition and management of Wormsloe took place within the context of a national and local environmental movement and the historical commemorations of the late 1960s and early 1970s and reflected these public discourses. Academic and popular concern regarding the state of Georgia's coastal lands encouraged conservation of the estate, as did excitement about the upcoming bicentennial

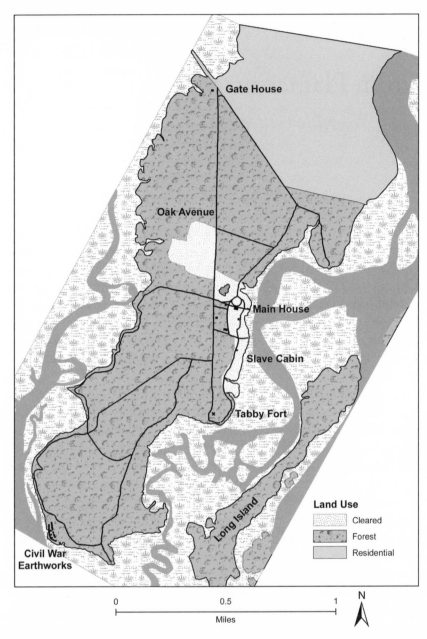

Wormsloe 1960. Map by Dr. Thomas R. Jordan, Center for Remote Sensing and Mapping Science, Department of Geography, University of Georgia, Athens, Georgia.

of the American Revolution. The Wormsloe that state officials envisioned was thus the seat of one of Georgia's founding fathers and a piece of relatively undisturbed coastal real estate. Wormsloe was one expression of a Lowcountry regionalism that blended environmental and historic preservation into a distinctive sense of place.

These interpretations of Wormsloe's history and landscape, while not completely accurate, may have saved the plantation from further development; neighboring coastal tracts fell under the bulldozer blade, while Wormsloe survives relatively undeveloped to this day. But this colonial emphasis also ensured that the site would survive in a particular form that obfuscated much of the plantation's long history. After the De Rennes designated Wormsloe a colonial site, the Barrows and the Georgia Department of Natural Resources, which managed the park, were unlikely to change course and emphasize other elements of the property's past. The forested landscape that evoked the initial years of white settlement held little room for stories of sea island cotton agriculture, memories of slavery, the struggles of emancipation, or extensive white and black usage of the marsh. These long-enduring human engagements with the Lowcountry environment were pushed into the interpretive background when they were not omitted completely.

Static interpretations of Wormsloe's history and environment could not prevent ongoing cultural and environmental change, however. Like much of the American South, the world around the old plantation was rapidly changing in the mid-twentieth century. Savannah continued to expand until the suburbs surrounding the Isle of Hope stretched almost unbroken across the solid ground. New piers projected into the estuarial marsh, as likely to provide berths for pleasure craft as for shrimp and crab boats. A new industry, paper manufacturing, led to loblolly pine plantations replacing great swaths of Georgia's surviving coastal forests, and the related factories polluted Savannah's water and air. And a small insect, the southern pine beetle, attacked Wormsloe's conifers, leading to the largest timbering episode in the plantation's long history. State officials' response to the southern pine beetle infestation again brought old relationships between human and insect to the forefront as logging operations contributed to a formidable mosquito outbreak on the Isle of Hope. These events served as a reminder that whatever the land's ownership status or interpretive framework, the plantation on the southern end of the Isle of Hope was still firmly rooted in the Lowcountry environment. Change was a constant on the old plantation, but the form of that change remained in part a product of mosquitoes, tides, hurricanes, and pine beetles.

Twentieth-century Wormsloe demonstrated both the power of the mind and the power of the natural world. As Wormsloe's stewards worked to interpret the site's past, they also created a specific image of the Lowcountry environment. The erasure of large portions of the plantation's past through omission also removed generations of land use from the public purview and gradually from public and family understandings of the landscape. These interpretive decisions, whether intentional or inadvertent, made preservation and management of Wormsloe's natural and cultural resources a challenging task, a reality that state officials continue to face in the early twenty-first century.

Although they came to Wormsloe through Wymberley Wormsloe and Augusta De Renne's financial misfortune, Craig and Elfrida Barrow were the plantation's most active owners since the days of George W. Jones. Wormsloe's new masters moved into the manor house in 1938. The Barrows made some immediate changes to the plantation's appearance, remodeling the historic plantation house and stripping away much of the Victorian trappings that Wymberley J. De Renne had commissioned in the 1890s. Like Wymberley Wormsloe and Augusta's gardening efforts, this remodeling emphasized—or interpreted—the property's history, whether or not the Barrows intended such an impression. The new facade sported simple lines evocative of the antebellum structure, but the Barrows built a substantial, two-story columned porch that conjured up images of a gracious Old South. Gone were the attached ornate pavilion, stair tower, lacy woodwork, and massive servants' wing. The Barrows also made similar architectural alterations to the estate's dependencies. Although the resulting structure was not a faithful re-creation of the 1850s manse—the antebellum house had a lower, simpler porch—this remodeling brought the historic building closer to its antebellum appearance than it had been since George W. Jones's death.[1]

The house remodeling and the Barrows' continued interest in Wormsloe's historic landscape reflected the couple's attraction to Georgia history in general, especially the state's colonial past. Like her father and grandfather before her, Elfrida was an active member of the Georgia Historical Society. She also served as president of the Georgia Society of Colonial Dames during the 1930s, and she was a founding member of the Savannah Historical Research Association, an organization that celebrated local history.[2] Membership in the Colonial Dames, organized in 1894, required that Elfrida express an interest not only in Georgia's colonial history but also in her own early lineage. The society limited membership to the descendants of colonial officials, military officers, and "Landed Proprietors" who had received Crown grants of at least "five hundred acres in one tract."[3] In Noble and Noble Wimberly Jones, Elfrida had at least two ancestors who met all three requirements. Drawing on these interests and a long family tradition of collecting and recording state history, Elfrida was an amateur historian as well as a poet. Her works dealt primarily with Georgia's early years. She would go on to support the publication of a number of colonial texts under the auspices of the Wormsloe Foundation, a nonprofit formed following World War II.[4] Elfrida was not alone in her interest in the past: Craig Barrow served as the "governor" of the Society of Colonial Wars in the State of Georgia, the male equivalent of the Society of Colonial Dames.[5] As it had for decades, Wormsloe served as both a home to and an inspiration for these intellectual activities.

While the Barrows continued to remake and preserve Wormsloe in selective ways, the old plantation largely escaped one of the most transformative trends of the midcentury Georgia Lowcountry. From the 1940s forward, the pulp-paper industry and cooperating private landowners planted vast swaths of the state's coastal plain in pine plantations. The Savannah area in particular served as a model for the nascent southern pine industry. By 1947, the Union Bag plant just west of Savannah employed forty-two hundred workers in transforming coastal pines into kraft (brown) paper for use in packaging and cardboard products. The company also set about purchasing local tracts on which to plant more pines and encouraged landowners to do the same. The resulting pine plantations were the start of the vast monocultural forests that cover much of the southeastern coastal plain today. These "forests" were in essence silvicultural fields, where tree farmers planted slash or loblolly pines— species that grew rapidly in the region's sandy soils—in tight rows that shaded out competing understory plants. The resulting stands made poor habitat for most plant and animal species but produced tremendous quantities of wood. In 1941, as a part of these pine-procurement efforts, Union Bag purchased a portion of Skidaway Island across the river from Wormsloe and established an extensive loblolly plantation.[6]

There are strong indications that the Barrows at least considered transforming their property into a commercial pine plantation after moving to Wormsloe. During the mid-1930s, the Barrows and De Rennes had experimented with slash pines on the plantation. And Craig Barrow corresponded with officials from the Georgia Department of Forestry, which, in its role as a timber industry supporter, billed its agency as the "Pine Kindergarten of the South." Over the following decade, Barrow ordered fire signs, requested instructional literature, and discussed his property's forestry potential.[7] The Barrows' forestry activities extended beyond their relationships with state agencies. In 1941, an official of the Forest Farmers Association Cooperative tried to enlist the Barrows in the organization, based in Valdosta, Georgia. The cooperative sought conservation payments under the Agricultural Adjustment Act, loans for timber plantations at low agricultural rates, and reduced federal oversight of timber lands. The Barrows eventually declined to join and by the mid-1940s seem to have lost interest in making Wormsloe a pine plantation.[8] It is unclear if the family's rejection of industrial forestry resulted from an awareness of the paper industry's growing impact on the Lowcountry environment in the form of timbering and pollution or from some other reason, such as Craig's 1945 death.

Wormsloe's forests, though heavily used since the colonial era, remained a mixture of pines, live oaks, palmettos, hickories, and assorted understory species. A timber survey taken at some point during the first decades of the twentieth century, perhaps as the family considered cutting trees in preparation for planting pines, revealed that more than half of the estate was still forested. Pine timber, likely a mixture of original and secondary growth, covered an estimated 460 acres of the property. The survey included only longleaf and shortleaf pine stands; an additional but undocumented portion of Wormsloe was covered in live oak hammock and other hardwood stands. By 1945, roughly 800 acres of Noble Jones's old estate was forested. The pine woods were composed of a mix of small trees (ten inches or less in diameter) and mature trees more than two feet in diameter. Though the surveyor made no comments on the processes that had affected plantation forest composition, these varied tree measurements suggest a forest that had been subject to some timber cutting as well as natural forces of disturbance, including hurricanes and lightning storms. All told, the surveyor estimated that Wormsloe's forest contained 2.5 million board feet of pine timber. This abundant stand was a substantial economic resource that the family chose not to fully exploit.[9] If anything, woods were quickly reclaiming plantation land that had previously been devoted to row crops and pasture. An aerial photograph taken sometime around World War II reveals saplings and shrubs colonizing land used to feed dairy cows only a few years earlier.[10]

Craig and Elfrida Barrow closed Wormsloe Gardens to the public once they assumed control of the plantation, but the property continued to draw visitors during and after World War II. Like Wormsloe Gardens under Wymberley Wormsloe and Augusta De Renne, Elfrida Barrow's special events and tours emphasized a particular plantation history and landscape.[11] Elfrida remained most interested in the property's colonial era. A flyer she printed to give to occasional tour groups touted Noble Jones and his contributions to early Georgia and described the current Wormsloe landscape as a relatively untouched extension of the eighteenth-century coastal environment: "Although at first the raising of silk-worms was carried on to a certain extent, as elsewhere in the colony, this attempt was soon abandoned, and little of the estate was ever placed under cultivation afterwards. Therefore, with the exception of the enhancement which age and the work of successive generations have lent to its gardens and avenues, Wormsloe is much the same today as it was two centuries ago."[12] This pamphlet, along with Elfrida's tours, suggested that the De Rennes' and Barrows' primary role had been as preservers of a plantation and a legacy rather than as active agents in shaping Wormsloe's past and present. This interpretation emphasized the importance of Noble Jones's plantation but defined subsequent generations as "enhancers" rather than creators.

Visiting Elfrida Barrow's Wormsloe was much less formal than touring Wormsloe Gardens. She opened her home and gardens to friends and special groups and for fund-raising purposes but did not permit the general public to enter Wormsloe. The plantation reverted to a place of family leisure and entertainment, much as it had under the control of Elfrida's father, although the old estate maintained a much greater presence in the public awareness thanks to its years as a tourist attraction. The landscape served at once as a retreat and a showpiece. Elfrida often hosted historians, poets, and novelists, including such southern luminaries as Allen Tate and Andrew Lytle. She also allowed tours by or for the benefit of such groups as the Audubon Society, the Woman's Auxiliary of Christ Episcopal Church, and Savannah's Juliette Gordon Low Birthplace, and she opened her home on occasion to college groups from across the state. These special groups explored the plantation's gardens, roamed the colonial ruins, and soaked up the Lowcountry environment. These and similar tours and meetings kept Wormsloe in the Savannah newspapers and garnered Barrow a reputation as one of the area's most gracious hostesses.[13]

Barrow might have expected visitors from Savannah and the surrounding Lowcountry to appreciate Wormsloe as a colonial space, but guests from much greater distances also came away from the plantation with a sense that it was a preserved cameo of southern history. In 1964, author Irving Fineman, educated at Harvard and the Massachusetts Institute of Technology, described Wormsloe as a piece "of the antebellum world more than a century ago . . . which Mrs. Barrow has devotedly preserved for us."[14] Although Fineman did not emphasize the property's colonial history per se, he accepted Barrow's presentation of Wormsloe as a place valuable for its early history rather than its post–Civil War activities or its evolution as an estate. Fineman's assessment missed a great deal of history on the property, but it did capture an important element of Barrow's Wormsloe—the idea that the plantation as witnessed by guests was a place created by preservation. Without acknowledging the creative aspect of the act of preservation, his statement alludes to the fact that preservation was itself a process—in this case, quite a vigorous one.

These interpretations of Wormsloe as a colonial site trapped in amber, unchanged since Noble Jones set foot on Georgia soil, worked to obscure or eliminate generations of labor on the land. This erasure of the postcolonial past was not an intentional slight of events since 1776—labeling the plantation as one of Georgia's oldest Euro-American sites made for good press—but it did simplify the land's cultural and natural histories in ways that gave little credit to certain people and events for the contemporary face of the land. The story line of a re-created colonial Wormsloe had little room for slaves working in sea island cotton fields or harvesting the marsh's bounty, offered no space for complicated descriptions of an ever-evolving agricultural economy, and allowed no mention of land that had seen forests come and go and come again over more than two centuries. Thus the conception of Wormsloe as Noble Jones's estate was a satisfying idea for family attempts to identify the property as a special and significant place but did little to explain how or why the plantation landscape looked the way that it did in the mid-twentieth century. These omissions mattered because Wormsloe was increasingly being treated as a preserved landscape: As at most preservation sites before the midcentury rise of social history, Wormsloe's interpreters were most interested in well-known figures and eras deemed historically significant.

By the second half of the twentieth century, Savannah's urban growth and the popularity of the coast as a recreational ground posed a new challenge to Wormsloe. Rising land values led to a steady increase in the historic plantation's property taxes, testing Elfrida Barrow's ability to maintain the estate. In 1951, Barrow created the Wormsloe Foundation, a nonprofit entity organized to preserve Georgia history and fund regional publications. Ten years later, she ceded control over 750 acres of Wormsloe to the foundation to avoid the ever-increasing tax burden.[15] Foundation lands were open to the public by appointment, and archeologists, historians, and other scholars could use the plantation's facilities for academic research. In some respects, the Wormsloe Foundation provided a formal framework for the sort of efforts that had long taken place in the estate's library and gardens. The foundation supported various scholarly endeavors that further tied the plantation to colonial history. The vast majority of the publications that the foundation funded through a relationship with the University of Georgia Press were reprints of colonial documents or accounts of the revolution. The first book in the Wormsloe Foundation series was noted historian E. Merton Coulter's *Wormsloe: Two Centuries of a Georgia Family* (1955), a biography of Noble, Noble Wimberly, and George Jones.[16]

The foundation's most ambitious project took place in 1968, when archeologist William Kelso surveyed and explored the ruins of Noble Jones's fortified house. Kelso went on to become the director of archeological work at

Virginia's Jamestown and Monticello, home of Thomas Jefferson. On the Isle of Hope, Kelso and a team of researchers uncovered the outlines of the original tabby fort, unearthed and cataloged hundreds of colonial artifacts, and created a rendering of the complete structure as it likely appeared in the mid-eighteenth century. Kelso published his findings in the Wormsloe Foundation's series as *Captain Jones's Wormslow* (1979). These efforts solidified Wormsloe's significance in early Georgia history but, like so many interpretations of the site, failed to elaborate on the land's nineteenth- and twentieth-century history. Kelso ended his description of plantation history at 1820.[17] Kelso's emphasis on the discovery and preservation of Wormsloe's colonial history was understandable in light of growing local and national interest in the upcoming bicentennial of the American Revolution, a trend of which archeologists were fully aware. As Kelso was writing his report on Wormsloe's eighteenth-century significance, the Society for American Archeology released a booklet for primary educators and their students touting archeology as the best discipline for exploring and interpreting colonial and revolutionary America. *Above Ground Archeology* encouraged students to engage in basic archeology and claimed that "archeology can be a path extending from the present toward 1776."[18] Kelso's work seemed in part a scholarly expression of popular demand.

Barrow's creation of the Wormsloe Foundation as a solution to the property's tax burdens proved a temporary fix. Within a few years of the organization's founding, Chatham County challenged the Wormsloe Foundation's nonprofit status, arguing that it was in reality a tax shelter for the Barrow family and that the arrangement did little to ensure the long-term preservation of the property. County attorneys claimed that under the current terms of the nonprofit, the family could still sell the land to developers if the foundation were dissolved. In such a case, Chatham would be out a good deal of tax revenue, and one of the coast's most valuable historic sites and green spaces would be lost forever. The Barrows countered that they received no profit from foundation lands, that the whole of the estate was available for public use upon request, and that they were actively preserving the property's historic and natural resources. Following a protracted lawsuit that ultimately reached the Georgia Supreme Court, the county won. The court ordered the Barrows to resume payment of the property's taxes in 1972. By that time the family owed a quarter of a million dollars in back taxes and fines, a sum that was increasing at a rate of fifteen thousand dollars per year.[19] Part of the county's case against the foundation rested on the importance of preserving Wormsloe's history and environment from development, but Chatham's victory placed the survival of the plantation as a single, unified property in question.

The Barrows' interpretation of Wormsloe as a colonial site seemed well entrenched, but following the Georgia Supreme Court's ruling, the plantation's future was very much in limbo. Elfrida Barrow had died in 1970, and her son, Craig Jr., and his wife, Laura, sought a solution that would keep the historic landscape intact while reducing its financial burden. In late 1972, Craig approached the Nature Conservancy about donating the land to Georgia for a new state park. It is unclear why Barrow took this indirect approach, though it seems likely that he retained hard feelings toward the state in the wake of the lawsuit and thus used the Nature Conservancy as an intermediary. State officials believed the site had tremendous historic and natural value as a park, and Governor Jimmy Carter supported the purchase because the site was "rich in history and beauty."[20] With the Nature Conservancy steering the negotiations, on December 31, 1972, the state's Department of Natural Resources (DNR) formally acquired 750 acres of Wormsloe plantation in exchange for a payment of $250,000 to the Nature Conservancy and the assumption of all outstanding tax bills and liens attached to the property.[21]

The terms of the donation reflected Craig Barrow Jr.'s worry that state control might lead to the creation of a tawdry "tourist attraction."[22] This concern likely stemmed from the tensions between Wymberley Wormsloe De Renne and Elfrida Barrow regarding the commercialism of Wormsloe Gardens in the late 1930s. State officials worked to assuage the Barrows' concerns while justifying their decision to acquire the property for the public. The DNR promised that the property was "to be held in perpetuity for the general public as an historical and ecological nature preserve for scientific, educational and esthetic purposes."[23] The DNR stressed that Wormsloe was important as both a cradle of Georgia history and as a slice of the coastal environment. Although officials considered the colonial period the most significant historical era in Wormsloe's history, their valuation of the plantation's natural environment was much less cogent. The dual-purpose nature of the property would provide park officials with management challenges over the following decades. Although the Barrow family retained about eighty acres of the historic plantation—including the big house, farmyard, and the land around the old slave village—the state's acquisition ended the family's control over the bulk of the land after almost a quarter of a millennium of stewardship.

One of the ironies of government preservation is that it often brings about great change. Such was the case on Wormsloe. The state's first actions were to make practical alterations to the plantation's infrastructure that would make the park more accessible to the public. Along these lines, the DNR commissioned a suitability report that examined the peninsula's soils, hydrology, and biota and made recommendations on park design and layout. This report recommended that the DNR build an interpretive museum near the historic tabby fort, a superintendent's house and maintenance facility in the forest on the western edge of the site, a parking lot, and nature trails traversing the park's woodlands. Connecting all of these facilities was a network of new roads cut across second-growth forests and historic fields. The DNR followed all of these suggestions, resulting in the most intensive restructuring of Wormsloe since George W. Jones's agricultural improvement campaign of the 1850s.[24] As had previously been the case, Wormsloe was remade to conserve the past.

Although state acquisition led to a remodeled physical landscape, the change in land tenure did not necessarily mean that established understandings of the plantation would begin anew. After the state assumed control of the bulk of Wormsloe, DNR officials worked to determine exactly how they would manage the landscape and present it to the public. Early on, management opted for a two-pronged interpretive approach, combining conservation of the property's natural environment with selected interpretations of its cultural past. Even during the months preceding acquisition, the DNR viewed the plantation as a valuable natural site where visitors could enjoy the coastal environment as a retreat from the surrounding city. The site's recreational potential also meshed nicely with the new Skidaway Island State Park just across the river. DNR planning and development director Chuck Parrish stressed Wormsloe's biological value, declaring that the estate's "virgin or climax forest, [and] natural game and plant habitats" warranted its preservation in perpetuity.[25] Wormsloe became a useful green space and biological refuge amid Savannah's suburbs. In this role, the property served the public and Lowcountry wildlife much as it had generations of the Jones/De Renne/Barrow family: as an escape.

Parrish's description of Wormsloe's ecosystems ignored a great deal of cultural land use and avoided discussions of ongoing environmental change. The lands surrounding Wormsloe were undergoing rapid transition in the early 1970s, a trend that contributed to Georgia officials' eagerness to acquire and preserve the historic plantation. Savannah's suburban growth continued to gobble up open land west and north of the property; by 1970, the city essentially stretched unbroken from the downtown squares to the Isle of Hope. East of the site, the new Skidaway Island State Park was joined by the Skidaway Institute of Oceanography, a research and educational station affiliated with the University System of Georgia. The island also faced more commercial uses, as the Branigar Corporation worked to develop part of its Skidaway forestland as a resort modeled on South Carolina's Hilton Head, complete with an eighteen-hole golf course designed by Arnold Palmer. The Branigar Corporation was a branch of Union Camp (the descendant of Union Bag and Paper), which in 1941 had purchased a substantial tract of land on the island to raise pines for kraft paper production.[26] In 1973, Governor Carter declared that

Wormsloe's transfer to the DNR marked a victory in the struggle against "the bulldozer of misguided progress [that] is awaiting the signal to destroy your heritage and mine."[27]

Park visitors experienced the site's biology and history through an interpretive framework crafted by DNR managers but firmly rooted in the plantation's past interpretation. In many ways, the interpretive focus for the nascent park reflected the De Rennes' and Barrows' conceptualization of the landscape as it had evolved over the decades following the Civil War. In fact, during the first months following the state's acquisition of the estate, new park superintendent Ralph Reed and DNR planners downplayed the importance of the site's antebellum history. They argued that Wormsloe had never served as "a working plantation in the traditional sense" and that this lack of intense cultivation was beneficial, permitting the land's colonial features to survive more completely than at similar Georgia sites.[28] The meaning of the word *traditional* here remained unclear. If park officials meant that the Joneses had not relied on Wormsloe's fields and slaves for their primary source of income, then the assessment had merit. If, instead, Reed meant that plantation agriculture had not existed on Wormsloe in any significant fashion, the term was deceptive at best. Whereas family tales of Wormsloe had slighted the cotton plantation period, the state's early interpretation completely erased nineteenth-century agricultural efforts. A 1978 interpretive site plan followed this lead, prioritizing Wormsloe's cultural and natural history in setting the agenda for how visitors would encounter and experience the plantation: Wormsloe's primary purpose was "the interpretation of the Development of the English colony, 1733–1775 (Political), and the American Revolution 1775–1783, particularly Politics and Diplomacy."[29]

This emphasis was understandable in light of broader national events as well. Like archeologists working in the early 1970s, site managers wanted to tap into public excitement about the Bicentennial, and this desire dovetailed nicely with established portrayals of the plantation. Kelso's recent archeological investigation, which focused on Wormsloe as a colonial/military site, provided the DNR with a source for this interpretation.[30] The interpretive plan argued that Wormsloe should be managed and presented to visitors in the same manner as other southeastern colonial/military sites, such as Castillo de San Marcos in Florida and Georgia's Fort Frederica and Fort King George. Like these popular attractions, the new park would focus its interpretive displays on and guide visitor traffic to Wormsloe's colonial sites, especially locations of military interest. The prospectus went on to give a thumbnail sketch of the plantation's history through the reduction of the tabby fort in the 1820s and suggested that Civil War activities on the Isle of Hope might prove of interest to tourists, but the authors reiterated that the era of Noble Jones was the most significant of the site's past epochs. Park interpreters believed that Wormsloe's value lay in its role as a seat of one of Georgia's founding fathers.[31]

An interpretation of Wormsloe's environment as a relatively undisturbed stretch of coastline accompanied this familiar portrayal of Wormsloe's past. Wormsloe State Historic Site echoed Wormsloe Gardens, publishing literature and preparing interpretive guidelines that suggested that the marsh and forest surrounding the fort ruins were ancient and largely untouched. This interpretation was all but inevitable based on the property's historic tourism and the DNR's interpretive activities at other state-owned sites of colonial activity. The De Rennes and Barrows had already developed pamphlets, walkways, talks, and landscaping that emphasized the colonial era and associated landscapes, an intellectual and physical framework that DNR interpreters would have been hard-pressed to ignore. State historic sites, like private tourist attractions, were designed to draw visitors, and in Savannah and the adjacent Lowcountry, colonial history sold tickets.

Among the park's managers, this popular perception of a pristine Wormsloe coexisted uneasily with an understanding that the Isle of Hope was hardly a stable, climax environment. Park managers knew that people had long lived and worked on the land—this history was in fact part of the reason the state had acquired Wormsloe—yet found the power of past interpretations of the surrounding environment difficult to overcome. The 1978 master interpretive plan acknowledged that areas of the park had experienced a great deal of human activity. The document pointed to the necessity of selective tree thinning, the maintenance of fruit and nut trees planted by earlier plantation residents, and the management of exotic and invasive plants that coexisted with native species. Although they went unmentioned in the plan, environmental disturbances stemming from natural sources also made the existence of an untouched forest and marsh, stable since the Trustees landed in 1733, an illusion.[32]

The DNR's efforts to downplay the property's historic land use were in keeping with contemporary national park policy and perhaps drew on management of these federal lands for inspiration. An influential National Park Service internal document, the 1963 Leopold Report (officially titled "Wildlife Management in the National Parks") had set the national parks on a course that emphasized "the condition that prevailed [at a given site] when the area was first visited by the white man." The report's authors believed that preserved public land "should represent a vignette of primitive America."[33] In the wild backcountry of Yosemite or Yellowstone, this policy meant prohibiting roads, allowing occasional wildfires, and removing vestiges of ranching, small-scale farming, and in many cases Native American use. On Wormsloe,

DNR officials sought to do much the same thing by following the De Renne/Barrow interpretive theme. Like the private landowners who preceded them, park management emphasized the contact-era features of Wormsloe's landscape while working to erase or diminish the estate's more recent history.

The DNR's interest in Wormsloe as a piece of "pristine" coastal nature was also in part a product of scholarly, public, and political interest in America's southeastern coastline in the late 1960s and early 1970s. Throughout the second half of the twentieth century, the estuarial environment of the Georgia coast was the research ground of one the nation's most influential ecologists, Eugene P. Odum. Odum was a professor at the University of Georgia who conducted much of his formative research at the university's Marine Institute (originally named the Marine Biological Laboratory) on Sapelo Island. While at Sapelo, Odum popularized the concept of the ecosystem. With the help of his brother, Howard, also an ecologist, Eugene Odum published the first textbook in the field, *Fundamentals of Ecology*, in 1953.[34] Odum's book went through four editions, appeared in thirteen languages, and sold more than forty thousand copies annually by the early 1970s.[35] Early in his study of coastal ecosystems, Odum became convinced that the marsh was "a remarkable energy-absorbing natural system whose heart was the pumping action of the tides," and he devoted his work to providing "the basis for man to design with, rather than against, nature on this remarkable sea coast."[36] By the early 1970s, Odum believed that the "uses and abuses of [the estuarial coast] by man are becoming so critical that it is important that the unique features of estuaries become widely understood." To this end, he included an entire chapter on estuarine ecology in the third edition of *Fundamentals of Ecology*.[37]

Two of Odum's colleagues at the Marine Institute would popularize the ecological value of and threats to America's coastal marshlands. John and Mildred Teal worked with Odum on Sapelo in the mid-1950s to calculate energy flow in the marsh; their work treated the marsh ecosystem as a unified entity working in a cooperative equilibrium. In 1946, the couple wrote *Portrait of an Island*, a book intended for a general audience that explained the ecological functioning and significance of Georgia's salt marsh.[38] Five years later, the Teals released *Life and Death of the Salt Marsh*, an impassioned plea for Americans to recognize the importance of salt marshes and the dangers of pollution and overdevelopment. *Life and Death of the Salt Marsh* tapped into a rising public environmentalism centered on concerns about public health and well-being, catalyzed to no small extent by Rachel Carson's enormously influential 1962 book, *Silent Spring*. Echoing Odum, the Teals identified eastern America's salt marshes as "unusually productive places" and outlined the challenges posed by modern pesticides (like Carson, they were especially troubled by the effects of

DDT on wildlife), shoreline development, garbage, the heavy metals released by an industrial society, and reclamation. Like *Silent Spring*, *Life and Death of the Salt Marsh* linked the health of natural spaces to the health of human bodies, though this message was more implicit in the Teals' text than in Carson's book.[39] *Life and Death of the Salt Marsh* garnered popular acclaim and went through multiple editions.

The Teals' books and Odum's research, along with a debate between environmentalists and developers, helped bring about state and then federal support for coastal conservation in the early 1970s. Plans for a phosphate mine that would have devastated twelve thousand acres of salt marsh near Savannah galvanized popular conservation sentiment throughout coastal Georgia beginning in 1967. Odum sided with mine opponents, using a 1969 article in *Life* magazine to lay out his belief that legislation ensuring coastal preservation was vital. Odum's environmental advocacy proved critical to the mine's defeat and Georgia's creation of innovative coastal environmental legislation. In 1970, the state legislature passed the Coastal Marshlands Protection Act, which established a state agency to oversee development of Georgia's wetlands.[40] Two years later, the federal government followed Georgia when Congress passed the Coastal Zone Management Act (CZMA), which acknowledged the fragile nature of the nation's coastlines and pledged federal funds to restoring and preserving important stretches of shoreline. The CZMA pointed to a number of problems plaguing coasts from Georgia to the Great Lakes, including rapid and poorly planned residential and commercial development, flooding, declining fisheries, the loss of recreational space, decreasing biodiversity, and a general deterioration of water quality, among others. Many of these issues were extremely relevant to the greater Savannah area. The CZMA made clear Congress's determination to conserve areas "rich in a variety of natural, commercial, recreational, ecological, industrial, and esthetic resources of immediate and potential value to the present and future well-being of the Nation."[41] Although the Georgia DNR did not draw on federal funds to acquire Wormsloe, the agency's portrayal of Wormsloe as a biological and recreational refuge meshed nicely with several of the CZMA's emphases.

The conflict in Wormsloe's interpretive plans between the site as a pristine environment and the site as a historical and agricultural landscape reflected an emerging divide in contemporary ecology. Beginning with an influential 1973 article by William H. Drury and Ian C. T. Nisbet, a group of scientists challenged existing thinking concerning ecosystem ecology. Following in the footsteps of Frederic Clements, the most heralded ecologist of the early twentieth century, Odum had played an influential role in defining ecology in terms of equilibrium. In this paradigm, plant succession led to increasing species diversity and eventually to mature ecosystems that functioned in basic balance absent human action, which was defined as a disturbing or destructive intrusion.[42] Drury and Nisbet challenged the foundation of Odum's theory, arguing that there was no such thing as a cooperative ecosystem, no tendency toward greater diversity over time, and no equilibrium. Instead, they claimed that disturbance kept ecosystems in constant flux: Fire, drought, wind, and invasive plants and animals altered relationships among species, all of which sought every possible advantage. In the words of historian Donald Worster, this new ecology described a given habitat as "lots of individual species, each doing its thing, but . . . no emergent collectivity, nor any strategy to achieve one."[43] The world according to this new theory of individualistic or disturbance ecology was "a nature that has been undergoing profound and constant change for as far back as we can look."[44] By the late twentieth century, disturbance ecology was winning the debate over ecosystem ecology, but the victory was still not complete.[45] Wormsloe's interpretive planning made no direct reference to the upheavals in ecology, but whether cognizant of the changing of the scientific guard or not, the DNR's management and its plans reflected contemporary debates regarding the definition of the environment. The site's interpreters found themselves struggling to reconcile Wormsloe's long history of natural and human disturbance with their vision of a stable (and preserved) colonial environment.

The emphasis on the value of Wormsloe's natural resources also drew on a growing state and local environmentalism that defined the Lowcountry as a unique and valuable place. Coastal environmentalists had a powerful ally in Carter, who assumed Georgia's governorship in 1970. As president beginning in 1977, Carter would reveal his conservationist sentiment: He blocked federal dam projects, pushed for wilderness preservation in Alaska, touted programs to conserve energy and reduce pollution, and created the Superfund program to clean up the nation's most despoiled sites. The Alaska Lands Act of 1980 alone "more than doubled the size of America's national parks and wildlife refuges and almost tripled the amount of U.S. land designated as wilderness."[46] Carter's actions as Georgia's governor presaged his national agenda. In the statehouse, Carter often turned his full attention to conservation issues. He called in experts, including Eugene Odum, for advice on improving efficiency and reducing pollution. Even as Carter streamlined and reduced most state agencies, he oversaw the expansion of the DNR, increasing its budget by almost 25 percent and making the agency "the most successful department in his reorganized state government."[47] In 1972, he created the Georgia Heritage Trust Commission, which identified and purchased areas of historic and natural significance. Carter was particularly enamored with the sea islands and marshlands, writing to a friend on Sapelo, "I love the Georgia coast."[48] He affirmed his belief in the importance of the coast's cultural and environmental heritage when he visited Wormsloe in 1972. Carter came away from his tour of the property convinced that Wormsloe was well worth preserving, and he declared the landscape a reminder of the importance of the region's human history and the value of its natural resources for future generations.[49]

As was the case in much of the nation during the second half of the twentieth century, concerns about resource shortages, health, quality of life, and economic conditions stimulated regional environmentalism along the southeastern U.S. coast. Air and water pollution were the most galvanizing environmental concerns of Savannah-area residents during the late 1960s and early 1970s. Dirty rivers, smoke, and industrial stenches not only affected health and quality of life but also drove away tourists. Pollution concerns thus brought together environmental activists with Chamber of Commerce members. Savannah had its fair share of industrial polluters by the early 1970s. Union Camp and Continental Can operated paper mills that discharged oxygen-consuming solids into the Savannah River and smoke into the air, fouling local breezes and choking oyster beds and fish spawning grounds. American Cyanamide's facility for producing titanium dioxide released "six million gallons of [acid-contaminated] waste water to the Savannah every day."[50] The Savannah River Plant, a South Carolina nuclear facility upstream from Savannah, also relied heavily on river water and returned water used to cool radioactive materials to the stream, creating various concerns.[51]

Despoiled water and air prompted complaints and action from a wide range of Lowcountry residents. Officials with the U.S. Coast Guard and the Georgia Water Quality Control Board noted the poor state of the Savannah River, and Eugene Odum and other experts described the dangers of water pollution for coastal ecosystems. A group of activists under the auspices of environmental crusader and consumer advocate Ralph Nader visited the city and in 1971 published a scathing indictment of the industrial "Water Lords" who were polluting the Lowcountry.[52] Less prominent local residents also worried about pollution. In 1971, Homer Ray, a lifelong Savannah citizen, confided to a reporter that the river had become the site of "dump and oil and garbage, that's all. . . . It's a shame, just a damned shame."[53] Likewise, fisherman Arthur Ruffin declared pollution a concern of all Lowcountry residents: The polluted water "stinks and it's dirty and it gets on my trout lines and in my fish traps and it costs me a heap of money." The river used to look "pretty good, smelled good, and was chock full of all kinds of fishes. . . . Now the cows got more sense than to drink from that stinkin' river."[54]

Opposition to industrial growth and the accompanying pollution concerns further drew together Lowcountry activists interested in environmental quality and historic preservation. Activism could on occasion make for strange bedfellows, as in 1970, when the German company BASF proposed building a dye plant on land adjacent to Hilton Head Island, just across the South Carolina line from Savannah. Local environmentalists opposed the plant because of projected air pollution, fishermen worried about the impact on local waters, historic preservationists believed the plant would sully the scenery, and Hilton Head developers argued that smoke and odor from the plant would harm their investment properties.[55] The fight against the BASF facility epitomized an emerging Lowcountry conservationist sentiment that linked natural and historic preservation with economic interests.

Wormsloe's interpretive framework as envisioned by the DNR was thus no accident but rather reflected this growing regionalism tied up in issues of environmental conservation and historic preservation. The historic plantation both offered area residents a place where they could escape the crowded city and enjoy the tranquility of the marsh and shady forest and constituted a place that commemorated parts of the Lowcountry's long historical legacy. Both aspects of the park attracted tourists, a lure of no small importance in a region increasingly reliant on tourism dollars to fuel the local economy. When DNR interpreters crafted a narrative that portrayed Wormsloe as a repository of colonial history and a valuable ecological sanctuary, they were simultaneously following the evolving model of the Barrow family and responding to the public desires of many Lowcountry residents. Such a portrayal would have appealed to the Barrows' midcentury guests as well as to contemporary environmentalists. Wormsloe the park was part and parcel with a growing sense of Lowcountry regional identity that tied together beliefs in the uniqueness of the coastal environment and the region's long history.

A more material manifestation of the connections between the Isle of Hope's cultural and natural history challenged the DNR soon after the agency took possession of Wormsloe. An insect pest, the southern pine beetle (*Dendroctonus frontalis*), appeared in the plantation's forests.[56] The beetle is a native of the Southeast that attacks weakened pine trees of various species. Ralph Reed, the new park's superintendent, was the first to notice the infestation. Arriving at Wormsloe in January 1974, Reed immediately observed that a number of longleaf and loblolly pines on the southern end of the Isle of Hope appeared diseased. Concerned about the state of the site's forestland, Reed contacted a forester with the Georgia Forestry Commission (GFC), who surveyed the park and informed Reed that southern pine beetles had infested several stands of timber.

Commission officials laid the blame for the infestation on natural causes even as they characterized the situation as an unnatural ecological imbalance. They speculated that a series of lightning strikes two years earlier had weakened Wormsloe's pines, allowing beetle populations—naturally occurring in the forest in small numbers—to increase to levels that threatened all of Wormsloe's pines as well as timber tracts on adjoining land.[57] Alston Waylor, director of operations for the DNR's parks and historic sites branch, also blamed the infestation on a mistaken understanding of the plantation's forest. He wrote to his superior, Henry Struble, that "Wormsloe is a climaxed [*sic*] forest, and this type of forest is more susceptible to beetles and diseases than an emergent growth area."[58] Waylor's critique was firmly rooted in the industrial timber paradigm of the late-twentieth-century Georgia coast. Although this statement ignored almost three centuries of forest use and management on site, Waylor's assertion was an assessment more of Wormsloe's lack of large-scale management for timber production than of the site's land use history.

Waylor and the GFC's understanding of Wormsloe's forest reflected one general line of thought among contemporary forestry professionals. American foresters at the time tended to view a senescent (old-growth) forest as an inefficient woodland. Old-growth trees fell and rotted in the woods, damaging their healthy neighbors and creating conditions conducive to insect infestations. The same processes created forest diversity and habitat for a wide variety of plant and animal life, though this development often went unstated in forestry manuals. Many foresters believed that the ideal forest was a young, even-aged stand of trees that rapidly increased its timber volume.[59] Waylor's representation of Wormsloe as a "climaxed" forest was not entirely accurate. The southern end of the plantation, where agriculture was never dominant, likely had a number of mature pines and oaks, but the timber cruise from a few decades earlier indicated that the peninsular woodlands contained trees of a wide variety of ages and sizes. Many stretches of Wormsloe's forest were more mature than they had been in the early twentieth century, largely as a result of the end of farming on the estate, but to define them as climax forests stretched truth to the breaking point. Accurate or not, Waylor's declaration and officials' subsequent willingness to cut Wormsloe's timber reflected at least in part an acceptance of the critiques of old-growth forests.

Once the DNR and the GFC identified the beetle infestation as a threat, the two agencies moved with unusual decisiveness. GFC director Ray Shirley convinced DNR director Joe Tanner that all infected trees must be removed immediately, and Tanner authorized GFC foresters to arrange to have small portions of the new park selectively timbered. Tanner made this decision with some hesitation, as timbering on any scale went against the agency's general management policies. He wrote that Wormsloe must be an exception: DNR officials "regret very much that the cutting of the timber in certain areas on Wormsloe is required." The GFC had convinced Tanner that a policy of removing all infected trees was the only effective way to save the site's remaining pines.[60] On February 25, 1974, a little over one month following the identification of southern pine beetles on Wormsloe, the GFC solicited bids from private timber companies to cut pine stands on the state historic site. Three weeks later, chainsaws roared to life on Wormsloe as loggers began cutting longleaf and loblolly pines on the peninsula's southern end. The commission planned to remove all pines from approximately twenty-five acres of Wormsloe's forest in the hopes that this culling would eliminate the worst of the infestation and bring beetle numbers under control.[61]

DNR officials worried about how the public might interpret timbering operations, particularly in light of the fact that the state had argued that Wormsloe was an important purchase because of the land's environmental as well as historic value. The agency launched a full-scale public relations campaign to accompany the logging efforts. Since the park was not yet open for visitation, the logging would not interfere with tourism or present a safety issue, but officials deemed public opinion critical to Wormsloe's future success. The GFC invited local reporters to tour the forest and used the occasion to present their justifications for cutting plantation pines. They argued in effect that a failure to aggressively attack Wormsloe's beetles would jeopardize forests in Skidaway Island State Park as well as trees to the west that shaded Savannah's suburbs. Officials also organized a press conference with the television and print media. Waylor declared these efforts a resounding success, telling Struble that "the meeting went very well with all persons present understanding the situation fully. I saw the T.V. report and it was very good."[62] The decision to eradicate Wormsloe's beetles came as much out of the values of regional nature and history tourism as it did out of the GFC officials' understandings of forest ecology.

The GFC's auction of Wormsloe's timber finally gave a local economic force access to the plantation's most abundant natural resource. Union Camp won the Wormsloe contract and the right to cut the park's pines more than thirty years after the Barrows contemplated converting the land into a pine plantation to feed the Savannah River mill. Union Camp's victory was no surprise, since the company remained the dominant timber consumer along the Georgia coast and owned substantial stretches of adjacent Skidaway Island. Union Camp would ultimately prove to be a poor choice for the beetle eradication campaign. The company failed to faithfully follow the GFC's original cutting plan, and after timbering concluded, it failed to adequately repair damage to the park caused by logging operations.[63]

Union Camp quickly pushed the GFC and DNR to agree to cutting more of Wormsloe's pines than the initial estimates had specified. Within a few months of the first cuts, the operation expanded from a few stands of pines on the southern end of the peninsula to a campaign to remove all of the pines throughout the entire park with the exception of a few trees around the archeologically sensitive fort ruins and the plantation house. Tanner wrote to Carter that foresters had assured him that the wholesale cutting of the park's pines was the only way to control beetle populations. According to the DNR director, the beetles "spread so rapidly that it was impossible for the crews which were harvesting the timber to overtake the infestation." When the timbering was completed in the fall, Union Camp had cut 750 acres of Wormsloe and harvested approximately three million board feet of high-quality pine timber.[64]

This rapid deforestation of Wormsloe raises a number of questions. Did the southern pine beetle population really expand so fast? Were park officials overly concerned that neighboring property owners might blame them for beetle damage and thus undermine support for the new park? Was the timbering a simple case of Union Camp greed? The surviving records do nothing to answer these questions. If southern pine beetles did blaze through Wormsloe's forests with astonishing rapidity in the summer of 1974, it is at least possible that logging efforts spread rather than eradicated the insects. The beetles favor weak pines, but when a host dies or is cut down by loggers, the insects will move to healthy trees in search of food. Union Camp's workers hauled off loads of pine logs and with them millions of beetles, but insects in the limbs and treetops left on the forest floor would have quickly dispersed in search of living habitat. Union Camp thus may have driven the southern pine beetle from one stretch of Wormsloe's forest to another. At its most basic, the DNR and GFC's decision came down to choosing whether to allow Wormsloe's forests to be consumed by southern pine beetles or by Union Camp. They opted for the latter.[65]

In addition to stripping Wormsloe of almost all of its pine trees, Union Camp's expanded logging efforts presented state officials with a number of unexpected environmental challenges. Mosquitoes, ever a pest along the marshy coast, proved particularly prolific on Wormsloe during the summer of 1974. DNR officials contacted Chatham County's Mosquito Control Commission in the hopes that agency could do something to combat the problem. Mosquito Control worked to eliminate standing water and treated potential breeding pools with insecticides, and the agency had laborers and funding earmarked to keep the county's mosquito populations suppressed.[66] After surveying the park, Thomas Fultz Jr., director of the commission, wrote to the DNR that the infestation was a direct result of timbering operations. Fultz informed Waylor that the mosquito population had mushroomed because of blocked drainage across Wormsloe and Long Island. Union Camp's loggers had left tons of debris in the form of limbs and treetops blocking the plantation's historic ditch network, and the stagnant water that built up behind these barricades created perfect incubation pools for mosquito larvae. The ditches were full of decomposing organic matter and lacked fish that might prey on the larvae. Compounding the problem, the cutover land was crisscrossed by "thousands of ruts left by vehicles and equipment," which also attracted female mosquitoes intent on laying eggs. Fultz agreed that the mosquito population on Wormsloe was a problem and worried that it might become a general nuisance or even a health threat to greater Savannah. But Fultz did not believe the outbreak was Mosquito Control's problem. He argued that Union Camp (and by extension the DNR itself) had a "moral" if not a contractual obligation to solve the site's drainage issues.[67]

Wormsloe's mosquito problem brought colonial concerns about health and nature into the late twentieth century and proved that historic relationships with the environment lurked under the modern world. The same low ground, marshes, and insects that so worried Noble Jones and his fellow colonists re-emerged to plague DNR officials following Union Camp's operations. Malaria and yellow fever were no longer major health concerns on the Georgia coast, but swarms of mosquitoes proved noisome and could transmit diseases such as heartworms in domestic pets and equine encephalitis. More than a health threat, though, swarms of biting mosquitoes had the potential to keep park visitors away and to annoy adjacent landowners, thereby damaging the new park's reputation and appeal. Wormsloe's mosquitoes were more than symbolic; like the hurricanes that continued to affect both people and landscape, the insects' life cycles and habits remained a durable if unpredictable element of life on the Isle of Hope. And in both the colonial era and the late twentieth century, human action ultimately increased mosquito populations. Rice culture, deforestation, and herds of livestock fueled mosquito reproduction in the eighteenth century, while more than two hundred years later, blocked ditches and skidder ruts had much the same results. Of course, significant differences existed between the two eras. Twentieth-century medicine had largely conquered deadly mosquito-borne diseases, people had a much greater understanding of where and how mosquitoes bred, and agencies such as the Mosquito Control Commission existed to combat the insect. However, Wormsloe's mosquito outbreak illustrated just how fragile generations of landscaping and design could prove in the face of human disturbance coupled with environmental forces.

The landscape disturbance created by logging extended beyond the nuisance of mosquito swarms. Logging trucks used the 1890s oak alley for hauling timber, and the heavy traffic damaged a number of the historic trees by compacting their root systems and tearing off low-hanging branches. The trucks carved deep ruts in the roadbed itself, making the historic plantation drive all but impassable.[68] The DNR was ultimately forced to spend almost sixteen thousand dollars for tree services to stabilize the live oaks.[69] The plantation's other roads suffered as well. The Barrows complained to Reed that Union Camp had obstructed most of the old farm roads that connected various portions of the plantation. Equipment ruts and debris-choked ditches turned low dirt roads into sticky morasses. By the end of August, as timbering operations neared completion, only 1.5 of the park's 8 miles of forest road was accessible to conventional vehicles.[70] Forty-three logging decks that Union Camp left behind presented another difficulty. These decks were sites where equipment loaded cut timber onto trucks, and each of the decks suffered from severe compaction caused by heavy machine traffic and was choked with wood debris. DNR planners worried that the decks would become temporary dead spots in the successional forest, with new trees failing to take hold.[71]

As part of its contract, Union Camp had agreed to remove timber debris and repair any damaged ditching on site, but cleaning up the mess fell to Wormsloe's small staff—just Reed and a few seasonal laborers—who were also readying the park for the public. In response, the DNR again brought unfree labor to Wormsloe's landscape, arranging with the county for eight prisoners to begin burning and chipping wood debris and clearing blocked ditches. After three months of backbreaking labor, these workers had cleared only 25 of the 750 acres. This slow cleanup ground to a complete halt as a shortage of guards, prisoner complaints about the hard labor, and DNR fears that the prisoners might present a danger to park employees led the county to remove the work detail. Faced with hundreds of acres of remaining slash, Tanner requested thirty convicts and three guards in addition to twenty thousand dollars in emergency funds from Governor Carter. This request was refused. Reed and his staff worked slowly to clear the park's ditches and to resolve the site's drainage issues, but the vast majority of the logging debris, much of which would have contained southern pine beetles, slowly rotted on the ground.[72]

Exactly how to reforest the denuded landscape was a contested issue as well. The DNR's archeologist responsible for surveying Wormsloe recommended that the agency plant the cutover plantation in longleaf pines, which he believed had been the dominant species during Noble Jones's era and would thus help create a more "authentic" experience for park visitors. Union Camp employees advised the DNR to plant Wormsloe in loblollies, the standard tree of the pulp paper industry. Union Camp did not elaborate on its logic, but the company's recommendation may have simply been a boilerplate response to all landowners contemplating reforestation. Then, if pine beetles again attacked the park's forest, vast stands of loblollies would be ideal fodder for paper mills. Thanks to the failure of cleanup operations, however, the site remained unplanted (with the exception of an old agricultural field along the oak avenue, which had not been part of the logging effort and which was put in loblollies as a test plot), and succession alone worked to fill the massive blank spaces where the plantation's pines once stood. This succession led to a more varied forest than replanting would have created; rather than monocultural stands of pine, a mix of pine, live oak, and other hardwood saplings filled in the forest gaps, interlaced with understory and shrub species such as saw palmetto and yaupon holly.[73]

The reduction of Wormsloe's forests and the ecological and economic consequences raise an obvious question: Why did state officials perceive the southern pine beetle, a native insect, to be such a dire threat? Like the individual pine beetles, pine beetle population outbreaks are regular elements of most southern mixed forests. These outbreaks remain poorly understood, but they happen in cyclical patterns. Pine beetles infest weakened trees, and temporary population explosions result in damage to healthy trees until the outbreak subsides—again, for unknown reasons. These outbreaks are both damaging and renewing for southern forests. Along with such forces as fire, hurricanes, floods, and landslides, southern pine beetles create openings of various sizes in affected forests. These disturbances promote biodiversity as successional shrubs and trees take advantage of gaps in the forest canopy, and beetle outbreaks ensure woodlands that are full of both species and age diversity. This diverse cover in turn creates a forest favorable for a wide variety of wildlife. Although the records are silent on the subject, Wormsloe's forests had certainly been through pine beetle outbreaks in the past, and they would have survived the 1970s event in some fashion as well. And Wormsloe's managers were not working blind: They had a basic knowledge of southern pine beetle ecology at their disposal.[74]

The state's response to the beetle outbreak owed more to the economic and social relationships of the 1970s Lowcountry than it did to the dynamic between insect and pine tree. Union Camp's economic motivation to cut as many of Wormsloe's pines as possible is understandable, but the panic exhibited by the DNR and the GFC was rooted in a much more nuanced conception of forests, timber, property value, and nature tourism, and their response to the beetle infestation was a product of the times. The DNR felt obligated to remove Wormsloe's pines not because the pine beetle would destroy the park's forests but because the outbreak would decimate the land's pine timber value and, more important, might threaten valuable timber and recreational woods on Skidaway Island and ornamental trees in Savannah's suburbs. Just as DNR officials worried about the public reaction to logging the newly acquired site, they also feared a public backlash if parklands served as an incubator for a regional beetle outbreak. Timber had long been a vital economic resource in the region, but pine lumber became even more valuable with the coming of the paper industry. And tourism rooted in the regional environment had become one of the driving economic engines of the Lowcountry. To be a responsible neighbor, park officials believed that they had no choice but to cut the site's pines. Wormsloe and the world around it had changed, and this transformation altered the threat of the southern pine beetle.[75]

In 1979, within a few years of Wormsloe's logging, the park was opened to the general public, complete with the facilities and interpretive programs proposed in the original planning documents. Despite the destruction of the southern pine beetle and the tremendous social and land use changes of the twentieth century, interpretations of Wormsloe as a strictly colonial site persisted into the new millennium. A 2006 flyer for the state historic site included only colonial events when describing the site's attractions. The flyer invited visitors to tour the ruins of the tabby fort and to partake in a number of special events, including a "Colonial Faire and Muster," a festival celebrating the War of Jenkins's Ear, a program on "Tools and Skills That Built a Colony," and a "Colonial Christmas." The live oak avenue planted in the 1890s appears on the leaflet's cover, but the text gives no date for the impressive drive. Instead, the flyer explains that the avenue is significant because it "leads to the tabby ruins of Wormsloe."[76] Wymberley J. De Renne would likely have been pleased that his landscaping has been so seamlessly integrated into Wormsloe's colonial past.

The interpretive campaigns of Wormsloe's owners and managers have met with extraordinary success. To all appearances, modern Wormsloe is the epitome of a well-preserved colonial (or perhaps to some an antebellum) plantation, and this "history in amber" perception of the property helped attract 71,513 guests to the state historic site in 2007. All the classic southern plantation elements are present on Wormsloe: a massive stone entrance gate, the mile-long drive paved with crushed oyster shells and overarched by stately live oaks that filter the southern sun, a manor house, ornamental gardens, and (nonthreatening) remnants of a slave past. Instead of presenting visitors with the divisive image of a plantation on the eve of a Civil War, however, the avenue so reminiscent of the Old South delivers visitors to the colonial ruins that likely appeal to the majority of the site's guests, though African American and Native American visitors undoubtedly have a less nostalgic take than many white guests on the results of Georgia's European colonization. Wormsloe may appear classically southern, but our look at the property's past has revealed a landscape of unceasing change.

Wormsloe offers an insightful case study of southern environmental history because the property is a place to explore the interconnected nature of the early American South and the greater Atlantic world, connections long noted by a variety of eminent historians.[77] In this regard, Wormsloe was a quite representative large southern plantation. Tobacco, rice, cotton, sugar, and indigo were commodities destined more often than not for European markets, and like the Joneses, the majority of substantial southern planters turned to Africa and the Caribbean for labor. Wormsloe's exceptionality lies in its remarkable sources concerning these economic ties and the ideas that connected the Lowcountry and distant environments. The Isle of Hope was a place where understandings of the natural world, among them English timber concerns and European epidemiological discourses, incorporated thinking from Europe, North America, and Africa. Wormsloe also demonstrates that these ideas stemming from transatlantic contact were surprisingly durable.[78]

If Wormsloe is an exemplar of broad environmental and intellectual threads, it equally demonstrates the utility of studying plantation-scale locales. Much of Wormsloe's story reveals natural/historical forces that paid little attention to property lines: insects and seeds drifted across fence lines just as hurricanes and tariffs affected broad swaths of the Southeast.[79] But the plantation as it has taken shape also directly reflects the decisions made by individuals treating the land as a discrete piece of private property. The proliferation of camellias and ivy around the big house, the orientation of the magnificent live oak avenue, and the crumbling formal gardens are the end products of Noble Jones's and his descendants' conceptions of the plantation as a discrete estate. Microhistories are best capable of taking into account both individual and societal thinking that contributed to the creation of particular landscapes. A close look at Wormsloe reveals the power of individual people and environments over the course of local history.

Microhistory is also vital for understanding a site that so often followed its own course, a landscape that defied certain conventions. Wormsloe fit within a broad southern model—that of a staple-producing plantation—but much less frequently mirrored immediate, local trends. During the colonial period, when most coastal Georgia planters turned to rice or indigo (including the Joneses on their other plantations), Wormsloe was home to a mixture of experimental subtropical crops, livestock ranging, and sericulture. After the revolution, the Joneses turned to sea island cotton cultivated by a growing slave population, but by the antebellum period George W. Jones increasingly rejected many of the conventions of traditional plantation agriculture and sought connections to other regions and agricultural practices. Although Wormsloe moved rapidly through wage labor, sharecropping, and rental regimes during Reconstruction, the plantation became a place of retreat and escape over the second half of the nineteenth century. The exceptional nature of Wormsloe's pleasure grounds and gardens made the landscape a public attraction in the early twentieth century. The plantation thus illustrates the maxim that there is no such thing as a typical plantation. The paths of landscapes come from multitudinous interactions among ideas, environment, economy, and individuals, punctuated periodically by social and environmental upheavals such as wars and hurricanes, but they are often shaped by individuals acting on the land.

Wormsloe's story also raises intriguing questions concerning the ties between the economic success of a landscape and its long-term survival in a stable form. Continuously productive agricultural landscapes are commonly thought of as successful spaces, their methods of land use proven by time. Dairies or grain fields persist from one century to the next by consistently turning a profit—preferably one large enough to prevent the temptations of land division. This is sustainability of a sort. Wormsloe, however, was rarely a place of successful economic activity. Noble Jones's sericultural efforts and his attempts to discover lucrative tropical crops for the most part flopped; sea island cotton culture brought Wormsloe into the world of the southern plantation, but George W. Jones's efforts to make the plantation a truly modern operation resulted in failure; postbellum Wormsloe agriculture, from rentals to dairying, did little more than contribute to the maintenance of the estate; and Wormsloe Gardens, while popular, could not rescue Wymberley Wormsloe and Augusta De Renne's claims to the land. Even the modern state historic site is the product of government subsidies. Instead, the durability of the Wormsloe landscape as a discrete entity stemmed from the land's ability to stimulate the imaginations of nine generations of Joneses, De Rennes, and Barrows. Since the first permanent English settlement in Georgia, the family has possessed a willingness to see the Wormsloe landscape as more than just the sum of its economic parts: timber, seafood, and agricultural produce. The family members have long treated history, beauty, memory, and legacy as equally important if less tangible components of Wormsloe's value and have usually had the financial wherewithal to do so.

For much of Wormsloe's history, the family seat was a place to be preserved, but in practice this preservation was not static; it included the notion of improvement or betterment of the landscape. The beauty of Wormsloe's natural and human-created environments played a large role in the Jones/De Renne/Barrow family's attachment to the plantation. Historians of wilderness have long recognized the power of this concept of the aesthetic value of landscape to shape management and preservation. Advocates of preserving wildlands from John Muir to Dave Foreman have argued that wilderness is vital for preserving the beauty of the natural world. Although exceptions exist, environmental historians have less frequently acknowledged the importance of aesthetics in the history of agricultural spaces.[80] A preference for the aesthetics of wilderness over the pastoral or tended landscape was a Romantic development and was far from universal.[81] For many Americans, particularly residents of the agricultural South, the pastoral landscape remained a more attractive and durable ideal than that of wilderness. On the Isle of Hope this "middle" landscape was the ideal of landowners from Noble Jones to Wymberley Wormsloe and Augusta De Renne.[82] Early generations of the Joneses found beauty in utility, yet as agriculture faded from the plantation scene, the aesthetics of an ornamental landscape, another sort of improvement, almost seamlessly filled the void. Wormsloe's survival may have been a product of its beauty and the way in which that beauty appealed to a particular family as much as of any utilitarian quality of the environment. A historian might be tempted to call this affection a "sense of place." From the colonial period, the Jones/De Renne/Barrow family consistently expressed an appreciation and love of the family seat. This affection often surpassed the property's economic importance and over the decades became intimately tangled with its history. As the family left layer upon layer of memories on the plantation, its members came to associate the landscape with their lineage. Wormsloe thus came to matter to so many Georgians because it first mattered to a single founding family intent on defining its ties to a particular place.

The creation of history and the creation of landscapes and how we value and preserve them go hand in hand. As Wormsloe's masters thought about, recorded, and interpreted their history, they simultaneously worked to shape the land into a form that matched their understandings of themselves. Wormsloe the plantation reflected people who thought of themselves as planters. Wormsloe the historic site, with its thickening forests and abandoned fields, reflected a family and a public that believed themselves to be preservers of Georgia's early history. What mattered for the way in which the Joneses, De Rennes, and Barrows perceived the peninsular landscape was not so much the actual history of the environment but rather the stories and traditions they had recorded about the environment. These two accounts did not always mesh. Thus, two hundred years of agriculture could be transformed into a virtually untouched forest that echoed with the report of colonial guns and Spanish steel.

This process is hardly unique to Wormsloe. Historic sites and parks throughout the region and nation have selected and continue to select for particular histories and with them particular landscapes, and vice versa. The nation's Civil War battlefield parks are prime examples of this process. Sites from Antietam to Chickamauga to Shiloh are preserved as slices of mid-nineteenth-century landscape. Features relevant to a particular battle—a cornfield, fence-row, meadow, or creek crossing—remain preserved year after year through the labor of park staff, who mow, plant, and repair so that the land appears in virtual stasis save for the changing seasons. Park managers have calculated that visitors want to be temporally transported and work to provide a Civil War experience.[83] Management of eastern national parks such as the Great Smokies and Shenandoah engaged in similar efforts to eliminate or minimize historic land use. Human history did not entirely disappear from these parks but appeared through the interpretation of carefully selected primitive sites and structures, such as rustic log cabins and re-creations of pioneer barns and split-rail fences.[84] More germane to Wormsloe's case, historic sites along the southeastern coast, from Virginia's Colonial Williamsburg to the Lowcountry plantations of South Carolina and Georgia, followed the familiar Wormsloe formula, emphasizing early or military history at the expense of long-term analyses of landscape or agricultural history.[85]

Despite its associations with similar sites of historic or natural preservation, Wormsloe followed its own course. This atypicality remains today. A drive along the sloughs and creeks surrounding the plantation reveals a thoroughly suburban landscape, reflecting more than a century of Savannah's growth. Houses cluster on most reaches of high ground, and countless docks jut into the channels that cut through the salt marsh. The greater Isle of Hope is home, playground, and work space for thousands of people. Wormsloe's shady forest, massive live oaks, and stately entrance gate seem a piece of the rural Lowcountry stranded in coastal Georgia's largest metropolitan area. The estate is as easy to spot on satellite images of the region as it is from the ground. The property's emerald green forests and unbroken marshes sit amid a sea of rooftops and hardscape, a tranquil piece of ground just north of the earthen embankments and concrete bridges of the Diamond Causeway, which slashes across the tidal flats to connect Savannah to Skidaway Island. Wormsloe appears under siege in these images, encroached on all sides by development, with obvious siltation of the Skidaway River where the Diamond Causeway bridges the water.[86] If for no other reason, the plantation holds great value as a place of retreat—for people, plants, and animals—from the relentless onslaught of coastal development.

Wormsloe has survived relatively intact from the founding of Georgia to the present day through a generous amount of luck and because of countless family decisions as well as because of the flexibility of its land use. As properties devoted specifically to rice, cotton, or cattle disappeared one by one, Wormsloe's owners never ceased adapting their land to the contingencies of the times. In part, this flexibility reflected the financial resources of the Jones/De Renne/Barrow family: Not every plantation owner could accept less than maximum profit or survive the ups and downs of cotton or dairy markets. But the adaptability of Wormsloe land use was also the product of family members' intense desire to retain a piece of land that they loved and of an association between preserving memories and preserving a particular place. From George W. Jones to Elfrida Barrow, Wormsloe's owners believed that their historic family seat was part of what made them who they were. Wormsloe exists today as an exemplar of the Lowcountry plantation precisely because the Joneses, De Rennes, and Barrows were never content to be only Lowcountry planters but thought about preserving the old plantation even as they changed it. This decision, the determination to preserve, fueled Wormsloe's conservation as a historic and natural landscape.

Perhaps the greatest value of Wormsloe's history resides in the lessons it offers for present and future park management and by extension for the conservation of similar sites across the South and the nation. Careful microhistories are critical if managers wish to present as thorough a story as possible of a particular site, and no small part of that presentation is the conservation and management of landscapes. On Wormsloe, even if DNR officials judge that the best use of the site is as a colonial showpiece (as they have in the past), managers can have little success in presenting an accurate interpretation of colonial Georgia without a thorough knowledge of intervening land use. A quarter millennium of Euro-American cultivation and management has done much to cloak the Wormsloe of Noble Jones's day—drainage ditches have dried the oak hammocks, modern causeways have changed the hydrology of the Skidaway River, insecticides keep mosquito populations at artificially low levels, Civil War earthworks form the highest point on the peninsula, and introduced plants from the forests of Japan and China grow next to longleaf pines and saw palmetto. Through all of these human alterations, basic ecological forces, from the dramatic disturbances of hurricanes and ice storms to the slow and steady work of plant succession and soil erosion, worked to create a particular place. Left unopposed, these forces will lead not back to the woods and marshes of colonial Wormsloe but instead to a new environment. Nature works relentlessly, and its interpreters have proven just as tireless. And like ecological forces, interpretation will never faithfully re-create the past but will instead shape a new history.

Of course it can be argued that most visitors to Wormsloe or similar historic sites are not terribly interested in environmental accuracy: They want to see ruins (or better yet, re-creations) of historic forts or buildings, green space, and perhaps a nice gift shop where they can purchase souvenirs. If this is the case, why should managers care about the environmental history of Wormsloe or of any other site, for that matter? The most convincing argument lies in the value of Wormsloe as a place cultural resource managers define as a "historic vernacular landscape": a site where "through social or cultural attitudes of an individual, family or a community, the landscape reflects the physical, biological, and cultural character of those everyday lives."[87] Wormsloe's landscape, then, is a place to see the everyday of history, the timbering, oystering, gardening, and ditching that have dropped from our collective conscious. Preserved in bits and pieces throughout the site are hidden scraps of history that can show visitors just how different (or similar) the past was from today. Of course, many tourists at historical sites seek out the unique—the site of an important battle, the birthplace of a president, the workshop where a craftsman created a critical technology—and an interpretation of the site's environmental history can go a long way toward explaining singularities as well. The fort that serves as centerpiece for the park is difficult to understand absent an explanation of shifting river channels: Thanks to the Diamond Causeway, the ruins guard nothing at all today. Perhaps no other feature on Wormsloe is as memorable as the live oak avenue; it is reproduced endlessly on postcards, on park brochures, on the Wormsloe website, and, judging from the number of tourists who stop at the head of the avenue and get out their cameras, in thousands of scrapbooks and photograph albums. Visitors who want to know the history of such a beautiful feature are in essence asking for a description of Wormsloe as a vernacular landscape. They are asking for an interpretation of Wormsloe's environmental history.

In 2010, Touchstone Pictures released a movie set in part on Wormsloe's grounds. *The Last Song*, a romantic film based on a Nicholas Sparks novel of the same name and starring actress and musician Miley Cyrus, was set in part against the backdrop of the historic plantation.[88] In the film, Cyrus plays Ronnie Miller, a wayward New York City teen sent to live with her estranged father for the summer on the Georgia coast. Ronnie falls for Will Blakelee (played by Liam Hemsworth), the son of a wealthy family that resides on Wormsloe. Although the plantation is not named and its past (real or fictional) is not explained for the audience, Wormsloe's natural and cultural landscape steals several scenes. More than the impressive architecture of the big house or the family's collection of antique furniture, the estate's broad swaths of green forest amid the urbanized coastal landscape signify wealth and luxury. As Will drives Ronnie through the massive arched gate and down the live oak avenue, she stares in wonder and asks if he lives at Graceland. The plot takes the couple inside the mansion house, onto the Skidaway pier, around the landscaped grounds, and into the historic library. Like much of the estate's history since World War II, the film's interpretation of Wormsloe makes no reference to its agricultural past. Will's father is no planter; instead, he owns a chain of brake repair shops.

The authenticity of *The Last Song*'s portrayal of Wormsloe is not vital here, but it does illustrate the enduring natural and cultural beauty of the Isle of Hope. It is fitting that Cyrus's character compares Wormsloe to Graceland—a cultural construction if ever one existed—even as she stares at such exemplars of Lowcountry nature as Spanish moss, live oaks, yaupon holly, and the mixed pine forest. Whether or not the audience realizes it, the comparison is apt. The entrance avenue, created from the living native materials of the Lowcountry, is as much a human construction as a natural one, and it is freighted with a great deal of cultural power. Ronnie sees the avenue and the woods beyond as living plants, but she also interprets the scene in a way that might have pleased the avenue's designer, Wymberley J. De Renne. Like his predecessors and descendants, De Renne created a landscape of such beauty and majesty that it today serves effectively as a symbol of the wild coast and of the colonial/Old South as well as a recreational space.

This Disney-funded film contains a kernel of sage advice on conserving cultural landscapes. Beauty and impressions matter. That is, careful, successful conservation must remain mindful not only of how a landscape came to be but also why people have cared for and preserved it. If we want to ensure that there will be a green and lovely Wormsloe plantation a hundred years from today, we could do worse than look to its history for lessons in how it survived to the present. These lessons will not always reveal how to best manage the land; few people would contest that slavery proved a poor land management scheme in addition to a moral evil. Yet Wormsloe's environmental history illustrates that thinking about the past—as Wormsloe's owners so often did—can lead to the preservation of land as well as to memory. Like other lived-in landscapes, Wormsloe is important because of all its historic and contemporary components, its human and natural histories. It is nothing less than the sum of its past. What went wrong, what is a product of interpretation, what is sustainable—all have a place in creating the Wormsloe that charms today. Live oaks, oyster beds, the ruins of the tabby fort, slave cabins, and historic gardens contribute to Wormsloe's significance, but the historic search for meaning in human actions in a particular landscape, the search for a sense of place, makes the land special—a place worth preserving.

NOTES

ABBREVIATIONS

CBFP	Craig Barrow Family Papers (ms. 3090), Hargrett Rare Book and Manuscript Library, University of Georgia, Athens
DRFP 1064	De Renne Family Papers (ms. 1064), Hargrett Rare Book and Manuscript Library, University of Georgia, Athens
DRFP 2819	De Renne Family Papers (ms. 2819), Hargrett Rare Book and Manuscript Library, University of Georgia, Athens
GWJ Farm Journal	Farm Journal of George W. Jones, De Renne Family Papers (ms. 1064), box 12, folder 27, Hargrett Rare Book and Manuscript Library, University of Georgia, Athens
GWJDR Account Book	George W. J. De Renne Account Book, 1854–1875, De Renne Family Papers (ms. 1064), box 57, folder 1, Hargrett Rare Book and Manuscript Library, University of Georgia, Athens
GWJDR DIARY	George W. J. De Renne Diary, 1876–1880, De Renne Family Papers (ms. 1064), box 13, folder 7, Hargrett Rare Book and Manuscript Library, University of Georgia, Athens
NJFP	Noble Jones Family Papers (ms. 1127), Hargrett Rare Book and Manuscript Library, University of Georgia, Athens
SPBR	Southern Pine Beetle Reports, RG 30, subgroup 1, box 16, Georgia State Archives, Morrow
WJDR Account Book	W. J. De Renne Account Book, 1899–1916, De Renne Family Papers (ms. 1064), box 15, folder 1, Hargrett Rare Book and Manuscript Library, University of Georgia, Athens
WWDFP	Wymberley Wormsloe De Renne Family Papers (ms. 1788), Hargrett Rare Book and Manuscript Library, University of Georgia, Athens

INTRODUCTION. The Last Plantation

1. Rackham, *Last Forest*, 271.

2. The direct inspiration here is Rackham's *Last Forest*. In this wonderful history, Rackham, an English botanist, traces the evolution of Essex County's Hatfield Forest over more than nine hundred years, from the Domesday survey of 1086 to its contemporary management by the National Trust.

3. The classic school of history here is the French Annales, who call for *longue durée*

(long-duration) history, although the Annales school was often all but deterministic when discussing the role of the environment in history. Famous practitioners include Marc Bloch, Lucien Febvre, Fernand Braudel, and Emmanuel Le Roy Ladurie.

4. For a comprehensive yet graceful introduction to American perceptions of nature as wilderness, see Nash, *Wilderness and the American Mind*. There are reams of scholarly literature concerning the utility of the wilderness ideal (or lack thereof) in history and conservation, but the most influential essay remains William Cronon's "The Trouble with Wilderness; or, Getting Back to the Wrong Nature," in *Uncommon Ground*, ed. Cronon, 69–90. For a survey of European environmental and landscape history prior to 2000, see Cioc, Linnér, and Osborn, "Environmental History Writing in Northern Europe," 396–406; Bess, Cioc, and Sievert, "Environmental History Writing in Southern Europe," 545–56.

5. Levi, *Inheriting Power*, xv.

6. Lynn A. Nelson, *Pharsalia*, 13.

7. In addition to Lynn A. Nelson's *Pharsalia*, recent self-consciously agroecological studies include Soluri, *Banana Culture*; McCann, *Maize and Grace*.

8. This assessment paraphrases Richard White in *Organic Machine*, esp. chap. 1. For more of his thoughts on the appropriate place of labor in environmental history, see Richard White, "'Are You an Environmentalist or Do You Work for a Living?': Work and Nature," in *Uncommon Ground*, ed. Cronon, 171–85.

9. For an entrée into the South as a particularly agrarian region of America and the implications of this past for environmental history, see Stewart, "If John Muir."

10. Works that to varying extents explore the relationships between slavery and nature include Silver, *New Face*; Stewart, *"What Nature Suffers to Groe"*; Cecelski, *Waterman's Song*; Glave and Stoll, *"To Love the Wind"*; Kirby, *Mockingbird Song*; Lynn A. Nelson, *Pharsalia*.

11. Lewis, *Abolition of Man*, 35. For an example of a recent environmental history embracing Lewis's maxim, see James D. Rice, *Nature and History*, 8.

12. I thank an anonymous reviewer for the University of Georgia Press for this observation concerning the inversion of Lewis's statement.

13. Some prominent examples include Crosby, *Columbian Exchange*; Crosby, *Ecological Imperialism*; Chaplin, *Subject Matter*; Kelton, *Epidemics and Enslavement*; Valencius, *Health of the Country*; Curtin, *Migration and Mortality*; Curtin, "Epidemiology and the Slave Trade"; Chaplin, "Climate and Southern Pessimism"; Stewart, "'Let Us Begin.'"

14. "Wormsloe Tour," flyer, n.d., CBFP, box 30, folder 1.

15. Key among the collections documenting Wormsloe's past are the De Renne Family Papers (mss. 1064, 1064a, 2819, and oversize drawers), Noble Jones Family Papers (ms. 1127), Wymberley Wormsloe De Renne Family Papers (ms. 1788), and the Craig Barrow Family Papers (ms. 3090), all in the Hargrett Rare Book and Manuscript Collection.

ONE. A Lowcountry Experiment

1. Coulter, *Wormsloe*, 1–4; Kenneth Coleman, *Colonial Georgia*, 13–25; Harold Earl Davis, *Fledgling Province*, 9–10; Betty Wood, *Slavery in Colonial Georgia*, 2.

2. Cobb, *Georgia Odyssey*, 4.

3. Coulter, *Wormsloe*, 1–4.

4. Harold Earl Davis, *Fledgling Province*, 27–28, 30; Fraser, *Savannah in the Old South*, 5–7; Sweet, *Negotiating for Georgia*, 30.

5. Coulter, *Wormsloe*, 4–5; Harold Earl Davis, *Fledgling Province*, 11; Land Grant of Noble Jones and Noble Wimberly Jones, December 21, 1733 (copy), DRFP 1064, box 9, folder 4.

6. Coulter, *Wormsloe*, 21–22; Betty Wood, *Slavery in Colonial Georgia*, 8; Kenneth Coleman, *Colonial Georgia*, 127. For its first hundred years, the plantation was usually spelled *Wormslow*. I have elected to use the modern spelling throughout the book.

7. Kelso, *Captain Jones's Wormslow*, 1–10.

8. For a description of the live oak forest ecosystem, see Wallace, "Archeological, Ethnohistoric, and Biochemical Investigation," 32–33.

9. Michael Williams, *Americans and Their Forests*, 47–48; Silver, *New Face*, 17–19; Stewart, *"What Nature Suffers to Groe,"* 66–67, 199–200; Pyne, *Fire in America*, 148–49; Shores, *On Harper's Trail*, 128–38; Albert G. Way, "Burned to Be Wild: Herbert Stoddard and the Roots of Ecological Conservation in the Southern Longleaf Pine Forest," in *Environmental History*, ed. Sutter and Manganiello, 285.

10. Neel, with Sutter and Way, *Art of Managing Longleaf*, 155; see also chap. 4.

11. Wallace, "Archeological, Ethnohistoric, and Biochemical Investigation," 35–36.

12. Ibid., 24.

13. Batista and Platt, "Tree Population Responses"; Batista and Platt, *Old-Growth Definition*; Bruce P. Allen, Pauley, and Sharitz, "Hurricane Impacts."

14. Courtemanche, Hester, and Mendelsohn, "Recovery"; Shepherd et al., "Impact."

15. For the prevailing perceptions of insalubrious landscapes in England, which carried over to the New World, see Dobson, *Contours*.

16. Crosby, *Ecological Imperialism*, 6.

17. For the Georgia Lowcountry as "an extended Caribbean," see Philip D. Morgan, "Lowcountry Georgia and the Early Modern Atlantic World, 1733–ca. 1820," in *African American Life*, ed. Philip D. Morgan, 14.

18. Lewis H. Larson Jr., "Historic Guale Indians of the Georgia Coast and the Impact of the Spanish Mission Effort," in *Tacachale*, ed. Milanich and Procter, 120; Hudson, *Southeastern Indians*, 433–34; Swanton, *Indians*, 135–36; Hann, "Twilight," 2. On the coalescence of a "Creek" people in the late 1600s and early 1700s, see Ethridge, *Creek Country*, esp. 22–31; Kelton, *Epidemics and Enslavement*, 125, 147.

19. Thomas et al., "Anthropology," 178, 195.

20. Wallace, "Archeological, Ethnohistoric, and Biochemical Investigation," 211–15, 222–23, 267; Hutchinson et al., "Regional Variation," 398; Larson, "Historic Guale Indians," 122. Wallace concludes that oysters were a supplementary rather than primary food source.

21. Caldwell, McCann, and Hulse, *Irene Mound Site*, 53–54, 60.

22. Bratton, "Vegetation History," 134–35; Bratton and Miller, "Historic Field Systems"; Pyne, *Fire in America*, 148–49; Stewart, *"What Nature Suffers to Groe,"* 199–200.

23. Michael Williams, *Americans and Their Forests*, 47.

24. Wallace, "Archeological, Ethnohistoric, and Biochemical Investigation," 174–

80, 266–67, 270. See also Thomas and Pendleton, "Archaeology," 61; Thomas et al., "Anthropology," 178–79, 188–94.

25. The "ecological Indian" concept has been effectively debunked by Shepherd Krech, among others. See Krech, *Ecological Indian*.

26. Cronon, *Changes in the Land*, 34.

27. Hudson, *Southeastern Indians*, 433–34.

28. Thomas et al., "Anthropology," 181–85; Thomas and Pendleton, "Archaeology," 102.

29. Wallace, "Archeological, Ethnohistoric, and Biochemical Investigation," 266. See also Hutchinson et al., "Regional Variation," 408–9.

30. Larson, "Historic Guale Indians," 122–23, 133; Thomas et al., "Anthropology," 188–94; Wallace, "Archeological, Ethnohistoric, and Biochemical Investigation," 236.

31. Hutchinson et al., "Regional Variation," 398. Isotopic analysis involves dissolving bone material and measuring levels of various chemical elements to determine historic nutrition.

32. Larson, "Historic Guale Indians," 133.

33. Kelton, *Epidemics and Enslavement*, 130–31; Garrison, Baker, and Thomas, "Magnetic Prospection," 301–2; Swanton, *Indians*, 63, 135–36; Ramsey, *Yamasee War*, 74; Thomas et al., "Anthropology," 186, 211–12; Hudson, *Southeastern Indians*, 434–36.

34. Kelton, *Epidemics and Enslavement*, 130–31, 223; Hann, "Twilight," 4; Sweet, *Negotiating for Georgia*, 1.

35. Map of Wormsloe, Isle of Hope, Georgia, 2008, available at http://crms.uga .edu/files/Wormsloe_maps3.pdf.

36. Kelso, *Captain Jones's Wormslow*, 91, 133 n. 65, 95.

37. Ralph Reed to Alston Waylor, March 4, 1974, Wormsloe Master Plan Documents, RG 30, subgroup 1, box 16, Georgia State Archives, Morrow.

38. This distinction between site and situation comes from Kelman, *River and Its City*, 5–7. For similar observations, see Colten, *Unnatural Metropolis*, 1–6.

39. Sickels-Taves, "Understanding Historic Tabby Structures," 23–24; Sickels-Taves and Sheehan, *Lost Art*, esp. 17–27; W. H. H., "Sea Island Compost," 358; *Historic Savannah*, 43; Sullivan, *Tabby*, 2.

40. Kelso, *Captain Jones's Wormslow*, 73–90.

41. Von Reck, *Von Reck's Voyage*, 33–34.

42. Noble Jones to James Oglethorpe, July 6, 1735, DRFP 1064, box 6, folder 2; "Itinerant Observations in America," 15.

43. Muir, *Thousand-Mile Walk*, 60.

44. Noble Jones to James Oglethorpe, July 6, 1735, DRFP 1064, box 6, folder 2.

45. S. Max Edelson, "Clearing Swamps, Harvesting Forests: Trees and the Making of a Plantation Landscape in the Colonial South Carolina Lowcountry," in *Environmental History*, ed. Sutter and Manganiello, 112. For an authoritative overview of historic English forests and their management, see Rackham, *History of the Countryside*, 62–154; Rackham, *Trees and Woodland*; Rackham, *Last Forest*.

46. Leigh Shaw-Taylor, "The Management of Common Land in the Lowlands of Southern England, circa 1500 to circa 1850," in *Management*, ed. De Moor, Shaw-Taylor, and Warde, 75–77; Cantor, *Changing English Countryside*, 97–118; Brian Short,

"Forests and Wood-Pasture in Lowland England," in *English Rural Landscape*, ed. Thirsk, 126–28.

47. Rackham, *History of the Countryside*, 78, table 5.1.

48. Shaw-Taylor, "Management of Common Land," 61.

49. Rackham, *History of the Countryside*, 297; Cantor, *Changing English Country-side*, 59, 96; Short, "Forests and Wood-Pasture," 141–42.

50. Kelso, *Captain Jones's Wormslow*, 6; Jones, *Dead Towns of Georgia*, 251–52.

51. Cashin, *Beloved Bethesda*, 1–23.

52. Account of Thomas Rasberry, October 21, 1763, NJFP. Rasberry sold Jones six "felling axes" in 1763.

53. Fraser, *Lowcountry Hurricanes*, 14–26.

54. "Itinerant Observations in America," 15.

55. Kimber in Coulter, *Wormsloe*, 16–20.

56. Von Reck, *Von Reck's Voyage*, 34–37, 50.

57. Kelton, *Epidemics and Enslavement*, 11–28. The presence of dysentery-causing bacteria in pre-Columbian America is certain, and Kelton postulates that typhoid and tuberculosis were indigenous diseases as well.

58. Fraser, *Savannah in the Old South*, 10; Cashin, *Beloved Bethesda*, 20; William Stephens, *Journal*, 1:44.

59. Kenneth Coleman, *Colonial Georgia*, 33–34.

60. For a recent treatment of the importance of these two diseases in the history of the New World, see McNeill, *Mosquito Empires*, esp. chaps. 1, 2.

61. Kelton, *Epidemics and Enslavement*, 30–31; Curtin, "Epidemiology and the Slave Trade," 209–10, 212; Philip D. Curtin, "Disease Exchange across the Tropical Atlantic," in *Migration and Mortality*, 344–45; Peter H. Wood, *Black Majority*, 86–87; Carney, *Black Rice*, 147–48; Stewart, *"What Nature Suffers to Groe,"* 54, 139–40; Bell, *Mosquito Soldiers*, 10–14.

62. William Stephens, *Journal*, 1:253–54.

63. Ibid., 270. Every member of Von Reck's group of Salzburger immigrants in 1736 survived the Atlantic voyage in good health, but shortly following their arrival in Georgia, the population was attacked by severe intermittent fevers, almost certainly malaria. See Von Reck, *Von Reck's Voyage*, 50.

64. Equiano, *Interesting Narrative*, 127.

65. Curtin, *Rise and Fall*, 39; Curtin, "Disease Exchange," 347–48; Peter H. Wood, *Black Majority*, 73–75; Bell, *Mosquito Soldiers*, 15; McNeill, *Mosquito Empires*, 40–44; Kelton, *Epidemics and Enslavement*, 33–34.

66. Both Jones and his son, Noble Wimberly Jones, served as physicians. See Harold Earl Davis, *Fledgling Province*, 86–87; Kenneth Coleman, *Colonial Georgia*, 33–34; Bassett, *Medical Biography*, 3.

67. Note of Medical Treatments, n.d. (bound with material from 1760), NJFP.

68. Noble Jones to David Murray, August 1754, NJFP. While this letter is unsigned, it is in Noble Jones's hand and is bound with other of Jones's papers.

69. James D. Rice, *Nature and History*, 73.

70. Byrd, *William Byrd's Natural History*, 14. Though his comments reflected wide-spread concerns about southern weather, Byrd's criticisms of the Georgia colony were

also motivated at least partly by self-interest, as during the mid-1730s he was engaged in securing European colonists for his planned town along the southern branch of the Roanoke River, in the Virginia Piedmont.

71. Megan Kate Nelson, *Trembling Earth*, 14–17; Stewart, *"What Nature Suffers to Groe,"* 63. For discussions of colonial views of the southern climate and its effects on white bodies, see Chaplin, *Subject Matter*; Chaplin, "Climate and Southern Pessimism"; Stewart, "'Let Us Begin'"; Kupperman, "Fear." For the continuation of these beliefs about the connections between bodily health and the southern environment into the nineteenth century, see Valencius, *Health of the Country*.

72. McNeill, *Mosquito Empires*, 48, 55–57. Sutter has described this process in detail for the Panama Canal Zone in the early twentieth century. See Sutter, "Nature's Agents," 740–47.

73. Bell, *Mosquito Soldiers*, 15.

74. Lockley, *Lines in the Sand*, 3; Philip D. Morgan, "Lowcountry Georgia," 15–16; Stewart, *"What Nature Suffers to Groe,"* 63–64. The initial Trustees' grants, such as Jones's 1733 indenture for a Savannah lot and outlying garden, forbade slaveholding. See Trustees' Grant to Noble and Noble W. Jones, December 21, 1733, DRFP 1064, box 9, folder 4.

75. Curtin, "Epidemiology and the Slave Trade," 194.

76. Ibid., 198; Peter H. Wood, *Black Majority*, 88–89; Bell, *Mosquito Soldiers*, 12–13; McNeill, *Mosquito Empires*, 53–54; Curtin, *Rise and Fall*, 38–39. People living in malarial environments can also accrue relative but incomplete acquired resistance to the disease through surviving repeated infections. See McNeill, *Mosquito Empires*, 53–54.

77. Shawn William Miller, *Environmental History of Latin America*, 55; Curtin, *Rise and Fall*, 39; Peter H. Wood, *Black Majority*, 86–91.

78. Curtin, "Epidemiology and the Slave Trade," 204–7; McNeill, *Mosquito Empires*, 44–46.

79. For influential works on the cultural construction of racial slavery, see Jordan, *White over Black*; Edmund S. Morgan, *American Slavery, American Freedom*; Breen and Innes, *"Myne Owne Ground"*; Barbara J. Fields, "Ideology and Race in American History," in *Region, Race, and Reconstruction*, ed. Kousser and McPherson, 143–77; Kathleen Brown, *Good Wives*; Betty Wood, *Origins of American Slavery*; Eltis, *Rise*; Vaughan, *Roots of American Racism*.

80. Jacoby, "Slaves by Nature?"

81. Menard, "Transitions," 29. See also Betty Wood, *Slavery in Colonial Georgia*.

82. Bolzius in David S. Williams, *From Mounds to Megachurches*, 22.

83. Thomas Stephens, *Hard Case*, 2.

84. Thomas Stephens, *Brief Account*, 8.

85. Lockley, *Lines in the Sand*, 5.

86. Cobb, *Georgia Odyssey*, 6.

87. Lockley, *Lines in the Sand*, 23.

88. Notes of George W. J. De Renne, n.d. (probably 1870s), DRFP 1064, box 12, folder 22. These notes consist of transcripts from the "Publick Record Office, London."

89. Betty Wood, *Slavery in Colonial Georgia*, 94–95.

90. Noble Jones to James Oglethorpe, July 6, 1735, DRFP 1064, box 6, folder 2.

91. Account of Noble Jones with the Estate of Thomas Rasberry, October 21, 1763, NJFP.

92. Noble Jones's Will, 1775, DRFP 1064, box 6, folder 10; Estate Claims of Noble Jones, May 3, 1783, NJFP; Tax Return of Noble W. Jones, 1770, DRFP 1064, box 9, folder 26. Noble Jones's will does not record exact slave numbers, but an estimate of fifty or more seems safe, as a tax return for his estate ten years later listed forty-eight slaves although some had already been willed to his daughter, Mary Jones. See Tax Return of Estate of Noble Jones, 1785, DRFP 1064, box 6, folder 9.

93. Petition by Noble Jones, March 31, 1746 (transcript), CBFP, box 19, folder 19; Notes of George W. J. De Renne, n.d. (probably 1870s), DRFP 1064, box 12, folder 22; Coulter, *Wormsloe*, 108–9. Coulter attributes the acquisition of Lambeth to Noble Wimberly, but the family's notes transcribed from London records indicate that Noble requested the plantation. The Trustees originally leased Wimberly to John Fallowfield around the same time Jones acquired Wormsloe. Fallowfield aligned himself with the malcontents and was banished from the colony in the early 1740s. See Abstract of Title to Wymberley Lots, March 1, 1906, James S. Richmond Collection on Wymberley Tract, folder 2, Georgia Historical Society; Lindsey and Britt, *Isle of Hope*, 2–3.

94. Coulter, *Wormsloe*, 22–23, 108–9; Noble Jones's Will, n.d., NJFP.

95. Tax Return of Noble W. Jones, 1770, DRFP 1064, box 9, folder 26; Tax Return of Inigo and Noble W. Jones, 1785, DRFP 1064, box 9, folder 27.

96. Betty Wood, *Slavery in Colonial Georgia*, 108.

97. For a detailed treatment of early husbandry efforts in and around Savannah, see Stewart, "'Whether Wast, Deodand, or Stray.'"

98. Crosby, *Columbian Exchange*, 77–79. According to Deb Bennett and Robert Hoffman, feral hogs could reproduce six times as fast as wild cattle. See Bennett and Hoffman, "Ranching in the New World," ed. Viola and Margolis, in *Seeds of Change*, 101–3.

99. Kimber in Coulter, *Wormsloe*, 19.

100. Equiano, *Interesting Narrative*, 141.

101. Virginia De John Anderson, *Creatures of Empire*, 75–140; Crosby, *Ecological Imperialism*, 178–80; Silver, *New Face*, 172–75; Stewart, "'Whether Wast, Deodand, or Stray,'" 22–23. This system of cavalier stock management persisted in the Savannah area well into the mid-nineteenth century. See Burke, *Reminiscences of Georgia*, 127.

102. Robert C. Allen, *Enclosure and the Yeoman*, 107–129; Cantor, *Changing English Countryside*, 38–39, 174–75.

103. Clay, *Rural Society*, 171–83.

104. Edelson, *Plantation Enterprise*, 47.

105. Trustees' Grant to Noble and Noble W. Jones, December 21, 1733, DRFP 1064, box 9, folder 4.

106. Noble Jones to James Oglethorpe, July 6, 1735, DRFP 1064, box 6, folder 2.

107. "To Be Sold," *Georgia Gazette*, July 7, 1763, 4. Animals were also easily lost or stolen on the commons, despite the standard practice of branding or cutting the ears of stock in proprietary patterns. In 1791, Noble W. Jones lost two of his horses near the city, and he feared that they had been "stolen off the Common." See George Jones to William Gibbons, July 5, 1791, Jones Family Papers, box 1, folder 1, Georgia Historical Society, Savannah.

108. Bullard, *Cumberland Island*, 69–70; Edelson, *Plantation Enterprise*, 47; Stewart, "'Whether Wast, Deodand, or Stray,'" 6.

109. "Marsh and Its World," 39.

110. Anne Reeves and Tom Williamson, "Marshes," in *English Rural Landscape*, ed. Thirsk, 151, 158–59; Cantor, *Changing English Countryside*, 57; Edelson, *Plantation Enterprise*, 47–48.

111. Jensen, "Effect"; Andresen et al., "Long-Term Changes," 137–38.

112. Stewart, "From King Cane to King Cotton"; Silver, *New Face*, 179–80; Donald E. Davis, *Where There Are Mountains*, 71–73.

113. For English meadow agriculture and its transition to North America, see Donahue, *Great Meadow*, 59–60, 166–71.

114. Holder, Johnson, and Baker, "Cattle Grazing," 107–8.

115. Kelso, *Captain Jones's Wormslow*, 6.

116. Coulter, *Wormsloe*, 29–30.

117. Stephens Journal, Colonial Records, 4:619 (transcript), CBFP, box 19, folder 20.

118. Stewart, "'Whether Wast, Deodand, or Stray,'" 13–14.

119. William Stephens, *Journal*, 1:69.

120. Rackham, *History of the Countryside*, 34–36; Cowdrey, *This Land, This South*, 49–50; Jon T. Coleman, *Vicious*, esp. 39–42; Silver, *New Face*, 175–77; James D. Rice, *Nature and History*, 116.

121. Von Reck, *Von Reck's Voyage*, 37.

122. Stephens, *Journal*, 1:69, 414.

123. Ibid., 1:417.

124. "Ila of Hope" Map, Surveyor John M. Kinnon, 1802 (WPA Copy, 1941), CBFP, box 46.

125. Account of Thomas Rasberry, December 31, 1760, NJFP. Rasberry was a Savannah merchant who sold a "horse bell" in a lot of other goods to Jones. William Kelso's 1968–69 excavation of the tabby fort ruins on Wormsloe provided confirmation that the plantation stock wore bells, unearthing two well-preserved brass cowbells, perhaps used for selected milk cows. See Kelso, *Captain Jones's Wormslow*, 145–46.

126. Bennett and Hoffman, "Ranching in the New World," 110.

127. Silver, *New Face*, 179–81; Ethridge, *Creek Country*, 164–65; Virginia De John Anderson, *Creatures of Empire*, 185–86; Cowdrey, *This Land, This South*, 49–50; Pearson and Whitaker, "Forage and Cattle Responses," 445; Duvall and Hilmon, "New Grazing Research Programs," 132.

128. Horticultural gardens and botanical experimentation were a fairly common practice among well-educated and well-off colonial southerners. Traveler and botanist William Tatham documented this trend shortly after the Revolution, describing "private Botanic collections; & private Gentlemen who are particularly fond of this study, and whose circumstances and rural residences are favorable to the pursuit." See William Tatham's notebook, 1796, ms. 325, Hargrett Rare Book and Manuscript Library, University of Georgia, Athens.

129. Oglethorpe, *New and Accurate Account*, 17–20.

130. William Stephens, *Journal*, 1:48–49, 188, 193; Coulter, *Wormsloe*, 27.

131. Cobb, *Georgia Odyssey*, 3–5; Stewart, *"What Nature Suffers to Groe,"* 34–37; Betty Wood, *Slavery in Colonial Georgia*, 9. For an example of local residents drawn

to Wormsloe's exotic cultivars, see an article describing visits to the property to view a century plant in bloom: "Savannah, July 11," *Georgia Gazette*, July 11, 1765, p. 2. According to the article, "Numbers of people from this place [Savannah] have gone within these eight days past to the plantation of the Hon. Noble Jones, Esq. a few miles from town, to see an Agave plant, now in blossom there, which is said to be 27 and a half feet high, and has 33 branches, which contain a vast number of blossoms." For evidence that the Joneses grew plums, see Hannah Vincent to Noble W. Jones, February 16, 1771 (copy), DRFP 1064, box 9, folder 10. For evidence of the other species, see the following paragraph.

132. Coulter, *Wormsloe*, 27.

133. John Bartram, "Diary of a Journey," 30 (some punctuation added). While Bartram never names the property discussed here, the description of the plantation and its relationship to Bethesda almost certainly make it Wormsloe, a conclusion supported by Harper (John Bartram, "Diary of a Journey," 66).

134. Ibid., 30.

135. Benjamin Franklin to Noble W. Jones, October 7, 1772 (copy), CBFP, box 19, folder 14.

136. Noble W. Jones to Benjamin Franklin, in Malcolm Bell III, "Some Notes and Reflections upon a Letter from Benjamin Franklin to Noble Wimberly Jones" (manuscript article draft), n.d., 7, 9, CBFP, box 21, folder 3. Franklin obtained the rice seed from Irish naturalist John Ellis, who had a history of introducing Oriental plants to the West (3–4).

137. "Chinese Tallow Tree," 1; Godfrey and Wooten, *Aquatic and Wetland Plants*, 289.

138. Notes of George W. J. De Renne, n.d. (probably 1870s), DRFP 1064, box 12, folder 22.

139. Bonner, "Silk Growing," 143; Ewan, "Silk Culture in the Colonies," 130, 138; Van Horne, "Joseph Solomon Ottolenghe," 400.

140. Trustee Grant to Noble and Noble W. Jones, December 21, 1733 (copy); Bonner, "Silk Growing," 143–44.

141. James Habersham to Benjamin Martyn, December 19, 1750 (transcript), CBFP, box 19, folder 20.

142. James Habersham's letterbook, January 25, 1751 (transcript), CBFP, box 19, folder 20.

143. James Habersham to Benjamin Martyn, March 4, 1751 (transcript), CBFP, box 19, folder 20. For the mechanics of cocoon sorting, see Bonner, "Silk Growing," 146.

144. Ewan, "Silk Culture in the Colonies," 138; Bonner, "Silk Growing," 144.

145. Lockley, *Lines in the Sand*, 14–15.

146. Bonner, "Silk Growing," 147.

147. Van Horne, "Joseph Solomon Ottolenghe," 401.

148. Lockley, *Lines in the Sand*, 14–16. This white-female-centered sericulture thwarted attempts by the Trustees to draw silk production into the emerging slave economy. See Coulter, *Wormsloe*, 33.

149. Noble Jones to James Oglethorpe, July 6, 1735, DRFP 1064, box 6, folder 2.

150. Duncan and Duncan, *Trees*, 198; Petrides, *Field Guide to Eastern Trees*, 269.

151. Kelso, *Captain Jones's Wormslow*, 6; Account of Thomas Rasberry, October 21,

1763, NJFP. In this account with Rasberry, Jones purchased fourteen broad hoes and six sickles as well as a substantial amount of rough cloth for making slave clothing.

152. Petition by Noble Jones, March 31, 1746 (transcript), CBFP, box 19, folder 19.

153. Notes of George W. J. De Renne, n.d. (probably 1870s), DRFP 1064, box 12, folder 22.

154. Colonial subsistence production suffers from a paradox: Raising crops for home consumption was so vital that almost everyone did so to some extent, but because these products usually failed to enter a defined economic structure (they were not generally taxed, exported, or manufactured outside the home), they were rarely recorded.

155. Reese, *Colonial Georgia*, 129–30; Carney, *Black Rice*, 83–84, 121–22, 78.

156. While the mill seems a potentially strong piece of evidence supporting the presence of rice culture on Wormsloe, it was built in 1856, during a period of extremely detailed records for the property. No rice was grown on Wormsloe during this period, and George W. Jones must have built the mill to husk rice from his other plantations or his neighbors' crops. Modern GIS maps based on satellite imagery have failed to reveal any residual earthworks related to tidal rice cultivation.

157. Stewart, *"What Nature Suffers to Groe,"* 89; Harvey, "Development," 38–46, 55, 72; Range, "Agricultural Revolution," 253; Coon, "Eliza Lucas Pinckney," 62; Sandberg, *Indigo Textiles*, 30–31; Sharrer, "Indigo in Carolina," 94, 96–97; Sharrer, "Indigo Bonanza," 447–48, 453–55.

158. Sharrer, "Indigo Bonanza," 449–53, 455; Reese, *Colonial Georgia*, 130; Sharrer, "Indigo in Carolina," 95.

159. Account of Thomas Rasberry, December 31, 1760, NJFP. Throughout the colonial period, Noble and Noble Wimberly Jones's various holdings in Savannah and in neighboring parishes often make it difficult to determine exactly where they raised specific crops or kept slaves. See photostats of Noble W. Jones, eighteen-hundred-acre grant, St. George Parish, 1771, Noble Jones, eight-hundred-acre grant, St. Matthew Parish, 1772, Noble Jones, one-thousand-acre grant, St. Matthew Parish, 1772, all in DRFP 2819, box 13, folder 9.

160. Sarah Jones to George Jones, November 18, 1796, NJFP.

161. Philip D. Morgan, "Lowcountry Georgia," 36–37; Vincent Carretta, "'I Began to Feel the Happiness of Liberty, of Which I Knew Nothing Before': Eighteenth-Century Black Accounts of the Lowcountry," in *African American Life*, ed. Philip D. Morgan, 81–82.

162. "Advices from America, the East and West Indies, &c.," published in the *London Gazette* (pamphlet), 1779, CBFP, box 25, folder 2; Fraser, *Savannah in the Old South*, 129.

163. Fraser, *Savannah in the Old South*, 135–36.

164. Note of Noble W. Jones, March 30, 1801, NJFP.

165. Ibid., 130–33. The American and French forces landed on the banks of the Vernon River roughly two miles south of Wormsloe and marched north through the swampland to attack Savannah.

166. Court Summons, July 10, 1780, NJFP.

167. *Georgia Gazette*, June 8, 1780, in family history notes, W. J. De Renne, 1876, CBFP, box 1, folder 7.

168. Estate Claims of Noble Jones, Noble W. Jones executor, May 3, 1783, NJFP.

169. Bullard, *Cumberland Island*, 89–91.

170. Kenneth Coleman, *American Revolution in Georgia*, 144–46.

171. Fraser, *Savannah in the Old South*, 139–40. Lewis Gray's influential study of southern agriculture sides with Fraser's interpretation of Savannah's wartime experience. See Gray, *History of Agriculture*, 2:596.

172. Poem of Noble W. Jones, February 6, 1781, DRFP 1064, box 9, folder 33.

173. In this regard, events on Wormsloe reflect Philip D. Morgan's assessment of the revolution as a temporary disruption of Lowcountry agriculture and slavery. The threat of British emancipation was very real, but the plantation system emerged from the turmoil of war more firmly entrenched than ever. See Philip D. Morgan, "Lowcountry Georgia," 36–37.

174. Fraser, *Savannah in the Old South*, 129, 133.

175. Return of the taxable estate of Noble Jones, 1785, DRFP 1064, box 6, folder 9. At that date, Wimberly was outside of immediate family ownership. George W. Jones would reunite the plantation during the 1850s.

TWO. Becoming a Plantation

1. Estate Inventory of Mary Bullock, n.d., DRFP 1064, box 6, folder 1; *Georgia Gazette*, February 18, 1796, 2, CBFP, box 19, folder 18.

2. Kelso, *Captain Jones's Wormslow*, 12–13.

3. George Jones to Dr. John Grimes, June 2, 1805, DRFP 1064, box 9, folder 15.

4. John Abbot's Birding Notebook, ms. 1654, Hargrett Rare Book and Manuscript Library, University of Georgia, Athens.

5. Ibid.

6. Krech, *Spirits of the Air*, 176–77.

7. Statistics compiled from the University of Virginia Library's Historical Census Data Browser.

8. Ibid.; Fraser, *Savannah in the Old South*, 241–340. For Savannah's winter tourism, see Olmsted, *Cotton Kingdom*, 1:227–28.

9. Josiah Whitney to George Jones, December 10, 1806, DRFP 1064, box 8, folder 33.

10. George Jones also owned a substantial rice plantation on Onslow Island, four miles upriver from Savannah, for at least a few years around the turn of the century. The property included 250 acres of high ground and 200 acres of "rice land," but there are no references to the plantation after 1800 (Indenture of George Jones, May 25, 1798, DRFP 1064, box 7, folder 11).

11. S. G. Stephens, "Origin of Sea Island Cotton," 394–99; Porcher and Fick, *Story of Sea Island Cotton*, 78–79; Coulter, *Wormsloe*, 29; Chaplin, "Creating," 175.

12. Porcher and Fick, *Story of Sea Island Cotton*, 91.

13. William Bartram, *Travels of William Bartram*, 44–45.

14. Chaplin, "Creating," 178–81.

15. Works Progress Administration, *Story of Sea Island Cotton*, 6–7; Seabrook, *Memoir*, preface, 18; Reese, *Colonial Georgia*, 129; Aiken, *Cotton Plantation South*, 57; Porcher and Fick, *Story of Sea Island Cotton*, 91; Stephens, "Origin of Sea Island Cotton," 393. In an 1844 article, Thomas Spalding of Sapelo offered an alternative history of the ar-

rival of sea island cotton. Spalding claimed that the first seed came to the Georgia coast from Bahamian planters in 1778. See Spalding, "On the Cotton Gin," 83.

16. E. C. Spary, "Of Nutmegs and Botanists: The Colonial Cultivation of Botanical Identity," in *Colonial Botany*, ed. Schiebinger and Swan, 190; Balick and Cox, *Plants, People, and Culture*, 139; William H. McNeill, "American Food Crops in the Old World," in *Seeds of Change*, ed. Viola and Margolis, 48, 55; Sidney W. Mintz, "Pleasure, Profit, and Satiation," in *Seeds of Change*, ed. Viola and Margolis, 120; Dodge, *Plants That Changed the World*, 10–30; Haughton, *Green Immigrants*, 326.

17. Pollan, *Botany of Desire*, 14–15; Haughton, *Green Immigrants*, 173–74.

18. Hedrick, *History*, 431.

19. Ibid., 431–36; Edgar Anderson, *Plants, Man, and Life*, 28.

20. Hedrick, *History*, 431–36.

21. Works Progress Administration, *Story of Sea Island Cotton*, 7; Vance, *Human Factors*, 42; Gray, *History of Agriculture*, 2:732–33. While irrigation was unnecessary, drainage ditches were a necessary expenditure on most sea island cotton plantations, including Wormsloe. See Porcher and Fick, *Story of Sea Island Cotton*, 148–50. Frances Kemble, a temporary resident of Butler and St. Simons Islands in 1838–39, remarked that sea island cotton once brought as much as half a guinea per pound on the London market. See Kemble, *Journal*, 202.

22. Porcher and Fick, *Story of Sea Island Cotton*, 76, 80–81, 99; Gray, *History of Agriculture*, 2:731–33; Yafa, *Cotton*, 86–87; John Singleton, "The Lancashire Cotton Industry, the Royal Navy, and the British Empire, c. 1700—c. 1960," in *Fibre That Changed the World*, ed. Farnie and Jeremy, 67–68; Keber, *Seas of Gold*, 194, 213.

23. Dodge, *Cotton*, 52–53. For accounts of the immense growth of the early English cotton manufacturing industry, see Douglas A. Farnie, "The Role of the Cotton Industry in Economic Development," in *Fibre That Changed the World*, ed. Farnie and Jeremy, 557–60; Hobhouse, *Seeds of Change*, 148–49.

24. Beckert, "Emancipation and Empire," 1405–9.

25. Bullard, *Cumberland Island*, 106.

26. Hobhouse, *Seeds of Change*, 143; Stewart, *"What Nature Suffers to Groe,"* 116–18; Porcher and Fick, *Story of Sea Island Cotton*, 148–54; Gray, *History of Agriculture*, 2:734–35; Rogers and Saunders, *Swamp Water and Wiregrass*, 156; Keber, *Seas of Gold*, 209–10; Shepard, "Sea Island Cotton," 195–96; Spalding, "On the Cotton Gin," 83.

27. For slave knowledge as the driving force of Lowcountry rice agriculture, see Carney, *Black Rice*, esp. 164–68; Peter H. Wood, *Black Majority*, 35–62.

28. Berlin, "From Creole to African." Though the number of creole slaves imported in these "charter generations" was small in comparison to the slaves brought directly from Africa as the Lowcountry's demand for laborers grew, Creel has argued that these initial slaves played a disproportionately large role in shaping the fusion culture of the region's African Americans. See Creel, *"Peculiar People,"* 43–44.

29. McFeely, *Sapelo's People*, 32–43; Gomez, *Exchanging Our Country Marks*, 77; Gomez, "Africans, Culture, and Islam in the Lowcountry," in *African American Life*, ed. Philip D. Morgan, 107–9.

30. Littlefield, *Rice and Slaves*; Carney, *Black Rice*; Judith A. Carney, "Out of Africa: Colonial Rice History in the Black Atlantic," in *Colonial Botany*, ed. Schiebinger and Swan, 187–203; Carney and Rosomoff, *In the Shadow of Slavery*, esp. 150–54; Peter H.

Wood, *Black Majority*, 61. These scholars' arguments for the dominant role of African customs and rice technology in the creation of Lowcountry rice agriculture have not gone unchallenged. See Eltis, Morgan, and Richardson, "Agency and Diaspora," 1353–56.

31. Gomez, *Exchanging Our Country Marks*, 69; Gomez, *Black Crescent*, 143, 152–153.

32. For these names and their derivations, see Noble Jones's Will, 1767, DRFP 1064, box 6, folder 10 (copy); list of slave names in GWJ Farm Journal; Turner, *Africanisms in the Gullah Dialect*, 31–190.

33. Gomez, *Black Crescent*, 149–52; Keith E. Baird and Mary A. Twining, "Names and Naming in the Sea Islands," in *Crucible of Carolina*, ed. Michael Montgomery, 23–37.

34. Spalding, "On the Cotton Gin," 83.

35. Rogers and Saunders, *Swamp Water and Wiregrass*, 156; Burke, *Reminiscences of Georgia*, 117, 145.

36. Gray, *History of Agriculture*, 2:731.

37. Ibid., 2:735.

38. Creel, *"Peculiar People,"* 190–192.

39. Ibid., 116.

40. Tax Return of George Jones, 1812, DRFP 1064, box 7, folder 65; Tax Return of George Jones, 1816, DRFP 1064, box 7, folder 66.

41. During the early 1800s, Jones occasionally left the Savannah area entirely and traveled to the Sandhills to seek "the smiles of health." See Edward Campbell to George Jones, December 1, 1806, DRFP 1064, box 8, folder 32.

42. George Jones to Noble W. Jones II, September 20, 1803, Jones Family Papers, box 1, folder 1, Georgia Historical Society, Savannah.

43. Receipt, George Jones to Noble W. Glen, February 15, 1809, DRFP 1064, box 7, folder 47. In 1809, Jones paid Glen $450 to oversee Wormsloe and a plantation on Skidaway. Based on an announcement in the *Public Intelligencer*, July 21, 1807, 3, Sims seems to have managed Wormsloe during 1807.

44. Contract between George Jones and John Rawls, January 2, 1810, DRFP 1064, box 29, folder 1. The contract's provision for Rawls's food, lodging, and a servant probably explain the difference between his and Glen's wages.

45. Kelso, *Captain Jones's Wormslow*, 13–14.

46. Lockley, *Lines in the Sand*, 32.

47. Sarah Jones to George Jones, November 18, 1796, NJFP.

48. Ibid. For the growth of Georgia exports of shingles and barrel staves to the Caribbean, see Reese, *Colonial Georgia*, 127; Kenneth Coleman, *Colonial Georgia*, 219–20.

49. For some of the artifacts that support these activities, see a list of items auctioned from Noble W. Jones's estate, N. W. Jones Estate Receipt Book, 1810–1816, DRFP 1064, box 9, folder 23. For the cotton gin on the Joneses' Skidaway property, see Receipt of George Jones, February 15, 1809, DRFP 1064, box 7, folder 47.

50. Sarah Jones to George Jones, November 18, 1796, NJFP.

51. Philip D. Morgan, "Work and Culture," 576; Philip D. Morgan, *Slave Counterpoint*, 179–87; Betty Wood, *Gender, Race, and Rank*, 8; Betty Wood, *Women's Work, Men's Work*, 17; Cashin, *Wilderness*, 62–63; Olmsted, *Cotton Kingdom*, 1:246–49; Creel,

"Peculiar People," 191; Burke, *Reminiscences of Georgia,* 117; Keber, *Seas of Gold,* 211–12; Spalding, "On the Cotton Gin," 83–84; Lockley, *Lines in the Sand,* 58–61.

52. Carney and Rosomoff, *In the Shadow of Slavery,* 123–38.

53. Stewart, *"What Nature Suffers to Groe,"* 134–37; Theresa Singleton, "Reclaiming the Gullah-Geechee Past," in *African American Life,* ed. Philip D. Morgan, 170–74. Ras Michael Brown has argued that especially for the colonial era, Lowcountry slaves' usage of coastal forests reflected African cultural and environmental understandings of woodlands. See Brown, "'Walk in the Feenda': West-Central Africans and the Forest in the South Carolina-Georgia Lowcountry," in *Central Africans and Cultural Transformation,* ed. Heyward, 289–317.

54. Stewart, *"What Nature Suffers to Groe,"* 128–29.

55. Account of George Jones with Edward Telfair's Estate, April 12, 1813, DRFP 1064, box 7, folder 48.

56. George Jones to Manning Spradley, December 16, 1831, DRFP 1064, box 8, folder 39. Spradley was overseer on Jones's Jefferson County plantation.

57. List of Lands, Lots, Improvements, Dwelling Houses, and Slaves Owned by George Jones, April 1, 1815, DRFP 1064, box 7, folder 36.

58. Estate Inventory of Noble W. Jones, April 1, 1815, NJFP.

59. Indenture, Ann Reid to George Jones, February 8, 1819, DRFP 1064, box 58, folder 15.

60. Deposition of John Hatcher to Isaac Russell, February 20, 1828, DRFP 1064, box 7, folder 4; Accounts of George Jones, 1827, DRFP 1064, box 7, folder 2.

61. Kelso, *Captain Jones's Wormslow,* 50.

62. Keber, *Seas of Gold,* 234–36.

63. Coulter, *Wormsloe,* 207.

64. For an earlier example of George Jones's fears concerning the dangers of the Lowcountry environment, see Edward Campbell to George Jones, December 1, 1806, DRFP 1064, box 8, folder 32.

65. Plan of Wormsloe House, 1829, De Renne Family Papers (ms. 1064a), oversize drawer, folder 15, Hargrett Rare Book and Manuscript Library, University of Georgia, Athens; Kelso, *Captain Jones's Wormslow,* 15.

66. Bragg, *De Renne,* 9–10, appendix 1, 400.

67. Records Ledger of George Jones's Estate, 1839–1849, DRFP 1064, box 12, folder 25.

68. Ibid.; GWJ Farm Journal. For Wormsloe's cotton production, see fig. 2.

69. Notebook of Estate Records, DRFP 1064, box 13, folder 9.

70. Receipt Book, n.d., De Renne Family Receipts and Remedies, ms. 1120, folder 11, Hargrett Rare Book and Manuscript Library, University of Georgia, Athens; Receipt Book, ca. 1840, CBFP, box 23, folder 9. De Renne Family Receipts and Remedies, folders 1–10, also include a number of period recipes in loose form.

71. Receipt Book, n.d., De Renne Family Receipts and Remedies, folder 11.

72. Ibid. For reference to benne on Wormsloe, see GWJ Farm Journal.

73. Jessica B. Harris, *Iron Pots and Wooden Spoons,* xii.

74. Hess, "Okra," 241.

75. Receipt Book, n.d., De Renne Family Receipts and Remedies, folder 11.

76. For the provenance of these ingredients and techniques, see Jessica B. Harris

and Robert L. Hall, "Savoring Africa in the New World," in *Seeds of Change*, ed. Viola and Margolis, 166–67.

77. Mink, "It Begins in the Belly," 313.

78. Ferris, "Edible South," 4.

79. The burgeoning "slow food" movement has echoed this philosophy, declaring that food consumers "become a part of and a partner in the production process" by eating (http://www.slowfood.com/about_us/eng/philisophy.lasso).

80. Stewart, *"What Nature Suffers to Groe,"* 135; Betty Wood, *Women's Work, Men's Work*, 38.

81. For another discussion of these food sources and the environment on Wormsloe, see Swanson, "Wormsloe's Belly."

82. GWJDR Account Book.

83. Farm notebook, DRFP 1064, box 13, folder 10. Ruffin's *An Essay on Calcareous Manures* was first published in 1832.

84. For an in-depth exploration of George W. Jones's character and interests, see Bragg, *De Renne*, 29–77.

85. Jones was not alone in reading agricultural periodicals; journals such as the *Farmers' Register* (Shellbanks, Va.), *Southern Cultivator* (Atlanta), and *Southern Planter* (Richmond, Va.) attracted wealthy planters, and articles from these publications were often reprinted in local newspapers across the region.

86. Taylor, *Arator*; Shelton and Hill, *Liberal Republicanism*; Ruffin, *Nature's Management*; Stoll, *Larding the Lean Earth*, 150–60; Mathew, *Edmund Ruffin*; Kirby, *Poquosin*, 61–85; Swanson, "Fighting over Fencing"; David R. Montgomery, *Dirt*, 129–130; Steffen, "In Search"; Cohen, *Notes from the Ground*, 43–47, 86–94. Jones was not the only Isle of Hope planter interested in agricultural improvement during the 1850s. An 1854 letter by William White from the peninsula indicated that White had published an article on southern farm improvement in a national agricultural journal, perhaps the *American Farmer* out of Baltimore. See William P. White to M. W. Phillips, January 9, 1854, Phillips (W. M.) Letter Collection, Special Collections Department, Mitchell Memorial Library, Mississippi State University, Starkville.

87. GWJ Farm Journal.

88. David R. Montgomery, *Dirt*, 185.

89. Ibid., 185–87; Wines, *Fertilizer in America*, 33–53; Kirby, *Mockingbird Song*, 89; Stoll, *Larding the Lean Earth*, 187–90; Shawn William Miller, *Environmental History*, 147–54.

90. GWJ Farm Journal.

91. George W. Jones to Col. Peter Firce (?), August 15, 1855, DRFP 1064, box 12, folder 22.

92. GWJ Farm Journal.

93. Ibid., November 27, 12, 1856.

94. Ibid., March 27, 1859.

95. Claire Strom, "Texas Fever and the Dispossession of the Southern Yeoman Farmer," in *Environmental History*, ed. Sutter and Manganiello, 221–25.

96. GWJ Farm Journal.

97. Keber, *Seas of Gold*, 194–204; Spalding, "On the Cotton Gin," 84; GWJ Farm Journal, February 3, 1860.

98. GWJDR Account Book.

99. Porcher and Fick, *Story of Sea Island Cotton*, 163.

100. GWJDR Account Book.

101. Bragg, *De Renne*, 78–89. Bragg's study of the De Renne family does an excellent job of parsing the entangled family connections and exploring their economic and social lives. In just one example of the complexity of the Jones family tree, George W. Jones married Mary Wallace Nuttall, who was the stepdaughter of his nephew, George Noble Jones (who was the son of George W. Jones's stepbrother, Noble W. Jones II, who died nine years before George W. Jones's birth), and the daughter of Mary Savage Nuttall. See Bragg, *De Renne*, appendix 1, tables 2, 6, 14.

102. GWJ Farm Journal, November 12, 1856. See also, for example, "Alderney Cows," 274; "Merino Sheep," 184.

103. GWJ Farm Journal, March 26, 1857.

104. Ibid.. The Fones McCarthy gin dated back to 1840, when McCarthy patented it in Demopolis, Alabama, but the gin only became popular with sea island cotton producers after an 1854 redesign.

105. Lynn A. Nelson, *Pharsalia*, 149–89.

106. Bragg, *De Renne*, 93.

107. GWJDR Account Book.

108. On "path dependency," see Melosi, *Sanitary City*, 4; Colten, *Unnatural Metropolis*, esp. 140–61.

109. GWJ Farm Journal, November 30, 1856.

110. GWJ Farm Journal; GWJDR Account Book. For the typicality of the diet of Wormsloe's slaves, see Hilliard, *Hog Meat and Hoecake*, 55–62; Jessica B. Harris, *Welcome Table*, 25–26; Betty Wood, *Women's Work, Men's Work*, 36–38.

111. For a discussion of slave gardens and hunting and fishing in Lowcountry Georgia, see Lockley, *Lines in the Sand*, 60–61; Betty Wood, *Women's Work, Men's Work*, 31–35. For slave and later freedpeople's reliance on woods and waters across the South for subsistence, see Giltner, *Hunting and Fishing*, chap. 1; Hahn, "Hunting, Fishing, and Foraging."

112. Redpath, *Roving Editor*, 75.

113. Burke, *Reminiscences of Georgia*, 112–13.

114. Olmsted, *Cotton Kingdom*, 1:233; for an additional description of local slave gardens and stock keeping, see 251.

115. Betty Wood, *Women's Work, Men's Work*, 35.

116. Cecelski, *Waterman's Song*, 67–76. For the popularity of oysters and marsh hen eggs among Lowcountry slaves, see Burke, *Reminiscences of Georgia*, 137, 140.

117. "Marsh and Its World," 38.

118. "Extract of Title, Long Island," n.d., DRFP 2819, box 10, folder 6.

119. GWJ Farm Journal, January 6, 1858, 1853.

120. GWJDR Account Book.

121. Bragg, *De Renne*, 96–97.

122. Singleton, "Reclaiming the Gullah-Geechee Past," 166; Foby, "Management of Servants," 227; "Plantation Management," 169–70; R. W. N. N., "Negro Cabins," 121–22; "Management of Slaves, &c.," 32–33; William H. Harrison, "Stoves for Negroes' Dwellings."

123. Aiken, *Cotton Plantation South*, 15. For the typicality of Wormsloe's slave cabins, see Porcher and Fick, *Story of Sea Island Cotton*, 219–21; for images of similar slave cabins on the South Carolina sea islands, see Westmacott, *African-American Gardens*, 43.

124. GWJ Farm Journal.

125. Aiken, *Cotton Plantation South*, 13–14; Singleton, "Reclaiming the Gullah-Geechee Past," 169–70; Vlach, *Back of the Big House*, esp. 183–227. Singleton describes dispersed slave settlements as more common in the Lowcountry than in the South in general, perhaps because of a high rate of absentee ownership along the coast. Wormsloe, with its separate but singular slave village, seems to have been an intermediate form between dispersed and nucleated plantation yards.

126. Miles, *House on Diamond Hill*, 75.

127. Vlach, *Back of the Big House*, 168–69.

128. For a description of this process, see Isaac, *Transformation of Virginia*, 52–53; Miles, *House on Diamond Hill*, 78–79.

129. Genovese, *Roll, Jordan, Roll*, 5.

130. Ibid., 524–35.

131. For examples of planter ideas concerning the compatibility of slavery and reform, see Mathew, *Edmund Ruffin*, 56–66; Lynn A. Nelson, *Pharsalia*, 104–8; Craven, *Edmund Ruffin:*, 86–87; Stoll, *Larding the Lean Earth*, 123–25, 190–91.

132. Mathew, *Edmund Ruffin*, 206–7. See also Stoll, *Larding the Lean Earth*, 158–59.

133. Fitzhugh, *Cannibals All!*, xiii.

134. Ruffin, *Essay on Calcareous Manures*, 162–64, 187–99.

135. Address of James C. Bruce to the Mecklenburg and Granville Agricultural Clubs, July 14, 1847, 7–15, Bruce Family Papers, Records of Antebellum Southern Plantations, series E, part 3, reel 14, University of Georgia Library, Athens.

136. Saikku, *This Delta, This Land*, 98–106; Siegel, *Roots of Southern Distinctiveness*, 105–19.

137. Gray, *History of Agriculture*, 2:739.

138. Figures drawn from U.S. Census Bureau, *Seventh Census*, 377–83; Kennedy, *Agriculture*, 24–26.

139. Fraser, *Savannah in the Old South*, 212, 239, 241–44, 247–54; Jacqueline Jones, "A Spirit of Enterprise: The African American Challenge to the Confederate Project in Civil War–Era Savannah," in *African American Life*, ed. Philip D. Morgan, 192; Johnson, *Black Savannah*, 55–58; Haunton, "Savannah in the 1850's," 5–33.

140. Olmsted, *Cotton Kingdom*, 1:230–31.

141. For a diagram and description of the Hermitage, see Vlach, *Back of the Big House*, 174–75.

142. For reference to a 7.5-foot alligator at Wormsloe, see GWJ Farm Journal, May 11, 1859.

THREE. Wormsloe Remade

1. Mary Jones in Coulter, *Wormsloe*, 232.

2. Receipt of George W. Jones, 1859, DRFP 1064, box 13, folder 16; GWJ Farm Journal, 1860, 1861.

3. GWJ Farm Journal; GWJDR Account Book.

4. Coulter, *Wormsloe*, 231–32. On lowland planters who temporarily sent their slaves to southern Appalachia, see Inscoe, *Race, War, and Remembrance*, 84.

5. Coulter, *Wormsloe*, 232; "Yankee News from the Georgia Coast," (unidentified newspaper clipping), December 30, 1861, DRFP 2819, box 35, scrapbook 4.

6. A local newspaper stated that "the cotton from all the islands around here has been removed to Savannah," probably because the staple made such an inviting target for Union raids. See "Yankee News from the Georgia Coast" (unidentified newspaper clipping), December 30, 1861, DRFP 2819, box 35, scrapbook 4.

7. Tax assessment, 1863, CBFP, box 19, folder 8; GWJDR Account Book. For Jones's direction of wartime care of his slaves, see medical receipts of George W. Jones, December 30, 1863, December 29, 1864, DRFP 1064, box 13, folder 12.

8. Contract between George W. Jones and Edward Nelson, January 10, 1864, DRFP 1064, box 58, folder 12.

9. Hay Receipt, February 1862, DRFP 1064, box 13, folder 12. Quartermasters usually paid for requisitioned goods, but they did so with inflated Confederate paper money or IOUs.

10. Bragg, *De Renne*, 100; Coulter, *Wormsloe*, 233; W. O. D. Rockwell, "Map of Wormsloe and Vicinity" (blueprint), April 20, 1908, DRFP 2819, oversize drawer; "Composite Suitability Map," University of Georgia Department of Geography, Center for Remote Sensing and Mapping Science, http://crms.uga.edu/files/Wormsloe_maps3.pdf; Dan Rice, Knudson, and Westberry, "Restoration." Coulter incorrectly placed the location of the southernmost Confederate earthworks at the sight of Noble Jones's colonial tabby fort.

11. "Autobiography of W. J. De Renne," ca. 1865, DRFP 1064, box 14, folder 20.

12. Receipts of George W. Jones, November 3, 5, 1862, November 4, 1863, all in DRFP 1064, box 13, folder 12.

13. Bragg, *De Renne*, 100–101.

14. W. B. Hodgson to George Washington Smith, March 29, 1865, DRFP 1064, box 12, folder 10.

15. Hahn et al., *Freedom*, 201; Perdue, *Negro in Savannah*, 8.

16. Bragg, *De Renne*, 104–5; Simus Howell, Land Title, July 13, 1865, DRFP 1064, box 26, folder 3.

17. List of Wormsloe slaves in GWJ Farm Journal. One hand was listed as "Prince" and another as "Prince Savage."

18. Simus Howell, Land Title, July 13, 1865, DRFP 1064, box 26, folder 3.

19. Hahn et al., *Freedom*, 466.

20. Reid, *After the War*, 132.

21. William Tecumseh Sherman in McFeely, *Sapelo's People*, 129.

22. W. B. Hodgson to George Washington Smith, March 29, 1865, DRFP 1064, box 12, folder 10.

23. Hahn et al., *Freedom*, 9; Allison Dorsey, "'The Great Cry of Our People Is Land!': Black Settlement and Community Development on Ossabaw Island, Georgia, 1865–1900," in *African American Life*, ed. Philip D. Morgan, 233–34; Blight, *Race and Reunion*, 44–45.

24. R. Habersham & Sons to George W. Jones, August 5, 1865, DRFP 1064, box 13, folder 12.

25. Estate Inventory Book of Wymberley J. De Renne, 1895, DRFP 1064, box 12, folder 26.

26. Bragg, *De Renne*, 106–7; Coulter, *Wormsloe*, 234; McFeely, *Sapelo's People*, 132.

27. Records of Savannah Area Property Restoration, Bureau of Refugees, Freedmen, and Abandoned Lands, Savannah Field Office, M1903, roll 85, National Archives and Records Administration, Morrow, Ga.; Dorsey, "'Great Cry,'" 239. A brief mention of a "Briston Drayton" as a witness for the prosecution in a case involving the condition of the Skidaway bridge suggests that at least one of the freedmen still lived on Long Island in 1866. See *Nichols v. Hammond Aves*, complaints registered, Records of Savannah Area Property Restoration, Bureau of Refugees, Freedmen, and Abandoned Lands, Savannah Field Office, M1903, roll 84.

28. Georgia Agricultural Census, Chatham County, 1870, T1137, roll 7, National Archives and Records Administration, Morrow, Ga.

29. J. William Harris, *Deep Souths*, 16–26, 50–51, 350, table 1; Perdue, *Negro in Savannah*, 105–8; Work, "Negroes of Warsaw, Georgia," 30; Rogers and Saunders, *Swamp Water and Wiregrass*, 163–64; Dorsey, "'Great Cry,'" 247–48. Dorsey traces the process of African American land acquisition from Ossabaw Island to the inland community of Pin Point, south of Savannah.

30. Perdue, *Negro in Savannah*, 108–9, 111–13.

31. Work, "Negroes of Warsaw, Georgia," 30.

32. "Buying Land," 58.

33. For the uses of these and other wild plants near Wormsloe, see Georgia Writer's Project, *Drums and Shadows*, 75.

34. Muir, *Thousand-Mile Walk*, 59; Perdue, *Negro in Savannah*, 116–18.

35. Bragg, *De Renne*, 56–60, 107; George W. Jones, Petition for Name Change, Chatham Superior Court, January 1866, DRFP 1064, box 12, folder 12.

36. For similar rentals, see McFeely, *Sapelo's People*, 140.

37. GWJDR Account Book; "Interesting Papers Found in Safety Box Long Unopened" (unidentified newspaper clipping), April 1, 1933, DRFP 1064, box 31, folder 9; Family History Notes, DRFP 1064, box 14, folder 14. After the 1865 contract, the firm was referred to as J. W. Teeple and R. T. Smillie. For the identification of the Smillie firm as northern, see Bragg, *De Renne*, 106–7.

38. Rental agreement between Allan L. Wyllie and N. B. Wilson, J. R. Pierce, and Jane Wilson, November 1, 1866, Wyllie Family Papers, Virginia Historical Society, Richmond.

39. J. William Harris, *Deep Souths*, 9.

40. Saikku, *This Delta, This Land*, 112; Lawrence N. Powell, *New Masters*, xvi.

41. GWJDR Account Book.

42. L. L. Knight, "Wormsloe," *Atlanta Constitution* (clipping), n.d., DRFP 2819, box 36, folder 2.

43. Megan Kate Nelson, *Trembling Earth*, 131–32; Porcher and Fick, *Story of Sea Island Cotton*, 327–28; J. William Harris, *Deep Souths*, 23–24.

44. Beckert, "Emancipation and Empire," 1411–22; Beckert, "From Tuskegee to Togo," 501–2, 504.

45. Saikku, *This Delta, This Land*, 134; Rogers and Saunders, *Swamp Water and Wiregrass*, 167.

46. Porcher and Fick, *Story of Sea Island Cotton*, 332–33, 328, table 13.11.

47. Vance, *Human Factors in Cotton Culture*, 13.

48. Contract between George W. J. De Renne and Brutus Butler, January 19, 1869, DRFP 1064, box 26, folder 3. Brutus's son, Bru'urs, also testified that his father worked the land for De Renne following the war. See Georgia Writer's Project, *Drums and Shadows*, 99.

49. Contract between George W. J. De Renne and James W. Jones, 1870, DRFP 1064, box 29, folder 4; slave list in George W. Jones Diary, DRFP 1064, box 12, folder 26. The contract does not specify whether Jones was allowed the use of Wormsloe's gin or other buildings.

50. GWJDR Account Book.

51. Ibid.; GWJDR Diary, June 1, 1880.

52. GWJDR Diary, March 8, May 7, December 31, 1876.

53. This lack of rearrangement of the plantation's living spaces likely resulted from the relatively short duration (less than twenty years) of tenantry on Wormsloe.

54. Georgia Agricultural Census, Chatham County, 1880, roll 11.

55. Cabins stereograph, neg. #3889, WWDFP, box 119. These stereographs are undated, but William Bragg believes they were made at some point during the 1870s. The appearance of Wormsloe's structures, fields, and woodlands throughout the collection supports Bragg's contention.

56. Westmacott, *African-American Gardens*, 17, 41–42. The form of side yards surrounded by palings was also a West African tradition (43). For other images of the continued use of paling lots next to area cabins following emancipation, see Wheeler, *Savannah River Plantations*, 102, 104.

57. There is a tremendous body of literature on this transition from slave labor to sharecropping in the rural South. Some of the most well known overviews include Hahn, *Nation under Our Feet*, chaps. 3, 4; Litwack, *Been in the Storm*; Ransom and Sutch, *One Kind of Freedom*. State and regional examples include Rodrigue, *Reconstruction in the Cane Fields*; Kerr-Ritchie, *Freedpeople in the Tobacco South*; Saville, *Work of Reconstruction*; Reidy, *From Slavery to Agrarian Capitalism*; Lynda Morgan, *Emancipation in Virginia's Tobacco Belt*; Ronald Davis, *Good and Faithful Labor*; Shlomowitz, "Origins of Southern Sharecropping," esp. 563–65. Although sharecropping as a labor system quickly prevailed in the majority of the South following Appomattox, wage labor persisted longer in the Lowcountry and Louisiana's sugar districts, probably because of the large average size of plantations and the political power of large planters.

58. Saville, *Work of Reconstruction*, 133–35; Foner, *Reconstruction*, 174–75; Hahn, *Nation under Our Feet*, 171–72; J. William Harris, *Deep Souths*, 15–17.

59. Foner, *Reconstruction*, 174–75.

60. Contract between William Gibbon and 120 Freedpeople, March 1, 1866, Labor Contracts, 1866–1867, Records of Savannah Area Property Restoration, Bureau of Refugees, Freedmen, and Abandoned Lands, Savannah Field Office, M1903, roll 82.

61. Stewart, "*What Nature Suffers to Groe*," 193–96.

62. McFeely, *Sapelo's People*, 88; Perdue, *Negro in Savannah*, 4–5. For examples of

Chatham County murders, see "Report of Persons Murdered in District of Savannah, Georgia," Miscellaneous Retained Reports, Records of Savannah Area Property Restoration, Bureau of Refugees, Freedmen, and Abandoned Lands, Savannah Field Office, M1903, roll 84.

63. Bragg, *De Renne*, 115–16. For another description of the bridge location, see Kelly, *Short History of Skidaway Island*, 46.

64. G. W. J. De Renne to G. Fenwick Jones, May 25, 1871, DRFP 1064, box 30, folder 6; Plat of Proposed Causeway from Isle of Hope to Long Island, 1871, De Renne Family Papers (ms. 1064a), oversize drawer, folder 26, Hargrett Rare Book and Manuscript Library, University of Georgia, Athens.

65. Porcher and Fick, *Story of Sea Island Cotton*, 119.

66. Estate Inventory Book of Wymberley J. De Renne, 1895, DRFP 1064, box 12, folder 26.

67. GWJDR Account Book.

68. Account Book of Estates, 1880, DRFP 1064, box 15, folder 4. Reconstruction rental of Wormsloe tended to show a slight profit each year, but only because De Renne invested almost nothing in maintaining or improving the land. See GWJDR Account Book.

69. For De Renne's Reconstruction-era historical society activity, see his correspondence in DRFP 1064, box 13, folder 5.

70. GWJDR Diary, June 6, 1879.

71. Estate Inventory Book of Wymberley J. De Renne, 1895, DRFP 1064, box 12, folder 26; GWJDR Diary, March 10, 1876, April 13, 1878;s Will of G. W. J. De Renne, 1880, DRFP 1064, box 12, folder 16.

72. GWJDR Diary, April 27, 1876, January 25, 1879, February 4, March 22, April 22, 1880.

73. Ibid., January 5, 1877, February 20, 1879.

74. Jones, "Sketch," 196–97. Jones had delivered the speech before the Georgia Historical Society in February 1881.

75. Bragg, *De Renne*, 231.

76. Ibid., 172.

77. Muir, *Thousand-Mile Walk*, 69.

78. John Bartram, "Diary," 30.

79. GWJDR Diary, November 28, 1878.

80. On the Virginia oyster's life cycle, requirements, and management issues, see Keiner, *Oyster Question*, esp. chap. 1. On population variability, see Hofmann and Powell, "Environmental Variability Effects," s27–s28.

81. Contracts between George De Renne and Edward Nelson, March 19, 1870, May 5, 1875, May 15, 1880, all in DRFP 1064, box 26, folder 3; Contract between George De Renne and Edward Nelson, 1870, DRFP 1064, box 29, folder 4; Contracts between Wymberley J. De Renne and Edward Nelson, 1892, January 1895, both in DRFP 1064, box 29, folder 6; Contract between Wymberley J. De Renne and Edward Nelson, April 1906, Contract between Wymberley J. De Renne and Clarence Nelson, October 1906, both in DRFP 1064, box 29, folder 9; Lawton and Cunningham to Wymberley J. De Renne, March 23, 1911, DRFP 1064, box 30, folder 1. By 1911, the annual rental rate

had increased to one hundred dollars, a sign that Nelson's harvesting efforts may have intensified.

82. *Code of the State of Georgia, 1867*, 322, §§ 1614–15; *Code of the State of Georgia, 1873*, 278–79, §§ 1618–23; *Code of the State of Georgia, 1882*, 347, §§ 1618–23.

83. *Code of the State of Georgia, 1895*, 463–68, §§ 1691–1711.

84. Ibid., 466, § 1700.

85. WJDR Account Book, October 30, 1901. Giltner has shown that white landowner prosecution of African American oyster and fish poachers was common in the South Carolina and Georgia Lowcountry around the end of the nineteenth century and often stemmed from white annoyance with blacks who used the region's rich natural resources to subsist largely outside of the wage labor market. See Giltner, *Hunting and Fishing*, 35–36.

86. U.S. Census, population schedule for Chatham County, Georgia, 1900.

87. For Nelson's contract, see Lawton and Cunningham to Wymberley J. De Renne, March 23, 1911, DRFP 1064, box 30, folder 1. For an enumeration of oystering court cases, see "Notes on Oyster Poaching and Illegal Fishing," DRFP 1064, box 30, folder 1. These low penalties suggest that local judges or juries were sympathetic to the plight of watermen, as the state code called for fines between fifty and five hundred dollars.

88. WJDR Account Book, October 10, 1907. It is unclear if Mauruel Williams was a former employee or simply a neighbor with whom De Renne was well acquainted.

89. Keiner, *Oyster Question*, 74–81; J. William Harris, *Deep Souths*, 143–44; Keiner, "W. K. Brooks," 383.

90. Work, "Negroes of Warsaw, Georgia," 32–37; J. William Harris, *Deep Souths*, 143–44; Piechocinski, *Once upon an Island*, 58–60. A similar oyster-packing plant opened on St. Catherines Island during the early 1900s. See Thomas et al., "Anthropology," 237.

91. For the early history of oyster aquaculture, see Keiner, *Oyster Question*, esp. 60–102. For a discussion of the importance of wildlife management in early conservation thought, see Reiger, *American Sportsmen*, esp. 50–72.

92. For this definition of a commons, see Warren, *Hunter's Game*, 99. See also Jacoby, *Crimes against Nature*.

93. GWJDR Diary, March 20, 1880; for a similar meal, see April 12, 1878.

94. Ibid., March 10, 1876.

95. For examples of these articles, see "Fences and Bonds," May 8, 1894, "The Fence Question," April 20, 1895, "Don't Want an Election," n.d., "They Want the Election," May 2, 1895, "There Will Be an Election," May 9, 1895, "Contest at Hand: Wednesday 'No Fence' Will Win Its Fight," June 29, 1895, "The No Fence Majority Declared by the Ordinary," July 5, 1895, "No Fence Law," July 4, 1895, "Cattle Must Be Fenced In," January 4, 1896, all clippings in DRFP 2819, box 35, scrapbook 5.

96. Hahn, *Roots of Southern Populism*; King, "Closing"; McDonald and McWhiney, "South"; Hahn, "Hunting, Fishing, and Foraging"; Hahn, "Response."

97. Kantor, *Politics and Property Rights*; Kantor and Kousser, "Common Sense or Commonwealth?"; Kantor, "Razorbacks."

98. A. Oemler, "The Issue in Chatham County" (clipping), June 2, 1895, DRFP 2819, box 35, scrapbook 5.

99. "Vote for No Fence" (clipping), June 30, 1894, in ibid.

100. "Fences and Bonds, Close Relation between the Two Elections" (clipping), May 4, 1895, in ibid.

101. See negatives 3592, 3593, 4141, and 4142, WWDFP, box 119; photo of longleaf pine stand, CBFP, box 42, folder 36.

102. Henderson, *History*, 2:40–50.

103. Ibid, 1:14–15; Barron, *Mixed Harvest*, 83–84, 89; Smith-Howard, "Perfecting Nature's Food," 28.

104. Receipt of W. J. De Renne, November 2, 1905, DRFP 1064, box 29, folder 8.

105. Bateman, "Improvement in American Dairy Farming," 267; Leavitt, "Attempts," 64.

106. Lemmer, "Spread," 88–89.

107. WJDR Account Book, 1899; Jesse Beach to Wymberley J. De Renne, September 7, 1905, DRFP 1064, box 29, folder 8.

108. Smith-Howard, "Perfecting Nature's Food," 44–46; Gardner, *Traditional American Farming Techniques*, 644–45.

109. Clippings, WJDR Account Book; Jesse Beach to Wymberley J. De Renne, September 7, 1905, DRFP 1064, box 29, folder 8.

110. Bateman, "Improvement in American Dairy Farming," 267–68.

111. Date Book, 1916, DRFP 1064, box 14, folder 13; WJDR Account Book, 1902, 1905, 1910; Wymberley J. De Renne Account Book, 1912–14, DRFP 1064, box 15, folder 2; field map of northern portion of Wormsloe, n.d., DRFP 2819, box 10, folder 8.

112. Risjord, "From the Plow to the Cow," 45–46; Fish, "History." On the slow adoption of silos in the South, see Ormie, "Ensilage at the South," 1.

113. Henderson, *History*, 1:v–vi; Bateman, "Improvement in American Dairy Farming," 259–60; Smith-Howard, "Perfecting Nature's Food," 72–74. Fluid milk became a more common Georgia dairy product during the 1920s. See Henderson, *History*, 1:v–vi.

114. Account Book of Wymberley J. De Renne, 1894, DRFP 2819, box 8, folder 1.

115. "Truck Farming around Savannah" (clipping), *Savannah Press*, February 11, 1896, DRFP 2819, box 35, scrapbook 5; "U.S. City Souvenir and Official Program," Savannah Military Inter-State Association, 1896, DRFP 2819, box 34, scrapbook 2.

116. For this progression of farm production over the course of the postbellum nineteenth century, see Kennedy, *Agriculture*, 24–26; Walker, *Ninth Census*, 120–23; *Report on the Productions of Agriculture*, 147, 183, 218; *Report on the Statistics of Agriculture*, 241, 281, 322, 360, 394, 426, 464, 504; *Census Reports, Twelfth Census*, 1:426–27, 595, 75, 2:192, 2:365, 2:431, 2:546. For the truck farming industry in early twentieth century Chatham County, see Latimer and Bucher, *Soil Survey*, 8–9; Savannah Board of Trade, *Agricultural Chatham*.

117. Stewart, *"What Nature Suffers to Groe,"* 224–29; Latimer and Bucher, *Soil Survey*, 6–7, 10. For southern truck farming in general, see McCorkle, "Agricultural Experiment Stations"; McCorkle, "Moving Perishables to Market."

118. Pete Daniel, *Breaking the Land*, 3–38; Kirby, *Rural Worlds Lost*, 26–29; Wright, *Old South, New South*, esp. 52–60; Shifflett, *Patronage and Poverty*; Hahn, *Roots of Southern Populism*.

119. Kennedy, *Agriculture*, xciii, xcvi; *Census Reports, Twelfth Census*, 412, 526. In 1859, the nation's farmers produced 5,387,052 bales of cotton and 434,209,461 pounds of tobacco. In 1899, those figures were 9,534,707 bales and 868,163,275 pounds.

FOUR. "Worth Crossing Oceans to See"

1. Fraser, *Lowcountry Hurricanes*, 187–90; neg. 7232, February 24, 1897, DRFP 1064, box 29, folder 11. For a letter discussing the storm's passage over Wormsloe, see J. G. Bulloch to W. J. De Renne, January 5, 1897, DRFP 1064, box 16, folder 7.

2. Fraser, *Lowcountry Hurricanes*, 14–16, 38–54, 121–32; GWJ Farm Journal, 1854; Robert Habersham to George N. Jones, September 4, 1854, Jones Family Papers, box 1, folder 10, Georgia Historical Society, Savannah.

3. Fraser, *Lowcountry Hurricanes*, 224–27; Craig Barrow Jr. to Craig Barrow, August 14, 1940, Hurricane Notes, August 11, 1940, both in CBFP, box 5, folder 51; Photographs of Storm Damage, CBFP, box 43, folder 1.

4. As Ted Steinberg notes, the damaging consequences of natural disasters, such as hurricanes, often spring from human decisions made with little regard for the power of the natural world. A hurricane's damage to Savannah or Wormsloe, for example, is both a natural process and a product of the decision to build along the southeastern coast, a choice often made despite copious evidence of the power of tropical storms. See Steinberg, *Acts of God*, esp. 47–68.

5. Bragg, *De Renne*, 144–45; Rental Contract between Wymberley De Renne and the Pennsylvania Company for Insurance on Lives and Granting Annuities, 1891, Rental Agreement between Wymberley De Renne and the Pennsylvania Company for Insurance on Lives and Granting Annuities, 1895, both in DRFP 1064, box 29, folder 6.

6. Bragg, *De Renne*, 223–30, 285; Postcards of House and Library, DRFP 1064, box 22, folder 11; Pier Architectural Plan, February 9, 1899, DRFP 2819, box 10, folder 5; Water Tower Photograph, neg. 6268, Map of Wormsloe, spring 1897, both in DRFP 2819, oversize drawer; Pier Construction Photograph, DRFP 2819, box 24, folder 5; Photograph Album, 1899, DRFP 2819, box 30; Elfrida De Renne to W. J. De Renne, February 17, 1898, WWDFP, box 1, folder: correspondence, 1898 February; W. W. De Renne to W. J. De Renne, March 6, 1901, WWDFP, box 3, folder: correspondence, 1901 March; Receipt of W. J. De Renne, 1905, DRFP 2819, box 7, folder 2.

7. Bragg, *De Renne*, 231.

8. Wormsloe Detail Plat, § A, Wormsloe Detail Plat, §§ B and C, both in DRFP 2819, oversize drawer.

9. W. J. Stevenson to W. J. De Renne, September 15, August 4, 1904, both in DRFP 1064, box 29, folder 7; WJDR Account Book, 1903.

10. Notes on Garden Layout, 1904, DRFP 1064, box 29, folder 7.

11. Bragg, *De Renne*, 225; Spirn, "Constructing Nature," 91.

12. Spirn, "Constructing Nature"; "Biltmore School of Forestry," 610–11; Jolley, "Biltmore Forest Fair," 7.

13. Spirn, "Constructing Nature," 102. For images of the grounds, see 1899 Photograph Album, DRFP 2819, box 30.

14. Chatham Hunt Club Minute Book, 1906–1909, 2, Georgia Historical Society, Savannah.

15. Audrey De Renne to W. J. De Renne, March 2, 1901, WWDFP, box 3, folder: correspondence, March 1901.

16. Chatham Hunt Club Minute Book, 31–33.

17. Race Track Diagram, n.d., DRFP 2819, box 10, folder 8; Bragg, *De Renne*, 233–

34. For images of the Hussars, stable, and horses at Wormsloe, see 1899 Photograph Album, DRFP 2819, box 30.

18. Elfrida De Renne to W. J. De Renne, February 13, 1901, WWDFP, box 3, folder: correspondence, February 1901; Elfrida De Renne to W. J. De Renne, May 17, 1903, WWDFP, box 6, folder: correspondence, May 11–20, 1903.

19. See, for example, Wymberley W. De Renne to W. J. De Renne, March 13, 1901, WWDFP, box 3, folder: correspondence, March 1901; Audrey De Renne to W. J. De Renne, December 1, 1901, WWDFP, box 3, folder: correspondence, December 1901.

20. Audrey De Renne to Wymberley J. De Renne, April 20, 1903, WWDFP, box 5, folder: correspondence, April 11–30, 1903; Elfrida De Renne to Wymberley J. De Renne, May 23, 1895, WWDFP, box 1, folder: correspondence, May 1895.

21. In 1800, Noble W. Jones had conveyed Wimberly to his daughter, Sarah, who divided it among her eight children in 1804. George W. Jones purchased the southernmost portion of the plantation during the antebellum period, but the remainder of the old colonial grant was split into lots by 1860 and eventually sold outside the family. See Abstract of Title to Wymberley Lots, March 1, 1906, Indenture between Ann G. Hunter and William Hunter, May 25, 1860, Indenture between Catharine S. Bulloch and William Hunter, May 25, 1860, and Indenture between William H. Bulloch et al. and Ann G. Hunter, May 25, 1860, all in James S. Richmond Collection on Wymberley Tract, Georgia Historical Society, Savannah.

22. Dupon Subdivision Plan, March 5, 1903, DRFP 2819, box 33.

23. *Wymberley, Isle of Hope, Georgia* (brochure), n.d., Richmond Collection, folder 3; Lindsey and Britt, *Isle of Hope.*

24. The one concrete record of De Renne procuring a specimen is that of a rare Georgia example of the saw whet owl. Hoxie killed the owl near Tybee in 1911 and gave the animal to De Renne, "owner of the Wormsloe collection." See Hoxie, "Saw-Whet Owl," 265–66. Hoxie's biographer contends that the ornithologist compiled a collection "of mounted birds of the region" for De Renne during his Savannah stay. See Fargo, "Walter John Hoxie," 179–80.

25. Barrow, "Specimen Dealer," 493–97, 499; Reiger, *American Sportsmen,* 65–66; Farber, "Development." For the popularity of birds as hats, see Price, *Flight Maps,* chap. 2; Merchant, "George Bird Grinnell's Audubon Society," 11–15.

26. List of Taxidermy Mounts, DRFP 1064, box 20, folder 7; John Abbot's Birding Notebook (ms. 1654), Hargrett Rare Book and Manuscript Library, University of Georgia, Athens. For the disappearance of ivory-billed woodpeckers (and their possible recent reemergence), Carolina parakeets, and passenger pigeons in the Southeast, see Krech, *Spirits of the Air,* 182–88; Price, *Flight Maps,* 1–55.

27. List of Taxidermy Mounts, DRFP 1064, box 20, folder 7; Photograph of Taxidermy Mounts, DRFP 2819, box 25, folder 1. The collection seems to have included several mammal and reptile species not listed in the inventory.

28. Timber Cruise, n.d., DRFP 2819, box 10, folder 9.

29. This list of Wormsloe livestock was compiled from the following sources: WJDR Account Book; Jesse Beach to W. J. De Renne, June 2, 1904, DRFP 1064, box 28, folder 7; Audrey De Renne to W. J. De Renne, May 8, 1898, WWDFP, box 1, folder: correspondence, 1898 May; Audrey De Renne to W. J. De Renne, March 12, 1901, W. W. De Renne to W. J. De Renne, March 13, 24, 1901, all in WWDFP, box 3, folder: cor-

respondence, 1901 March; Audrey De Renne to W. J. De Renne, December 1, 1901, WWDFP, box 3, folder: correspondence, 1901 December; Picture Album, WWDFP, box 66, folder: picture album; Account Book, 1895, DRFP 2819, box 8, folder 2. None of these records mention hogs on Wormsloe, though there is at least one picture from around 1940 showing the animals there. It seems likely that hogs always resided on the property and escaped mention because of either their ubiquity or their ability to make do on almost any type of feed.

30. Jesse Beach to W. J. De Renne, September 1, 1906, DRFP 1064, box 9; Dairy Picture, neg. 6265, DRFP 2819, box 24, folder 4.

31. Notes on Dairy Production, 1906, DRFP 1064, box 29, folder 9; Jesse Beach to W. J. De Renne, July 1, 1904, DRFP 1064, box 29, folder 7.

32. Map of Northern Portion of Wormsloe, DRFP 2819, box 10, folder 8.

33. WJDR Account Book, 1902, 1905; Account Book, 1912–16, DRFP 1064, box 15, folder 2; Jesse Beach to W. J. De Renne, September 1, 1906, DRFP 1064, box 28, folder 9. In a typical month, such as March 1913, De Renne purchased eighty-four bushels of animal feed from external sources.

34. Beach was a tenant on Wormsloe at least as early as the summer of 1880. See GWJDR Diary, June 1, 1880.

35. Compiled from the letters of Jesse Beach to W. J. De Renne, June 2, 1904–August 9, 1906, DRFP 1064, box 29, folders 7–9. For Texas fever and diminished milk production, see Claire Strom, "Texas Fever and the Dispossession of the Southern Yeoman Farmer," in *Environmental History*, ed. Sutter and Manganiello, 230.

36. Jesse Beach to W. J. De Renne, June 2, 1904, DRFP 1064, box 29, folder 7; Jesse Beach to W. J. De Renne, September 7, 1905 DRFP 1064, box 29, folder 8; Jesse Beach to W. J. De Renne, September 1, 1906, DRFP 1064, box 29, folder 9.

37. Jesse Beach to W. J. De Renne, August 1, September 1, 1905, DRFP 1064, box 29, folder 8; Jesse Beach to W. J. De Renne, August 9, 1906, DRFP 1064, box 29, folder 9.

38. Construction Photographs, DRFP 2819, box 24, folder 9; Wormsloe Worker Photographs, DRFP 2819, box 19, folder 31; Date Book, 1916, DRFP 1064, box 14, folder 13.

39. Bragg, *De Renne*, 315–17, 326–27.

40. "Savannah's Show Places Be Opened to Tourists" (clipping), *Savannah Press*, September 24, 1927, DRFP 1064, box 31, folder 1; "Wormsloe Opens Library to Public" (clipping), *Savannah Morning News*, March 17, 1928, 16, DRFP 1064, box 31, folder 2; "Many Visitors at Wormsloe Gardens, Bird and Animal Collection Is of Interest" (clipping), *Savannah Morning News*, March 23, 1929, DRFP 1064, box 31, folder 3.

41. This composite description was compiled primarily from the following: Photographs of Wormsloe's Grounds, DRFP 1064, box 24, folders 3, 6, 8, 13; Gardening Notebook of Augusta De Renne, n.d., WWDFP, box 113, folder 6; "Rambling Observations"; "Wormsloe Gardens," 2; *Atlanta Journal*, March 30, 1930, Rotogravure Section, 1; Elizabeth Wade White, "Wormsloe Plantation," 79; De Renne, "Formal Gardens at Wormsloe"; Savannah Unit, Federal Writers' Project, *Savannah*, 169.

42. Brickell, "Literary Landscape," 380.

43. Wormsloe Visitors' Register, 1934–1935, DRFP 1064, box 58, folder 33.

44. Account Book, 1928–37, DRFP 1064, box 30, folder 4.

45. Advertisement for the Seaboard Air Line Railway (clipping), 1928, Advertise-

ment for the Central of Georgia Railway (clipping), 1928, both in DRFP 1064, box 31, folder 2; "Beautiful Wormsloe Gardens" (clipping), n.d., CBFP, box 30, folder 1.

46. "Famous Wormsloe Gardens Now Open to Public" (clipping), *Albany Herald*, March 16, 1929, DRFP 1064, box 31, folder 4.

47. Sutter, *Driven Wild*, 23–41; Sellers, *Preserving Nature*, 59–61; Aron, *Working at Play*, 206–36.

48. For examples on all three levels, see Margaret Brown, *Wild East*; Silver, *Mount Mitchell*; Swanson, "Marketing a Mountain."

49. Bates, "Way Down South in Dixie," 8, 13; "Wormsloe Gardens, Savannah, Georgia," 19; "Beauty Spots," 12–13.

50. "Famous Wormsloe Gardens Now Open to Public" (clipping), *Albany Herald*, March 16, 1929, DRFP 1064, box 31, folder 4; "Visit Savannah," 11.

51. Pennington, "Wormsloe Gardens," 38.

52. Bragg, *De Renne*, 332.

53. Finlay, *Growing American Rubber*, 62, 102, 125–27; Rogers and Saunders, *Swamp Water and Wiregrass*, 205–7.

54. Rogers and Saunders, *Swamp Water and Wiregrass*, 206–12.

55. Ingram, "Dixie Highway," 107.

56. Jakle and Sculle, *Motoring*, 29, 114–20.

57. Stewart, *"What Nature Suffers to Groe,"* 216–224; McFeely, *Sapelo's People*, 146–48; J. William Harris, *Deep Souths*, 147–48, 255–56; Thomas et al., "Anthropology," 239; Hull, *St. Simons, Enchanted Island*, 99–102.

58. McCash, *Jekyll Island Cottage Colony*, 1; McCash and McCash, *Jekyll Island Club*.

59. Bullard, *Cumberland Island*, 184–265; J. William Harris, *Deep Souths*, 144–46.

60. Cuthbert and Hoffius, *Northern Money, Southern Land*, esp. xv–xvi.

61. "Wormsloe Gardens" (clipping), *Sumter (S.C.) Daily Item*, February 22, 1937, WWDFP, box 70, folder: Wormsloe.

62. Lattimore, *Fort Pulaski National Monument*, § P; Russell and Hines, *Savannah*, 161–62. Savannah's transformation into a tourist city was by no means completed during the interwar years. Russell and Hines have noted that many parts of the historic city remained shabby; they quote Lady Astor's 1946 declaration that Savannah was "a beautiful lady with a dirty face" (*Savannah*, 175).

63. T. Bignault to W. W. De Renne, February 16, 22, 1917, both in WWDFP, box 8, folder: correspondence, 1917 February.

64. R. A. Young to W. W. De Renne, September 26, 1929, DRFP 1064, box 36, folder 2.

65. T. H. McHatton to Augusta De Renne, November 15, 1930, WWDFP, box 107, folder: gardening material, correspondence, 1930.

66. Mr. Grossmauw to Augusta De Renne, September 29, 1931, WWDFP, box 11, folder: correspondence, 1931 September; David Griffiths to Augusta De Renne, October 14, 1931, O. M. Freeman to Augusta De Renne, October 16, 1931, both in WWDFP, box 11, folder: correspondence, 1931 October.

67. H. B. Skeele to Augusta De Renne, March 15, 1928, WWDFP, box 9, folder: correspondence, 1928 March; B. M. Lufburrow to Craig Barrow, July 10, 1935, CBFP, box 5, folder 26.

68. Granger, *Savannah River Plantations*, 450; Kelly, *Short History of Skidaway Island*, 103.

69. Margaret Davis Cate to Augusta De Renne, July 30, 1930, WWDFP, box 11, folder: correspondence, 1930 July; Fred Thompson to Augusta De Renne, February 22, 1933, WWDFP, box 11, folder: correspondence, 1933 February; *USDA Farmers' Bulletin*, nos. 810, 840, 1155, CBFP, box 30, folder 5.

70. Rasmussen, *Taking the University*; Langston, *Forest Dreams, Forest Nightmares*, 86–113; Kirby, *Rural Worlds Lost*, 21–22. The De Rennes' reliance on extension agents and affiliated USDA services supports Phillips's assertion that these programs disproportionately benefited wealthier rural residents. See Phillips, *This Land, This Nation*, 204.

71. De Renne, "Formal Gardens at Wormsloe," 24–25.

72. "Savannah and the Wormsloe Gardens," *Bulletin of the National Council of State Garden Clubs Incorporated* 6.5 (February 1936): 8.

73. Gardening Journal of Augusta De Renne, 1927–1929, WWDFP, box 112, folder: Gardening material, journal.

74. Fox, *American Conservation Movement*, 341. Merchant has suggested that women were much more active in the conservation movement than Fox credits. See Merchant, "Women."

75. Norwood, *Made from This Earth*, 98–142.

76. Ibid., 110–17; Merchant, "Women," 60–62, 68–73; Lawson, "Remarkable Foundations"; Hecht, "Flowers to Gladden the City," 694–96.

77. Hoelscher, "Making Place, Making Race," 658–59, 665–66.

78. "Wormsloe Rich in Georgia History" (clipping), *Macon Telegraph*, March 24, 1929, 1, DRFP 1064, box 31, folder 4; De Renne, "Formal Gardens at Wormsloe," 24.

79. E. Elizabeth Robinson to Augusta De Renne, April 1929, WWDFP, box 10, folder: correspondence, 1929 April; De Renne, "Formal Gardens at Wormsloe," 24–25.

80. "Wormsloe Gardens," 2; De Renne, "Formal Gardens at Wormsloe," 24–25.

81. Gardening Notebook of Augusta De Renne, n.d., WWDFP, box 113, folder 6; "Wormsloe Gardens, Savannah, Georgia," *Atlantic Coast Line News* 15.2 (March–April, 1934): 1; "Excursions to Wormsloe Planned" (clipping), *Savannah Press*, March 7, 1929, DRFP 1064, box 31, folder 3.

82. "Wormsloe Gardens" (clipping), *Tourist Topics*, March 29, 1930, "Elizabeth's Letter," *Savannah Morning News* (clipping), [1930?], both in DRFP 1064, box 31, folder 5.

83. Elizabeth Wade White, "Wormsloe Plantation," 79.

84. Bates, "Way Down South in Dixie," 13.

85. Savannah Unit, Federal Writers' Project, *Savannah*, 169–70.

86. "Wormsloe Is Home of Interest" (clipping), *Savannah Morning News*, 1928, DRFP 1064, box 31, folder 2; "Elizabeth's Letter" (clipping), *Savannah Morning News*, March 2, 1929, DRFP 1064, box 31, folder 3.

87. "Cabin of Woman's Birth Again Home" (clipping), DRFP 1064, box 39, folder 6; "Wormsloe Rich in Georgia History" (clipping), *Macon Telegraph*, March 24, 1929, 1, DRFP 1064, box 31, folder 4. Though it strains credulity, Liza's story may have been true. The last surviving register of slave names on Wormsloe dates from 1857, at least a year earlier than Liza claimed to have been born. The 1860 census recorded George W.

Jones as owning two unnamed female slaves approximately two years of age, either one of whom might have been Liza. See U.S. Census Bureau, Slave Schedule for Chatham County, Georgia, 1860.

88. "Liza's Cabin" (postcard), DRFP 2819, box 24, folder 12.

89. Jo-Ann Morgan, "Mammy the Huckster," 87–88.

90. Anthony J. Stanonis, "Just Like Mammy Used to Make: Foodways in the Jim Crow South," in *Dixie Emporium*, ed. Stanonis, 208–33.

91. Hale, *Making Whiteness*, 152; for an analysis of Aunt Jemima and the mammy image, see 151–53, 164–66.

92. Wayne, *Death of an Overseer*, 153–54. See also Blight, *Race and Reunion*, 286–87.

93. Hillyer, "Designing Dixie," 153, 160.

94. Ibid., 250–51, 306–9; Jo-Ann Morgan, "Mammy the Huckster," 94–96.

95. For image making and the process of reconciliation, see Silber, *Romance of Reunion*, 124, 131; Blight, *Race and Reunion*, 222–24.

96. Cullen, "Wormsloe," 1.

97. Cook, "Wormsloe Gardens," 19.

98. Giltner, *Hunting and Fishing*, chaps. 3, 4.

99. "Bayard Wooten to Visit Wormsloe" (clipping), January 29, 1934, "Historical Talk at Wormsloe Party" (clipping), *Savannah Evening Press*, February 2, 1934, both in DRFP 1064, box 39, folder 5; Cotten, *Light and Air*.

100. Bayard Wooten to Augusta De Renne, April 17, 1935, WWDFP, box 11, folder: correspondence, 1935 April; Glass Lantern Slides of Wormsloe, DRFP 2819, box 26.

101. A. W. Ziebold to Craig Barrow, November 12, 1929, CBFP, box 5, folder 16.

102. Lawrence Manning to N. J. Gillespie, October 20, 1920, DRFP 2819, box 3, folder 1.

103. "Potato Growers Visit Wormsloe" (clipping), April 8, 1930, DRFP 1064, box 31, folder 5.

104. "Statement of Fact," Wymberley W. De Renne, DRFP 2819, box 10, folder 7; Craig Barrow to Harry P. Marshall, February 4, 1935, CBFP, box 5, folder 16.

105. U.S. Army Air Corps, Aerial Photograph, n.d., CBFP, box 42, folder 29.

106. Bragg, *De Renne*, 323–26.

107. Ibid., 336–52.

108. Sears, *Sacred Places*, 72.

FIVE. From Plantation to Park

1. Bragg, *De Renne*, 370–71.

2. Ibid., 371–74, 381–83.

3. "By-Laws of the Georgia Society Colonial Dames of America," typescript, 1937, CBFP, box 30, folder 8.

4. Bragg, *De Renne*, 375–76, 388–89.

5. *Society of Colonial Wars in the State of Georgia: Officers, Standing Committees, and Members* (booklet), 1938, CBFP, box 30, folder 11.

6. Dick and Johnson, "Smell of Money," 309–10, 322; Fallows, *Water Lords*, esp. 58–61, 64–74, 157–59. The Union Bag plant was located on the site of the historic Her-

mitage Plantation. See Granger, *Savannah River Plantations*, 450; Kelly, *Short History of Skidaway Island*, 103.

7. B. M. Lufburrow to Craig Barrow, July 10, 1935, Craig Barrow to Georgia Department of Forestry, April 7, 1945, J. M. Tinker to Craig Barrow, April 11, 1945, all in CBFP, box 5, folder 26.

8. W. M. Oettmeier to Craig Barrow, September 30, 1941, *Answering Your Questions about the Forest Farmers Association Cooperative* (pamphlet), 1941, both in CBFP, box 5, folder 17.

9. Timber Cruise, n.d., DRFP 2819, box 10, folder 9; Craig Barrow to Georgia Department of Forestry, April 7, 1945, CBFP, box 5, folder 26.

10. Wormsloe, Aerial View, U.S. Army Air Corps, CBFP, box 42, folder 29. Though undated, the image was almost certainly taken between 1938, when dairy operations ceased, and 1947, when the Air Corps was absorbed into the new Air Force.

11. Bragg, *De Renne*, 386.

12. "Wormsloe Tour" (flyer), n.d., CBFP, box 30, folder 1.

13. Wormsloe Advertising Pamphlets, 1955, 1957, n.d., "Audubon Members Enjoy Wormsloe" (clipping) April 7, 1941, all in CBFP, box 30, folder 1; Bragg, *De Renne*, 371–74, 393.

14. Irving Fineman, "Author, Playwright Returns to Savannah, Wormsloe Revisited after 30 Years" (clipping), November 29, 1964, CBFP, box 30, folder 1.

15. "Wormsloe Foundation Gets 750 Acres," *Savannah Evening Press*, February 16, 1961.

16. See Coulter's comments in the foreword to Kelso, *Captain Jones's Wormslow*, xi–xiii.

17. Ibid.

18. Cotter, "Above Ground Archeology," 267.

19. "Wormsloe's Head Denies Acquisition," *Savannah Evening Press*, October 7, 1972; Bragg, *De Renne*, 395–96, appendix 3.

20. Frank Daniel, *Addresses of Jimmy Carter*, 176.

21. Barbara Dlugozima, "Plantation Considered 'Endangered,' Heritage Trust Meets on Wormsloe Priority," *Savannah Evening Press*, October 24, 1972; Barbara Dlugozima, "Governor's Commission Urges Wormsloe Acquisition," *Savannah Morning News*, October 25, 1972; "750 Acres Donated to Conservancy," *Jacksonville Times-Union and Journal*, December 31, 1972; Jan Reetz, "Wormsloe Land Donated to Group," *Savannah News-Press*, December 31, 1972; "Wormsloe," *Outdoors in Georgia* (clipping), January 1973, CBFP, box 30, folder 1.

22. "Wormsloe's Head Denies Acquisition," *Savannah Evening Press*, October 7, 1972.

23. "750 Acres Donated to Conservancy," *Jacksonville Times-Union and Journal*, December 31, 1972.

24. Wormsloe Preliminary Master Plan, 1974, Wormsloe Master Plan Documents, RG 30, subgroup 1, box 16, Georgia State Archives, Morrow; Coy L. Ballard, "Wormsloe Master Plan," 1974 Intern Study Reports of the Governor's Special Affairs Office, Georgia State Archives.

25. Barbara Dlugozima, "Plantation Considered 'Endangered,' Heritage Trust Meets on Wormsloe Priority," *Savannah Evening Press*, October 24, 1972. On the DNR's in-

tention that Wormsloe and Skidaway Island State Park would serve as complementary sites, see Ballard, "Wormsloe Master Plan," 4–5.

26. Francher, *Savannah*, 127–32; Kelly, *Short History of Skidaway Island*, 103.

27. "Governor Outlines $1.6 Billion Budget, Chatham Property Cited," *Savannah Evening Press*, January 11, 1973.

28. Ralph Reed, "Development of the Ruins at Wormsloe," December 11, 1973, SPBR; Ballard, "Wormsloe Master Plan," 1–2.

29. Deveau and Reed, *Interpretive Prospectus*, 1.

30. For a direct statement connecting Wormsloe to Bicentennial excitement, see Ralph Reed to Alston Waylor, January 21, 1974, Wormsloe Master Plan Documents, RG 30, subgroup 1, box 16. Reed argued that the park should open in 1976 to capitalize on public sentiment.

31. Deveau and Reed, *Interpretive Prospectus*, 15, 19–20. Contemporary publications such as Hartje, *Bicentennial USA*, provided historic sites with guidelines on how to best commemorate (or perhaps exploit) the upcoming Bicentennial.

32. Deveau and Reed, *Interpretive Prospectus*, 3, 14.

33. A. Starker Leopold et al., "Wildlife Management in the National Parks," in *Great New Wilderness Debate*, ed. Callicott and Nelson, 106.

34. Craige, *Eugene Odum*, 54–58; Odum, *Fundamentals of Ecology*.

35. Craige, *Eugene Odum*, 40–47.

36. Odum in Brower, *Guale*, 20.

37. Odum, *Fundamentals of Ecology*, 352.

38. For John Teal's research at the Marine Institute, see Odum in Brower, *Guale*, 21; Teal and Teal, *Portrait of an Island*, 6.

39. Teal and Teal, *Life and Death*, 198; see also chaps. 13, 15.

40. Craige, *Eugene Odum*, 100–102.

41. Coastal Zone Management Act, 16 U.S.C., §§ 1451–64 (1972). For the full text of the CZMA, see the National Oceanic and Atmospheric Administration's website, http://coastalmanagement.noaa.gov/about/media/CZMA_10_11_06.pdf.

42. Craige, *Eugene Odum*, 88–89; Worster, *Wealth of Nature*, 158–62; Drury and Nisbet, "Succession," 331–68.

43. Worster, *Wealth of Nature*, 162–65.

44. Ibid., 150.

45. Craige, *Eugene Odum*, 94–95. For a disturbance ecology take on the composition of the dominant type of old-growth forest in the southeastern coastal plain, see Batista and Platt, *Old-Growth Definition*.

46. Brinkley, *Unfinished Presidency*, 24–25.

47. Godbold, *Jimmy and Rosalynn Carter*, 189, 196.

48. Carter in ibid., 197.

49. "Stretch of River Studied," *Savannah News-Press*, December 31, 1972; "Governor Outlines $1.6 Billion Budget, Chatham Property Cited," *Savannah Evening Press*, January 11, 1973.

50. Fallows, *Water Lords*, esp. 64–74, 40.

51. Gary Thatcher, "Nuclear Controversy Sizzles in the South," *Christian Science Monitor*, November 26, 1976, 18–19; Jim Walser, "Along the Savannah: Round-the-Clock A-Bomb Production," *Washington Post*, December 27, 1979, A3.

52. Fallows, *Water Lords*, 212–13, 225–26.

53. Ray in James T. Wooten, "In River City of Savannah, Old-Timers Recall Pollution-Free Days," *New York Times*, January 28, 1971, 16.

54. Ruffin in Fallows, *Water Lords*, 242.

55. Eugene Warner and John Carmody, "Hilton Head Is Wondering about Its New Neighbor," *Washington Post*, April 26, 1970, 17, 19–20, 23–24, 49–50, 62.

56. Deveau and Reed, *Interpretive Prospectus*, 11.

57. Alston C. Waylor to Henry D. Struble, February 8, 11, 1974, Francis Palmer to Ralph Reed, February 12, 1974, Ray Shirley to Joe D. Tanner, February 18, 1974, all in SPBR.

58. Alston C. Waylor to Henry D. Struble, February 8, 1974, SPBR.

59. For examples of the power and durability of this ideal among federal foresters throughout the twentieth century, see Hirt, *Conspiracy of Optimism*; Langston, *Forest Dreams, Forest Nightmares*.

60. Ray Shirley to Joe D. Tanner, February 18, 1974, Ralph Reed to Alston C. Waylor, February 25, 1974, Joe D. Tanner to Ray Shirley, February 19, 1974, all in SPBR.

61. Joe D. Tanner to Governor Jimmy Carter, n.d., Wormsloe Timber Sale Flyer, February 25, 1974, both in SPBR; Ballard, "Wormsloe Master Plan," 15.

62. Carol Woodford, "Wormsloe Pines Infested" (clipping), *Savannah Morning News*, February 21, 1974, Alston Waylor to Henry D. Struble, February 22, 1974, both in SPBR.

63. Joe D. Tanner to Governor Jimmy Carter, n.d., Henry D. Struble to Alston Waylor, Ray Thomas, and Ralph Reed, March 12, 1974, both in SPBR.

64. Henry D. Struble to Allen L. Ault, August 30, 1974, Joe D. Tanner to Governor Jimmy Carter, n.d., both in SPBR.

65. For the DNR's concerns about pine beetles that remained in logging debris, see Joe D. Tanner to Governor Jimmy Carter, n.d., Henry D. Struble to Allen L. Ault, August 30, 1974, Ralph Reed to Alston Waylor, March 12, 1976, all in SPBR; Ralph Reed to Alston C. Waylor, June 18, 1975, Wormsloe Plantation Correspondence, Georgia State Archives.

66. For a history of the growth and operations of southern mosquito control agencies along the lines of the Chatham County Mosquito Control Commission, see Patterson, *Mosquito Wars*.

67. Thomas O. Fultz Jr. to Alston C. Waylor, September 27, 1974, SPBR.

68. Ralph Reed to Thomas A. Smith Jr., August 13, 1974, Wormsloe Plantation Correspondence.

69. Contract between the Georgia Department of Natural Resources and Waters Tree Service, July 18, 1977, SPBR.

70. Ralph Reed to Alston C. Waylor, August 30, 1974, Wormsloe Plantation Correspondence.

71. Ralph Reed to Alston C. Waylor, March 12, 1976, SPBR.

72. Joe D. Tanner to Governor Jimmy Carter, n.d., Henry D. Struble to Allen L. Ault, August 30, 1974, Ralph Reed to Alston Waylor, March 12, 1976, all in SPBR; Ralph Reed to Alston C. Waylor, June 18, 1975, Wormsloe Plantation Correspondence.

73. Joe Morgan to Alston Waylor, August 23, 1974, Wormsloe Clean-Up Meeting Memorandum, August 9, 1974, both in SPBR.

74. Waldron et al., "Simulating"; Rantis and Johnson, "Understory Development," 104, 110–13.

75. DNR and GFC officials never explicitly recorded these justifications, but their correspondence frequently expressed worries over the beetles spreading to Skidaway Island and beyond, and there never seemed to be any question that the state would use cutting to combat the beetle outbreak.

76. *Wormsloe State Historic Site.*

77. Selected examples especially relevant to this study include Littlefield, *Rice and Slaves*; Carney, *Black Rice*; Beckert, "Emancipation and Empire"; Edelson, *Plantation Enterprise*; Kelton, *Epidemics and Enslavement*; Silver, *New Face*; Stewart, *"What Nature Suffers to Groe."* Few studies of the colonial South fail to at least mention the region's reliance on foreign markets.

78. A few of the excellent works examining the intellectual connections between the Old World and the southern environment used for this study include Edelson, *Plantation Enterprise*; Silver, *New Face*; Stewart, *"What Nature Suffers to Groe"*; Chaplin, *Subject Matter*; Kupperman, "Fear"; Gomez, *Black Crescent*.

79. For an eloquent summary of the permeability of plantation boundaries, see Lynn A. Nelson, *Pharsalia*, 130–37.

80. Some notable exceptions include Marx, *Machine in the Garden*; Price, *Flight Maps*; Stoll, *Larding the Lean Earth*; Pollan, *Second Nature*. Historians of Europe have less of a wilderness fetish. For examples, see Kjaergaard, *Danish Revolution*; Berminham, *Landscape and Ideology*; Rackham, *History of the Countryside*; Rackham, *Last Forest*; Rackham, *Trees and Woodland.*

81. Nash, *Wilderness and the American Mind*, esp. chaps. 3, 4.

82. This important conceptualization of American understandings of vernacular landscapes is from Marx, *Machine in the Garden*, 71.

83. Mackintosh, "National Park Service," 52; Synnott, "Disney's America."

84. Dunn, *Cades Cove*; Margaret Brown, *Wild East*; Katrina M. Powell, *"Answer at Once"*; Katrina M. Powell, *Anguish of Displacement*; Reich, "Re-Creating the Wilderness." Western national parks also conducted a great deal of historical land use erasure, though they often interpreted the land as unsettled wilderness. See Spence, *Dispossessing the Wilderness*; Warren, *Hunter's Game*; Jacoby, *Crimes against Nature*; Kenneth R. Olwig, "Reinventing Common Nature: Yosemite and Mount Rushmore—A Meandering Tale of a Double Nature," in *Uncommon Ground*, ed. Cronon, 379–408; Sellars, *Preserving Nature.*

85. On Colonial Williamsburg, see James S. Miller, "Mapping the Boosterist Imaginary"; Tyler-McGraw, "Becoming Americans Again."

86. Governor Carter recognized the impact of the Diamond Causeway from the early years of the roadway's construction. During a December 1972 visit to the newly acquired property, Carter noted that the causeway had obviously worked to silt in some of the marshland at the peninsula's southern tip. See "Stretch of River Studied" (clipping), *Savannah News-Press*, December 31, 1972, CBFP, box 30, folder 1.

87. On historic vernacular landscapes, see Birnbaum with Peters, *Secretary of the Interior's Standards*, 5; Messick, Joseph, and Adams, *Tilling the Earth*; Birnbaum, *Protecting Cultural Landscapes.*

88. Robinson, *Last Song*; Sparks, *Last Song.*

BIBLIOGRAPHY

MANUSCRIPTS

Georgia Historical Society, Savannah
    Chatham Hunt Club Minute Book, 1906–1909
    Jones Family Papers
    James S. Richmond Collection on Wymberley Tract

Georgia State Archives, Morrow
    1974 Intern Study Reports of the Governor's Special Affairs Office
    Southern Pine Beetle Reports
    Wormsloe Master Plan Documents
    Wormsloe Plantation Correspondence

Hargrett Rare Book and Manuscript Library, University of Georgia, Athens
    John Abbot's Birding Notebook (ms. 1654)
    Craig Barrow Family Papers (ms. 3090)
    De Renne Family Papers (mss. 1064 and 2819)
    De Renne Family Papers Oversize (ms. 1064a)
    De Renne Family Receipts and Remedies (ms. 1120)
    De Renne Historical Manuscripts (ms. 1136)
    Wymberly Wormsloe De Renne Family Papers (ms. 1788)
    Noble Jones Family Papers (ms. 1127)
    William Tatham's Notebook (ms. 325)

Library of Congress, Washington, D.C.
    American Memory Collection: FSA/OWI Photographs

National Archives and Records Administration, Southeastern Branch, Morrow, Ga.
    Agricultural Census Manuscript Schedules, 1860, 1870, 1880
    Bureau of Refugees, Freedmen, and Abandoned Lands, Records of the Savannah,
        Georgia, Field Office

Special Collections Department, Mitchell Memorial Library, Mississippi State University, Starkville
    Phillips (W. M.) Letter Collection

University of Georgia Library, Athens
    Records of Antebellum Southern Plantations (microfilm), Bruce Family Papers

Virginia Historical Society, Richmond
    Wyllie Family Papers

PERIODICALS AND NEWSPAPERS

AAA Travel
Albany Herald
Atlanta Constitution
Atlanta Journal
Atlantic Coast Line News
The Auk
Carolina Resorts
Chatham Home Owner
Christian Science Monitor
Farmers' Register
Georgia Gazette
Halifax Topics
Horticulture Illustrated
Isle of Hope Weekly
Jacksonville Times-Union and Journal
Junior League Magazine
Macon Telegraph
Motor Bus Traveler
New York Times
Orange Disc
Outdoors in Georgia
Progressive Farmer
Public Intelligencer
Savannah Evening Press
Savannah Morning News
Savannah News-Press
Savannah Press
Southern Cultivator
Southern Planter
Sumter Daily Item
Tourist Topics
Washington Post

GOVERNMENT DOCUMENTS

Batista, William B., and William J. Platt. *An Old-Growth Definition for Southern Mixed Hardwood Forests.* USDA Forest Service General Technical Report, SRS-9. Asheville, N.C.: Southern Research Station, 1997.

Birnbaum, Charles A. *Protecting Cultural Landscapes: Planning, Treatment and Management of Historic Landscapes.* Washington, D.C.: U.S. Department of the Interior, National Park Service, 1994. Available online at http://www.nps.gov/history/hps/tps/briefs/brief36.htm.

Birnbaum, Charles A., with Christine Capelle Peters, eds. *The Secretary of the Interior's Standards for the Treatment of Historic Properties with Guidelines for the Treatment of Cultural Landscapes*. Washington, D.C.: U.S. Department of the Interior, National Park Service, 1996.

Coastal Zone Management Act. 16 U.S.C., §§ 1451–64 (1972).

Census Reports, Twelfth Census of the United States, Taken in the Year 1900. Agriculture Part II: Crops and Irrigation. Washington, D.C.: U.S. Census Office, 1902.

"Chinese Tallow Tree, *Triadica sebifera*." In USDA Natural Resources Conservation Service Plant Guide. Washington, D.C.: U.S. Government Printing Office, n.d.

The Code of the State of Georgia, 1867. Atlanta: Franklin, 1867.

The Code of the State of Georgia, 1873. Macon: Burke, 1873.

The Code of the State of Georgia, 1882. Atlanta: Harrison, 1882.

The Code of the State of Georgia, Adopted December 15th, 1895. Vol. 1. Atlanta: Foote and Davies, 1896.

Compendium of the Enumeration of the Inhabitants and Statistics of the United States, as Obtained at the Department of State, from the Returns of the Sixth Census. Washington, D.C.: Allen, 1841.

Daniel, Frank, comp. *Addresses of Jimmy Carter: (James Earl Carter) Governor of Georgia, 1971–1975*. Atlanta: Georgia Department of Archives and History, 1975.

Deveau, Patricia Carter, and Ralph Reed. *Interpretive Prospectus for Wormsloe, Savannah, Georgia*. Atlanta: Georgia Department of Natural Resources, 1978.

Historical Census Data Browser. University of Virginia. Available online at http://fisher.lib.virginia.edu/collections/stats/histcensus/index.html.

Kennedy, Joseph C. G. *Agriculture of the United States in 1860, Compiled from the Original Returns of the Eighth Census, under the Direction of the Secretary of the Interior*. Washington, D.C.: U.S. Government Printing Office, 1864.

Latimer, W. J., and Floyd S. Bucher. *Soil Survey of Chatham County, Georgia*. Washington, D.C.: U.S. Government Printing Office, 1912.

Lattimore, Ralston B. *Fort Pulaski National Monument, Georgia*. Historical Handbook Series 18. Washington, D.C.: National Park Service, 1954.

Loughridge, R. H. *Report on the Cotton Production of the State of Georgia, with a Description of the General Agricultural Features of the State*. Washington, D.C.: U.S. Government Printing Office, 1880.

Messick, Denise P., J. W. Joseph, and Natalie P. Adams. *Tilling the Earth: Georgia's Historic Agricultural Heritage—A Context*. Atlanta: Georgia Department of Natural Resources, Historic Preservation Division, 2001.

Report on the Productions of Agriculture, as Returned at the Tenth Census. Washington, D.C.: U.S. Government Printing Office, 1883.

Report on the Statistics of Agriculture in the United States at the Eleventh Census: 1890. Washington, D.C.: U.S. Government Printing Office, 1895.

U.S. Census Bureau. *The Seventh Census of the United States: 1850*. Washington, D.C.: Armstrong, 1853.

———. Slave Schedule for Chatham County, Georgia, 1850.

———. Slave Schedule for Chatham County, Georgia, 1860.

Walker, Francis. *Ninth Census*. Vol. 3, *The Statistics of the Wealth and Industry of the United States*. Washington, D.C.: U.S. Government Printing Office, 1872.

Works Progress Administration. *The Story of Sea Island Cotton*. Tallahassee: Florida Department of Agriculture, 1941.

Wormsloe State Historic Site. N.p.: Georgia Department of Natural Resources, 2006.

PUBLISHED PRIMARY SOURCES

"Alderney Cows." *Southern Planter* 7.9 (September 1847): 274.

Bartram, John. "Diary of a Journey through the Carolinas, Georgia, and Florida, from July 1, 1765, to April 10, 1766." Annotated by Francis Harper. *Transactions of the American Philosophical Society* 33.1 (December 1942): 1–120.

Bartram, William. *The Travels of William Bartram: Naturalist Edition*. Edited by Francis Harper. Athens: University of Georgia Press, 1998.

Bates, Erland Wallace. "Way Down South in Dixie: New Roads—New Sights—New Thrills." *AAA Travel* 3.4 (January 1933): 8, 13.

"Beauty Spots of the True South." *Ohio Motorist*, March 1934, 12–13.

Burke, Emily P. *Reminiscences of Georgia*. Oberlin, Ohio: Fitch, 1850.

"Buying Land." *Southern Workman* 3.8 (August 1874): 58.

Byrd, William. *William Byrd's Natural History of Virginia, or the Newly Discovered Eden*. Edited by Richard Croom Beatty and William Mulloy. Richmond, Va.: Dietz, 1940.

Cashin, Edward J., ed. *A Wilderness Still the Cradle of Nature: Frontier Georgia*. Savannah, Ga.: Beehive, 1994.

Cook, J. C. "Wormsloe Gardens." *Orange Disc*, March–April 1937, 19.

De Renne, Augusta Floyd. "The Formal Gardens at Wormsloe." *Junior League Magazine* 16.9 (June 1930): 24–25.

Equiano, Olaudah. *The Interesting Narrative and Other Writings*. Edited by Vincent Carretta. New York: Penguin, 2003.

Fitzhugh, George. *Cannibals All!; or, Slaves without Masters*. Richmond, Va.: Morris, 1857.

Foby. "Management of Servants." *Southern Cultivator* 11.8 (August 1853): 226–28.

Genealogical Committee of the Georgia Historical Society. *The 1860 Census of Chatham County, Georgia*. Easley, S.C.: Southern Historical, 1979.

Georgia Writers' Project. *Drums and Shadows: Survival Studies among the Georgia Coastal Negroes*. Athens: University of Georgia Press/Brown Thrasher, 1986.

Hahn, Steven, et al., eds. *Freedom: A Documentary History of Emancipation, 1861–1867*. Ser. 3, vol. 1, *Land and Labor, 1865*. Chapel Hill: University of North Carolina Press, 2008.

Harrison, William H. "Stoves for Negroes' Dwellings." *Farmers' Register* 8.4 (April 30, 1840): 212–13.

Hoxie, W. J. "The Saw-Whet Owl in Georgia." *The Auk* 28.2 (April 1911): 265–66.

"Itinerant Observations in America." In *Collections of the Georgia Historical Society*, vol. 4. Savannah, Ga.: Estill, 1878.

Jones, Charles C., Jr. "Sketch of Dr. G. W. De Renne." *Southern Historical Society Papers* 11.4 (April–May 1883): 193–201.

Kemble, Frances A. *Journal of a Residence on a Georgian Plantation in 1838–1839*. Edited by John A. Scott. Athens: University of Georgia Press/Brown Thrasher, 1984.

"Management of Slaves, &c." *Farmers' Register* 5.1 (May 1, 1837): 32–33.

"Merino Sheep." *Southern Planter* 14.6 (June 1854): 184.

"The Marsh and Its World." *Southern Cultivator* 20.2 (February 1862): 38–39.

Muir, John. *A Thousand-Mile Walk to the Gulf.* New York: Houghton Mifflin, 1916.

Oglethorpe, James Edward. *A New and Accurate Account of the Provinces of South-Carolina and Georgia: With Many Curious and Useful Observations on the Trade, Navigation, and Plantations of Great-Britain, Compared with Her Most Powerful Maritime Neighbours in Ancient and Modern Times.* London: Worrall, 1733.

Olmsted, Frederick Law. *The Cotton Kingdom: A Traveler's Observations on Cotton and Slavery in the American Slave States.* 2 vols. New York: Mason, 1861.

Ormie, W. P. "Ensilage at the South." *Progressive Farmer* 1.10 (April 14, 1886): 1.

Pennington, Edgar L. "Wormsloe Gardens." *Motor Bus Traveler* 2.2 (April 1930): 16–17, 38.

"Plantation Management." *Southern Cultivator* 17.6 (June 1859): 169–70.

R. W. N. N. "Negro Cabins." *Southern Planter* 16.4 (April 1856): 121–22.

"Rambling Observations of a Roving Gardener." *Horticulture Illustrated*, March 15, 1931, 125–26.

Redpath, James. *The Roving Editor; or, Talks with Slaves in the Southern States, by James Redpath.* Edited by John R. McKivigan. University Park: Pennsylvania State University Press, 1996.

Reid, Whitelaw. *After the War: A Southern Tour: May 1, 1865, to May 1, 1866.* Cincinnati: Moore, Wilstach, and Baldwin, 1866.

Ruffin, Edmund. *An Essay on Calcareous Manures.* Edited by J. Carlyle Sitterson. Cambridge: Belknap Press of Harvard University Press, 1961.

———. *Nature's Management: Writings on Landscape and Reform, 1822–1859.* Edited by Jack Temple Kirby. Athens: University of Georgia Press, 2000.

"Savannah and the Wormsloe Gardens." *Bulletin of the National Council of State Garden Clubs Incorporated* 6.5 (February 1936): 8.

Savannah Board of Trade. *Agricultural Chatham: Savannah, Georgia.* Savannah, Ga.: Commercial, 1924.

Seabrook, Benjamin Whitemarsh. *A Memoir on the Origin, Cultivation, and Uses of Cotton, from the Earliest Ages to the Present Time, with Especial Reference to the Sea-Island Cotton Plant, Including the Improvements in Its Cultivation, and the Preparation of the Wool, &c. in Georgia and South Carolina.* Charleston, S.C.: Miller and Browne, 1844.

Shepard, Charles Upham. "Sea Island Cotton—Statistics—Report of Prof. Charles U. Shepard, &c." *Southern Cultivator* 11.7 (July 1853): 195–97.

Spalding, Thomas. "On the Cotton Gin and the Introduction of Cotton." *Southern Cultivator* 2.11 (May 1844): 83–84.

Stephens, Thomas. *A Brief Account of the Causes That Have Retarded the Progress of the Colony of Georgia, in America.* London: n.p., 1743.

———. *The Hard Case of the Distressed People of Georgia.* London: n.p., 1742.

Stephens, William. *A Journal of the Proceedings in Georgia, Beginning October 20, 1737.* 2 vols. London: Meadows, 1742.

Taylor, John. *Arator: Being a Series of Agricultural Essays, Practical and Political.* Georgetown: Carter and Carter, 1813.

"Visit Savannah and Wormsloe Gardens on Your Way North." *Halifax Topics* 6.6 (March 8, 1935): 11.

Von Reck, Philip Georg Friedrich. *Von Reck's Voyage: Drawings and Journal of Philip Georg Friedrich von Reck.* Edited by Kristian Hvidt. Savannah, Ga.: Beehive, 1990.

W. H. H. "Sea Island Compost—'Tabby' Houses, &c." *Southern Cultivator* 17.12 (December 1859): 358.

White, Elizabeth Wade. "Wormsloe Plantation and the De Renne Georgia Library." *Junior League Magazine* 16.9 (June 1930): 79.

"Wormsloe Gardens." *Carolina Resorts* 1.12 (March 20, 1930): 2.

"Wormsloe Gardens, Savannah, Georgia." *Delaware Motorist* 7.2 (February 1935): 19.

SECONDARY SOURCES

Aiken, Charles S. *The Cotton Plantation South since the Civil War.* Baltimore: Johns Hopkins University Press, 1998.

Allen, Bruce P., Eric F. Pauley, and Rebecca R. Sharitz. "Hurricane Impacts on Liana Populations in an Old-Growth Southeastern Bottomland Forest." *Journal of the Torrey Botanical Society* 124.1 (January–March 1997): 34–42.

Allen, Robert C. *Enclosure and the Yeoman.* New York: Oxford University Press, 1992.

Anderson, Edgar. *Plants, Man, and Life.* Boston: Little, Brown, 1952.

Anderson, Virginia De John. *Creatures of Empire: How Domestic Animals Transformed Early America.* New York: Oxford University Press, 2004.

Andresen, H., J. P. Bakker, M. Brongers, B. Heydemann, and U. Irmler. "Long-Term Changes of Salt Marsh Communities by Cattle Grazing." *Vegetatio* 89.2 (October 1990): 137–48.

Aron, Cindy S. *Working at Play: A History of Vacations in the United States.* New York: Oxford University Press, 1999.

Balick, Michael J., and Paul Alan Cox. *Plants, People, and Culture: The Science of Ethnobotany.* New York: Scientific American Library, 1996.

Barron, Hal S. *Mixed Harvest: The Second Great Transformation in the Rural North, 1870–1930.* Chapel Hill: University of North Carolina Press, 1997.

Barrow, Mark V., Jr. "The Specimen Dealer: Entrepreneurial Natural History in America's Gilded Age." *Journal of the History of Biology* 33.3 (Winter 2000): 493–534.

Bassett, Victor H. *A Medical Biography of Dr. Noble Wymberley Jones of Georgia, First President of the Georgia Medical Society of Savannah.* Savannah: Georgia Historical Society, 1936.

Bateman, Fred. "Improvement in American Dairy Farming, 1850–1910: A Quantitative Analysis." *Journal of Economic History* 28.2 (June 1968): 255–73.

Batista, William B., and William J. Platt. "Tree Population Responses to Hurricane Disturbance: Syndromes in a South Eastern USA Old-Growth Forest." *Journal of Ecology* 91.2 (April 2003): 197–212.

Beckert, Sven. "Emancipation and Empire: Reconstructing the Worldwide Web of Cotton Production in the Age of the American Civil War." *American Historical Review* 109.5 (December 2004): 1405–38.

———. "From Tuskegee to Togo: The Problem of Freedom in the Empire of Cotton." *Journal of American History* 92.2 (September 2005): 498–526.

Bell, Andrew McIlwaine. *Mosquito Soldiers: Malaria, Yellow Fever, and the Course of the American Civil War*. Baton Rouge: Louisiana State University Press, 2010.

Berlin, Ira. "From Creole to African: Atlantic Creoles and the Origins of African-American Society in Mainland North America." *William and Mary Quarterly*, 3rd ser., 53.2 (April 1996): 251–88.

Bermingham, Ann. *Landscape and Ideology: The English Rustic Tradition, 1740–1860*. Berkeley: University of California Press, 1986.

Bess, Michael, Mark Cioc, and James Sievert. "Environmental History Writing in Southern Europe." *Environmental History* 5.4 (October 2000): 545–56.

"The Biltmore School of Forestry." *Outlook*, March 21, 1914, 610–11.

Blight, David W. *Race and Reunion: The Civil War in American Memory*. Cambridge: Belknap Press of Harvard University Press, 2001.

Bonner, James C. "Silk Growing in the Georgia Colony." *Agricultural History* 43.1 (January 1969): 143–48.

Bragg, William Harris. *De Renne: Three Generations of a Georgia Family*. Athens: University of Georgia Press, 1999.

Bratton, Susan P. "The Vegetation History of Fort Frederica, Saint Simons Island, Georgia." *Castanea* 50.3 (September 1985): 133–45.

Bratton, Susan P., and Scott G. Miller. "Historic Field Systems and the Structure of Maritime Oak Forests, Cumberland Island National Seashore, Georgia." *Bulletin of the Torrey Botanical Club* 121.1 (January–March 1994): 1–12.

Breen, T. H., and Stephen Innes. *"Myne Owne Ground": Race and Freedom on Virginia's Eastern Shore, 1640–1676*. New York: Oxford University Press, 1980.

Brickell, Herschel. "The Literary Landscape." *North American Review* 235.4 (April 1933): 376–84.

Brinkley, Douglas. *The Unfinished Presidency: Jimmy Carter's Journey beyond the White House*. New York: Viking, 1998.

Brower, Kenneth, ed. *Guale, the Golden Coast of Georgia*. New York: Friends of the Earth, 1974.

Brown, Kathleen. *Good Wives, Nasty Wenches, and Anxious Patriarchs: Gender, Race, and Power in Colonial Virginia*. Chapel Hill: University of North Carolina Press, 1996.

Brown, Margaret. *The Wild East: A Biography of the Great Smoky Mountains*. Gainesville: University Press of Florida, 2000.

Bullard, Mary R. *Cumberland Island: A History*. Athens: University of Georgia Press, 2003.

Caldwell, Joseph, Catherine McCann, and Frederick S. Hulse. *Irene Mound Site: Chatham County, Georgia*. Athens: University of Georgia Press, 1941.

Callicott, J. Baird, and Michael P. Nelson, eds. *The Great New Wilderness Debate: An Expansive Collection of Writings Defining Wilderness from John Muir to Gary Snyder*. Athens: University of Georgia Press, 1998.

Cantor, Leonard. *The Changing English Countryside, 1400–1700*. New York: Routledge and Kegan Paul, 1987.

Carney, Judith A. *Black Rice: The African Origins of Rice Cultivation in the Americas*. Cambridge: Harvard University Press, 2001.

Carney, Judith A., and Richard Nicholas Rosomoff. *In the Shadow of Slavery: Africa's Botanical Legacy in the Atlantic World*. Berkeley: University of California Press, 2009.

Carson, Rachel. *Silent Spring*. Boston: Houghton Mifflin, 1962.

Cashin, Edward. *Beloved Bethesda: A History of George Whitefield's Home for Boys, 1740–2000*. Macon, Ga.: Mercer University Press, 2001.

Cecelski, David S. *The Waterman's Song: Slavery and Freedom in Maritime North Carolina*. Chapel Hill: University of North Carolina Press, 2001.

Chaplin, Joyce E. *An Anxious Pursuit: Agricultural Innovation and Modernity in the Lower South, 1730–1815*. Chapel Hill: University of North Carolina Press, 1993.

———. "Climate and Southern Pessimism: The Natural History of an Idea, 1500–1800." In *The South as an American Problem*, edited by Larry Griffin and Don Doyle. Athens: University of Georgia Press, 1995.

———. "Creating a Cotton South in Georgia and South Carolina, 1760–1815." *Journal of Southern History* 57.2 (May 1991): 171–200.

———. *Subject Matter: Technology, the Body, and Science on the Anglo-American Frontier, 1500–1676*. Cambridge: Harvard University Press, 2001.

Chester, Robert N., III, and Nicolaas Mink. "Having Our Cake and Eating It Too: Food's Place in Environmental History: A Forum." *Environmental History* 14.2 (April 2009): 309–44 (includes essays by Jane Dusselier and Nancy Shoemaker).

Cioc, Mark, Björn-Ola Linnér, and Matthew Osborn. "Environmental History Writing in Northern Europe." *Environmental History* 5.3 (July 2000): 396–406.

Clay, Christopher, ed. *Rural Society: Landowners, Peasants, and Labourers, 1500–1750*. Vol. 2 of *Chapters from the Agrarian History of England and Wales*, edited by Joan Thirsk. New York: Cambridge University Press, 1990.

Cobb, James C. *Georgia Odyssey: A Short History of the State*. 2nd ed. Athens: University of Georgia Press, 2008.

Cohen, Benjamin. *Notes from the Ground: Science, Soil, and Society in the American Countryside*. New Haven: Yale University Press, 2009.

Coleman, Jon T. *Vicious: Wolves and Men in America*. New Haven: Yale University Press, 2004.

Coleman, Kenneth. *The American Revolution in Georgia, 1763–1789*. Athens: University of Georgia Press, 1958.

———. *Colonial Georgia: A History*. New York: Scribner's, 1976.

Colten, Craig. *An Unnatural Metropolis: Wresting New Orleans from Nature*. 2nd ed. Baton Rouge: Louisiana State University Press, 2006.

Coon, David L. "Eliza Lucas Pinckney and the Reintroduction of Indigo Culture in South Carolina." *Journal of Southern History* 42.1 (February 1976): 61–76.

Cotten, Jerry W. *Light and Air: The Photography of Bayard Wooten*. Chapel Hill: University of North Carolina Press, 1998.

Cotter, John L. "Above Ground Archeology." *American Quarterly* 26.3 (August 1974): 266–80.

Coulter, E. Merton. *Thomas Spalding of Sapelo*. Baton Rouge: Louisiana State University Press, 1940.

———. *Wormsloe: Two Centuries of a Georgia Family*. Athens: University of Georgia Press, 1955.

Courtmanche, Richard, Jr., Mark W. Hester, and Irving A. Mendelssohn. "Recovery of a Louisiana Barrier Island Marsh Plant Community Following Extensive Hurricane-Induced Overwash." *Journal of Coastal Research* 15.4 (Autumn 1999): 872–83.

Cowdrey, Albert E. *This Land, This South: An Environmental History.* Rev. ed. Lexington: University Press of Kentucky, 1996.

Craige, Betty Jean. *Eugene Odum: Ecosystem Ecologist and Environmentalist.* Athens: University of Georgia Press, 2001.

Craven, Avery O. *Edmund Ruffin: Southerner.* Baton Rouge: Louisiana State University Press, 1991.

Creel, Margaret Washington. *"A Peculiar People": Slave Religion and Community-Culture among the Gullahs.* New York: New York University Press, 1988.

Cronon, William. *Changes in the Land: Indians, Colonists, and the Ecology of New England.* Rev. ed. New York: Hill and Wang, 2003.

———, ed. *Uncommon Ground: Rethinking the Human Place in Nature.* New York: Norton, 1995.

Crosby, Alfred W. *The Columbian Exchange: Biological and Cultural Consequences of 1492.* Westport, Conn.: Greenwood, 1972.

———. *Ecological Imperialism: The Biological Expansion of Europe, 900–1900.* 2nd ed. New York: Cambridge University Press, 2004.

Cullen, Virginia F. "Wormsloe, Two Centuries in the Making." *Chatham Home Owner* 1.4 (April 1930): 1.

Cunningham, Cornelia. *Wormsloe: An Historic Plantation Dating from 1733.* Wormsloe, Ga.: n.p., 1937.

Curtin, Philip D. "Epidemiology and the Slave Trade." *Political Science Quarterly* 83.2 (June 1968): 190–216.

———. *Migration and Mortality in Africa and the Atlantic World, 1700–1900.* Burlington, Vt.: Ashgate, 2001.

———. *The Rise and Fall of the Plantation Complex: Essays in Atlantic History.* 2nd ed. New York: Cambridge University Press, 1998.

Cuthbert, Robert B., and Stephen G. Hoffius, eds. *Northern Money, Southern Land: The Lowcountry Plantation Sketches of Chlotilde R. Martin.* Columbia: University of South Carolina Press, 2009.

Daniel, Pete. *Breaking the Land: The Transformation of Cotton, Tobacco, and Rice Cultures since 1880.* Urbana: University of Illinois Press, 1985.

Davis, Donald E. *Where There Are Mountains: An Environmental History of the Southern Appalachians.* Athens: University of Georgia Press, 2000.

Davis, Harold Earl. *The Fledgling Province: Social and Cultural Life in Colonial Georgia, 1733–1776.* Chapel Hill: University of North Carolina Press, 1976.

Davis, Jack E. *An Everglades Providence: Marjory Stoneman Douglas and the American Environmental Century.* Athens: University of Georgia Press, 2009.

Davis, Ronald. *Good and Faithful Labor: From Slavery to Sharecropping in the Natchez District, 1860–1890.* Westport, Conn.: Greenwood, 1982.

De Moor, Martina, Leigh Shaw-Taylor, and Paul Warde, eds. *The Management of Common Land in North West Europe, c. 1500–1850.* Turnhout, Belgium: Brepols, 2002.

Dick, Susan E., and Mandi D. Johnson. "The Smell of Money: The Pulp and Paper-Making Industry in Savannah, 1931–1947." *Georgia Historical Quarterly* 84.2 (Summer 2000): 308–23.

Dobson, Mary J. *Contours of Death and Disease in Early Modern England.* New York: Cambridge University Press, 1997.

Dodge, Bertha S. *Cotton: The Plant That Would Be King.* Austin: University of Texas Press, 1984.

———. *Plants That Changed the World.* Boston: Little, Brown, 1959.

Donahue, Brian. *The Great Meadow: Farmers and the Land in Colonial Concord.* New Haven: Yale University Press, 2004.

Drury, William H., and Ian C. T. Nisbet. "Succession." *Journal of the Arnold Arboretum* 54 (July 1973): 331–68.

Duncan, Wilbur H., and Marion B. Duncan. *Trees of the Southeastern United States.* Athens: University of Georgia Press, 1998.

Dunlap, Thomas R. *Faith in Nature: Environmentalism as Religious Quest.* Seattle: University of Washington Press, 2004.

Dunn, Durwood. *Cades Cove: The Life and Death of a Southern Appalachian Community, 1818–1937.* Knoxville: University of Tennessee Press, 1988.

Duvall, V. L., and J. B. Hilmon. "New Grazing Research Programs for Southern Forest Ranges." *Journal of Range Management* 18.3 (May 1965): 132–36.

Edelson, S. Max. *Plantation Enterprise in Colonial South Carolina.* Cambridge: Harvard University Press, 2006.

Eltis, David. *The Rise of African Slavery in the Americas.* New York: Cambridge University Press, 2000.

Eltis, David, Philip Morgan, and David Richardson. "Agency and Diaspora in Atlantic History: Reassessing the African Contribution to Rice Cultivation in the Americas." *American Historical Review* 112.5 (December 2007): 1329–58.

Ethridge, Robbie. *Creek Country: The Creek Indians and Their World.* Chapel Hill: University of North Carolina Press, 2003.

Ewan, Joseph. "Silk Culture in the Colonies." *Agricultural History* 43.1 (January 1969): 129–42.

Fallows, James M. *The Water Lords: Ralph Nader's Study Group Report on Industry and Environmental Crisis in Savannah, Georgia.* New York: Grossman, 1971.

Farber, Paul Lawrence. "The Development of Taxidermy and the History of Ornithology." *Isis* 68.4 (December 1977): 550–66.

Fargo, William G. "Walter John Hoxie." *Wilson Bulletin* 46.3 (September 1934): 169–96.

Farnie, Douglas A., and David J. Jeremy, eds. *The Fibre That Changed the World: The Cotton Industry in International Perspective, 1600–1990s.* New York: Oxford University Press, 2004.

Ferris, Marcie Cohen. "The Edible South." *Southern Culture* 15.4 (Winter 2009): 3–27.

Finlay, Mark R. *Growing American Rubber: Strategic Plants and the Politics of National Security.* New Brunswick, N.J.: Rutgers University Press, 2009.

Fish, N. S. "The History of the Silo in Wisconsin." *Wisconsin Magazine of History* 8.2 (December 1924): 160–70.

Foner, Eric. *Reconstruction: America's Unfinished Revolution, 1863–1877*. New York: Perennial Classics, 2002.

Fox, Stephen. *The American Conservation Movement: John Muir and His Legacy*. Madison: University of Wisconsin Press, 1981.

Francher, Betsy. *Savannah: A Renaissance of the Heart*. Garden City, N.Y.: Doubleday, 1976.

Fraser, Walter, Jr. *Lowcountry Hurricanes: Three Centuries of Storms at Sea and Ashore*. Athens: University of Georgia Press, 2006.

———. *Savannah in the Old South*. Athens: University of Georgia Press, 2003.

Gaillard, Frye. *Prophet from Plains: Jimmy Carter and His Legacy*. Athens: University of Georgia Press, 2007.

Gardner, Frank D. *Traditional American Farming Techniques: A Ready Reference on All Phases of Agriculture for Farmers of the United States and Canada*. 1916; Guilford, Conn.: Lyons, 2001.

Garrison, Ervan G., James G. Baker, and David Hurst Thomas. "Magnetic Prospection and the Discovery of Mission Santa Catalina de Guale, Georgia." *Journal of Field Archeology* 12.3 (Autumn 1985): 299–313.

Genovese, Eugene D. *Roll, Jordan, Roll: The World the Slaves Made*. New York: Pantheon, 1974.

Giltner, Scott E. *Hunting and Fishing in the New South: Black Labor and White Leisure after the Civil War*. Baltimore: Johns Hopkins University Press, 2008.

Glave, Dianne, and Mark Stoll, eds. *"To Love the Wind and the Rain": African Americans and Environmental History*. Pittsburgh: University of Pittsburgh Press, 2005.

Godbold, E. Stanly, Jr. *Jimmy and Rosalynn Carter: The Georgia Years, 1924–1974*. New York: Oxford University Press, 2010.

Godfrey, Robert K., and Jean W. Wooten. *Aquatic and Wetland Plants of Southeastern United States: Dicotyledons*. Athens: University of Georgia Press, 1981.

Gomez, Michael A. *Black Crescent: The Experience and Legacy of African Muslims in the Americas*. New York: Cambridge University Press, 2005.

———. *Exchanging Our Country Marks: The Transformation of African Identities in the Colonial and Antebellum South*. Chapel Hill: University of North Carolina Press, 1998.

Granger, Mary, ed. *Savannah River Plantations*. Savannah, Ga.: Oglethorpe, 1997.

Gray, Lewis C. *History of Agriculture in the Southern United States to 1860*. 2 vols. Washington, D.C.: Carnegie Institution, 1933.

Haunton, Richard H. "Savannah in the 1850's." Ph.D. diss., Emory University, 1968.

Hahn, Steven. "Hunting, Fishing, and Foraging: Common Rights and Class Relations in the Postbellum South." *Radical History Review* 1982.26 (October 1982): 37–64.

———. *A Nation under Our Feet: Black Political Struggles in the Rural South from Slavery to the Great Migration*. Cambridge: Belknap Press of Harvard University Press, 2003.

———. "A Response: Common Cents or Historical Sense?" *Journal of Southern History* 59.2 (May 1993): 243–58.

————. *The Roots of Southern Populism: Yeoman Farmers and the Transformation of the Georgia Upcountry, 1850–1890*. New York: Oxford University Press, 1983.

Hale, Grace Elizabeth. *Making Whiteness: The Culture of Segregation in the South, 1890–1940*. New York: Vintage, 1999.

Hann, John H. "Twilight of the Mocamo and Guale Aborigines as Portrayed in the 1695 Spanish Visitation." *Florida Historical Quarterly* 66.1 (July 1987): 1–24.

Harper, Francis, and Delma E. Presley. *Okefinokee Album*. Athens: University of Georgia Press, 1981.

Harris, J. William. *Deep Souths: Delta, Piedmont, and Sea Island Society in the Age of Segregation*. Baltimore: Johns Hopkins University Press, 2001.

Harris, Jessica B. *Iron Pots and Wooden Spoons: Africa's Gifts to New World Cooking*. New York: Atheneum, 1989.

————. *The Welcome Table: African-American Heritage Cooking*. New York: Simon and Schuster, 1995.

Hartje, Robert G. *Bicentennial USA: Pathways to Celebration*. Nashville: American Association for State and Local History, 1973.

Harvey, Diane. "The Development of Indigo in Colonial South Carolina." Master's thesis, University of Georgia, 1970.

Haughton, Claire S. *Green Immigrants: The Plants That Transformed America*. New York: Harcourt Brace Jovanovich, 1978.

Hecht, Arthur. "Flowers to Gladden the City: The Takoma Horticultural Club, 1916–1971." *Records of the Columbia Historical Society, Washington, D.C.* 71–72 (1971–72): 694–711.

Hedrick, U. P. *A History of Horticulture in America to 1860*. New York: Oxford University Press, 1950.

Henderson, H. B., ed. *A History of the Dairy Industry in Georgia*. 2 vols. N.p., 1981.

Hess, Karen. "Okra in the African Diaspora of Our South." In *Cornbread Nation 1: The Best of Southern Food Writing*, edited by John Egerton. Chapel Hill: University of North Carolina Press, 2002.

Heyward, Linda, ed. *Central Africans and Cultural Transformations in the American Diaspora*. New York: Cambridge University Press, 2002.

Hilliard, Sam B. *Hog Meat and Hoecake: Food Supply in the Old South, 1840–1860*. Carbondale: Southern Illinois University Press, 1972.

Hillyer, Reiko. "Designing Dixie: Landscape, Tourism, and Memory in the New South, 1870–1917." Ph.D. diss., Columbia University, 2007.

Hirt, Paul W. *A Conspiracy of Optimism: Management of the National Forests since World War Two*. Lincoln: University of Nebraska Press, 1994.

Historic Savannah. Savannah, Ga.: Historic Savannah Foundation, 1968.

Hobhouse, Henry. *Seeds of Change: Five Plants That Transformed Mankind*. London: Sidgwick and Jackson, 1985.

Hoelscher, Steven. "Making Place, Making Race: Performances of Whiteness in the Jim Crow South." *Annals of the Association of American Geographers* 93.3 (September 2003): 657–86.

Hofmann, E. E., and T. M. Powell. "Environmental Variability Effects on Marine Fisheries: Four Case Histories." *Ecological Applications* 8.1 (February 1998): S23-S32.

Holder, Gregory L., Mark K. Johnson, and James L. Baker. "Cattle Grazing and Management of Dusky Seaside Sparrow Habitat." *Wildlife Society Bulletin* 8.2 (Summer 1980): 105–9.

Hudson, Charles. *The Southeastern Indians*. Knoxville: University of Tennessee Press, 1976.

Hull, Barbara. *St. Simons, Enchanted Island: A History of the Most Historic of Georgia's Fabled Golden Isles*. Atlanta: Cherokee, 1980.

Hutchinson, Dale, Clark Spencer Larsen, Margaret J. Schoeninger, and Lynette Norr. "Regional Variation in the Pattern of Maize Adoption and Use in Florida and Georgia." *American Antiquity* 63.3 (July 1998): 397–416.

Ingram, Tammy. "Dixie Highway: Private Enterprise and State Building in the South, 1900–1930." Ph.D. diss., Yale University, 2007.

Inscoe, John C. *Race, War, and Remembrance in the Appalachian South*. Lexington: University Press of Kentucky, 2008.

Isaac, Rhys. *The Transformation of Virginia, 1740–1790*. New York: Norton, 1988.

Jacoby, Karl. *Crimes against Nature: Squatters, Poachers, Thieves, and the Hidden History of American Conservation*. Berkeley: University of California Press, 2001.

———. "Slaves by Nature? Domestic Animals and Human Slaves." *Slavery and Abolition* 15.1 (April 1994): 89–99.

Jakle, John A., and Keith A. Sculle. *Motoring: The Highway Experience in America*. Athens: University of Georgia Press, 2008.

Jensen, A. "The Effect of Cattle and Sheep Grazing on Salt-Marsh Vegetation at Skallingen, Denmark." *Vegetatio* 60.1 (March 1985): 37–48.

Johnson, Whittington B. *Black Savannah, 1788–1864*. Fayetteville: University of Arkansas Press, 1996.

Jolley, Harley E. "Biltmore Forest Fair, 1908." *Forest History* 14.1 (April 1970): 6–17.

Jones, Charles C., Jr. *The Dead Towns of Georgia*. Collections of the Georgia Historical Society, vol. 4. Savannah, Ga.: Morning News, 1878.

Jordan, Winthrop D. *White over Black: American Attitudes toward the Negro, 1550–1812*. Chapel Hill: University of North Carolina Press, 1968.

Kantor, Shawn. *Politics and Property Rights: The Closing of the Open Range in the Postbellum South*. Chicago: University of Chicago Press, 1998.

———. "Razorbacks, Ticky Cows, and Closing the Open Range: The Dynamics of Institutional Change Uncovered." *Journal of Economic History* 51.4 (December 1991): 861–86.

Kantor, Shawn, and J. Morgan Kousser. "Common Sense or Commonwealth? The Fence Law and Institutional Change in the Postbellum South." *Journal of Southern History* 59.2 (May 1993): 201–42.

Keber, Martha L. *Seas of Gold, Seas of Cotton: Christophe Poulain DuBignon of Jekyll Island*. Athens: University of Georgia Press, 2002.

Keiner, Christine. *The Oyster Question: Scientists, Watermen, and the Maryland Chesapeake Bay since 1880*. Athens: University of Georgia Press, 2009.

———. "W. K. Brooks and the Oyster Question: Science, Politics, and Resource Management in Maryland, 1880–1930." *Journal of the History of Biology* 31.3 (Autumn 1998): 383–424.

Kelly, V. E. *A Short History of Skidaway Island*. N.p.: Branigar, 1994.

Kelman, Ari. *A River and Its City: The Nature of Landscape in New Orleans*. Berkeley: University of California Press, 2003.

Kelso, William M. *Captain Jones's Wormslow: A Historical, Archeological, and Architectural Study of an Eighteenth-Century Plantation Site near Savannah, Georgia*. Athens: University of Georgia Press, 2008.

Kelton, Paul. *Epidemics and Enslavement: Biological Catastrophe in the Native Southeast, 1492–1715*. Lincoln: University of Nebraska Press, 2007.

Kerr-Ritchie, Jeffrey. *Freedpeople in the Tobacco South: Virginia, 1860–1900*. Chapel Hill: University of North Carolina Press, 1999.

King, J. Crawford, Jr. "The Closing of the Southern Open Range: An Exploratory Study." *Journal of Southern History* 68.1 (February 1982): 53–70.

Kirby, Jack Temple. *Mockingbird Song: Ecological Landscapes of the South*. Chapel Hill: University of North Carolina Press, 2006.

———. *Poquosin: A Study of Rural Landscape and Society*. Chapel Hill: University of North Carolina Press, 1995.

———. *Rural Worlds Lost: The American South, 1920–1960*. Baton Rouge: Louisiana State University Press, 1985.

Kjaergaard, Thorkild. *The Danish Revolution, 1500–1800: An Ecohistorical Interpretation*. New York: Cambridge University Press, 1994.

Knight, Lucian Lamar. *Georgia's Landmarks, Memorials, and Legends*. 2 vols. Atlanta: Byrd, 1913–14.

Kousser, J. Morgan, and James M. McPherson, eds. *Region, Race, and Reconstruction: Essays in Honor of C. Vann Woodward*. New York: Oxford University Press, 1982.

Krech, Shepherd, III. *The Ecological Indian: Myth and History*. New York: Norton, 1999.

———. *Spirits of the Air: Birds and American Indians in the South*. Athens: University of Georgia Press, 2009.

Kupperman, Karen O. "Fear of Hot Climates in the Anglo-American Colonial Experience." *William and Mary Quarterly* 41 (April 1984): 213–40.

Langston, Nancy. *Forest Dreams, Forest Nightmares: The Paradox of Old Growth in the Inland West*. Seattle: University of Washington Press, 1995.

Lawson, Joanne Seale. "Remarkable Foundations: Rose Ishbel Greely, Landscape Architect." *Washington History* 10.1 (Spring–Summer 1998): 46–69.

Leavitt, Charles T. "Attempts to Improve Cattle Breeds in the United States, 1790–1860." *Agricultural History* 7.2 (April 1933): 51–67.

Lemmer, George F. "The Spread of Improved Cattle through the Eastern United States to 1850." *Agricultural History* 21.2 (April 1947): 79–93.

Levi, Giovanni. *Inheriting Power: The Story of an Exorcist*. Chicago: University of Chicago Press, 1988.

Lewis, C. S. *The Abolition of Man*. New York: Macmillan, 1947.

Lindsey, Elizabeth Chaplin, and Albert Sidney Britt Jr. *Isle of Hope, 1736–1986*. Savannah, Ga.: Isle of Hope Historical Association, 1986.

Littlefield, Daniel C. *Rice and Slaves: Ethnicity and the Slave Trade in Colonial South Carolina*. Baton Rouge: Louisiana State University Press, 1981.

Litwack, Leon. *Been in the Storm So Long: The Aftermath of Slavery*. New York: Knopf, 1979.

Lockley, Timothy James. *Lines in the Sand: Race and Class in Lowcountry Georgia, 1750–1860*. Athens: University of Georgia Press, 2001.

Lowrance, Richard, Paul F. Hendrix, and Eugene Odum. "A Hierarchical Approach to Sustainable Agriculture." *American Journal of Alternative Agriculture* 1.4 (1986): 169–73.

Mackintosh, Barry. "The National Park Service Moves into Historical Interpretation." *Public Historian* 9.2 (Spring 1987): 50–63.

Marx, Leo. *The Machine in the Garden: Technology and the Pastoral Ideal in America*. New York: Oxford University Press, 1967.

Mathew, William M. *Edmund Ruffin and the Crisis of Slavery in the Old South: The Failure of Agricultural Reform*. Athens: University of Georgia Press, 1988.

McCann, James C. *Maize and Grace: Africa's Encounter with a New World Crop, 1500–2000*. Cambridge: Harvard University Press, 2005.

McCash, June Hall. *The Jekyll Island Cottage Colony*. Athens: University of Georgia Press, 1998.

McCash, June Hall, and William Barton McCash. *The Jekyll Island Club: Southern Haven for America's Millionaires*. Athens: University of Georgia Press, 1989.

McCorkle, James L., Jr. "Agricultural Experiment Stations and Southern Truck Farming." *Agricultural History* 62.2 (Spring 1988): 234–43.

———. "Moving Perishables to Market: Southern Railroads and the Nineteenth-Century Origins of Southern Truck Farming." *Agricultural History* 66.1 (Winter 1992): 42–62.

McDonald, Forrest, and Grady McWhiney. "The South from Self-Sufficiency to Peonage: An Interpretation." *American Historical Review* 85.5 (December 1980): 1095–1118.

McFeely, William. *Sapelo's People: A Long Walk into Freedom*. New York: Norton, 1994.

McNeill, J. R. *Mosquito Empires: Ecology and War in the Greater Caribbean, 1620–1914*. New York: Cambridge University Press, 2010.

Melosi, Martin V. *The Sanitary City: Environmental Services in Urban America from Colonial Times to the Present*. Abridged ed. Pittsburgh: University of Pittsburgh Press, 2008.

Menard, Russell. "Transitions to African Slavery in British America, 1630–1730: Barbados, Virginia and South Carolina." In *Slavery in America: A Reader and Guide*, edited by Kenneth Morgan. Athens: University of Georgia Press, 2005.

Merchant, Carolyn. "George Bird Grinnell's Audubon Society: Bridging the Gender Divide in Conservation." *Environmental History* 15.1 (January 2010): 3–30.

———. "Women of the Progressive Conservation Movement: 1900–1916." *Environmental Review* 8.1 (Spring 1984): 57–85.

Milanich, Jerald T., and Samuel Procter, eds. *Tacachale: Essays on the Indians of Florida and Southeastern Georgia during the Historic Period*. Gainesville: University Press of Florida, 1994.

Miles, Tiya. *The House on Diamond Hill: A Cherokee Plantation Story*. Chapel Hill: University of North Carolina Press, 2010.

Miller, James S. "Mapping the Boosterist Imaginary: Colonial Williamsburg,

Historical Tourism, and the Construction of Managerial Memory." *Public Historian* 28.4 (Autumn 2006): 51–74.

Miller, Shawn William. *An Environmental History of Latin America*. New York: Cambridge University Press, 2007.

Mink, Nicolaas. "It Begins in the Belly." *Environmental History* 14.2 (April 2009): 312–22.

Montgomery, David R. *Dirt: The Erosion of Civilizations*. Berkeley: University of California Press, 2007.

Montgomery, Michael, ed. *The Crucible of Carolina: Essays in the Development of Gullah Language and Culture*. Athens: University of Georgia Press, 2008.

Morgan, Edmund S. *American Slavery, American Freedom: The Ordeal of Colonial Virginia*. New York: Norton, 1975.

Morgan, Jo-Ann. "Mammy the Huckster: Selling the Old South for the New Century." *American Art* 9.1 (Spring 1995): 87–109.

Morgan, Lynda. *Emancipation in Virginia's Tobacco Belt, 1850–1870*. Athens: University of Georgia Press, 1992.

Morgan, Philip D., ed. *African American Life in the Georgia Lowcountry: The Atlantic World and the Gullah Geechee*. Athens: University of Georgia Press, 2010.

———. *Slave Counterpoint: Black Culture in the Eighteenth-Century Chesapeake and Lowcountry*. Chapel Hill: University of North Carolina Press, 1998.

———. "Work and Culture: The Task System and the World of Lowcountry Blacks, 1700 to 1880." *William and Mary Quarterly*, 3rd ser., 39.4 (October 1982): 564–99.

Nash, Roderick F. *Wilderness and the American Mind*. 3rd ed. New Haven: Yale University Press, 1982.

Neel, Leon, with Paul S. Sutter and Albert G. Way. *The Art of Managing Longleaf: A Personal History of the Stoddard-Neel Approach*. Athens: University of Georgia Press, 2010.

Nelson, Lynn A. *Pharsalia: An Environmental Biography of a Southern Plantation, 1780–1880*. Athens: University of Georgia Press, 2007.

Nelson, Megan Kate. *Trembling Earth: A Cultural History of the Okefenokee Swamp*. Athens: University of Georgia Press, 2005.

Norwood, Vera. *Made from This Earth: American Women and Nature*. Chapel Hill: University of North Carolina Press, 1993.

Odum, Eugene P. *Fundamentals of Ecology*. 3rd ed. Philadelphia: Saunders, 1971.

Odum, Eugene P., and Howard T. Odum. *Fundamentals of Ecology*. Philadelphia: Saunders, 1953.

Patterson, Gordon. *The Mosquito Wars: A History of Mosquito Control in Florida*. Gainesville: University Press of Florida, 2004.

Pearson, H. A., and L. B. Whitaker. "Forage and Cattle Responses to Different Grazing Intensities on Southern Pine Ridge." *Journal of Range Management* 27.6 (November 1974): 444–46.

Perdue, Robert E. *The Negro in Savannah, 1865–1900*. New York: Exposition, 1973.

Petrides, George A. *A Field Guide to Eastern Trees: Eastern United States and Canada, Including the Midwest*. New York: Houghton Mifflin, 1998.

Phillips, Sarah T. *This Land, This Nation: Conservation, Rural America, and the New Deal*. New York: Cambridge University Press, 2007.

Piechocinski, Elizabeth Carpenter. *Once upon an Island: The Barrier and Marsh Islands of Chatham County, Georgia*. Savannah, Ga.: Oglethorpe, 2003.

Pollan, Michael. *The Botany of Desire: A Plant's-Eye View of the World*. New York: Random House, 2001.

———. *Second Nature: A Gardener's Education*. New York: Atlantic Monthly Press, 1992.

Porcher, Richard Dwight, and Sarah Fick. *The Story of Sea Island Cotton*. Charleston, S.C.: Wyrick, 2005.

Powell, Katrina M. *The Anguish of Displacement: The Politics of Literacy in the Letters of Mountain Families in Shenandoah National Park*. Charlottesville: University of Virginia Press, 2007.

———, ed. *"Answer at Once": Letters of Mountain Families in Shenandoah National Park, 1934–1938*. Charlottesville: University of Virginia Press, 2009.

Powell, Lawrence N. *New Masters: Northern Planters during the Civil War and Reconstruction*. New York: Fordham University Press, 1998.

Price, Jennifer. *Flight Maps: Adventures with Nature in Modern America*. New York: Basic Books, 2000.

Pyne, Stephen J. *Fire in America: A Cultural History of Wildland and Rural Fire*. Princeton: Princeton University Press, 1988.

Rackham, Oliver. *The History of the Countryside*. London: Dent, 1986.

———. *The Last Forest: The Story of Hatfield Forest*. London: Dent, 1989.

———. *Trees and Woodland in the British Landscape*. Rev. ed. London: Dent, 1990.

Ramsey, William L. *The Yamasee War: A Study of Culture, Economy, and Conflict in the Colonial South*. Lincoln: University of Nebraska Press, 2008.

Range, Willard. "The Agricultural Revolution in Royal Georgia, 1752–1775." *Agricultural History* 21.4 (October 1947): 250–55.

Ransom, Roger L., and Richard Sutch. *One Kind of Freedom: The Economic Consequences of Emancipation*. New York: Cambridge University Press, 1977.

Rantis, Polly-Anne, and James E. Johnson. "Understory Development in Canopy Gaps of Pine and Pine-Hardwood Forests of the Upper Coastal Plain of Virginia." *Plant Ecology* 159.1 (2002): 103–15.

Rasmussen, Wayne D. *Taking the University to the People: Seventy-Five Years of Cooperative Extension*. Ames: Iowa State University Press, 1989.

Reese, Trevor R. *Colonial Georgia: A Study in British Imperial Policy in the Eighteenth Century*. Athens: University of Georgia Press, 1963.

Reich, Justin. "Re-Creating the Wilderness: Shaping Narratives and Landscapes in Shenandoah National Park." *Environmental History* 6.1 (January 2001): 95–117.

Reidy, Joseph P. *From Slavery to Agrarian Capitalism in the Cotton Plantation South: Central Georgia, 1800–1880*. Chapel Hill: University of North Carolina Press, 1992.

Reiger, John F. *American Sportsmen and the Origins of Conservation*. New York: Winchester, 1975.

Rice, Dan, Susan Knudson, and Lisa Westberry. "Restoration of the Wormsloe Plantation Salt Marsh in Savannah, Georgia." In *Proceedings of the 2005 Georgia Water Resources Conference*, University of Georgia, April 25–27, 2005. Available online at http://cms.ce.gatech.edu/gwri/uploads/proceedings/2005/RiceD-GWRCpaper%20revised.pdf.

Rice, James D. *Nature and History in the Potomac Country: From Hunter-Gatherers to the Age of Jefferson*. Baltimore: Johns Hopkins University Press, 2009.

Risjord, Norman K. "From the Plow to the Cow: William D. Hoard and America's Dairyland." *Wisconsin Magazine of History* 88.3 (Spring 2005): 40–49.

Robinson, Julie Anne. *The Last Song*. Movie. Touchstone Pictures, 2010.

Rodrigue, John C. *Reconstruction in the Cane Fields: From Slavery to Free Labor in Louisiana's Sugar Parishes, 1862–1880*. Baton Rouge: Louisiana State University Press, 2001.

Rogers, George A., and R. Frank Saunders. *Swamp Water and Wiregrass: Sketches of Coastal Georgia*. Macon, Ga.: Mercer University Press, 1984.

Rome, Adam. *The Bulldozer in the Countryside: Suburban Sprawl and the Rise of American Environmentalism*. New York: Cambridge University Press, 2001.

Rosenbaum, Walter A. *Environmental Politics and Policy*. 5th ed. Washington, D.C.: CQ Press, 2002.

Rosengarten, Theodore. *Tombee: Portrait of a Cotton Planter*. New York: Morrow, 1986.

Russell, Preston, and Barbara Hines. *Savannah: A History of Her People since 1733*. Savannah, Ga.: Bell, 1992.

Saikku, Mikko. *This Delta, This Land: An Environmental History of the Yazoo-Mississippi Floodplain*. Athens: University of Georgia Press, 2005.

Sandberg, Gösta. *Indigo Textiles: Techniques and History*. Asheville, N.C.: Lark, 1989.

Savannah Unit, Federal Writers' Project. *Savannah*. Savannah, Ga.: Review, 1937.

Saville, Julie. *The Work of Reconstruction: From Slave to Wage Laborer in South Carolina, 1860–1870*. New York: Cambridge University Press, 1994.

Schiebinger, Londa, and Claudia Swan, eds. *Colonial Botany: Science, Commerce, and Politics in the Early Modern World*. Philadelphia: University of Pennsylvania Press, 2005.

Sears, John F. *Sacred Places: American Tourist Attractions in the Nineteenth Century*. New York: Oxford University Press, 1989.

Sellars, Richard West. *Preserving Nature in the National Parks: A History*. New Haven: Yale University Press, 1997.

Sharrer, G. Terry. "The Indigo Bonanza in South Carolina, 1740–1790." *Technology and Culture* 12.3 (July 1971): 447–55.

———. "Indigo in Carolina, 1671–1796." *South Carolina Historical Magazine* 72.2 (April 1971): 94–103.

Shelton, Garret Ward, and C. William Hill Jr. *The Liberal Republicanism of John Taylor of Caroline*. Madison, N.J.: Fairleigh Dickinson University Press, 2008.

Shepherd, Philippa, Tanja Crockett, Toni L. De Santo, and Keith L. Bildstein. "The Impact of Hurricane Hugo on the Breeding Ecology of Wading Birds at Pumpkinseed Island, Hobcaw Barony, South Carolina." *Colonial Waterbirds* 14.2 (1991): 150–57.

Shifflett, Crandall A. *Patronage and Poverty in the Tobacco South: Louisa County, Virginia, 1860–1900*. Knoxville: University of Tennessee Press, 1982.

Shlomowitz, Ralph. "The Origins of Southern Sharecropping." *Agricultural History* 53.3 (July 1979): 557–75.

————. "Plantations and Smallholdings: Comparative Perspectives from the World Cotton and Sugar Cane Economies, 1865–1939." *Agricultural History* 58.1 (January 1984): 1–16.

Shores, Elizabeth Findley. *On Harper's Trail: Roland McMillan Harper, Pioneering Botanist of the Southern Coastal Plain.* Athens: University of Georgia Press, 2008.

Sickels-Taves, Lauren B. "Understanding Historic Tabby Structures: Their History, Preservation, and Repair." *Association for Preservation Technology Bulletin* 28.2–3 (1997): 22–29.

Sickels-Taves, Lauren B., and Michael Sheehan. *The Lost Art of Tabby Redefined: Preserving Oglethorpe's Architectural History.* Southfield, Mich.: Architectural Conservation, 1999.

Siegel, Frederick F. *The Roots of Southern Distinctiveness: Tobacco and Society in Danville, Virginia, 1780–1865.* Chapel Hill: University of North Carolina Press, 1987.

Silber, Nina. *The Romance of Reunion: Northerners and the South, 1865–1900.* Chapel Hill: University of North Carolina Press, 1993.

Silver, Timothy. *Mount Mitchell and the Black Mountains: An Environmental History of the Highest Peaks in Eastern America.* Chapel Hill: University of North Carolina Press, 2003.

————. *A New Face on the Countryside: Indians, Colonists, and Slaves in South Atlantic Forests, 1500–1800.* New York: Cambridge University Press, 1990.

Smith-Howard, Kendra D. "Perfecting Nature's Food: A Cultural and Environmental History of Milk in the United States, 1900–1970." Ph.D. diss., University of Wisconsin–Madison, 2007.

Soluri, John. *Banana Culture: Agriculture, Consumption, and Environmental Changes in Honduras and the United States.* Austin: University of Texas Press, 2005.

Sparks, Nicholas. *The Last Song.* New York: Grand Central, 2009,

Spence, Mark David. *Dispossessing the Wilderness: Indian Removal and the Making of the National Parks.* New York: Oxford University Press, 2000.

Spirn, Anne Whiston. "Constructing Nature: The Legacy of Frederick Law Olmsted." In *Uncommon Ground: Rethinking the Human Place in Nature*, edited by William Cronon. New York: Norton, 1995.

Stanonis, Anthony J., ed. *Dixie Emporium: Tourism, Foodways, and Consumer Culture in the American South.* Athens: University of Georgia Press, 2008.

Steffen, Charles G. "In Search of the Good Overseer: The Failure of the Agricultural Reform Movement in Lowcountry South Carolina, 1821–1834." *Journal of Southern History* 63.4 (November 1997): 753–802.

Steinberg, Ted. *Acts of God: The Unnatural History of Natural Disaster in America.* Rev. ed. New York: Oxford University Press, 2006.

Stephens, S. G. "The Origin of Sea Island Cotton." *Agricultural History* 50.2 (April 1976): 391–99.

Stewart, Mart A. "From King Cane to King Cotton: Razing Cane in the Old South." *Environmental History* 12.1 (January 2007): 59–79.

————. "If John Muir Had Been an Agrarian: Environmental History West and South." *Environment and History* 11.2 (May 2005): 139–62.

———. "'Let Us Begin with the Weather': Climate, Race and Cultural Distinctiveness in the American South." In *Nature and Society in Historical Context*, edited by Mikuláš Teich, Roy Porter, and Bo Gustafsson. New York: Cambridge University Press, 1997.

———. *"What Nature Suffers to Groe": Life, Labor, and Landscape on the Georgia Coast, 1680–1920.* Athens: University of Georgia Press, 1996.

———. "'Whether Wast, Deodand, or Stray': Cattle, Culture, and the Environment in Early Georgia." *Agricultural History* 65.3 (Summer 1991): 1–28.

Stoll, Steven. *Larding the Lean Earth: Soil and Society in Nineteenth-Century America.* New York: Hill and Wang, 2002.

Strom, Claire. *Making Catfish Bait out of Government Boys: The Fight against Cattle Ticks and the Transformation of the Yeoman South.* Athens: University of Georgia Press, 2009.

Sullivan, Buddy. *Tabby: A Historical Perspective of an Antebellum Building Material in McIntosh County, Georgia.* Darien, Ga.: n.p., 1998.

Sutter, Paul S. *Driven Wild: How the Fight against Automobiles Launched the Modern Wilderness Movement.* Seattle: University of Washington Press, 2002.

———. "Nature's Agents or Agents of Empire?: Entomological Workers and Environmental Change during the Construction of the Panama Canal." *ISIS: Journal of the History of Science in Society* 98.4 (December 2007): 724–54.

Sutter, Paul S., and Christopher Manganiello, eds. *Environmental History and the American South: A Reader.* Athens: University of Georgia Press, 2009.

Swanson, Drew A. "Fighting over Fencing: Agricultural Reform and Antebellum Efforts to Close the Virginia Open Range." *Virginia Magazine of History and Biography* 117.2 (2009): 103–39.

———. "Marketing a Mountain: Changing Views of Environment and Landscape on Grandfather Mountain, North Carolina." *Appalachian Journal* 36.1–2 (Winter–Spring 2009): 30–54.

———. "Wormsloe's Belly: The History of a Southern Plantation through Food." *Southern Cultures* 15.4 (Winter 2009): 50–66.

Swanton, John R. *The Indians of the Southeastern United States.* Washington, D.C.: Smithsonian Institution Press, 1979.

Sweet, Julie Anne. *Negotiating for Georgia: British-Creek Relations in the Trustee Era.* Athens: University of Georgia Press, 2005.

Synnott, Marcia G. "Disney's America: Whose Patrimony, Whose Profits, Whose Past?" *Public Historian* 17.4 (Autumn 1995): 43–59.

Teal, John, and Mildred Teal. *Life and Death of the Salt Marsh.* Boston: Little, Brown, 1969.

———. *Portrait of an Island.* Athens: Brown Thrasher Books/University of Georgia Press, 1981.

Thirsk, Joan, ed. *The English Rural Landscape.* New York: Oxford University Press, 2000.

Thomas, David Hurst, Grant D. Jones, Roger S. Durham, Clark Spencer, Larsen, and Clarence B. Moore. "The Anthropology of St. Catherines Island: 1. Natural and Cultural History." *Anthropological Papers of the American Museum of Natural History* 55.2 (October 1978): 157–248.

Thomas, David Hurst, and Lorann S. A. Pendleton. "The Archaeology of Mission Santa Catalina De Guale: 1. Search and Discovery." *Anthropological Papers of the American Museum of Natural History* 63.2 (June 1987): 47–161.

Thompson, Victor D. "Questioning Complexity: The Prehistoric Hunter-Gatherers of Sapelo Island, Georgia." Ph.D. diss., University of Kentucky, 2006.

Turner, Lorenzo Dow. *Africanisms in the Gullah Dialect.* Chicago: University of Chicago Press, 1949.

Tyler-McGraw, Marie. "Becoming Americans Again: Re-Envisioning and Revising Thematic Interpretation at Colonial Williamsburg." *Public Historian* 20.3 (Summer 1998): 53–76.

Vance, Rupert B. *Human Factors in Cotton Culture: A Study in the Social Geography of the American South.* Chapel Hill: University of North Carolina Press, 1929.

Van Horne, John C. "Joseph Solomon Ottolenghe (ca. 1711–1775): Catechist to the Negroes, Superintendent of the Silk Culture, and Public Servant in Colonial Georgia." *Proceedings of the American Philosophical Society* 125.5 (October 1981): 398–409.

Valencius, Conevery Bolton. *The Health of the Country: How American Settlers Understood Themselves and Their Land.* New York: Basic Books, 2002.

Vaughn, Alden T. *Roots of American Racism: Essays on the Colonial Experience.* New York: Oxford University Press, 1995.

Viola, Herman J., and Carolyn Margolis, eds. *Seeds of Change: A Quincentennial Commemoration.* Washington, D.C.: Smithsonian Institution Press, 1991.

Vlach, John Michael. *Back of the Big House: The Architecture of Plantation Slavery.* Chapel Hill: University of North Carolina Press, 1993.

Waldron, J. D., C. W. Lafon, R. N. Coulson, D. M. Cairns, M. D. Tchakerian, A. Birt, and K. D. Klepzig. "Simulating the Impacts of Southern Pine Beetle and Fire on the Dynamics of Xerophytic Pine Landscapes in the Southern Appalachians." *Applied Vegetation Science* 10.1 (April 2007): 53–64.

Wallace, Ronald Lynn. "An Archeological, Ethnohistoric, and Biochemical Investigation of the Guale Aborigines of the Georgia Coastal Strand." Ph.D. diss., University of Florida, 1975.

Warren, Louis S. *The Hunter's Game: Poachers and Conservationists in Twentieth-Century America.* New Haven: Yale University Press, 1997.

Wayne, Michael. *Death of an Overseer: Reopening a Murder Investigation from the Plantation South.* New York: Oxford University Press, 2001.

Westmacott, Richard. *African-American Gardens and Yards in the Rural South.* Knoxville: University of Tennessee Press, 1992.

Wheeler, Frank T. *Savannah River Plantations: Photographs from the Collection of the Georgia Historical Society.* Charleston, S.C.: Arcadia, 1998.

White, Richard. *The Organic Machine: The Remaking of the Columbia River.* New York: Hill and Wang, 1995.

Williams, David S. *From Mounds to Megachurches: Georgia's Religious Heritage.* Athens: University of Georgia Press, 2008.

Williams, Michael. *Americans and Their Forests: A Historical Geography.* New York: Cambridge University Press, 1990.

Wines, Richard A. *Fertilizer in America: From Waste Recycling to Resource Exploitation.*
Philadelphia: Temple University Press, 1985.

Wood, Betty. *Gender, Race, and Rank in a Revolutionary Age: The Georgia Lowcountry,
1750–1820.* Athens: University of Georgia Press, 2000.

———. *The Origins of American Slavery: Freedom and Bondage in the English
Colonies.* New York: Hill and Wang, 1997.

———. *Slavery in Colonial Georgia, 1730–1775.* Athens: University of Georgia Press,
1984.

———. *Women's Work, Men's Work: The Informal Slave Economies of Lowcountry
Georgia.* Athens: University of Georgia Press, 1995.

Wood, Peter H. *Black Majority: Negroes in Colonial South Carolina from 1670 through
the Stono Rebellion.* New York: Knopf, 1974.

Work, Monroe N. "The Negroes of Warsaw, Georgia." *Southern Workman* 37.1
(January 1908): 29–40.

Worster, Donald. *Nature's Economy: A History of Ecological Ideas.* New York:
Cambridge University Press, 1977.

———. *The Wealth of Nature: Environmental History and the Ecological Imagination.*
New York: Oxford University Press, 1993.

Wright, Gavin. *Old South, New South: Revolutions in the Southern Economy since the
Civil War.* Baton Rouge: Louisiana State University Press, 1996.

Yafa, Stephen. *Cotton: The Biography of a Revolutionary Fiber.* New York: Penguin,
2006.

INDEX

Texas fever, 80, 140
Thomas, Tom, 109
Thunderbolt, Georgia, 120
Toller, Martin, 49
Tomochichi, 14, 20
tourism, 9–10, 145–47, 155, 181;
    contemporary, 186–87; interwar, 142,
    143–45
Townshend, Charles, 77
Trustees, 26, 42; prohibition of slavery,
    15, 32; vision for Georgia, 14, 15, 19, 44
Tull, Jethro, 77–78
Tybee Island, 98, 129
Tyler, Frank, 119, 120

Union Bag and Paper Company, 147,
    161, 167, 176–79, 180
Union Camp. *See* Union Bag and
    Paper Company
University of Georgia, 167, 170
University of Georgia Press, 164

Vanderbilt, George, 134
vernacular landscapes, 187
von Reck, Philip Georg Friedrich,
    28, 29

Walker, Isaac, 109
Wallace, Ronald, 18
Waring, Frederick, 86
War of Jenkins's Ear, 17, 25, 181
Washington, George, 78
Waylor, Alston, 175, 176
White, Elizabeth Wade, 150
Whitefield, George, 27, 59
Whitehall Plantation, 146
wilderness, 183–84
Williams, Julius, 119
Williams, Mauruel, 119
Williamsburg, Colonial, 185

Wilmington Island, 120
Wimberly Plantation, 70, 86
wolves, 39–40
Wooten, Bayard, 153
Wormsloe Foundation, 161, 164–65
Wormsloe Gardens: advertising,
    143–44, 153; attendance, 143; black
    labor at, 150–53, 155; closure, 162;
    descriptions of, 4–5, 142–43; opening,
    132, 142
Wormsloe Plantation: agriculture,
    44–48, 51–52, 55, 62–67, 139–41, 153–54,
    182–83; agricultural reform on, 76–84,
    86–87, 89; the big house, 71, 89, 133,
    160; effects of revolution on, 49–51;
    family attachment to, 86–87, 99–100,
    114, 136–37; international ties, 19, 25,
    51, 62, 82–83, 97, 182; landscaping and
    design, 88–90, 114–17, 133–36; library,
    11, 87, 133, 141; origin of name, 15;
    Reconstruction on, 102, 105–6,
    107–13; self-sufficiency, 69–70, 72,
    84–86, 140; as site of recreation, 131,
    136–37, 163; Trustee grant, 15, 24.
    See also cotton, sea island; slavery;
    Wormsloe Gardens; Wormsloe
    State Historic Site
Wormsloe State Historic Site, 1, 116;
    attendance, 181; creation, 5, 157,
    166; description, 1–3; development,
    166–67; mission, 166; timbering
    associated with southern pine beetle,
    176–77, 179; use of convict labor, 179.
    See also Georgia Department of
    Natural Resources; interpretation

Yamacraw, 14–15, 20, 26
Yamasee, 23
yellow fever. *See* disease
Young, R. A., 147

ENVIRONMENTAL HISTORY AND THE AMERICAN SOUTH